AIR, ARCHITECTURE + OTHER CLIMATES

STUDIO AS BOOK
NO. 07

SERIES INTRODUCTION

Studio as Book is a series of publications that tender the extraordinary creative work undertaken in the School of Architecture + Cities design studios – in detail. Each book in the series covers the work of a single design studio, either undergraduate or graduate, and sometimes both, over the course of at least two years. Its objectives are:

- To record, archive, and present the pedagogical programme and creative student outputs of a design studio.
- To position the work of a design studio within a broader intellectual, scientific or aesthetic field.
- To advance the design driven research being undertaken in the School's design studios.
- To provide a reference for future iterations and variations of a design studio.

Compressing the creative output of a multi-year design studio into a single volume, using a pre-designed book template is no easy undertaking, and it is necessarily selective. At the same time, it provides a consistent, sure platform for the wide range of approaches to the discipline of teaching architectural design which characterise the school.

Each Studio as Book has been peer-reviewed on the basis of a proposal submitted by the studio's tutors to an editorial committee. In addition to studio briefs and student work, each book includes content that draws out the studio's research and pedagogical agenda. The format that this takes varies from book to book – reflective essays by tutors or past students, interviews, theoretical essays from parallel fields, and so forth.

I wish to acknowledge the contribution of the following in bringing this project to fruition: Lindsay Bremner, Director of Research and Knowledge Exchange, who was the driving force behind the series when it was launched in 2016; Mark Boyce, author of Sizes May Vary, A workbook for graphic design (Lawrence King, 2008) – and the designer of Studio as Book; Filip Visnjic and Mirna Pedalo, who have given the books a presence on OpenStudiowWestminster: http://www.openstudiowestminster.org/studio-as-book/; and the design tutors and students who have given of their time and energy to collate and edit the books into this unique series.

Harry Charrington
Former Head of the School of Architecture + Cities
University of Westminster

AIR, ARCHITECTURE + OTHER CLIMATES

DS18 2019-2023

EDITED BY LAURA NICA, JOHN COOK & BEN POLLOCK

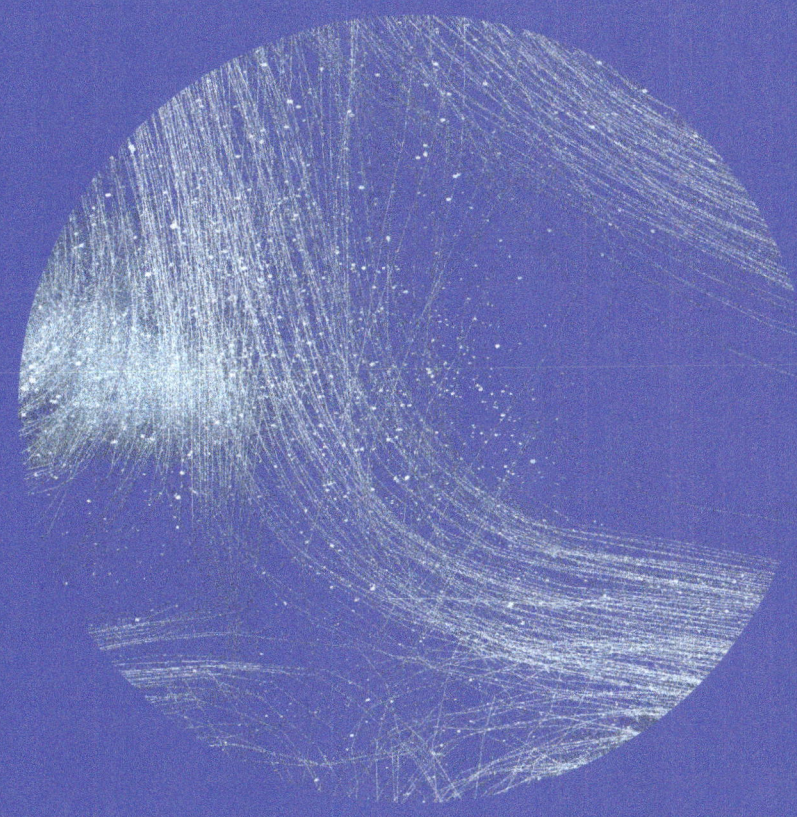

STUDIO AS BOOK
NO. 07

SCHOOL OF ARCHITECTURE + CITIES
UNIVERSITY OF WESTMINSTER

003

CONTENTS

PREFACE — 006

INTRODUCTION - ARCHITECTURING AIR — 008
Roberto Bottazzi

AIR + ATMOSPHERE

THINKING THROUGH AIR — 016
John Cook

CARTOGRAPHIC IMAGINARIES

MAPS OF THE ANTHROPOCENE — 032 & 062
Student work from global, to local and strategic atmospheric maps

COMPUTING CLIMATES — 042
Guy Sinclair

CLIMATE CARTOGRAPHIES — 050
Ben Pollock

SIMULATIONS

THERMODYNAMICS AND SIMULATIONS — 090
John Cook and Laura Nica

MODELLING AIR: ARROWS, POINT-CLOUDS AND THEIR WAYS OF KNOWING AIR — 100
Uri Wegman

MANUFACTURED ATMOSPHERE - A DIALOGUE ON CALIBRATION — 112
Laura Nica in conversation with ARUP (Olivia Ewing, Shahid Padhani and Dimple Rana)

FLUID SURFACES AND SATURATED SUBSTRATES — 120
Andreas Körner

MODEL BEHAVIOURS — 130
Student work from simulations, artefacts and apparatuses

ARCHIVES

THE EARTH AS AN ARCHIVE 162
Laura Nica

DIGITAL REPOSITORIES 178
Laura Nica and Ben Pollock

SELECTED STUDENT PROJECTS 188
Katherine Dechow (p. 190), Kate Hosking (p. 198), Gaby Bucknall (p. 206), Aimee Daniels (p. 212), Zixin (Tiffany) Yao (p. 218), Helen Windsor (p. 224), Daria Donovetsky (p. 232), Elizabeth Terry (p. 238), Kirsten Davis (p. 244), Chada Elalami (p. 250), Nicholas Tsangaris (p. 256), Justyna Lesny (p.262), and Seni Agunpopo (p.268)

BEYOND STUDIO

ANTHROPOGENIC PEDAGOGIES AND EXPERIMENTAL MEDIA 274
Lidia Gasperoni

ALTERNATIVE MODES OF SPATIAL PRACTICE 278
Ben Pollock in conversation with Georgios Malliaropoulos, Jamie Williams, Chada Elalami, Oscar McDonald, Tom Benson, Diana Fox, Tom Wildbore, Calvin Sin, and Aimee Daniels.

APPENDICES 288

Biographies
Students (2019 -2023)
Awards, Talks and Publications
Acknowledgements
Open Exhibition Photo Journal (2019 -2023)
Air Photo Journal (Field trips)
Thematics

PREFACE

Introduction

This edition of studio as book documents the period between 2019 to 2022 of Design Studio 18 (DS18) at the University of Westminster, tutored by John Cook, Ben Pollock and Laura Nica, through their investigations titled 'Air, Atmosphere and Other Climates'. This book contains an edited selection of student work produced under this theme, and is supported by a series of writings and reflections from our peers, collaborators and past students engaged with the studio over this period.

Studio Background

DS18 was established in 2013 by Professor Lindsay Bremner and Roberto Bottazzi, setting out to explore the intersection of architecture, urbanism and geology framed by three interrelated ideas. The first was around the then recent hypothesis that humanity had entered a new geological epoch, the Anthropocene, whereby the impacts of our society on the planet were so widespread and significant they would materially register within future geologic strata along their associated deep geologic time scales. The second in relation to this, was the recognition that humanity's accelerated and mass mobilisation of Earth's materials and energies had now interfered with the planets stratigraphy, oceans and atmosphere to such an extent, that what was once considered a geologic system, a hydrologic system, and an urban or infrastructural system, were so deeply entangled they were no longer distinguishable. [01] And finally methodologically, was in thinking about these architectural, urban and infrastructural systems as intensities of data, energy and matter amongst these wider interlinked material systems, how we could enlist computational tools and data to analyse, simulate and visualise these processes in order to intervene in them through design.

These foundational ideas established a material framework that saw the studio commence its inaugural investigations under the title 'Architecture, Energy, Matter' (2013-15) via explorations of the ground – through the material and structural properties of geology, mineral resources, and extraction, the energy economies they generated, and towards the wider implications amongst the societies they fuelled. Following this the studio was partnered to the research agenda of the ERC funded project 'Monsoon Assemblages' (2016-18). Here the focus shifted to the fast and fluid fields of water - investigated across three sites around the South Indian monsoonal basin within the aqueous environments of marsh, delta, and river. [02]

Throughout these studios, the principle of their thematic framing was to provide a material frame of reference, a guiding perspective in which to read these contexts, across their historical development, present conditions and possible futures. The *matter* in question would necessitate investigations to explore across multiple scales and through time, whilst directing students to consider this materials far reaching presence across cultures, industries and politics, as well as its entanglements amongst human and non-human life. As we became custodians of the studio in 2019, there was an evident logic to evolve this developed framing into the realms of *air and atmosphere*, to close the final chapter of states, whilst offering new challenges and opportunities for investigation and design, alongside an ever more pressing urgency around matters of our climate.

Structure of Book

The book is organised as a set of three trajectories that move at different speeds, allowing readers a degree of flexibility in approaching it.

The first trajectory spans the entire arc of the

book and traces the feedback loop linking architecture, computational design and representation.

A second series of (medium speed) trajectories is found within the book chapters. Each chapter traces the feedback between specific concepts and methodologies, illustrated and developed through examples from internal and external practices and writings – ranging from conceptual interpretations of air, towards systems and techniques of engaging with the atmosphere and the environment.

Chapter 1, *Air + Atmosphere* introduces and explores the conceptual framing of the studio's agenda. The chapter explores air across its array of diverse terms, through their disparities of meaning, contrasting modes of perception, and diverse ways of understanding. From international politics, science and climatology, to local cultures and lived experiences of weather.

Chapter 2, *Cartographic Imaginaries* reflects on the development of the studio's use of mapping and cartographic methodologies, from the planetary scales of meteorological computing, to the localised impacts of climate change. The chapter covers more experimental explorations of data, informing new aerial approaches to site planning and strategic spatial design configurations. Mapping here is introduced as a design research method, a data-driven analytical tool, and a multi-scaled and temporal representational medium.

Chapter 3, *Simulations* introduces the use of the computational simulation tools (CFD), in attempts to capture and describe the complexities of air dynamics and behaviours across scales, space and time. From environmental simulations, geometrical optimisations to interactive modelling – the chapter outlines the use and calibration of digital simulation in practice, its notational history and development, as well as its potential future use in architectural surface exploration and artefact. Fluid simulations offer new aerial design methods for the development of architectural form, material investigations and detailing.

Chapter 4, *Archives* outlines architecture's potential role in recording, preserving and managing climatic information, registering volumes of air through various layers in flux, to create physical marks of memory and visualise new conditions of space. This chapter presents a series of student proposals, as well as other creative approaches developed by the studio to document, archive and utilise the generated content through various visual assemblies, to expand collaboration and multi-disciplinary dialogues.

Chapter 5, *Beyond Studio* reflects on the studio's pedagogical approach, told through contributions from past students who have each carved their own path into alternative modes of spatial practice, founded and building upon the studios' unique methodologies and thinking. The chapter highlights a network of intersecting fields, delving into broader themes such as sustainability, digital innovation, ethical practice, and design's evolving role as an agent of care.

The third trajectory is composed of an extensive array of student work, of various scales, programmes and detail. These range from strategic masterplans, retrofit schemes, micro interventions and quasi-infrastructural proposals, intended to allow for a more rapid perusal. Developed through a minimum of a seven-month period, these pages represent a sample of essential ideas describing air as a medium of design, research engagement and spatial enquiry.

Notes

(01) Bremner, L. and Bottazzi, R. 2016. Architecture, Energy, Matter. London Department of Architecture, University of Westminster
(02) Bremner, L., Cullen, B., Leigh Geros, C. Cook, J., Bhat, H., Powis, A., and Benson, T. (2022). Monsoon as Method. Actar D, Inc.

ARCHITECTURING AIR

ROBERTO BOTTAZZI

The second instalment of the Design Studio 18 (DS18) of the Studio as Book series documents and reflects on the students' work and tutors' research on the exploration of air as a medium, a piece of infrastructure, and a design object. This essay sets out to trace both the genealogy of the design agenda of DS18 and contextualise the elements of novelty introduced by Laura Nica, John Cook, and Ben Pollock since taking over DS18 in 2019. DS18 's agenda, in fact, was initially set up by Lindsay Bremner and myself in 2013 and concentrated on the impact of the Anthropocene on architecture. Each year the Studio analysed different global conditions (for instance, fracking in the UK and South Africa, Ocean levels raising in the Maldives) to eventually focus on the Monsoon region around the Bay of Bengal in closer alignment with Lindsay Bremner's own research project. [01] Since 2019 John Cook, Ben Pollock, and Laura Nica took over the agenda they develop it and expand it in such way to tackle with the most elusive, invisible, and yet essential material dimension of the planet: air. This publication takes stock of their achievements and the impressive students' work and acts as a prelude to the new phase of research DS18 will enter.

    Combined, the first and second volume can be imagined as drawing a large cross-section through the various matters that makes up the earth: from geology to the ground – first volume – and from the ground up to the end of the atmosphere – this volume. Both books also propose and discuss ideas, instruments, and designs on how architecture could be mobilised to attend to the Anthropocene and the climate emergency. Implicitly, they also outline a pedagogy on how we could teach architecture in the age of climate crisis. Such pedagogy emerges from considering architecture as entangled with three conditions: the understanding of the earth as a metabolic system, the end of classical theories of nature and consequent the realisation that "human and natural forces have intertwined, so that the fate of one determines the fate of the other", [02] and need to develop instruments able to register transformations whose scale and speed does not match that of the human 'sensorium'. The realisation of such a profound shift indicates that traditional architectural approaches no longer hold. For this reason the Studio does not consider typological analysis, stylistic debates, or tectonic preoccupations which are either entirely overlooked

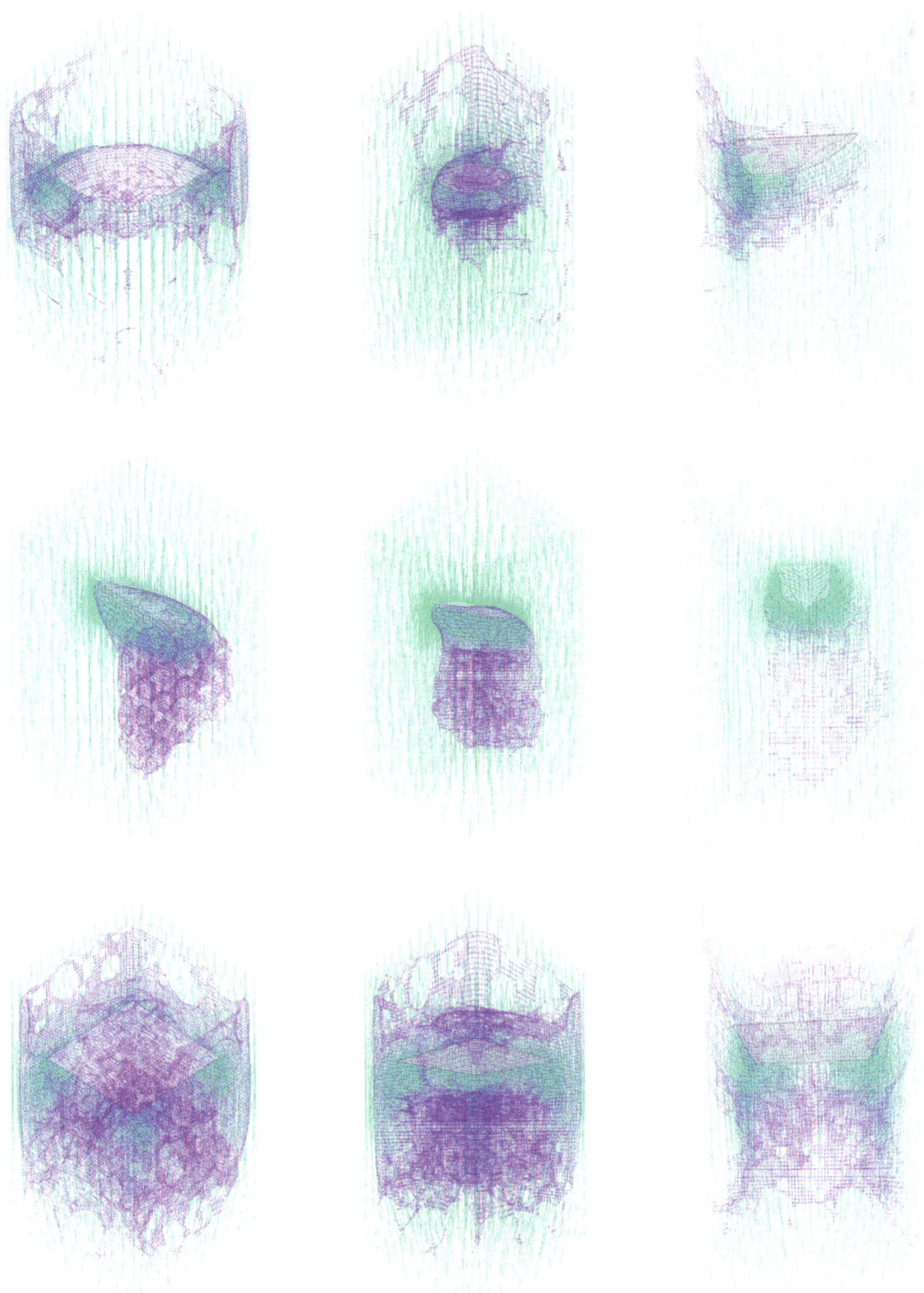

Alistair Orchard-Mitchell. Acid Britain. Simulations of air and acidification interactions with the surface and massing of tree leaves (2023).

Charlotte Grasselli. The Polar Wind Park. Simulating the meandering wave of the Jet Stream (2020).

or, at best, only considered as secondary preoccupations. What replaces them is the idea of architecture as an instrument able to negotiate forces and energies and operate across scales to catalyse change. The issue of scale, in particular, stands out: the projects developed by students, independently from the their actual physical size, attend to vast environmental or even cosmic scales that architecture normally avoids.

Air, Architecture + Other Climates marks a clear expansion of this line of research, well beyond the initial premises of the Studio, and the emergence of new positions, ideas, and instruments to equip future architects to confront the climate emergency. Architecture's own engagement with air is certainly a complex one, as the discipline has been invariably described through words that are antithetical to how we characterise air. Presence, fixity, and stability, which are often understood as the qualities of architecture, are simply unapplicable to air. For this reason, air has often been the forgotten element, as Luce Irigaray suggested, (03) that architecture has rarely engaged with. However, the small collection of projects which did focus on air represent some of the richest and most experimental works developed by the discipline.

Architecture's engagement with air has taken either an infrastructural approach, in which architecture works with air while renouncing to its qualities of stability and presence, or has attempted to absorb the characteristics of air in its vocabulary. Air could be understood as the very material of architecture, its most fundamental and the one that hold the promise to deliver social and physical freedom by eliminating forms of spatial control such as walls. More efficient and economic than bricks and mortar, air could be sufficient to provide that "well-tempered environment" (04) that appeared to constitute the minimal condition for the existence of architecture. Substituting the function of walls and windows by manipulating air has not just being a call for a more materially efficient architecture, but also a political move that suggested a different relation between humans and their environment and between technology and society. Some of the these preoccupations animated Yves Klein's and Claude Parent's Air Architecture project (1957-1962) which the pair pursued through a series of exceptional drawings and writings. They imagined spaces and a whole city designed around the manipulation of basic elements such as air and fire. The adequate conditions for inhabitation would be achieved without the use of static masses or structures and humans would be free to move without the need to wear clothes. Philippe Rahm's installation "Digestible Gulf Stream" – exhibited at the

Venice Biennale in 2008 – materialised some of these visions by having naked people inhabiting his piece. In 1972, Emilio Ambasz was determined to take a more pragmatic approach to the theme of air architecture when he tested the possibility of building a wall of air to separate different areas of his famous MoMa exhibition "Italy: The New Domestic Landscape". Though the project could not be realised, it indicated the ambition to use air not only to replace the conventional elements of architecture, but to also liberate its users from following imposed routes. The seduction of this approach also derived from the possibility to radically challenge architectural conventions through, at least on paper, the simplest of operations: the manipulation of air flows. Architects have also used air as a medium and an infrastructure to heighten spatial awareness or provide the necessary conditions for inhabitation. In this line of experimental work, architects have perhaps shown a clearer understanding of the multiple conditions of air. They played with the physics of air to realise that it consists of a mixture of gases that are not homogeneous, that particles of various other materials float in it, and that, under specific physical conditions, air itself can change its aspect. Gianni Pettena's drawing – such as Cancellation of a State (1970) – showed how air and smoke could be choreographed into vast territorial architectures that contested the exiting spatial order. The jet engine part of the piece is the architectural agent tasked to transform the appearance of air. Different physical phenomena that also result in changing the aspect of air were also exploited by Diller and Scofidio in their Blur Building in 2002. The building itself is the infrastructure necessary for fog to envelope the structure and alter visitors' perceptions.

These examples also indicate a different role played by technology in supporting architects' imagination. The early images of air architecture were characterised by strong political and aesthetic ambitions, with little or no technological tools to implement these intentions. Recent projects such as Diller and Scofidio's Blur Building are indicative of a different technological landscape in which imagination and implementation are no longer separated by technical limitations. The role of digital technologies in bridging the gap between ideas and actions has certainly been essential, particularly in the case of substances as elusive as air. Digital technologies have not only provided the means to achieved some of the spaces that architects could only imagine, but they have also articulated a different abstract space through which to rethink architecture's relation with air.

As for many of the technological changes we are experiencing today, the early experiments in understanding the physics of air and weather patterns date back to the nineteenth century. Luke Howard's taxonomy of clouds published in his Essay on the Modification of Clouds (1802) laid the foundations to meteorology. The classification of clouds was broadly shaped after Linnaeus' taxonomy and employed a descriptive approach developed through observations of the skies above London. Description is the pre-requisite to classification which, either implicitly or explicitly, requires the development of an explanatory theory. As we have briefly hinted above, the application of typological classifications to the earth's physics often returns unsatisfactory results as dynamic, cross-scalar phenomena such as the weather do not easily fit clear-cut distinctions. The technologies of air classification and weather description rather needed a more granular and continuous infrastructure for measurement that would pick up subtle differences and gradient variations. The introduction of a continuous infrastructure to capture data about the atmosphere was also the prerequisite to computing air and weather patterns. In 1922 Lewis Fry Richardson performed the first mathematical weather prediction by subdividing the volume of skies above Europe into a three-dimensional grid. The weather dynamics within each cubical portion – in computational parlance, voxels – could be computed independently using seven equations. The output of the calculations would constitute the input values for the adjacent voxels, and so on until all the voxels had been computed: in short, Richardson conceived a proto Finite Element Method (FME) for computing the weather. (05) The experiment, unsuccessful due to the scarcity of data on which to base the calculations and coarse grain of the voxel resolution, is nevertheless important in this context because it foregrounds the issue of models and methods of abstraction: both in terms of how they translate physical phenomena into a different language (i.e. mathematics) and how they allow different systems to converse with each other.

Though the quality and precision of weather models today has massively improved since Richardson's experiment, what has persisted is the search for abstract models to conceptualise the most elusive of earth's substances. Technological innovation has also been accompanied by intellectual discussions that have provided instruments to connect the abstraction of computational models with the materiality of lived experience and the phenomenological aspects of air. In this very fruitful context, the work of DS18 straddles between abstract and concrete, theoretical and practical, intelligible and sensible, as well as speculative and pragmatic to imagine the architecture of the climate emergency.

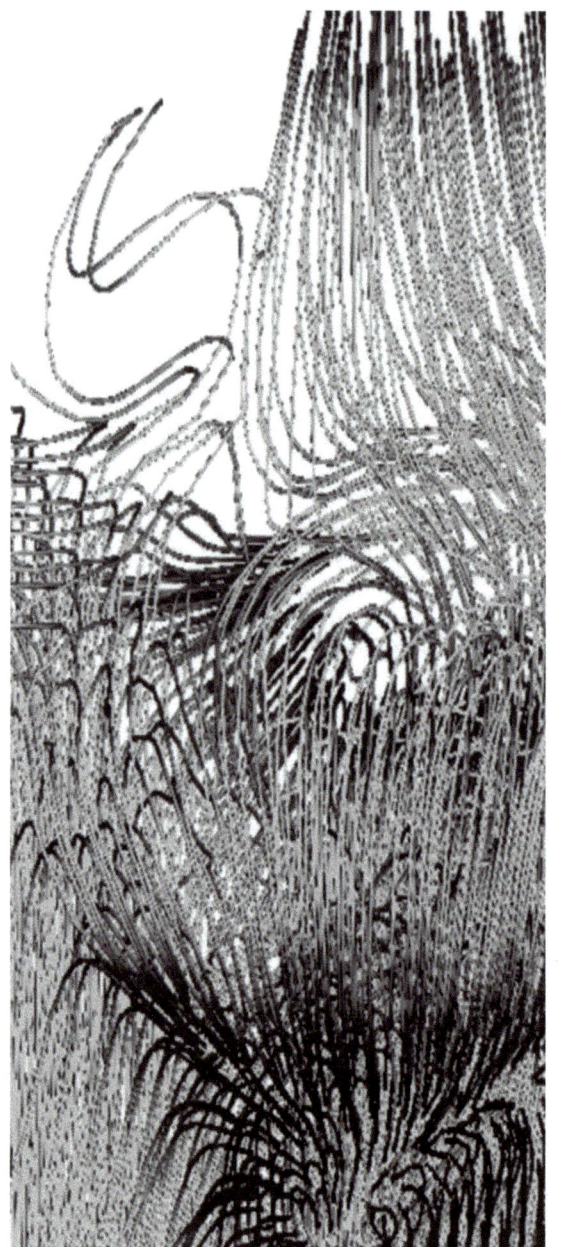

Notes

(01) L. Bremner, edited by. *Monsoon as a Method: assembling monsoonal multiplicities* (New York: ACTAR, 2022).
(02) M. Wark, *Molecular Red: Theory for the Anthropocene* (London: Verso, 2015), xxii.
(03) L. Irigaray, *The Forgetting of Air* in Martin Heidegger (London: The Athlone Press, 1999).
(04) R. Bahnam, *The Architecture of the Well-Tempered Environment* (Chicago: Chicago Press, 1969).
(05) https://en.wikipedia.org/wiki/Finite_element_method.

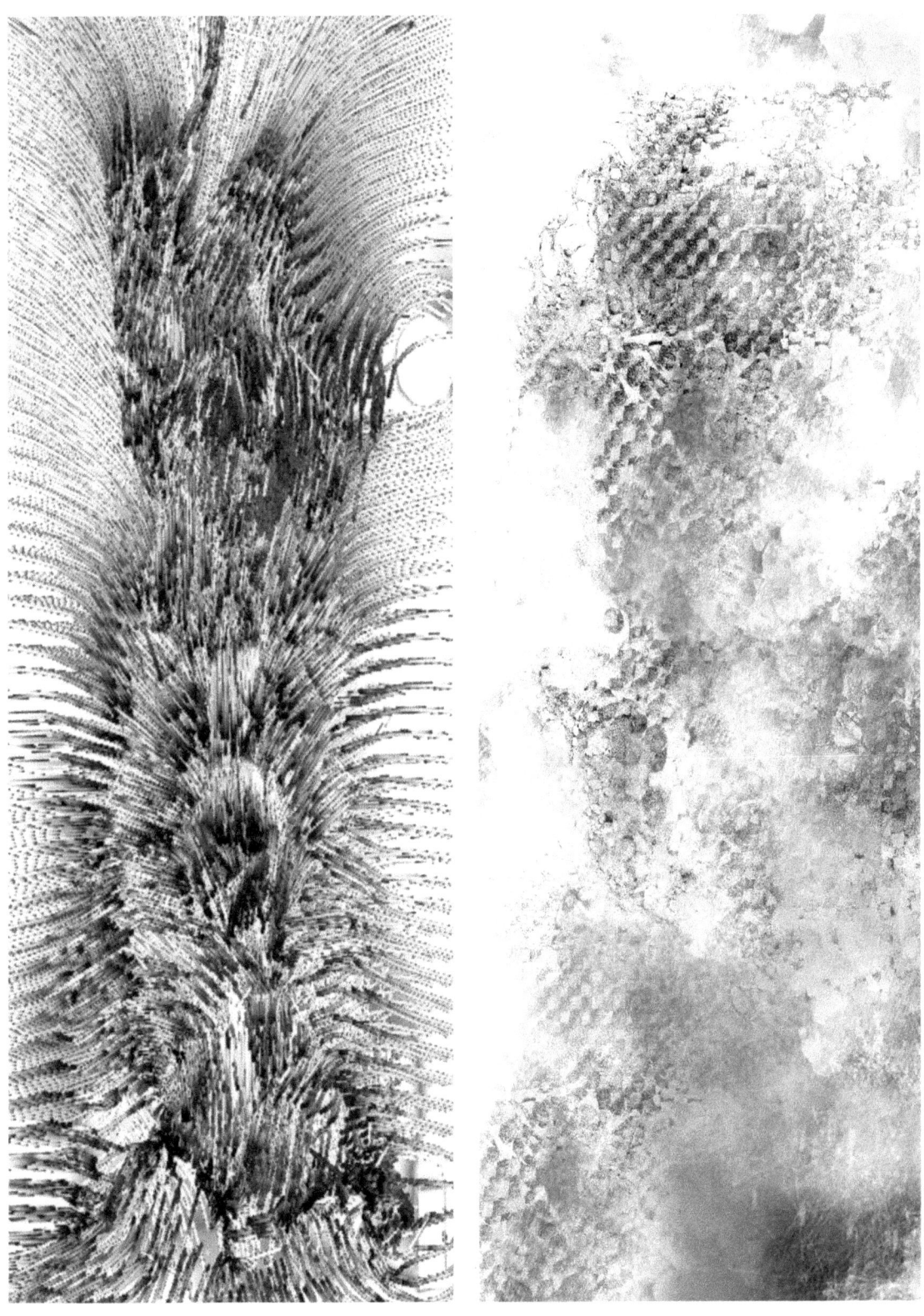

(left and top) Timea Iulia Kadar. The Atmospheric Harvesting Centre. Mist, fog and Cumulus cloud simulation in three different densities (2023).

AIR AND ATMOSPHERE

THINKING THROUGH AIR

JOHN COOK

This following thought-piece seeks to provide a narrative account of our *thinking through air*, as we conceptualised the studio's agenda and investigations during its evolution upwards into the atmosphere. It attempts to both capture and reflect on our thought processes at the time, the ways in which we used atmospheric phenomena as a pedagogical framework, a spatial locator, and the questions we asked of both air and architecture through explorations of design.

The Climate Around Air

Design Studio 18's aerial evolution to the medium of *air* in 2019 coincided with a significant rise in global awareness and concern around matters of our atmosphere and climate. Whilst the International Union of Geological Sciences (IUGS) sought to reject the commencement of the Anthropocene era, the Intergovernmental Panel on Climate Change (IPCC) released their landmark report providing a stark warning to the world that we had only 12 years to reduce global emissions to keep projected temperature rises within 1.5 degrees and prevent irreversible climate collapse. [01] Though clearly links between human activity and climate has existed and been warned of for decades, the sheer weight of scientific consensus ignited climatic debates further into public discourse.

Over this same year social movements grew, from Greta Thunberg's commencement of her "Skolstrejk för klimatet", to the formation of the global climate activist group Extinction Rebellion, and more locally even, the Architects Climate Action Network (ACAN). Each drove the wider global Rebellion Day movement culminating in one of the last memorable UN Climate Action Summits of that year. Scientific consensus coupled with social activist momentum, was further fuelled through a sequence of relentless extreme weather events around cities of the Global North. From 2018's California wildfires, the devastating landing and duration of Hurricane Sandy, Europe's anticyclonic cold front named 'the Beast from the East', to the record breaking heatwaves of June 2019 that followed. The indisputable impacts of climate change were brought to the doorstep of the industrial and consumerist world that birthed it. *Climate* and *weather, atmosphere* and *air* – often mingled terms with a plurality of meanings, were driven by new media and invaded public consciousness with new urgency.

But what did these terms mean and to whom? At the global extreme, 'climate' is understood as an abstracted planetary system. A statistical construct fed by observed and modelled meteorological data in attempts to replicate these complex dynamics, to reveal and predict their relationships and anomalies, whilst forecasting their trajectories across scales and time periods incomprehensible to the human experience. At the other end of the scale, the impacts of 'changes' to this climate are more often experienced at the human level through disturbance and irregularity, through weather extremes and events that bring the typically background and invisible atmospheric realm of air to the forefront with force, violence and consequence.

In our studio, we were interested in exploring *air* across all these terms, through their disparities of meaning, contrasting modes of perception and diverse ways of experiencing. Through this, we saw an opportunity to advance the methodologies and tools of DS18 by adapting them to this new material, whilst curious of the challenges, role and possibilities for architecture and design when explored through this medium, and all the scales and forms it presents itself in.

The Medium of Air

Our conception of air was widened and guided by a number of inspiring theorists and designers, their works provided ranging viewpoints across the many readings of this invisible and indispensable realm. These multiple modes are best captured by Evan Horn in her epistemology of air:

> *...not only an environment, but as an intrinsic element of human civilisation, human knowledge and phenomenological experience.* (02)

She presents air not merely as *matter*, but as *medium*. One that has fundamentally shaped, and in turn been shaped by, the civilisations and cultures grown within it.

As an object of scientific study, air is defined as a gaseous substance, formed by the chemical composition of nitrogen, oxygen, argon, carbon dioxide and other trace gases. This elemental substance forms the atmosphere of our planet, a thin enveloping layer of gases that circulate the globe within complex fluid dynamic systems driven by Earth's orbital physics and the alternating temperature differentials across the irregular distribution of landmass and sea. This air is a life bringing resource, operating simultaneously at the planetary and microscopic scales,

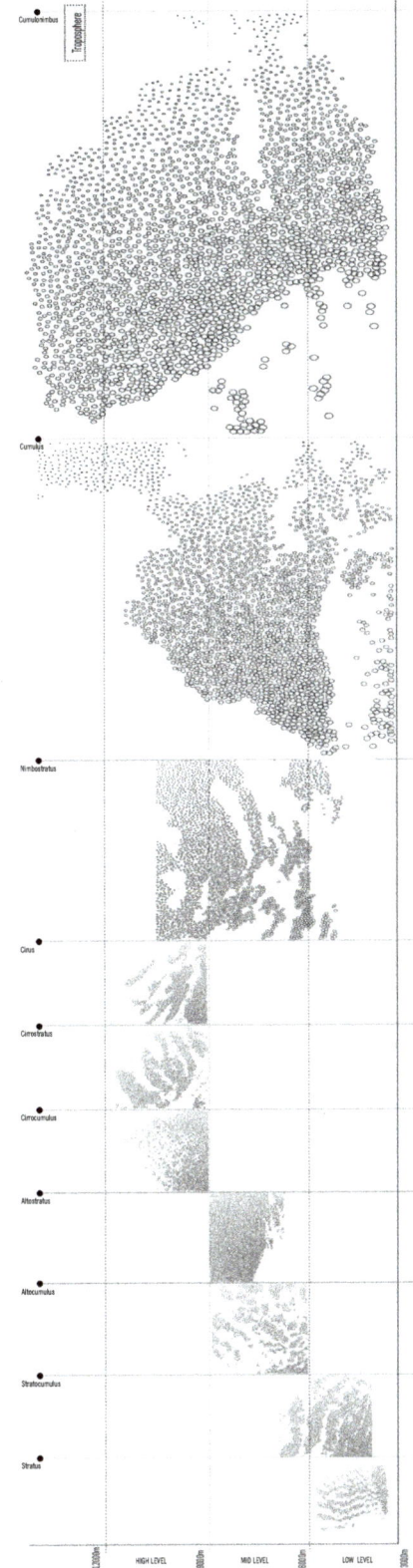

Seni Agunpopo. The Cloud Sanctuary. Formations through levels of atmosphere (2020).

Sara Kosanovic. The Nordkapp Dust Research Station. (top) Global mapping of dust and aerosol movement. (right) Global dust tracking, between Norway and Chad (2020).

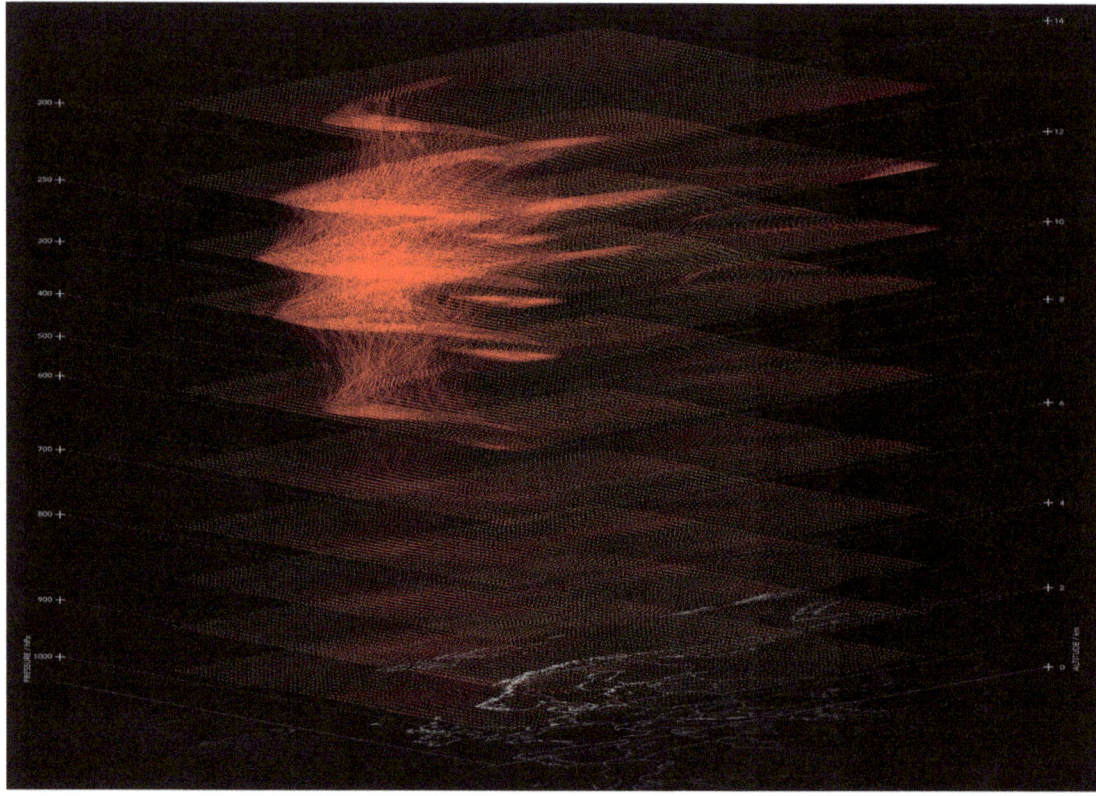

Charlotte Grasselli. The Polar Wind Park. Three dimensional wind profiles through the Polar Jet Stream (26th July 2019) (2020).

existing at once both within and outside of our bodies. It fuels the full spectrum of earth's flora and fauna from microbial to greater plant life, driving photosynthesis and energising our living planetary system within this habitable 'sphere of breath'. [03] Simultaneously air is a transmissive vehicle, one that carries a host of vapours, toxins, particulates and contagions, presenting unseen aerial dangers often necessitating filtration or capture, more often distributed inequitably towards the more vulnerable lives of our planet. In extreme cases our atmospheric environments are intentionally contaminated, mobilised against living beings as aerial weapons of warfare through acts of what Peter Sloterdijk calls 'atmoterrorism'. [04]

This all-encompassing and ubiquitous substance represents a global commons, a resource that defies ownership whilst unifying and linking every corner of humanity under a single and shared common climate. This material transcends nations, oblivious to our political borders in its circulation of the earth, whilst conversely debated, governed and administered through ever evolving, often defied, policies, legislations and treaties. Even the polluting of its composition has been commodified, to be taxed, penalised and fed back into the global economic system that poisoned it. Yet at the lived experience, air is the enabler of our senses. It carries the ingredients of our sight, our hearing and smell. We experience and feel air through its properties of temperature, pressure and humidity, as it is raised to our consciousness through disturbances, irregularities and extremes.

This medium would be the vehicle of our investigations, the atmospheres it operates in and climates it creates, explored through its extreme scales, polarised methods of understanding, and contrasting ways of perceiving. It would offer us an aerial framework to guide students research, one that was diverse and diffused across scales, forms and aspects of society. What architectural possibilities and experiences would emerge when thinking through and designing amongst this invisible, volatile and immersive medium.

Framing Through Air

To understand and provide the wider context of our investigations, we followed airs' pathways upwards to the outer layers of our atmosphere. We would form this aerial-spatial research framework around three interlinked and transforming climatic phenomena. The Arctic Circle, the boundary of the polar region defined by the limit of the

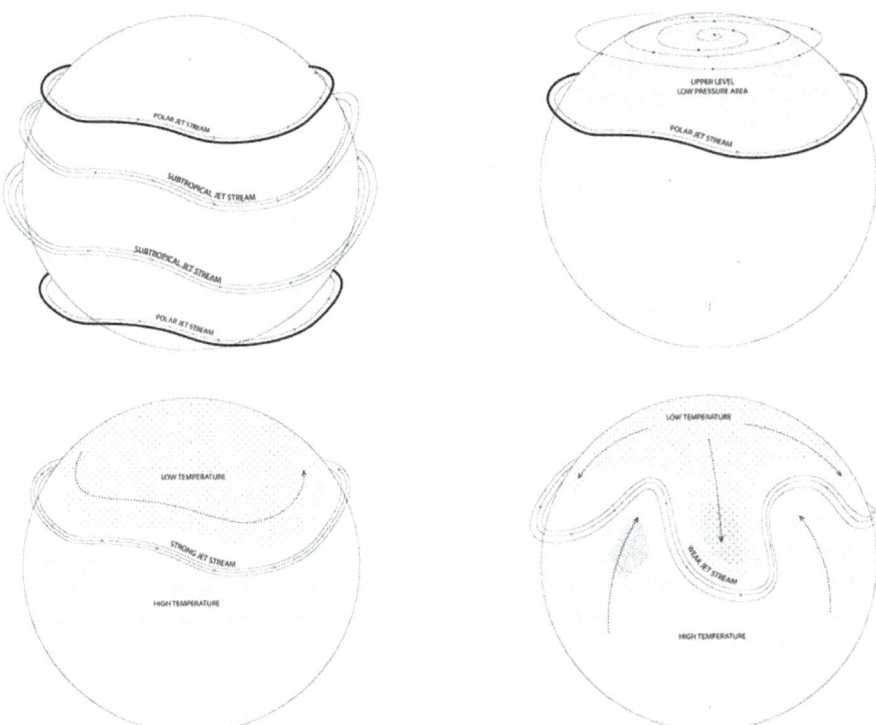

Charlotte Grasselli. (top) Diagrams of global jet streams and the Polar Vortex. (bottom) Diagrams of a 'strong' and 'weak' Polar Jet Stream (2020).

sun's visibility during the June and December solstices. The Ferrel and Polar air cells, two of the three global circulation systems that carry air, moisture and matter across the planet. And the Polar Jet Stream, the upper tropospheric westerly air flow generated at the boundary of these two systems – in turn dictating and influencing weather patterns throughout the majority of the Northern Hemisphere. Due to irregularities in the Earth's orbit and axial tilt, mankind's mass extraction and redistribution of materials around the globe, and the accelerated melting of the polar ice caps, these entwined atmospheric systems are destabilising, shifting and morphing in ever unpredictable ways. (05)

A weakening of the Polar Jet Stream, caused by a reduced temperature differential between the Arctic and tropical air fronts, leads to a more meandering pathway in its tropospheric circulation of the globe. Kinks, buckles and folds along this ribbons journey drags troughs and peaks of high and low pressure to increasingly southern and northern extremes, where they stall and linger for longer. The weather events associated with these zones are often severe and globally significant, grounding these upper air systems through land-based destruction and disruptions of our lived environment.

These entwined atmospheric phenomena would establish a spatial aerial transect, tethered loosely within this high latitudinal band, offering a horizontal swathe of linked but diverse sites to explore over the multiple years of the studio agenda. Through these we sought to study how these shifting lateral air systems transposed and revealed themselves upon the ground amongst these differing conditions and contexts. To witness how even 'marginal' global changes makes profound and permanent modifications to local climates, in turn reshaping the finely balanced organisational structures and ecologies evolved within them at rates far beyond their 'natural' evolution or possible pace of adaption. Within these shifting territories, as tensions and collisions arise between expanding settlements, mutating habitats and economic motives, what role could landscape or architectural interventions take amongst these transitions - to offer resistance, adaptation, measurement or control?

Siting Through Air

This aerial framework would direct the studio's territorial siting, scale and focus over the course of this period. It was however, somewhat ironically impacted in 2020 by the air dispersed spread of COVID-19, restricting the extents and

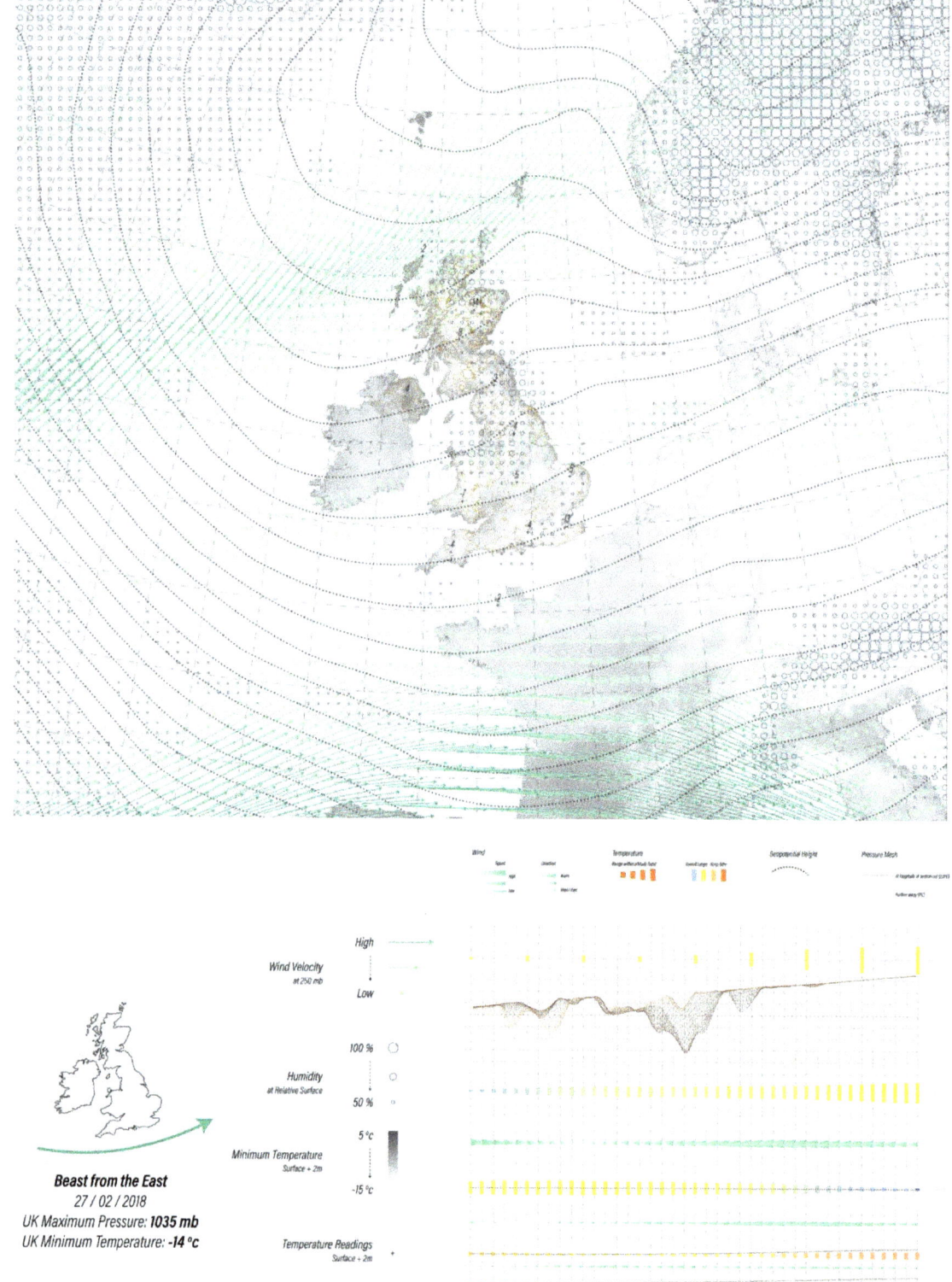

Kirsten Davis. Ferrel Periphery. The Jet Stream Archives. The 'Beast from the East' - February 2018 storm (2023).

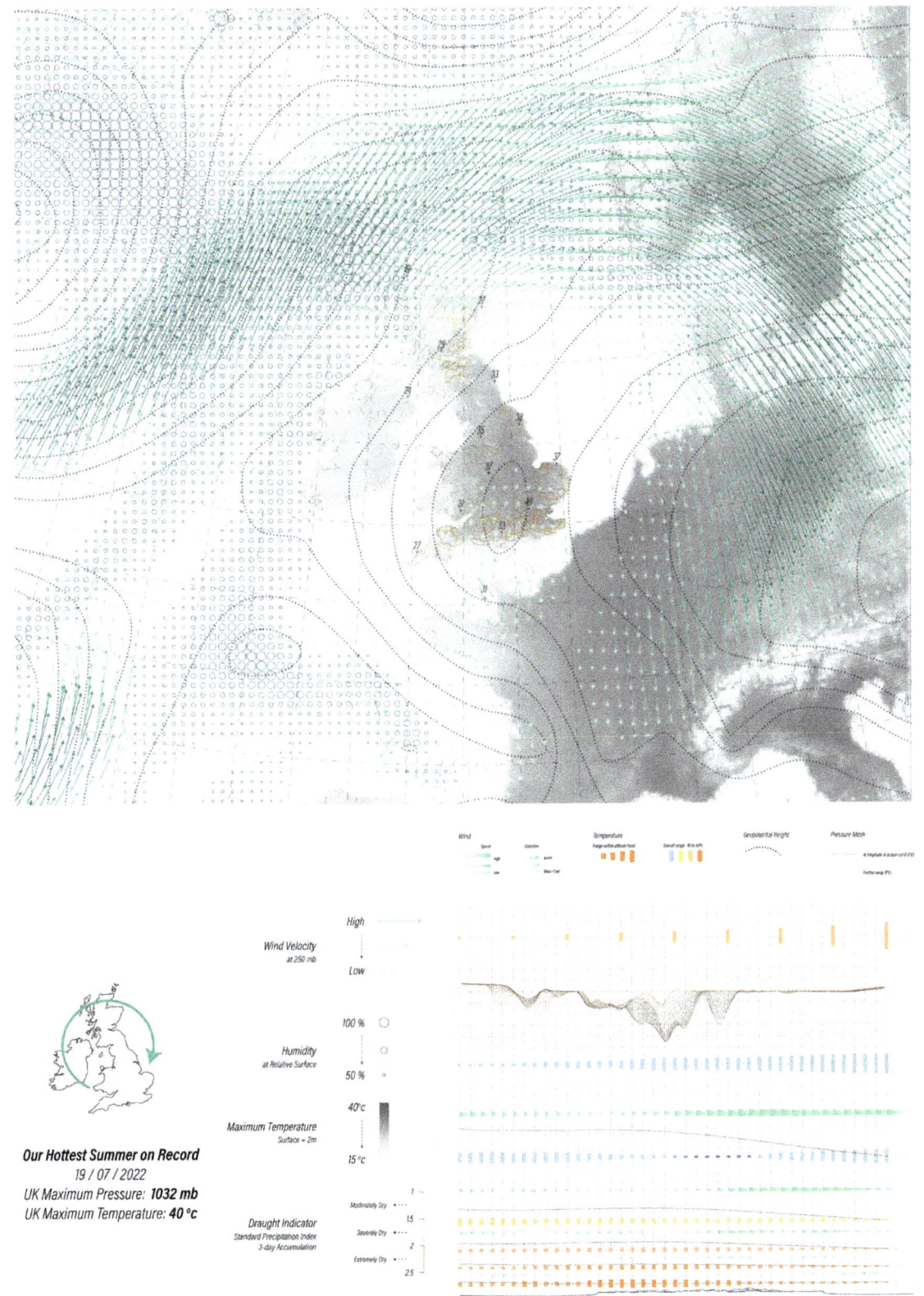

Kirsten Davis. Ferrel Periphery. The Jet Stream Archives. "Our Hottest Summer on Record" - July 2022 (2023).

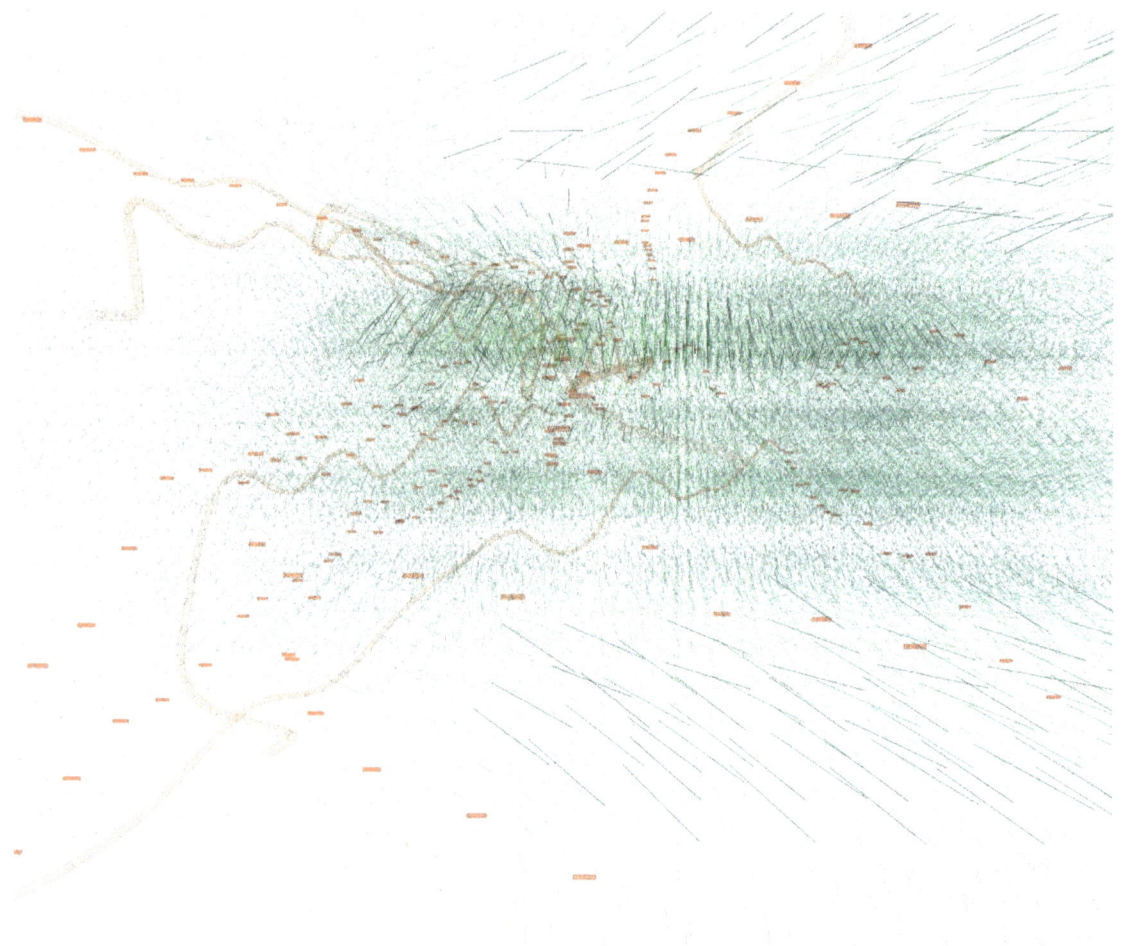

Gabrielle Bucknall. Moth Assembly. Moths journey through a forest (2020).

scope of our travels for study.

In 2019, *Arctic Transformations*, we travelled over the vast latitudinal stretches of Norway and its surrounding Arctic territories. We explored across the wide spectrum of its gradated climatic zones, to study the impacts and consequences of these now reconfigured boundaries and regions, as the country confronted the ramifications of ecological destruction amongst extractive opportunities.

In 2020, *Carbon Transitions*, we focused in on a particular ingredient of air, *Carbon* - at once considered the 'building block of life' and yet a measure of our climatic decline. Based within the UK at a time of significant political upheaval and supposed pathways to *de-carbonisation*, we studied this transformative entity across states, material type, energy and values. But also a spatial and cultural driver, one that had distributed and shaped the very fabric of our built environment, whilst catalysing the reciprocal energy consuming cycles it enabled. [06]

In 2021, *Climate Futures*, we shifted in scale to carry out a single place-based investigation, focused around the anomalous micro-climate of Dungeness on the southern coast of the UK. This precarious peninsula, colloquially termed 'Britain's only desert', lies at the very forefront of climate change and ecological collapse. We used this site as a proving ground, to test how speculative landscape infrastructures may provide hope for future climatic restoration and repair.

And finally in 2022, *Thermal Domains*, as the UK experienced record breaking temperatures rising above 40 degrees, we studied airs specific role as a vehicle and medium of heat. We used thermodynamic principles as tools of design, exploring how thermal conditions, thresholds and gradients become spatial and programmatic organisers, whilst imagining new societal relationships and practices around comfort, energy and heat.

Sara Kosanovic. The Nordkapp Dust Research Station. Computational magnetic field lines deposition of dust particles (2020).

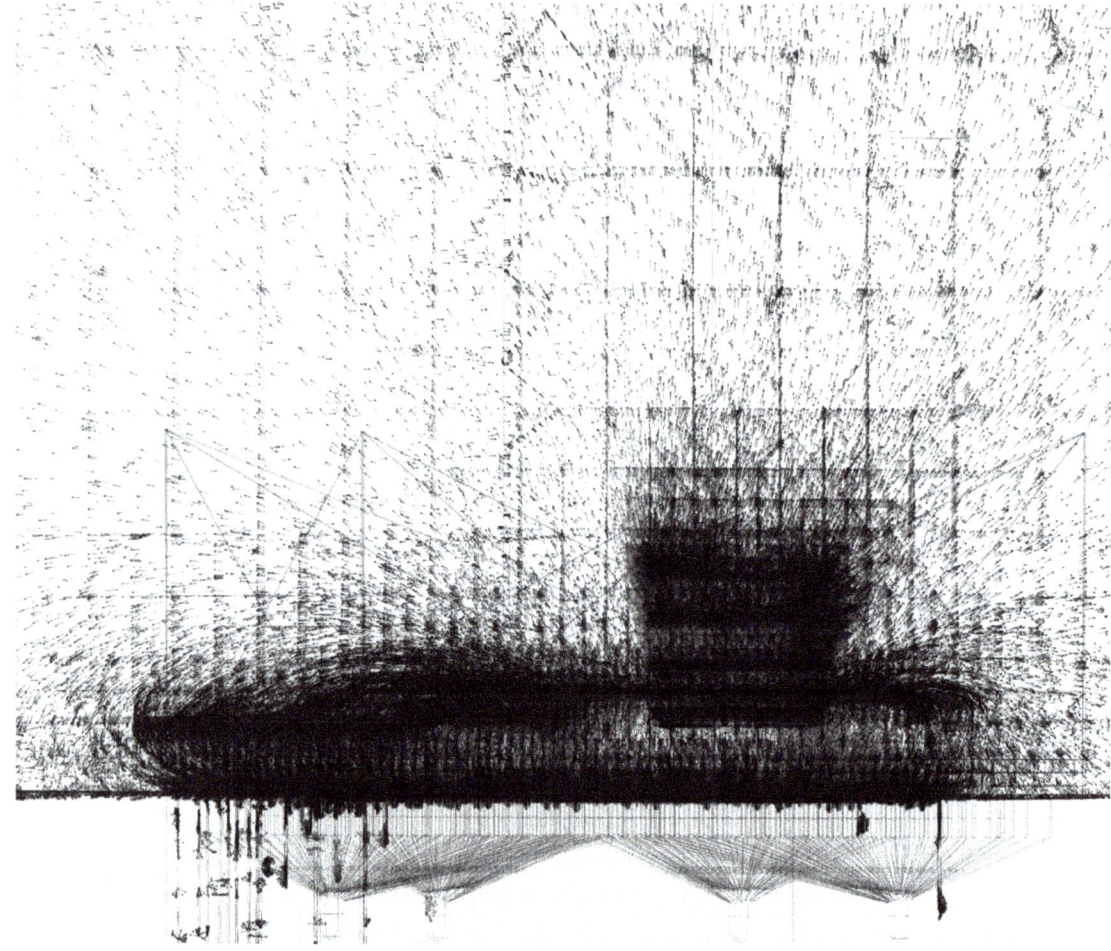

Seni Agunpopo. The Cloud Sanctuary. Overview massing simulation profile (2020).

Designing in Air

We recognise the practice of architecture has differing relationships towards environment, atmosphere and air, evolved over centuries specific and distinct to its context. Historically buildings have been orientated, shaped and detailed in ways that their form and fabric functioned as the primary moderator between external and internal atmospheres, techniques that became less critical with the advent of mechanical air conditioning and heating systems. [07] Through this recent history, buildings are typically considered as enclosures, enveloping and isolating one from their external environment, following the modernist separation of human and nature. Whether passive or technological, we were inspired to imagine buildings designed, integrated and responsive amongst their surrounding aerial environments. Architectures shaped and organised according to airs properties, its dynamics and aerial logics, perhaps even leading to an architecture of air itself. [08]

We looked to envisage architecture as a conduit between air's forms and scales, from global dynamics to micro interactions, from numerical datasets to weathering sensations, in attempts to ground and communicate incompressible long term global concerns through instantaneous human scale phenomenological experience. To explore how buildings themselves could materially reveal air, to augment its states, reactions and interactions for architectural, experiential and knowledge imparting effect. We wished to use these speculative projects to engage and centre matters of the air, to conceive public programmes forefronting aerial concerns, whether functionally, socially or politically, whilst envisaging buildings as mediators and active participants among these activities and debates. These ideas called for new design methods and tools, employing computational simulation software less focused upon the motion of physical particles through space (Next Limit's *Realflow*), but the node-based transferral of

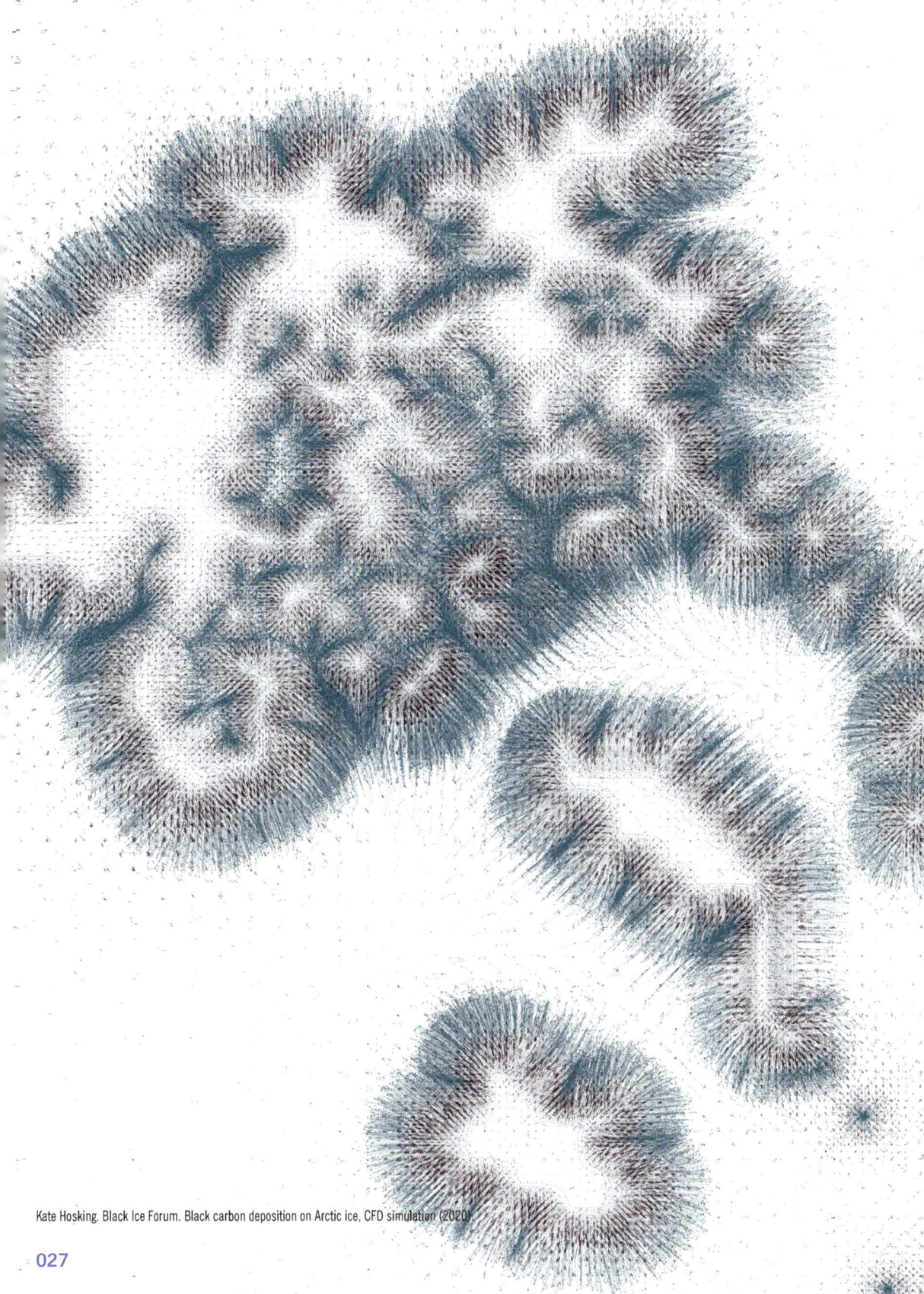

Kate Hosking. Black Ice Forum. Black carbon deposition on Arctic ice, CFD simulation (2020)

Seni Agunpopo. The Cloud Sanctuary. Atmospheric volumes and morphology studies (2020).

properties across gaseous volumetric environments and geometries within (Autodesk's *CFD*). In taking these often imperceivable outputs, we proposed new notations and modes of representation to *visualise the invisible*, to offer new intimacies and encounters with this data and matter. (09) And to format these within new drawing constructs, through Langranian frames of reference, in attempts to capture airs dynamics and relations across scales, space and time. (10)

Impacts of Air

The fore-fronting of climatic matters, as a concern for the architectural discipline and the design practices, is central to the education we try to offer. As graduates of DS18 ourselves, these priorities have had the most profound impact on our own individual practices and teaching. In reflecting on these years of aerial investigations, we recognise these themes as far reaching and ambitious. They depended on the talent, trust and creativity of our students, who were tasked to cover considerable research ground, around materials not widely considered in traditional architectural discourse. It demanded careful navigation and imagination to capture their findings, to translate them through building-scale design projects, whilst retaining the complexity and intrigue of their foundational reference points. Over the course the medium of air directed us towards design tools, methods and modes of communication outside of the traditional architectural toolkit – and ones we hope have equipped students uniquely to take into their latter architectural and wider forms of practice. We believe these themes encouraged and imparted a wider world view, one that called beyond the typically greenwashed, technological, or fetishised design 'solutions'. This subject offered space for critical discussion and debates, around our inadequate environmental metrics, our misguided definitions of 'sustainability', and fundamentally whether we should be building at all. To us we argue these are more than hypothetical student architectural projects. Through their conception and representation these become active tools in the world. (11) They offer new ways of materialising and communicating the wider critical issues of our time, explored through design, inciting new knowledge, responses and action, amongst the audiences, the students and ourselves.

Georgios Malliaropoulos. The Heat Exchange and Thermal Theatre. Melting wall elevation (2023).

Notes

(01) IPCC, Special Report on the Impacts of Global Warming of 1.5°C Above Pre-Industrial Levels. Intergovernmental Panel on Climate Change, 2018.
(02) E.Horn, *Air as Medium,* Grey Room 73, 2018, p.6-25.
(03) E.Coccia, 'In Open Air : Ontology of The Atmosphere', *in Log 60 : The Sixth Sphere,* Anyone Cooperation, 2024, p.61.
(04) P. Sloterdijk, *Terror From the Air,* Los Angeles, Semiotext(e), 2009.
(05) T. Woollings and M.Blackburn, 'The North Atlantic Jet Stream under Climate Change and Its Relation to the NAO and EA Patterns', in *Journal of Climate 25* (3), 2012 p. 886–902.
(06) I. Elisa, 'Architecture And the Death of Carbon Modernity', in *Log 47 : Overcoming Carbon Form*, Anyone Cooperation, 2019, p. 10–23.
(07) R.Banham, *The Architecture of the Well-Tempered Environment*, Chicago, University Of Chicago Press, 1984.
(08) P. Rahm, 'Meteorological Architecture', in *Architectural Design 79* (3), 2009, p.30–41.
(09) N. Cavillo, Sensing Aeropolis. Urban air monitoring devices in Madrid, 2006-2010. Thesis (Doctoral), E.T.S. Arquitectura (UPM), 2014.
(10) K.Moe, 'Non-Linear Perspective', in *Log 47 : Overcoming Carbon Form, Anyone Cooperation*, 2019, p. 118-130.
(11) R. Ghosn, and J. El Hadi, *Geostories: Another Architecture for the Environment,* New York - Barcelona: Actar Publishing, 2021.

CARTOGRAPHIC IMAGINARIES

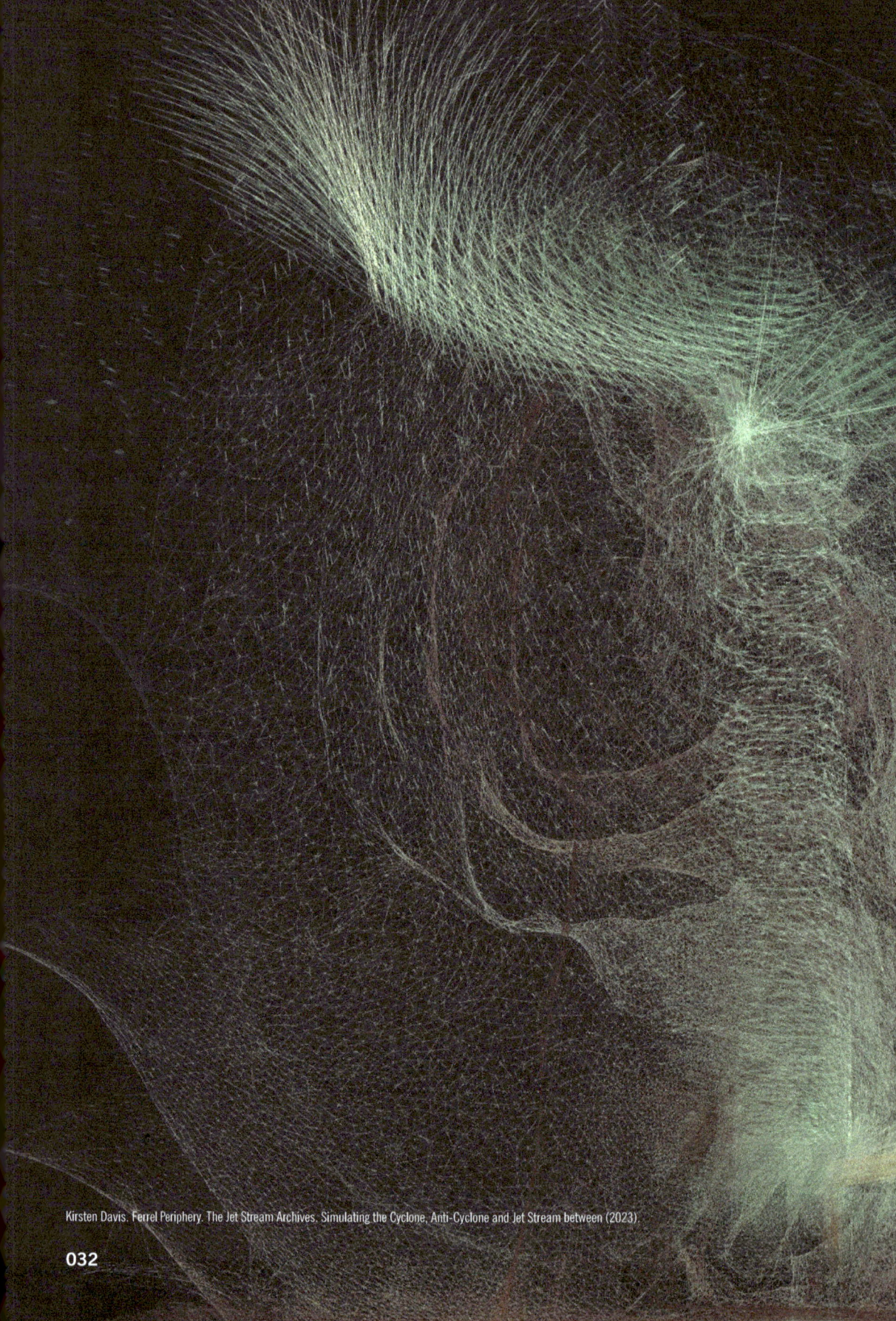

Kirsten Davis. Ferrel Periphery. The Jet Stream Archives. Simulating the Cyclone, Anti-Cyclone and Jet Stream between (2023).

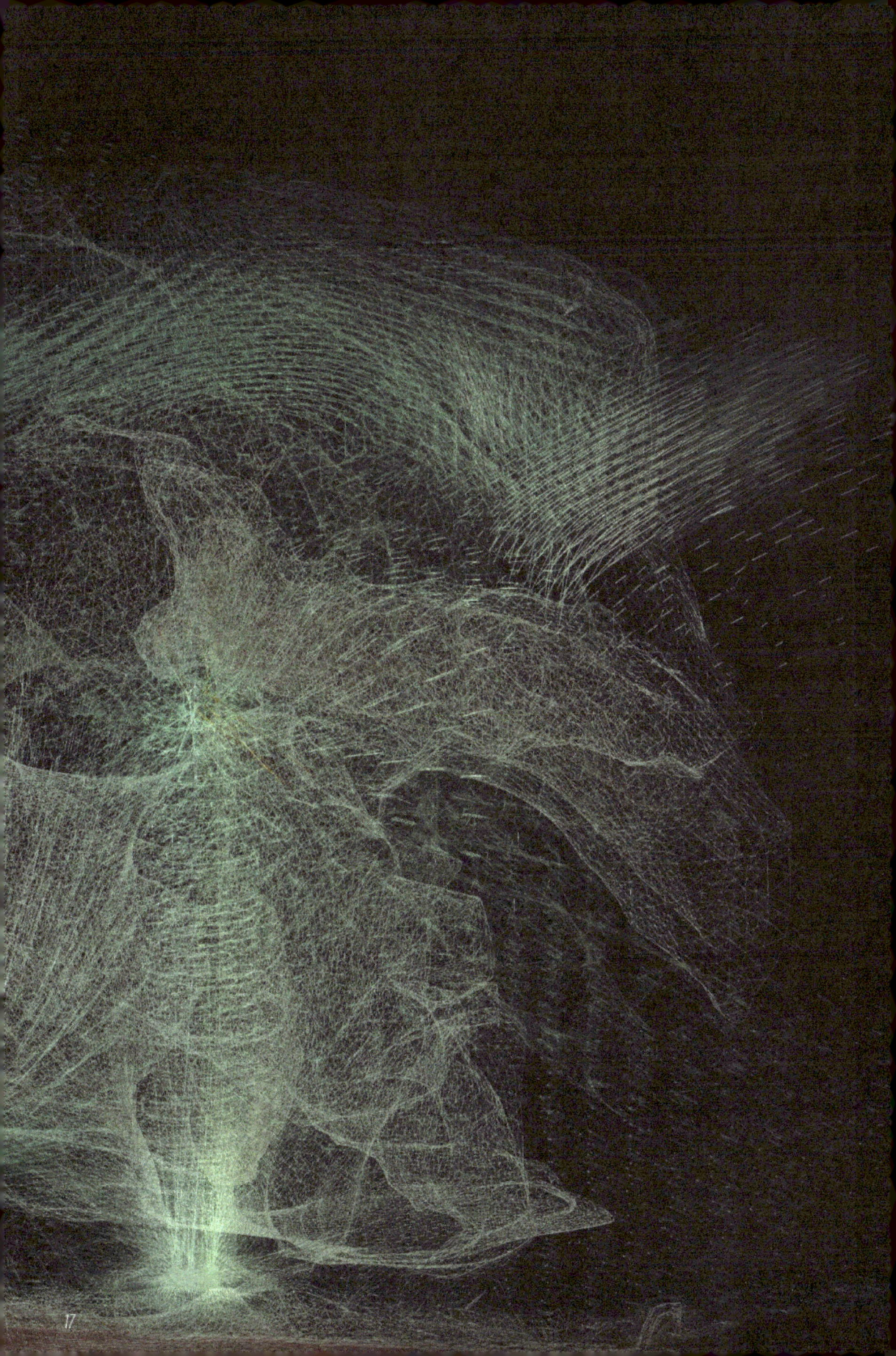

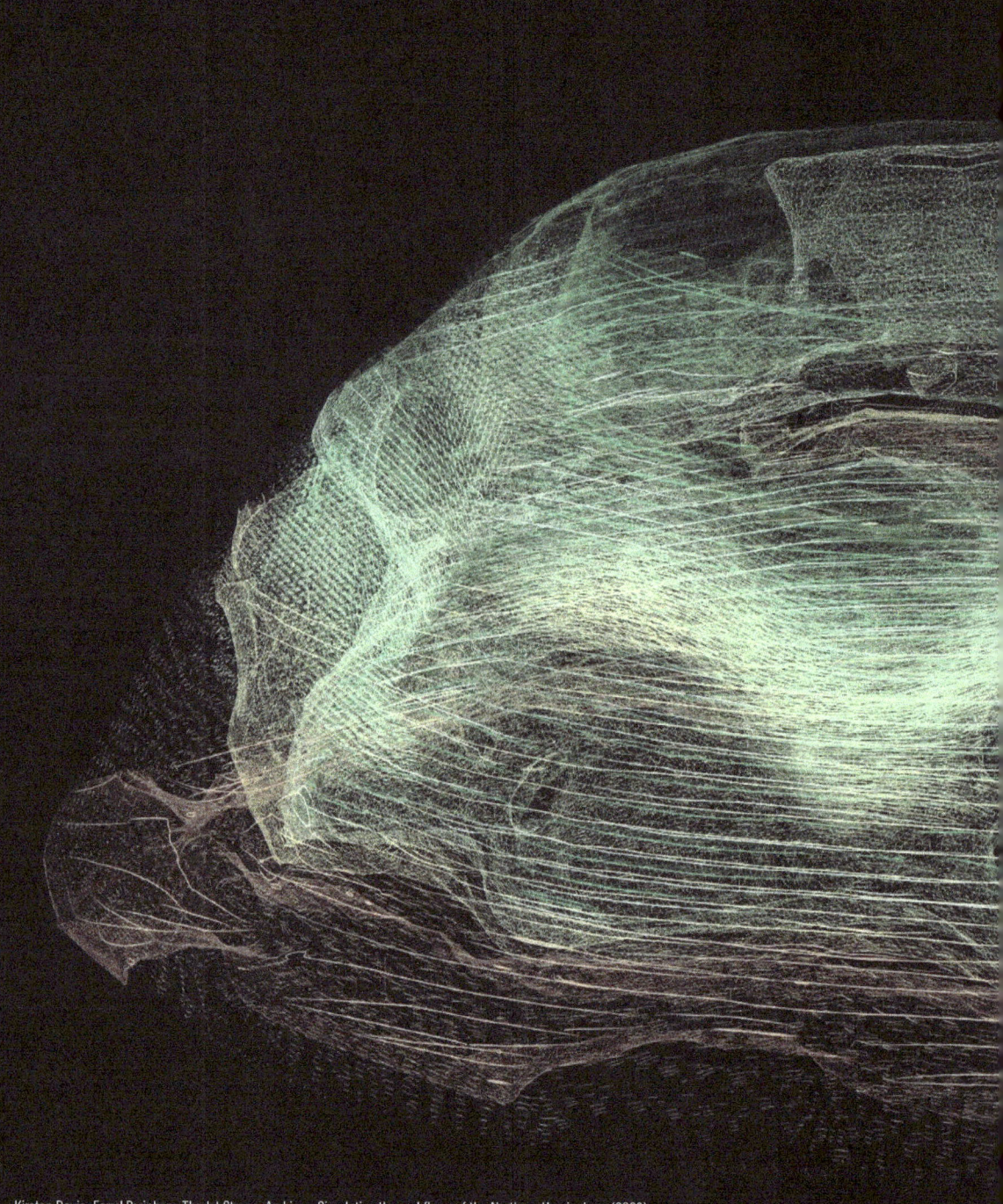

Kirsten Davis. Ferrel Periphery. The Jet Stream Archives. Simulating thermal flows of the Northern Hemisphere (2023).

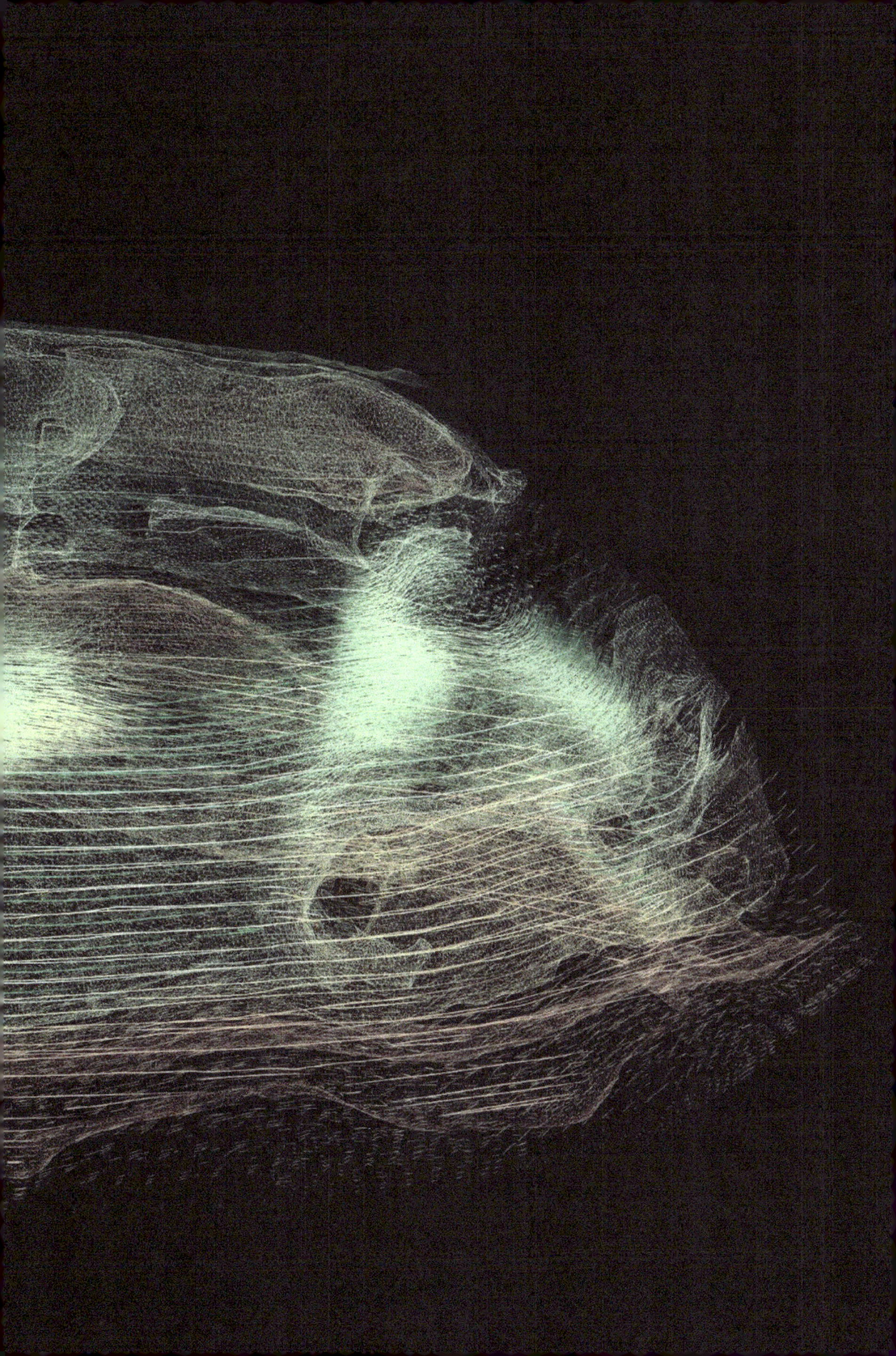

Kirsten Davis. Ferrel Periphery. The Jet Stream Archives. Dynamic weather patterns - the Atmospheric River (2023).

Kirsten Davis. Ferrel Periphery. The Jet Stream Archives. Storm Ciara (February 2020) - Correlating tropospheric wind and pressure levels to ground based temperature, humidity and flooding instances (2023).

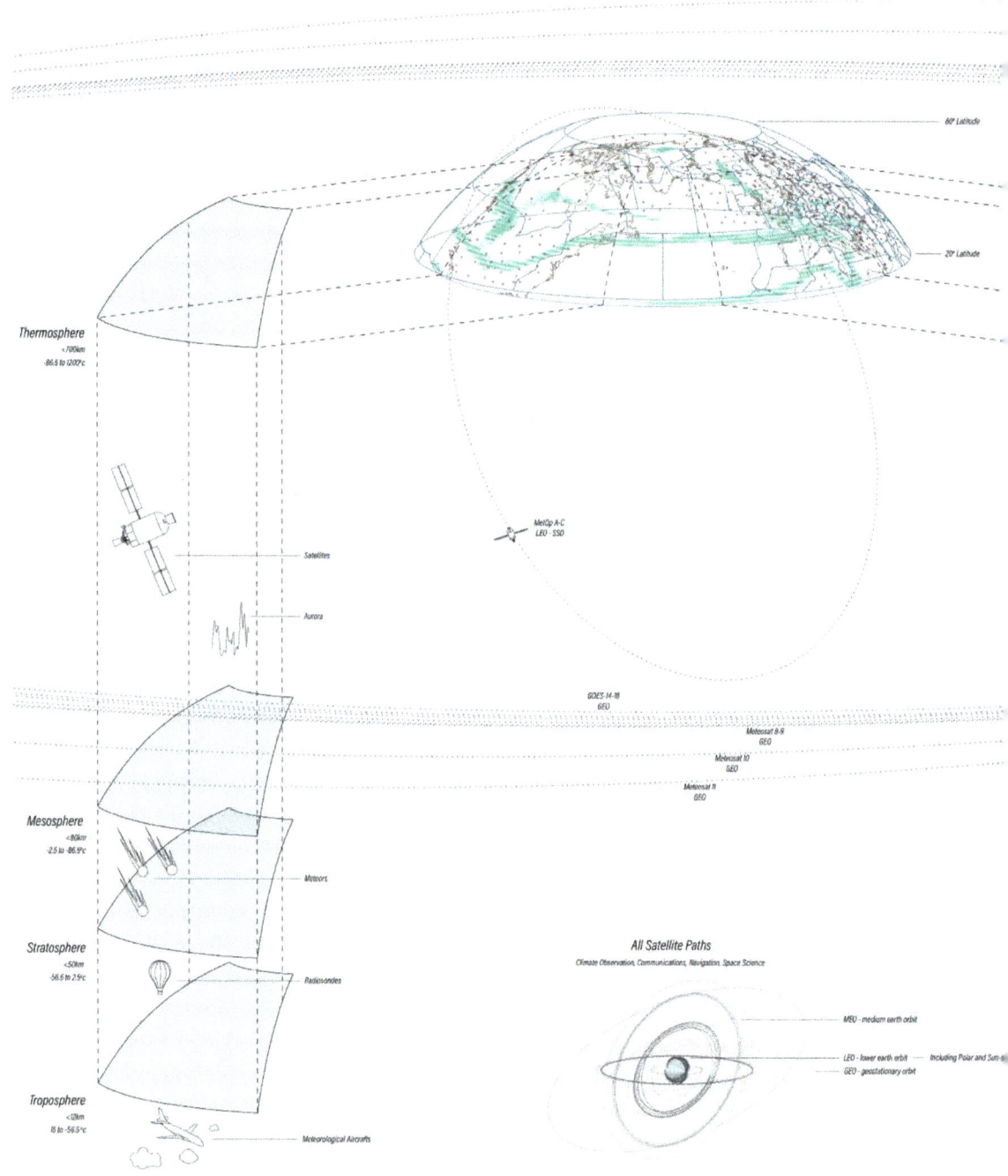

Kirsten Davis. Ferrel Periphery. The Jet Stream Archives. Understanding the Atmosphere : Meteorological Monitoring System.
Climate observation through apparatus at different layers of the atmosphere, and the management of airspace (2023).

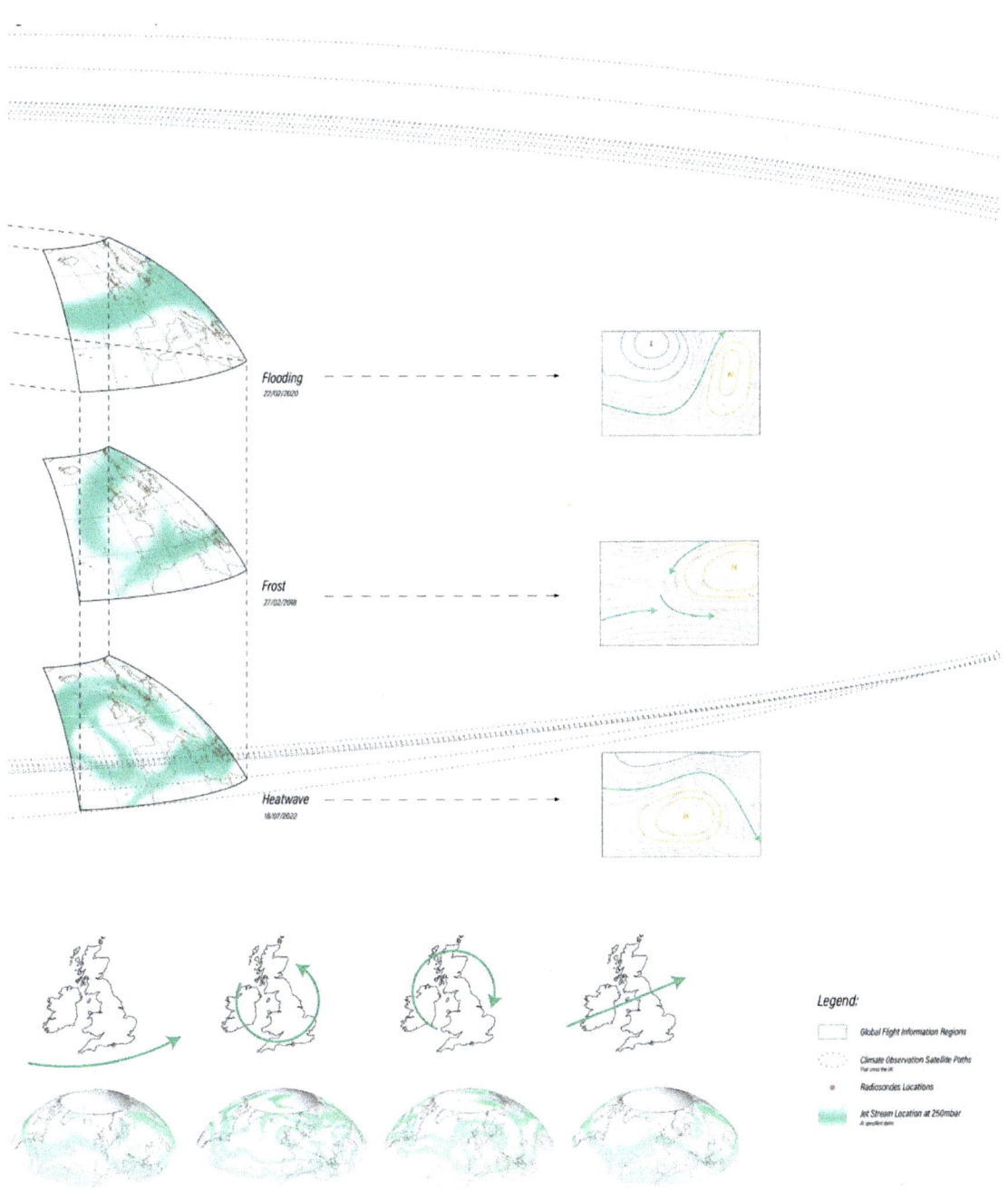

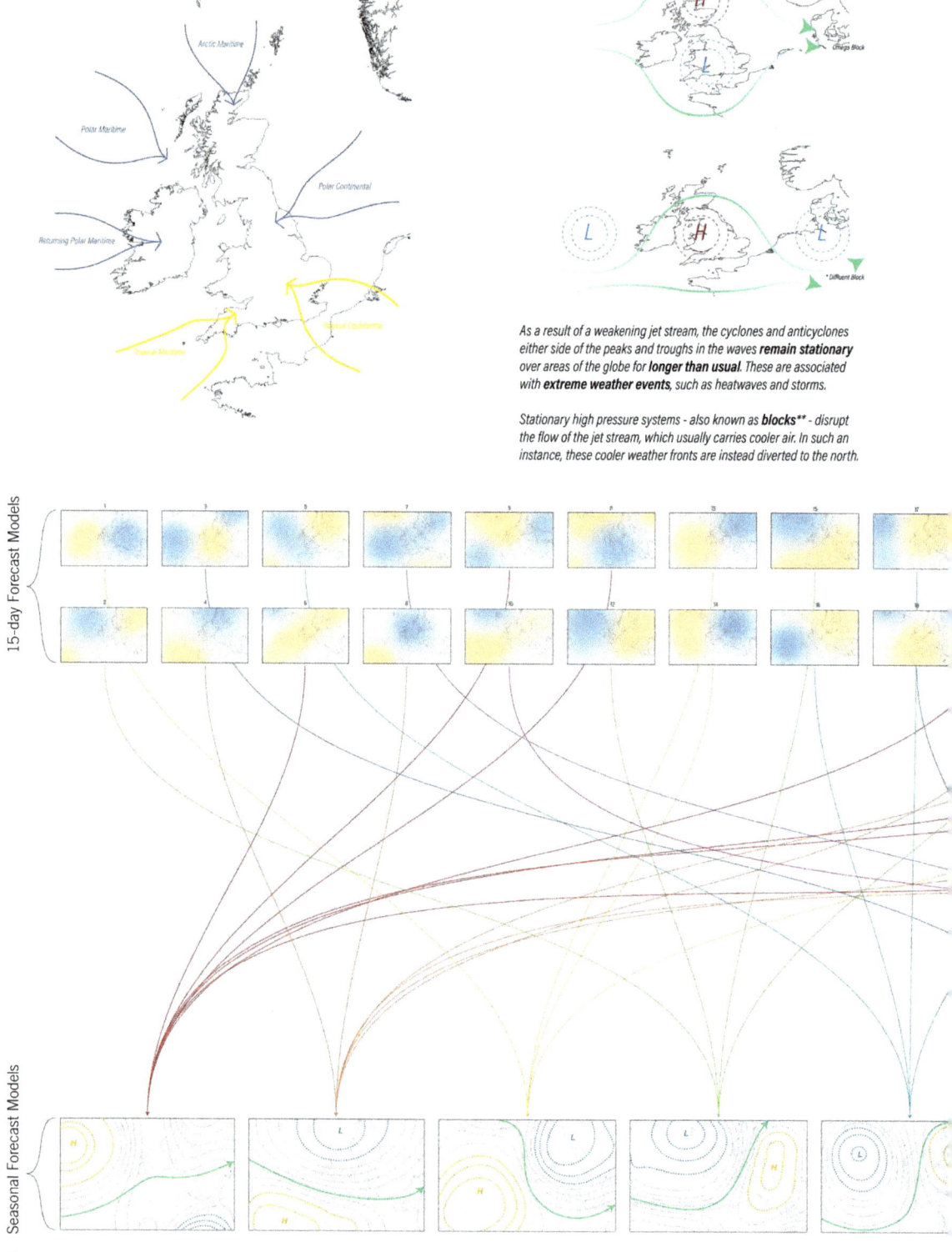

As a result of a weakening jet stream, the cyclones and anticyclones either side of the peaks and troughs in the waves **remain stationary** over areas of the globe for **longer than usual**. These are associated with **extreme weather events**, such as heatwaves and storms.

Stationary high pressure systems - also known as **blocks**** - disrupt the flow of the jet stream, which usually carries cooler air. In such an instance, these cooler weather fronts are instead diverted to the north.

Kirsten Davis. Ferrel Periphery. The Jet Stream Archives. Computing the Atmosphere : Climate Forecasting. UK Met Office classified pressure scenarios (2023).

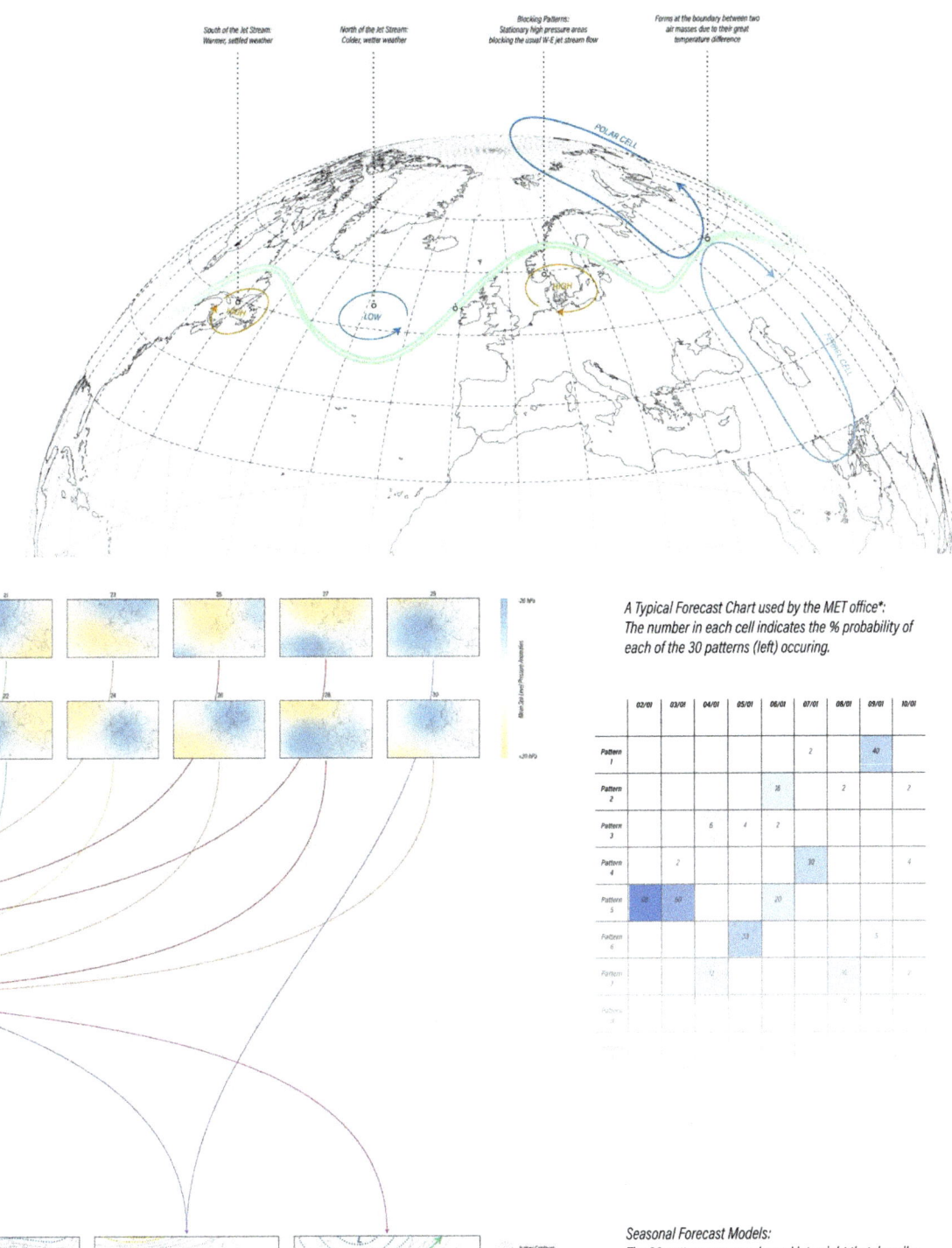

A Typical Forecast Chart used by the MET office*:
The number in each cell indicates the % probability of each of the 30 patterns (left) occuring.

Seasonal Forecast Models:
The 30 patterns are condensed into eight that describe longer term, seasonal weather patterns.

Transcribing these with the addition of the Jet Stream between the air masses serves as a key for the following more detailed climate cartographies.

* https://www.metoffice.gov.uk/research/news/2018/new-weather-patterns-for-uk-and-europe

COMPUTING CLIMATES

GUY SINCLAIR

Driving down the motorway at the junction turning into Exeter, south-west England, one passes within fifty metres of reputedly the "world's most powerful supercomputer dedicated to weather and climate." [01] Home to the U.K Meteorological Office and its interconnected suite of Cray XC40 supercomputing systems, this suburban campus is a critical centre in an unevenly globalised network of climate knowledge production and prediction. This network was once characterised, prophetically, by the Victorian polymath John Ruskin as a "vast machine" that wishes "its influence and its power to be omnipresent over the globe." [02]

This machine is now largely realised, through two centuries of work constructing the infrastructures of meteorology and climate science it observes, calculates and reproduces planetary climate and weather phenomena in silico. This desire for a systematic knowledge of global atmospheres expressed at the outset of meteorology as an organised scientific discipline exposes a core condition within the conception of climate – as a set of averages across spatial and temporal scales, climate can never be directly accessed through human experience. [03] It is inherently a beyond-human compact, not only because it refers to dynamic geophysical systems, but also because it can only be made knowable through hybrids between social and technological processes – or the sociotechnical.

Climates – historical, projected and contemporary - are now rendered legible and made governable at the Met Office and a select number of national weather and climate institutions operating primarily in the Global North (**Fig. 1**). Historian of climate science Paul Edwards describes this production of climate as a knowledge infrastructure, comprising instrumentation, computational capacity, scientific labour, international standards and technopolitical resources, which all generate and maintain a centralised and consensual scientific understanding of climate. [04]

The U.K Met Office is an historically significant institution within this knowledge infrastructure. It is notably one of a small number of centres contributing to the World Climate Research Program's Coupled Model Intercomparison Project (CMIP) as well as publishing the HadCRUT global surface temperature database via the Hadley Centre for Climate Science and Services, amongst a plethora of other scientific and technical work. Established as a national agency in service to British mariners around the world in the 19-th

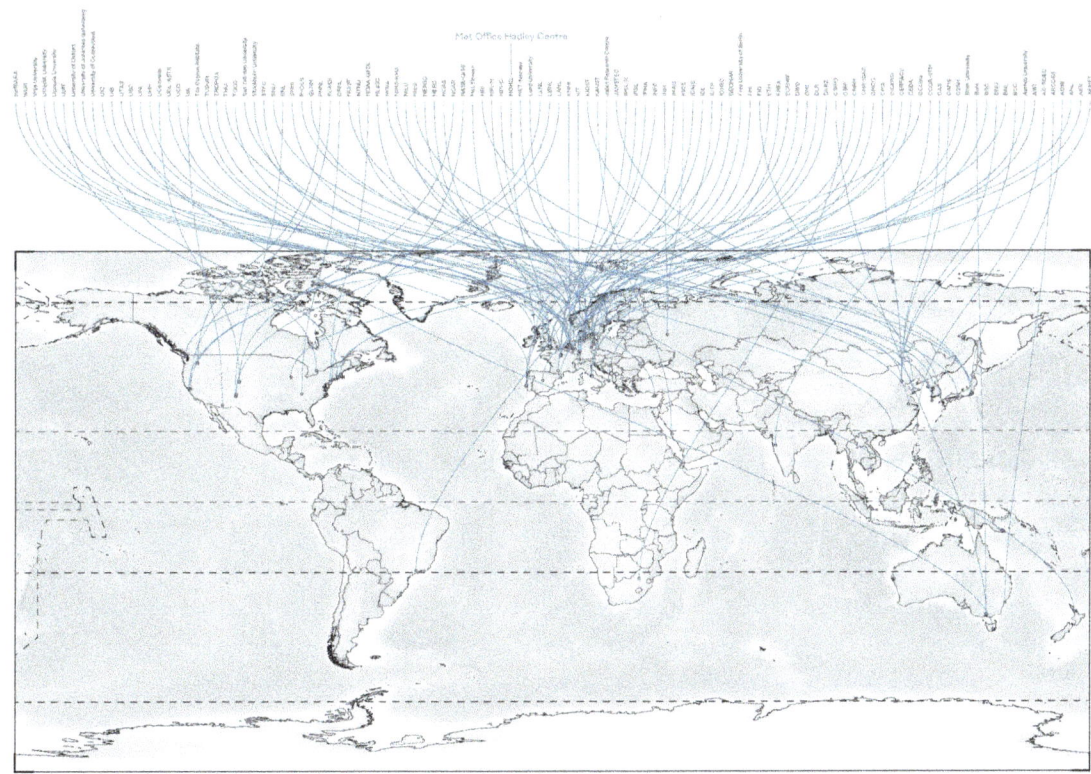

Figure 1 – Global distribution of CMIP 6 contributors.

century, the Met Office emerged as a national weather service within the milieu of military, colonial and imperial projects, in a similar vein to the development of other European meteorological organisations, and later grew with the development of numerical weather prediction models (NWP) in the context of cold war tensions between the US and USSR. [05] However, the Hadley Centre as a dedicated climate research unit at the Met Office was founded only in the 1980s during a shift towards the long term assessment of Earth's climate system with a specific goal – to measure, quantify, understand and project (anthropogenic) climatic changes. [06]

Sensing and making sense of the long-term climate change requires a co-production of planetary knowledge, bringing together a multitude of actors, amassing climate observations and modelling simulated Terran climates. Within this work though, one element stands out as critical to the development of the contemporary view of climate from the Global North – computational capacity. Cultural geographer of climate Mike Hulme goes as far to suggest that for the constituency of climate scientists, climate is primarily a numerical phenomenon "that exists virtually above all else." [07] The primacy of supercomputers to the production of climate knowledge is historically contingent, though given the complexity of fluid global circulatory systems and gathering worldwide climate information, only an apparatus such as the digital computer and its subsequent developments, like massively parallel processing, proffered a resolution to the problem of recording and modelling global climate data.

In the period following the birth of early digital computers during WWII, climatology rapidly became a science intimately connected to the growth of computational capabilities. Celebrated émigré mathematician John von Neumann explicitly supported the application of the first Electronic Computer Project, as well as the initial use of the prototypical ENIAC and EDVAC machines, to the problem of numerical weather prediction (NWP).[08] Weather and climate models presented an example par excellence for early computing applications that fulfilled three key criteria: mathematical and scientific interest; operational military value; and a use that would demonstrate the power of computers to the widest possible audience. Initial weather and climate modelling projects received strong backing from government and military resources through Von Neumann's advocacy. [09] At this point the previously empirical science of climatology had been supplemented by theoretical methods in meteorology that had begun to explain the fundamental physics of the atmosphere. Through the work of figures such as Vilhelm Bjerknes, who managed

Figure 2 - Lewis Fry Richardson's "forecast-factory" as illustrated by François Schuiten. Image permission: © Fraçois Schuiten & ATLANTIC 12.

to delineate a set of fluid dynamics equations describing atmospheric movement in just seven variables, a workable prerequisite in the physical science for computational modelling was established, one which presented an analytic method that would be impossible to solve without exceptionally large-scale calculation.

A contemporary of Bjerknes, Lewis Fry Richardson, saw the issues in the application of Bjerknes' equations to the reality of calculating weather and climate however. [10] In attempting a finite-difference calculation that could be initiated from data taken during an "international balloon day" in 1910, Richardson was confronted with the stark reality of the scale of the mathematical task – it took him six-weeks' worth of calculations to complete a single "retrospective weather forecast" of a six-hour period. [11] Given this imbalance, Richardson proposed an speculative image of a panoptic, global centre of calculation that foreshadows the later concentration of computing power within institutional weather forecasting and climate research facilities. He proposed a "forecast-factory" occupying the spherical interior of a global theatre (Fig. 2), consisting of 64,000 human computers, overseen by an elevated podium of clerical conductors managing the manual calculation of regional results. [12] These would be collected within the central pulpit and transported pneumatically to a separate room, whereby the weather forecast could be communicated to the world through means of telegraphy.

This description augured the global scope of early twentieth century climatology and the recognition of the planetary resolution required for an accurate forecast, or at least a more comprehensive understanding of weather and climate dynamics. Beyond the sheer calculating capacity that was imagined, the organisational requirements of such an apparatus are also apparent from Richardson's hypothetical world weather forecasting system. The improbability of such an operation of human computers stymied the application of numerical methods to weather and climate until the advent and rapid advancement of the electronic, digital computer in post-war America through programmes at the Institute for Advanced Studies, Princeton and the subsequent arrival of commercial manufacturers like IBM. The expense and scarcity of machine time in mid-century computing from 1948-1960 meant that initial experiments in numerical weather prediction and climate modelling were constrained to a very few laboratories in the United States and, through academic connections, in

Scandinavia. The U.K Met Office also pioneered the use of computing in the 1950s, employing the first stored-programme electronic computer at the University of Manchester and later a commercially available Ferranti Mk1 (**Fig. 3**). The Met Office did not acquire a dedicated digital computer until 1955, which came to be named Meteor. [13]

Deploying what was initially developed as a military technology, albeit with potentially universal applications, meant that a particular technoscientific culture emerged that brought together highly skilled mathematicians and trained meteorologists. Beyond the enormous expense and fragility of early computer technologies, the nascent discipline of computer science for numerical weather prediction created a somewhat esoteric academic community defined by the work of a handful of initial modelling projects based in the US, Europe, Japan and Australia. [14] It can be stated that "the concentration of computing resources at a few institutions probably affected no field more than it affected climatology". [15] This was true throughout the early stages of the introduction of digital computing technologies and is equally the case today. In describing the inescapable gravitational mass of computer technologies and their zenith in current high-performance parallel computing, Paul Edwards explains that as "modelers sought to increase model resolution and include more physical processes directly in the models, their models required more and more computer power. Every group building GCMs [General Circulation Models] either owned or had access to the largest, fastest supercomputers available". [16]

To compose accurate reproductions of the Earth's atmosphere within a simulated computer model, the exigencies of General Circulation Models required globally representative atmospheric and oceanographic data. As computational power increased inexorably, the paucities in the distribution and quality of climate data posed a challenge to ever gaining the long-desired omniscient view of planetary circulation and its driving effect on climate variability. Averaged climate data in a form that could become readable by machine only existed in a patchwork across temporal and geographic windows, with improving but generally problematic characteristics that made reconciling data from many different sources a substantial task in its own right. This compounded the underlying issue that most weather and climate observations had only documented the more populace northern-hemisphere and that there were significant regional omissions in the international record owing to political discord between nation states. This presented an inauspicious setting for what can be referred to as the dual projects of "making global data" and "making data global." [17] To make global data, denser networks of observation, with more reliable standards of collection, were installed to capture details from the Earth's upper atmosphere and the less well covered land and ocean surfaces. To make data global however, computer models had to take on a new aspect, implementing processes for "objective analysis" to create structured, gridded data across the complete spherical surface of the globe and ascending in a series of pressure layers vertically through the atmosphere. [18] Generating high quality, global gridded data derived from the locally variable measurements of radiosonde stations, weather ships and high-altitude flight paths created the necessity for data models. More than just a collection of calibrated observations, data models produced a complete, synthetic image of the Earth's climate or weather by an iterative process of interpolation and by re-analysing past data sets. A caveat to the advance of this putative God's-eye, computational image was that of resolution, the coarseness of the gridded data and the fidelity to climate behaviour that is implied.

Gridded data models posed a technopolitical dilemma. Increasing density in the observing networks that seed data for NWP models provides diminishing returns past a certain station separation, approximately five hundred kilometres. [19] Therefore, relatively sparse observational data is interpolated into complete gridded data models at resolutions which cover very large physical areas and can contain a diversity of human geographies. Gridding climate models to make them efficiently calculable or computable within reasonable timeframes means that a process called parametrisation is necessary in order to simulate a multiplicity of "sub-grid scale physics" which are often highly consequential at the human scale – rainfall, landforms and cloud cover for example. [20] Further, certain geographies such as small-island states often end up being represented solely as ocean within coarsely gridded, but consequential, long-run climate simulations. The technical trade-offs inherent in modelling planetary climate have political knock-ons for human lifeways, often more acutely affecting climate vulnerable nations in the Global South.

Reporting within the technical, political and scientific aegis of institutions such as the World Meteorological Organization (WMO) and the Intergovernmental Panel on Climate Change offers a potential corrective to structural imbalances in the process climate knowledge production. Profoundly imperfect inclusions and negotiations, through the Conference of Parties (COP), are offered to countries who are excluded from climate modelling by the very high human and material resource threshold that persists in the work of climate science. It has been noted that the "widespread perception that the issue of climate change 'belongs' to the developed [Global North] countries, not only because they are the initial (and still principal) sources of fossil fuel emissions but also because they are the 'owners' of knowledge about the problem"

Figure 3 - The Met Office's Ferranti computer, Meteor, in 1961.

endures. [21] Climates derived through computation are exclusionary in their creation, and foment a critique of climate knowledge generated in this mode that embodies a Western modernity in hock to, and perhaps uncritical of, dominant technoscientific practices.[22] These practices consist of those which make changing climates knowable, but also those which have made climates change through industrialised economies and extractive and emitting modes of production.

The continued dominance of this mode of knowledge production by institutions throughout the Global North is instantiated in the sociotechnical relations at the UK Met Office. The exclusive condition of the knowledge infrastructure of climate science are evidenced in situ at the Met Office's headquarters building in Exeter, where the critical role of the supercomputer as the locus of the climate model is materialised. Planetary climate is here made locally through the relationships between spatial arrangements, energetic armatures and human labour. The Met Office currently operates a linked set of three Cray XC40 high-performance computers (HPCs), with two focussed on modelling numerical weather prediction for operational, daily forecasts and a separate system that occupies an ancillary building, known only descriptively as the High-Performance Computer Facility (Fig. 4 -5), dedicated to climate modelling research.[23] In the hall that houses the supercomputers, the significant servicing requirement for thermally conditioning processing capacity can be seen through a panoply of ducts, vents, dials, and electrical units that serve the central hardware of the machine stacks. The investment in these physical infrastructures illustrates the complexity of the supercomputer as a sited and co-productive apparatus for contemporary climate science.

The spaces of the supercomputer localise and situate the research and observational network of climate science. In viewing the data halls and HPC facility at the Met Office as nodal point in this web, a view of the supercomputer as an instrument that engenders concentrations of power is reinforced. For example, the exterior of the separate data hall housing the climate research supercomputer (HPC 3 to the Met Office) appears as a blank mass without apertures, the interior is devoid of permanent human occupation, with only transitory visits by approved technicians. Reading this as a modern spatialisation of climate computing, the Cray supercomputer and its attendant systems manifest Lewis Fry Richardson's fantasy of global computation in a manner which is opposite to the fanciful scale, colourful cartography

Figure 4 - HPC data connections.

Figure 5 - Cray XC40 HPC 3.

and polite ushering of results by human clerks. Instead, the data hall is a nondescript space of infrastructure, belying the importance of the machines inside – rendering complex, global earth processes as projective models, vital tools in understanding the dynamics of climate and its accelerating degree of crisis around the world.

The Met Office data halls do not outwardly portray their interconnections to climate observing systems, nor any sense of its global significance or the scale of the data it computes. Like all infrastructures it operates silently and is consciously unseen, "transparent" in the sense used by theorists of large technical systems Susan Leigh Star and Karen Ruhleder. [24] What it does make explicit is the fundamental episteme of the climate scientist, the primacy of the digital simulation as a tool that can be predictive, reanalytic (i.e. assimilating incomplete or incongruous data sets), and informational. [25] The site of this activity is inescapably the supercomputer, a machine that has been developed to take on the huge and complex task (although reductively simplified from reality) of simulating the entire Earth System as understood through several key strata and geophysical cycles. This conception of climate as a phenomenon that plays out as digital simulacrum instead of a purely tangible stream of elapsing temperatures, eddies,

changing humidity levels and incident solar radiation etcetera, is indicated in the oddly referential, hexagonal form of the section of the building – it mimics the circuitry that makes up the computers that the building houses. [26]

As a sociotechnical apparatus, the supercomputer is built on the knowledge infrastructure of agreed scientific standards, data collection and programming from an international cohort of scientists and institutions, however it cannot physically operate without certain environmental, thermodynamic manipulations. Computing at the scale of the climate model requires not only financial and organisational resources, but fundamentally requires a controlled interior environment – models of planetary climate need a carefully conditioned climatic enclosure. This is delivered through air-conditioning technologies that were developed in the early twentieth century by engineer Willis H. Carrier as a means of producing "man-made weather." [27] This technology for interior climatic control in fact presupposes the productive ability of the supercomputer and the possibility for projected knowledge of future climate scenarios. In Climatic Media: Transpacific Experiments in Atmospheric Control media theorist Yuriko Furuhata proposes that with the advent of numerical weather prediction "adequate systems of air-conditioning

Figure 6 - HPC 3 Data hall interior, © Wilmott Dixon.

had to be constructed in order to provide an infrastructural support for these computers; the machines needed atmospheric pampering for their optimal performance." (28) In this history of climatic control and predictive computing across Japanese and American climate modelling groups, Furuhata posits that "without the production of indoor weather, numerical prediction of outdoor weather was impossible." Conventionally, it is understood that prediction precedes the desire for anthropic control over climates, but for Furuhata "this reversal of causality – that prediction is dependent on control – indicates the deeper epistemological and political stakes of the thermostatic desire". (29)

A further architectural and material question emerges from this observation. In serving the thermoregulatory requirements of such an advanced and resource intensive tool as the supercomputing system, how does the building envelope of the space of the supercomputer with its mechanical, electrical and plumbed services exemplify a modern architectural paradigm that relies on an entrenched, carbon intensive model of energy supply, despite superficial labels of sustainability? (30) Given that the foundational motivation of contemporary climate science is to rightly inform and alert the world to potentially catastrophic global heating and anthropogenic climate change, how does the architecture of climate science justify its recourse to "the closed world" of operationally intensive mechanical cooling? (31)

In developing probabilistic outcomes via computer simulation, compared and averaged through technopolitical methods such as CMIP6, an understanding of how the climate will change is underwritten by a faith in the veracity of the supercomputer as a tool of omniscient proportion. This results in publications from the IPCC that are couched as warnings but are co-opted towards a strategy of climate mitigation (summed up as 'given carbon emission reduction x we can achieve reduced global temperature increase y'). This logic follows a still dominant argument for "sustainability" or as Sarah Ichioka and Michael Palwyn write, the goal of making the climate crisis "100% less bad" and failing to conceive of unequivocally better or transformative futures. (32) Climate risk mitigation strategies that are driven by a sustainability agenda can emerge from the climate science knowledge infrastructure and its materialisations within the Met Office. This position is fuelled by the neoliberal desire to continue with an, albeit moderated, 'business as usual' approach in which growth is infinite, and the impacts of climate risks are computationally calculated to then be offset and outsourced. This deterministic thinking inflects the construction of a climate science knowledge defined by knowing and making climates quantifiable or modellable, and thus governable.

Climate supercomputing reproduces planetary systems as models from rarefied centres of calculation, which fulfil the machinic imaginaries developed by the sciences of weather and climate since the 19th century. The difficulty of making a complete image of planetary climate has concentrated the power to compose and predict those images at a small number of well-financed, and usually historically well-connected, institutions that can access the most cutting-edge computing technologies. However, these technologies are situated and contingent on environmental conditioning, the production of indoor climates enables the projection of planetary climates. In regulating and mediating an ostensibly bounded space, the Earth's climate appears to become governable through means of prediction, the intercomparison of models and the deployment of scientific knowledge into political, international processes. The limits of these processes founded in relationships between the technical, scientific and political spheres are now emerging. Without questioning and historicising the assumptions within the technoscientific practices of climate knowledge production in the Global North, climate becomes a separable object of study, external to the ways of life that change and manipulate it. Climates are constructed through social, technical and scientific practices that bring together non-human agents (i.e the supercomputer) (**Fig. 6**) and human mathematicians, modellers and meteorologists. These practices exist within a world that has sought to know in able to control climate from centres of military, economic or imperial power – a desire that may become futile in a world of erupting climate volatility.

Notes

(01) Press Office, 'Supercomputing Leap in Weather and Climate Forecasting', *Met Office* (2021) https://www.metoffice.gov.uk/about-us/news-and-media/media-centre/corporate-news/2021/met-office-and-microsoft-announce-supercomputer-project, (para. 3 of 21).

(02) P. N. Edwards, *A Vast Machine: Computer Models, Climate Data and the Politics of Global Warming* (Cambridge, MA: MIT Press 2013), p. vii.

(03) R. Staley et al., 'Making Climate History: Rationale', *University of Cambridge* (2019), https://www.hps.cam.ac.uk/research/projects/making-climate-history/rationale, (para. 1 of 3).

(04) Edwards, *A Vast Machine*, p.17-18.

(05) D. R. Coen, 'Climate', *Encyclopedia of the History of Science* (May 2024), doi: https://doi.org/10.34758/gx3d-364, p. 16-21.

(06) C. Folland, D. Griggs and J. Houghton, 'History of the Hadley Centre for Climate Prediction and Research', *Weather*, vol. 59, no. 11, 2004, p.317.

(07) M. Hulme, *Weathered: Cultures of Climate* (London, UK: Sage Publications, 2017), p.1.

(08) Edwards, *A Vast Machine*, pp.114-115.

(09) Edwards, *A Vast Machine*, p.113.

(10) Edwards, *A Vast Machine*, p.93.

(11) Edwards, *A Vast Machine*, p.94.

(12) L. F. Richardson, Weather Prediction by Numerical Process (Cambridge University Press, 1922).

(13) Archives of IT, 'The Met Office and supercomputers: a timeline' (*Archives IT*, 2016), https://archivesit.org.uk/the-met-office-and-supercomputers-a-timeline/.

(14) Edwards, *A Vast Machine*, p. 171.

(15) Edwards, *A Vast Machine*, p. 139.

(16) Edwards, *A Vast Machine*, p. 171.

(17) Edwards, *A Vast Machine*, p. 283.

(18) Edwards, *A Vast Machine*, p. 259.

(19) Edwards, *A Vast Machine*, p. 265.

(20) Edwards, *A Vast Machine*, p. 145.

(21) Edwards, *A Vast Machine*, p. 171.

(22) K. De Pryck and M. Hulme eds., *A Critical Assessment of the Intergovernmental Panel on Climate Change* (Cambridge University Press, 2022), doi: https://doi.org/10.1017/9781009082099.

(23) Met Office, 'The Cray XC40 Supercomputing System', *Met Office: About Us* [website], https://www.metoffice.gov.uk/about-us/who-we-are/innovation/supercomputer.

(24) S. L. Star and K. Ruhleder, 'Steps Toward an Ecology of Infrastructure: Design and Access for Large Information Spaces', *Information Systems Research*, vol. 7, no. 1, 1996, p.111-134.

(25) M. Heymann, G. Gramelsberger, M. Mahony eds., *Cultures of Prediction in Atmospheric and Climate Science: Epistemic and Cultural Shifts in Computer-based Modelling and Simulation* (London and New York: Routledge Environmental Humanities, 2017).

(26) R. James, 'The U.K Met Office Buildings' [Interviewed by Guy Sinclair], 20th April 2022.

(27) K. Moe and Princeton Architectural Press Staff, *Thermally Active Surfaces in Architecture*, (New York, NY: Princeton Architectural Press, 2010), p. 48.

(28) Y. Furuhata, *Climatic Media: Transpacific Experiments in Atmospheric Control* (Durham, NC: Duke University Press, 2022), p.53.

(29) Furuhata, *Climatic Media*, p.57.

(30) L. Yarina, 'Toward Climate Form' in C. Davidson and E. Iturbe (eds.), *Log 47: Overcoming Carbon Form*, (Anyone Corporation, 2019), p. 88.

(31) P. Anker, 'The Closed World of Ecological Architecture', *The Journal of Architecture*, vol. 10, no. 5, 2005, p. 539.

(32) S. Ichioka and M. Palwyn, *Flourish: Design Paradigms for Our Planetary Emergency* (Axminster, UK: Triarchy Press, 2021), p.9.

CLIMATE CARTOGRAPHIES

BEN POLLOCK

Mapping and cartography are traditionally considered as tools to help us interpret the physical world - its fixed masses, imposed borders, and typically static spatial configurations. Yet, amid intensifying climate and ecological crises within our advancing age of visual media, their role now takes on new purpose and responsibility. Though cartographic notation and techniques have developed in tandem with the advances in meteorological science and knowledge, the developing climate crisis and dissemination and communication of its evidence, requires mapping to increasingly expand and communicate the intangible, diffuse and complex phenomena – to non-specialist members of the public and decision makers.

This essay positions cartography and associated design research practice as more than static mediums of process and representation. Instead, mapping becomes a dynamic, speculative design tool - a mode of thinking that reveals interlinked global systems while suggesting new methods of engaging with climate and ecology through design. Under this lens, mapping in design transcends mere representation of statistical datasets, but facilitates design agency and visual storytelling, interweaving evidence with imagination. Two frameworks guide this exploration: climate as a medium for design, and cartography as a method to better understand, address, and communicate the intricacies of climate systems, amongst new and wide ranging audiences.

We see this as an emerging practice which this essay attempts to frame through ideas developed in MArch Design Studio 18 (DS18), a pedagogical environment in which mapping functions as both speculative and evidentiary methods for students to integrate climate thinking into architectural and territorial design. Following this, Climate Cartographics, a practice co-founded by John Cook and Ben Pollock, takes some of this experimentation and framing into real-world applications for NGOs, government authorities and commercial clients, as design research services.

Central to this thinking is the concept of mapping as both a producer of artefact and a process. As a visual artefact, a map intentionally represents a spatial domain. For many map makers, this static output marks the culmination of their engagement. Architecture, however, brings a distinctive viewpoint: mapping is not merely a final product but an initial means of inquiry, strategy, and provocation. Rather than ending a design process, mapping becomes the starting point for deeper investigations into the spatial, climatic, and ecological complexities it reveals.

It is also critical to recognise the inherent politics, histories, and limitations of mapping. Far from neutral, maps have long served as instruments of colonisation, control, and resource extraction, contributing to global power imbalances and industrial practices, particularly in the Global North, that underlie many of today's environmental and societal crises. Mapping is fundamentally a political act, shaped by the authors biases, choice of data, their sources, the vantage points adopted, and the intention embedded in each cartographic frame.

While acknowledging these critiques, this essay focuses on technical data driven geospatial mapping techniques—particularly those enabled by GIS (Geographical Information Systems) and computational workflows. These methods lend themselves to the complexity of climate and ecology fields, allowing multidimensional, data-rich systems to be visualised, analysed, and reimagined across varying scales. They also align with the evidence-based underpinnings of climate science, where measurable, repeatable, and verifiable principles are paramount.

This computational orientation does not dismiss other forms of map making, from counter-mapping or psycho-geographical approaches, which foreground lived experience and narrative. Indeed, these methods offer critical counterpoints to geospatial techniques. However, for the purposes of this essay, the emphasis remains on digitally driven mapping for engaging climate science data and frameworks - an approach that resonates with DS18's pedagogy, which forefronts data literacy, climate knowledge and computational design methods.

In exploring how computational mapping can grapple with the spatial and systemic complexities of climate and ecology, this essay ultimately posits cartography as an indispensable tool. It is neither mere artistic expression nor a purely personal statement, but a rigorous, evidence-based practice with profound implications for how we understand and respond to planetary crises. In doing so, it argues for an ongoing evolution of mapping as a speculative, strategic process - one that bridges the gap between measurable realities and imaginative design futures.

Climate, Complexity and Visioning

Climate is an ever-evolving construct, shaped by statistical patterns, empirical observations, and predictive models. At its simplest, climate is often defined as 'average weather', measured through parameters such as temperature, precipitation, and wind over a 30-year interval. [01] This, however, belies the true complexity of the climate system, which consists of five interlinked spheres: atmosphere, hydrosphere, cryosphere, lithosphere, and biosphere. These operate through continuous interplay - internally (e.g. oceanic and atmospheric circulation) and externally (e.g. solar variations, volcanic eruptions, and anthropogenic changes like land use or greenhouse gas emissions).

Climate is neither static nor on a preordained trajectory. While natural variability remains a factor, anthropogenic forces increasingly determine the direction and pace of change. Today's human-induced alterations to atmospheric chemistry and land use trigger uneven, unpredictable, and often catastrophic transformations. As of January 2025, global CO_2 concentrations hover around 425 ppm, [02] we have surpassed an average global temperature increase of 1.5°C over pre-industrial levels as of the end of 2024, [03] and the United States has just withdrawn from the Paris Agreement by executive order of President Trump with the catch phrase "We will drill, baby, drill". [04] The future of our climate is now more uncertain and bleaker than before.

Climate unfolds as an expansive network of interlocking systems, where perturbations in the atmosphere cascade through the hydrosphere, cryosphere, and biosphere. These ripple effects transfer energy, alter, move, transpose and drive phase changes of matter and forces. Crucially, these processes are intensifying due to human energy production and consumption, material extraction, pollution and changes in land use driven by socioeconomic patterns, growth and global supply chains. Within this system, the effects and impacts of a changing climate are not evenly spread, with various regions in the Global South facing the combination of exacerbating climate stressors despite being minor contributors to the pollutants (GHG) driving climate change.

Globally, frameworks like the Intergovernmental Panel on Climate Change (IPCC) and its Shared Socioeconomic Pathways (SSPs) attempt to distil this complexity into probabilistic "cones of prediction." [05] Although short-term projections can be more accurate, longer-term forecasts embed higher levels of uncertainty. Nonetheless, one conclusion remains uniform across models: average global temperatures will continue to rise. Such findings are frequently rendered as macro-scale global maps or diagrammatic figures that provide a planetary overview - our most common reference for gauging collective progress on these issues (or lack thereof).

Despite offering crucial insights, these global-scale visualisations rarely yield action at the local and territorial levels, where design interventions can be most effective. Each territory harbours unique climatic, geographic, and

Figure 1 – Regional combined climate map showing annual averages and the connection between topographical (contours), hydrological (river) and atmospheric (precipitation, wet bulb temperature) data. by Climate Cartographics, 2024.

socioeconomic conditions that shape vulnerability and resilience differently. Robust ecosystems may better absorb or adapt to disruptions, while resource-scarce, damaged or bio-depleted contexts risk compounding crises. Here, mapping is a crucial bridge: it translates macro-level projections into more granular understandings, illustrating how uneven warming patterns play out in specific locales.

Oversimplification remains a persistent challenge in climate communication. Sea-level rise, for instance, is often portrayed simply as an advancing blue mass that consumes a green land mass and usually stated a context 'sinking' into the sea. Though effective for raising awareness through possible shock, such maps can overshadow the intricate chain reactions that follow inundation or the temporal and spatial nature at which various elements of this happen - saltwater intrusion, displacement of human and non-human life, shifts in microclimates, and the loss or creation of different habitats. These second and third-order consequences are potentially more graspable yet often go unseen in simplified binary visual media.

Entangled with these physical changes is a broad spectrum of human systems: energy infrastructure, food production, urban development, and beyond. Climate change is thus a 'wicked problem', (06) a sprawling nexus of social, ecological, and technical factors that lack straightforward and easily comprehensible solutions. Mapping offers a method initially seeing and engaging with this complexity. Even though any single map is inherently partial, framed by the data, scale, and narrative selected by its curators, it can still illuminate multidimensional dynamics, informing clearer analysis, communication, and strategic planning.

Against this backdrop of intricacy, mapping becomes essential to visioning—that is, modelling, imagining, and storytelling about possible futures. Grappling with climate change requires both an understanding of current realities and an ability to project forward, charting pathways for adaptation and transformation. Maps enable us to confront and convey the complexity of climate crises while also articulating scenarios not yet fully realised, for better or for worse.

Two main strategies guide such visioning: mitigation and adaptation. Mitigation targets the root drivers of climate change - curbing emissions, shifting to renewable energy, and adopting low-carbon materials. Adaptation, by contrast, confronts the inevitability of certain changes, such as rising seas, desertification, or shifting agricultural zones, and devises resilient strategies to safeguard livelihoods and ecosystems. In both strategies, mapping proves indispensable by identifying areas of risk, pinpointing potential interventions, and setting these in broader ecological and societal intersections.

Historically, maps have served a projective role, guiding explorers into uncharted territories. In the era of climate upheaval, this projective function is vital: maps no longer merely document what exists but also speculate on what might be. By offering shared frameworks for collective imagination, mapping unites diverse audiences - scientists, designers, policymakers, and local communities - fostering the interdisciplinary collaborations required to address complex challenges.

Although data-driven mapping must rest on empirical foundations, it also demands imagination. Beyond presenting facts, maps can disrupt entrenched assumptions by highlighting new paradigms or potential. They should not be seen as final solutions but as catalytic tools, helping us probe complexities with stakeholders and communicate these entangled problems with wider audiences. Mapping thus becomes both an exploratory process and a platform for collective, more equitable action.

Climate As Medium: Data As Means Of Understanding

Climate, unlike weather, is not directly experienced. Weather events, heatwaves, storms, or an unusually mild November, manifest within day-to-day life. By contrast, climate is a cumulative statistical construct apprehended only through data aggregated over time and space, and the full complexities of this in one's mind are not comprehensible. Designing with climate, therefore, necessitates engagement with its evidence: the data itself, as well as its temporal scale and inherent complexities (**Fig. 1**).

Data is not a static record but an active, relational medium, embedded within a web of interconnected systems. Keller Easterling's concept of 'medium design' provides a valuable framework for understanding this complexity. Rather than focusing on individual objects—like a building, product, or isolated policy—medium design shifts attention to the relationships, exchanges, and feedback loops that shape larger systems. It considers how economic, political, cultural, and climatic systems interact, creating patterns that both perpetuate and resist change. (07)

When applied to climate data, this perspective is particularly illuminating. Climate data is not a standalone fact; it exists within socio-political and economic contexts, shaped by and shaping governance structures, financial interests, and cultural norms. (08) For example, tracking CO_2 emissions or ocean temperatures is only the first step. The real leverage lies in understanding how this data interacts with policies, subsidies, or material supply chains that amplify or mitigate climate challenges. This systemic view enables decision-makers to see where interventions might trigger ripple effects, reshaping not just individual outcomes

Figure 2 — Mapping the Rights of Nature. Produced in conjunction with Dr. Alex Putzer, spatially visualising research and collected data on global instances of the rights of nature. Image by Climate Cartographics, 2024.

but the larger networks sustaining climate crises.

Feedback loops are central to this approach. In a medium-design mindset, climate data becomes a dynamic tool, constantly updating and measuring change over time, such as rising sea levels or shifting weather patterns. These changes, in turn, inform adjustments elsewhere, such as revising building codes, which then influence urban development and energy consumption. By leveraging these loops, medium design enables strategic interventions that address not only immediate problems but their systemic causes.

Ultimately, medium design reframes climate data as a signal within an interconnected system. By focusing on relationships rather than isolated actions. As spatial and material designers in relation to medium design, observed climate data expresses energy, matter, and movement captured through observation and computation. It organises space, uncovers patterns, and delineates relationships. This spatial expression often follows established cartographic geometries:

- Points (specific observations at fixed locations, e.g., temperature readings).
- Vectors (flows and movements, e.g., wind directions or ocean currents).
- Rasters (continuous fields, e.g., pollutant concentrations or temperature gradients).
- 3D Geometries (volumetric domains like landforms or atmospheric layers).

Through computational processes, raw datasets can be transformed into dynamic visualisations, revealing hidden patterns and testing hypothetical scenarios. This process is critical for designers, as it bridges abstract, statistical constructs with more tangible and speculative design methods. Again the framing of 'medium design' provides a valuable lens for understanding this process. Rather than treating data as isolated facts, it emphasises the relational field in which systems, infrastructures, and feedback loops interact.

By tweaking gradients, simulating shifts, or layering multiple datasets, designers begin to develop a 'tactile and visual understanding' of data and its systemic behaviour. This process, cultivated through trial, error, and experience, builds an intuitive grasp of how data might behave - anticipating how datasets will contour, how clusters of points will reveal anomalies, or how feedback loops within the system might amplify or mitigate certain outcomes (**Fig. 1**). Medium design reframes these actions, encouraging designers to focus on how these individual elements interact within broader systems to create ripple effects or trigger larger shifts.

This tactile and relational engagement with data transforms visualisations into more than analytical tools; they become frameworks for speculative exploration and systemic intervention. Designers can use these processes to identify potential opportunities or threats, understanding not just localised outcomes but also how they are embedded within broader sociopolitical and ecological systems. By working with the 'medium' of interconnections—rather than isolated objects, designers can propose adaptive solutions informed by systemic relationships, navigating the complexities of climate data (**Fig. 2**).

In this sense, mapping transcends traditional cartography. Representing a matter like *air*—invisible, volatile, and dynamic—requires layered data and computational workflows to track interactions across diverse scales. A coarse grid of 100 sample points can grow to millions, enabling refined analysis or broader coverage. Likewise, temporal data moves mapping beyond static 'snapshots', modelling shifts in wind patterns, pollution dispersion, or seasonal changes. In doing so, the systemic nature of climate becomes clearer, bridging locally experienced phenomena such as a heat wave with globally scaled atmospheric mechanisms such as that of the jet stream.

Hyperobject

Along with medium, the idea and framing of climate as a hyperobject. As explained by Timothy Morton, hyperobjects refer to entities that are so vast in their temporal and spatial dimensions that they exceed typical human understanding. [09] Hyperobjects are not simply "large things"; instead, they challenge our usual frameworks for perceiving and interacting with the world. [10] Climate, and by extension climate data as our means to understand and define climate, fit this definition well; Climate spans deep time, unfolding over millennia and affecting every region of the planet in interconnected ways. Its vast scale and non-local nature mean shifts observed in one place are often driven by causes elsewhere, reflecting a complex tapestry of feedback loops and tipping points. We interact with climate through intangible and abstract data forms — graphs, projections, models—rather than a single physical entity. [11] These climate measurements, distributed across countless databases worldwide, highlight its temporally and spatially dispersed character. Overall, climate's enormous scale, invisibility, and intricate interdependencies make it a classic example of a hyperobject that challenges our conventional ways of perceiving and understanding the world. [12]

Mapping climate as a hyperobject also underscores the gaps in our observation. Detailed, local-scale data may be incomplete, demanding proxies, modelling, or interpolation. These lacunae often point to questions of

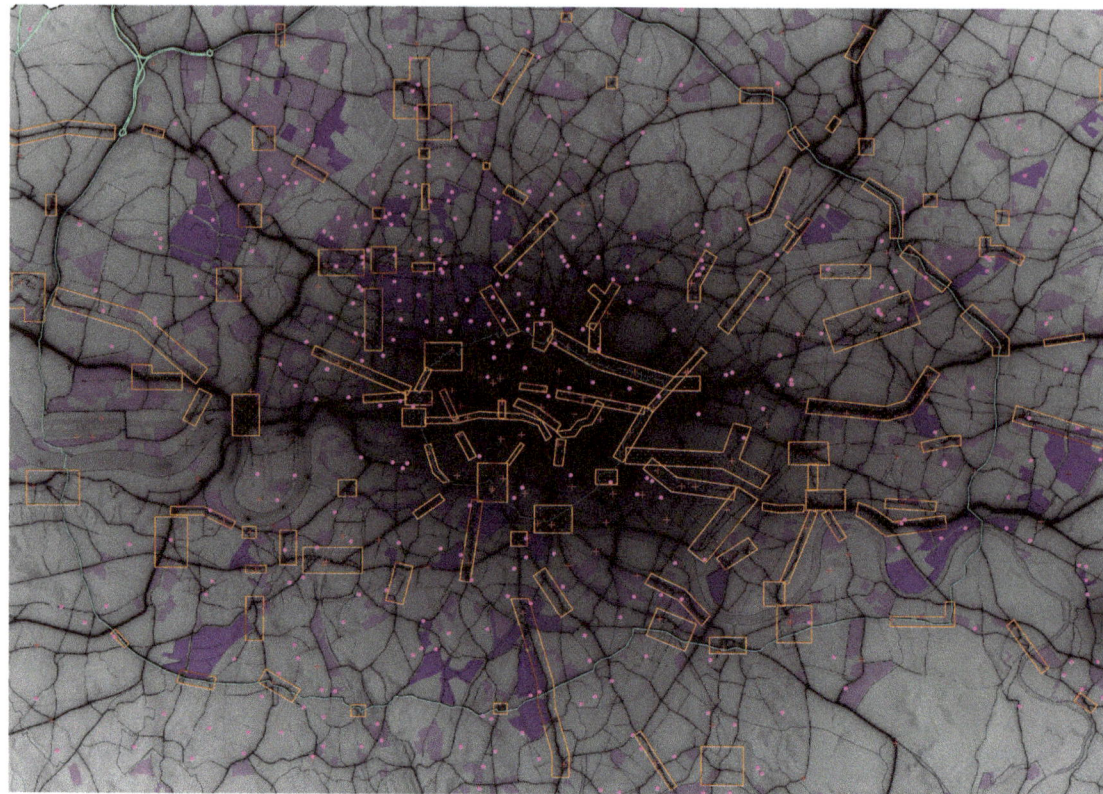

Figure 3 — Greater London air pollution, cycle infrastructure and low-traffic neighbourhood zones. For the Active Travel Academy, University of Westminster. Image by Climate Cartographics, 2024.

equity: well-resourced regions gather robust data, while those with fewer means blind spots remain, risking underestimation of critical vulnerabilities. Designers who work with climate data thus face the challenge of acknowledging these uncertainties, even as they strive to visualise climate in a legible, actionable form.

As a medium for design, climate data possesses a dual role: it is both evidentiary and speculative. Evidentiary data underpins our grasp of shifting temperature baselines or altered water cycles, offering a scientific grounding. Yet it also enables speculative thinking, where data is parsed and recombined to project possible futures or explore the systemic repercussions of an intervention. Ultimately, when treated as a medium, climate data can expand speculative design. It ushers practitioners beyond site-specific fixes and toward systemic engagements that account for nested, interconnected scales. Mapping in this expanded sense becomes more than a representational tool; it is an active mode of grappling with complexity, prototyping interventions, and imagining equitable futures.

What has been attempted here is to outline how climate's intangible phenomena, complexity, and data can guide new forms of practice. In the following sections, we shift from climate as a medium to cartography as a method.

Cartography as Method: Spatial Tools for Research and Design

Maps, past and present, offer powerful means to synthesise enormous amounts of information into understandable, action-oriented visualisations. While they cannot fully encapsulate multidimensional systems, maps excel at filtering complex phenomena, revealing patterns, vulnerabilities, and opportunities at scales both global and local.

Within the realm of climate-as-medium, a map's function goes beyond depiction. From the Renaissance onward, maps have framed knowledge and asserted power, fixing boundaries and shaping worldviews. Following this, Alexander von Humboldt's work pioneered a new way of visualising climate and ecology through cartography. By introducing isotherms—lines connecting points of equal average temperature—he effectively mapped global temperature patterns and illustrated how climate varies with latitude and elevation. In his extensive travels, particularly in South America, Humboldt collected and integrated meteorological, botanical, and zoological data, showing that plant and animal distributions are closely tied to both climate conditions and topography. This holistic perspective laid the necessary groundwork for modern fields such as biogeography, meteorology, and ecology. (13)

This capacity to coordinate spatial relationships across scales makes cartography indispensable for comprehending the complexity of climate change. In this context, maps act not as static images but as dynamic interfaces bridging diverse audiences.

A successful map begins with intention. The map-maker must identify the desired purpose, choose relevant data, and present it in an appropriate form. Decisions about what to include, exclude, or accentuate can reveal or mask insights, influencing how audiences interpret the map given cultural norms. Good cartographic practice requires careful attention to method, ensuring that the map clarifies rather than obscures. (14)

Contemporary cartography often relies on GIS and modelling to convert abstract datasets into spatial knowledge. Cartographers represent and enhance the legibility of intricate systems through adjustments in notation, colour palettes, line weights, vector overlays, or graduated symbologies. In addition, data visualisation techniques allow data to map intangible processes in ways that remain accessible to broader audiences, i.e. from a spreadsheet of numbers into a colour-coded pixel colour rendering. In this simplified sense, a map is a curated graphical and symbolised representation of reality. (15)

Beyond representation, mapping is a process of investigation mostly though the process of trial and error and reproduction. Spatialising data gives rise to new insights, exposing relationships, revealing emergent conditions, and clarifying territory-specific complexities. This is particularly important for climate data, which often involves knitting together meteorological, geographic, and socio-economic variables into layered visualisations.

A key strength of mapping is its capacity for multi-scalar or layered analysis. Climate operates across minuscule to planetary scales, from microscopic particulate matter in cities to global oceanic and atmospheric circulations. Maps can bridge between these scales, juxtaposing localised material understandings with immaterial strategic data visualisations. For example, this intentionality and curation could reveal how deforestation in one area might be connected in proximity to industrial service hubs and thus further connected to global supply chains. By capturing these links, mapping can help direct policy, guide design decisions, and facilitate public engagement in these large-scale issues.

Layering datasets is another hallmark of mapping methodologies. By overlaying, for example, temperature changes, biodiversity indices, and demographic data, designers can pinpoint zones of acute vulnerability or opportunity (**Fig. 3**). Such integrated visualisations become invaluable references for stakeholders - from municipal planners to grassroots organisers - transforming raw data into strategies for adaptation, mitigation, or resource management. This allows others' knowledge and understanding to be rendered within the same frame of reference or contextual data.

At the same time, data driven mapping must acknowledge uncertainty, anomalies or indeed missing data. By highlighting outliers or unexpected correlations, maps challenge entrenched assumptions. This interplay between predictable models and emergent phenomena underscores the importance of mapping as a dynamic research instrument rather than a static record.

Maps are more than technical outputs; they are communicative artefacts of design. Through symbolisation—colour, shapes, textures—designers translate geographical data into comprehensible stories that can spark emotional as well as intellectual responses. This is especially crucial when tackling 'hyperobjects' such as climate change: phenomena so vast and dispersed that they stretch beyond simple human comprehension. In addition to becoming their own medium of design for others to inhabit and project understanding.

Effective climate maps use visual storytelling to navigate this challenge. Perspective sections or 3D views can immerse the audience in hidden processes, such as pollutant flows or seasonal air currents. At the planetary scale, maps may highlight geopolitical disparities—showing, for instance, how certain regions bear the brunt of industrial emissions generated elsewhere. These techniques turn the map into a narrative device that fosters deeper engagement with climate complexities. (16)

Another critical aspect is limited-resolution cartographies. All maps omit something—due to data gaps, resolution limits, or design choices. Such omissions do not negate the utility of maps; instead, they highlight mapping's interpretive and speculative nature. Designers working with GIS, parametric models, or even hand-drawn sketches effectively transform quantitative abstractions into speculative methods, bridging raw data and design intuition.

Traditionally employed to order and define space, maps today function as instruments for navigating uncertainty. They simultaneously record and project, offering insights into possible futures shaped by the complex interplay of climate, society, and geography. As a contemporary design method, embraced both by DS18 and Climate Cartographics studio, mapping unveils how we see, know, and engage a rapidly changing world.

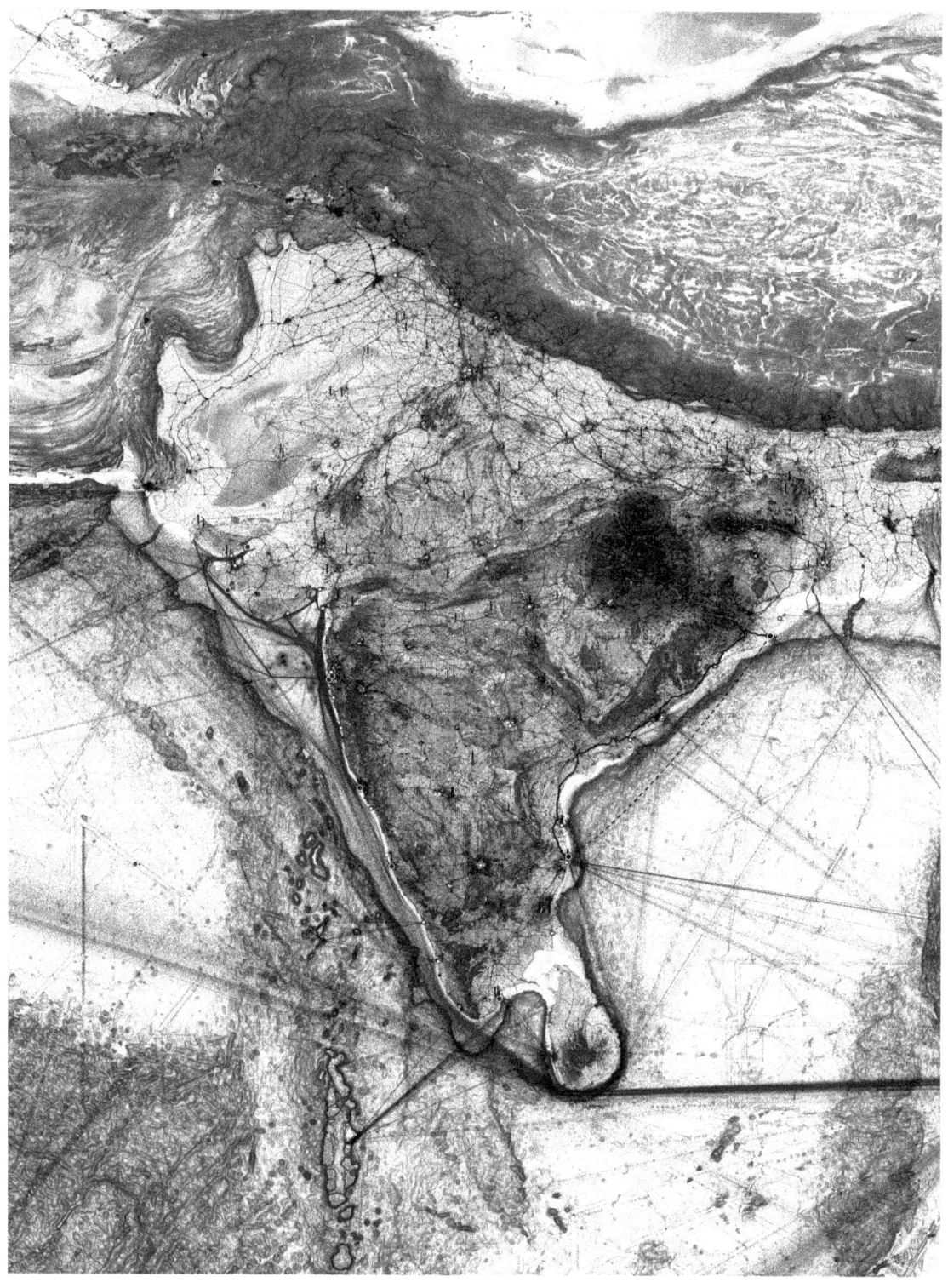

Figure 4 — Indian Extraction and Fossil Fuel Infrastructure. Map showing topography, coal deposits, population distribution, national energy networks and global shipping routes. British Academy Knowledge Frontiers International Interdisciplinary Research Grant (2022) No. KF6220264, titled *Reimagining the Good City from Ennore Creek*. Image by Climate Cartographics, 2024.

Climate Cartographics: Applied in Design Studio 18 and Practice

Cartography in design now extends from a representational tool to one of active inquiry and propositional thinking. In DS18, mapping functions as both a pedagogical framework and a spatial research method, enabling students to critically handle climate data and explore speculative design approaches. These methods bridge into Climate Cartographics, a nonprofit design research studio that applies cartographic principles to real-world ecological and climatic challenges.

This section shows how DS18's mapping pedagogy fosters climate literacy, speculative visioning, and systems thinking, before reflecting on how those methods inform professional practice. It also considers how speculative mapping can move beyond mere visualisation, directly influencing adaptive strategies in architecture and planning while balancing imaginative futures with the realities of climate science.

At DS18's core, mapping underpins both research and design. The studio introduces computational workflows, data literacy, and geospatial analysis as an iterative process, synthesising technical rigour with creative risk-taking. Students learn to see data not as a static or inherently objective entity, but as a material and medium for constructing new spatial stories or understandings.

Through workshops and structured exercises, students:
- Acquire GIS skills for sourcing, organising, and visualising geospatial data.
- Develop climate literacy, recognising dataset limitations and linking them to spatial, material realities.
- Produce layered maps merging climate data with architectural intentions, translating abstract phenomena into actionable design insights.

Rather than isolating a site and reviewing it through traditional site analysis (aspect, sun direction, or neighbouring facilities). Situating projects and mapping them within a wider territorial frame of climate data illuminates the flow lesser seen but essential to understand fluxes of gases, fluids, energies and forces - those elements that cross boundaries and interconnect broader ecological and socioeconomic systems. In so doing, students can better understand architecture as inhabiting this medium and the data construct of climate.

In DS18, mapping is posed as both evidential and speculative. Students synthesise empirical data with more imaginative interpretations, generating outputs that upend conventional perceptions. For example Kirsten's Jet Stream Maps (**P.40**) illustrate atmospheric flows at a planetary level, linking global patterns to local weather extremes. While Jamie's Carbon Economy Maps (**P. 66**) illuminate transnational carbon exchanges through carbon credit markets, revealing the practice of off-shoring verses national emission sources and natural carbon sinks. Such work transforms elusive climate dynamics into tangible spatial narratives. By weaving abstraction with storytelling and investigative insights, mapping becomes a design act - an intentional process that can expose injustices, highlight hidden patterns, or propose alternative futures.

Layered atop cartographic workflows, parametric or computational approaches enable propositional mapping. Traditional methods often document existing conditions; propositional mapping, in contrast, melds multiple data sources (e.g., topography, solar radiation, hydrology) to forge custom metrics. These metrics guide design decisions, bridging data-driven analysis and speculative thinking.

DS18's focus on multi-scalar awareness further extends this practice, linking local architecture to territorial or even planetary dynamics. Students learn to see each design gesture against the backdrop of flows of energy and matter. Conversely, at the end of projects, students are encouraged to produce what we refer to as 'hyper-drawings', which zoom out from local proposals to depict how, in summary, this fits within the global climatic or environmental systems of their research topics . This dual zooming fosters a deeper understanding of architecture as an active agent within these dynamic and complex systems rather than an isolated propositional object of specified programme and static material form.

In practice, Climate Cartographics emerged from the methodologies and insights part developed in DS18, with a mission to extend these approaches beyond academia. Formalised as a non-profit design research studio in 2024, Climate Cartographics builds on the foundational project Monsoon Assemblages (2016–2021), [17] and was piloted as a viable practice through a UKRI Proof of Concept Grant (2022–23). [18] The studio is dedicated to tackling the climate and ecological crisis through data-driven investigations, innovative visual communication, and map-based storytelling.

Operating beyond academia allows Climate Cartographics to attempt to address the increasing economic and societal costs of climate change directly amongst the commercial sphere. Its work provides tools and strategies for stakeholders - from policymakers to local communities - to understand risks, envision adaptive futures, and make informed decisions (**Fig. 4**).

The studio is guided by two emerging principles. Firstly, to expand climate knowledge by embedding environmental awareness across varied projects outputs

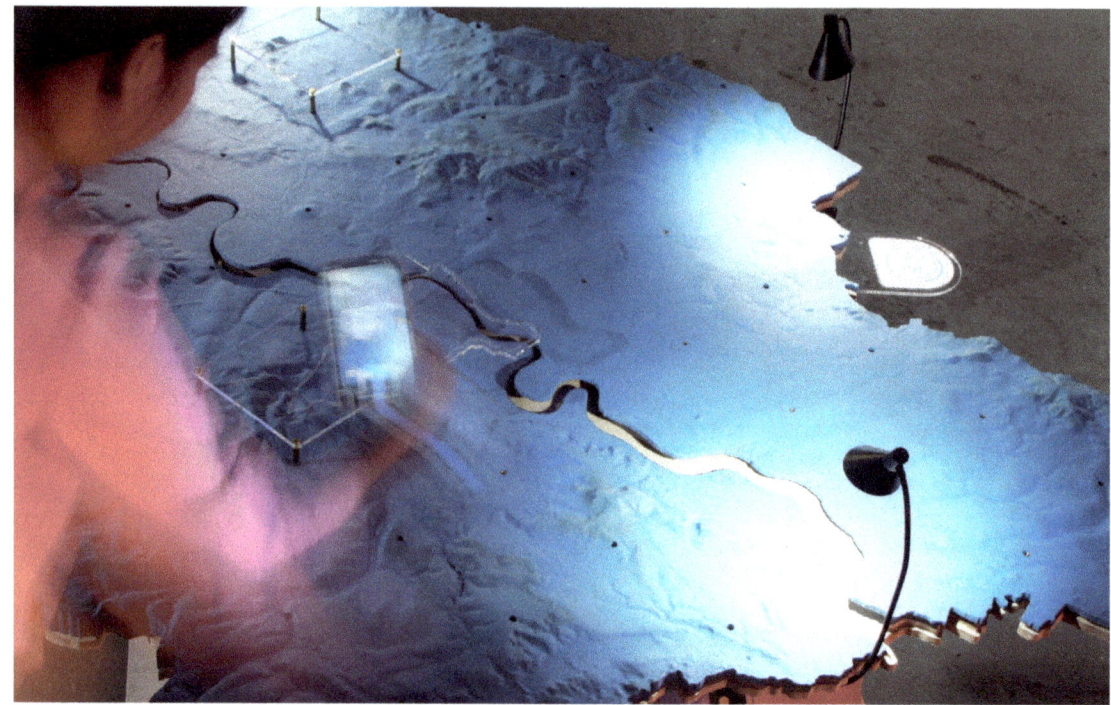

Figure 5 – Greater London Climate Interface Model. CNC topographic model with augmented reality overlays showing air pollution and socio-demographic data. Image by Climate Cartographics, 2024.

and sectors, the studio translates complex data into accessible visual tools, empowering stakeholders to integrate climate considerations into their decision-making. Secondly, by triggering emotional engagement with a recognition that raw data rarely inspires climate action, the studio adopts innovative aesthetics and narrative techniques to provoke emotional responses, fostering urgency and commitment to climate action.

Through spatial mapping, geospatial analysis, and storytelling, Climate Cartographics bridges the gap between climate science and public understanding. Its outputs, from data visualisations and 3D representations to animations and interactive platforms, are designed to clarify climate complexities, challenge traditional aesthetics, and inspire transformative responses. By reimagining how climate issues are communicated, Climate Cartographics provides actionable insights and frameworks for envisioning resilient, adaptive futures, helping stakeholders respond constructively to the climate crisis (Fig. 5).

End Notes

The practices of DS18 and Climate Cartographics exemplify how cartography can function as both an analytical and interdisciplinary projective tool to address the climate emergency. By blending computational precision with speculative creativity, mapping is recast as a dynamic method for navigating complexity, spurring interventions, and envisioning future possibilities. Throughout this essay, mapping is described not as a comprehensive solution but as a mechanism for understanding, communicating, and speculating. It engages with the nested systems of climate and ecology, energy and matter making unseen relations visible while guiding design strategies that transcending disciplinary silos. Moving fluidly from pedagogy to practice, mapping equips designers to confront the pressing realities of climate change while imagining more transformative outcomes. In balancing data, design, and narrative, cartography carries equal measures of evidence-based analysis and visionary reach.

DS18 and Climate Cartographics demonstrate how mapping can bridge academic inquiry and professional application, offering tools for grappling with the multi-scalar intricacies of climate systems. This work ultimately challenges conventional architectural approaches by situating design within broader ecological and systemic contexts. The legacy of these explorations positions mapping as a critical tool for designers to respond to the climate and ecological emergency - not by attempting to dominate or simplify it, but by engaging with complexity,

Figure 6 – Greater London Climate Interface Model. CNC topographic model with augmented reality overlays showing air pollution and socio-demographic data. Image by Climate Cartographics, 2024.

recognising climate data as a design medium, advocating for responsible agency and fostering imaginative yet grounded visions for the future and Other Climates.

Notes

(01) J. B. R. Matthews, V. Möller, R. van Diemen, J.S. Fuglestvedt, V. Masson-Delmotte, C. Méndez, S. Semenov, & A. Reisinger. (2021). 'Annex VII: Glossary', in *IPCC Sixth Assessment Report* (p. 2222), 24 January 2025, https://www.ipcc.ch.

(02) NOAA. (n.d.). 'Climate change: Atmospheric carbon dioxide', *NOAA Climate.gov*, 24 January 2025, https://www.climate.gov/news-features/understanding-climate/climate-change-atmospheric-carbon-dioxide.

(03) World Meteorological Organization (WMO). (2024). "WMO confirms 2024 as warmest year on record, about 1.55°C above pre-industrial levels", *wmo.int*, 24 January 2025, https://www.wmo.int/news/media-centre/wmo-confirms-2024-warmest-year-record-about-155degc-above-pre-industrial-level.

(04) M. McGrath, 'Trump vows to quit Paris climate pact and 'drill, baby, drill'' in BBCNews, 20 January 2025, https://www.bbc.co.uk/news/articles/c20px1e05w0o.

(05) IPCC. (2019). Summary for Policymakers. In Climate Change and Land: An IPCC special report on climate change, desertification, land degradation, sustainable land management, food security, and greenhouse gas fluxes in terrestrial ecosystems (P. R. Shukla, J. Skea, E. Calvo Buendia, et al., Eds.). In press.

(06) F.P. Incropera, *Climate Change: A Wicked Problem: Complexity and Uncertainty at the Intersection of Science, Economics, Politics, and Human Behavior*, Cambridge University Press, 2015.

(07-08) K. Easterling, *Medium Design: Knowing How to Work on the World*, New York: Verso, 2021.

(09-12) T. Morton, *Hyperobjects: Philosophy and Ecology after the End of the World*. University of Minnesota Press, 2013.

(13) A. Wulf, *The Invention of Nature: Alexander von Humboldt's New World*, Knopf, 2015.

(14-15) Ordnance Survey (n.d.). 'What is cartography?' in ordnancesurvey.co.uk, 14 November 2022, https://www.ordnancesurvey.co.uk/blog/what-is-cartography.

(16) R. Ghosn and El H. Jazairy/ Design Earth, *Geostories: Another Architecture for the Environment*, Actar Publishers, 2018.

(17) Bremner, L. (ed.), Cullen, B., Geros, C., Bhat, H., Powis, A., Cook, J., & Benson, T. Monsoon, *Monsoon as Method: Assembling Monsoonal Multiplicities,* Actar Publishers, 2022.

(18) This work was supported by UK Research and Innovation (n.d.), fEC GRANTS, Grant Ref: EP/X022528/1.

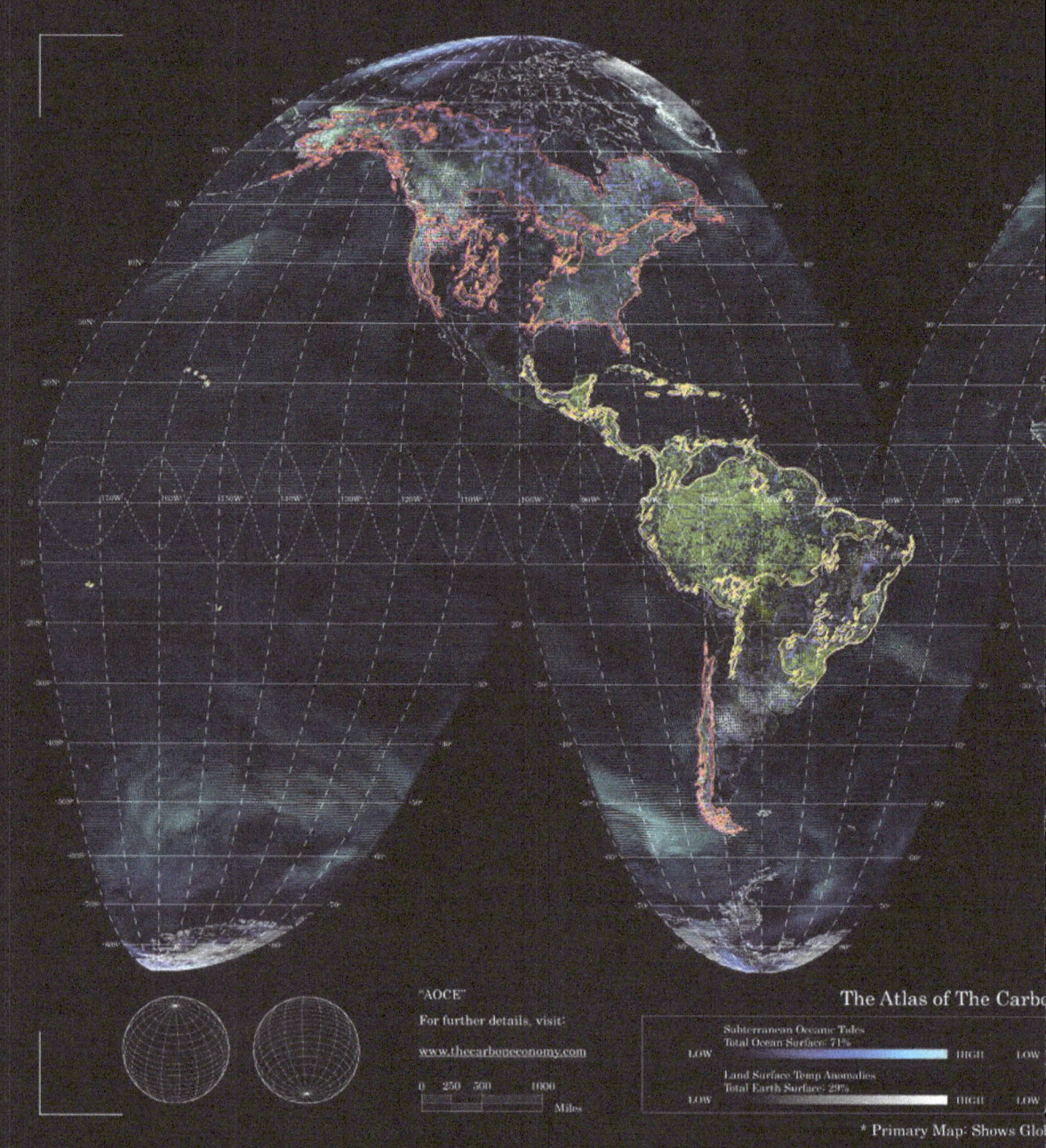

Jamie Williams. The Atlas of The Carbon Economy (Carbon sinks - Tree cover and ocean extents) (2021).

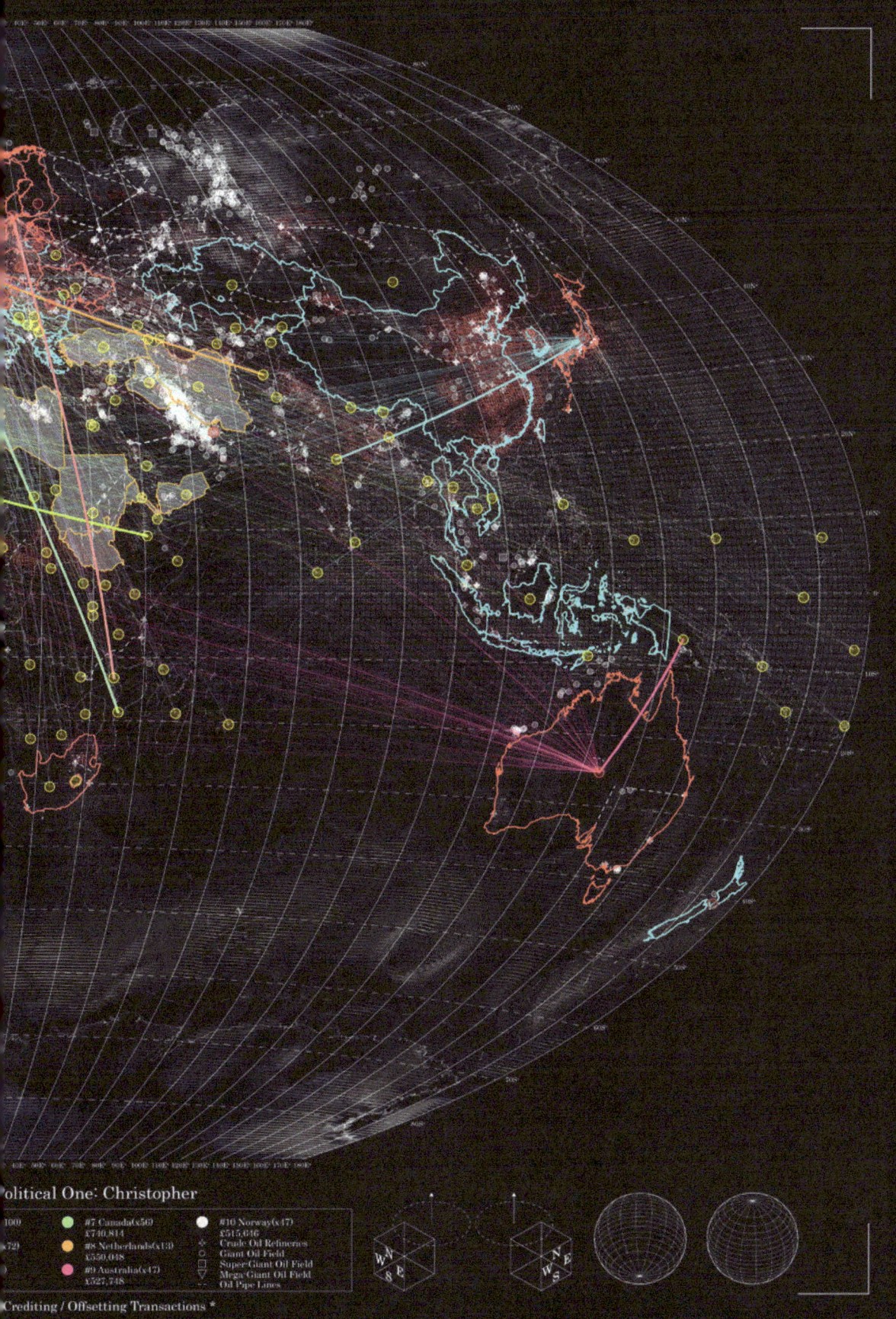

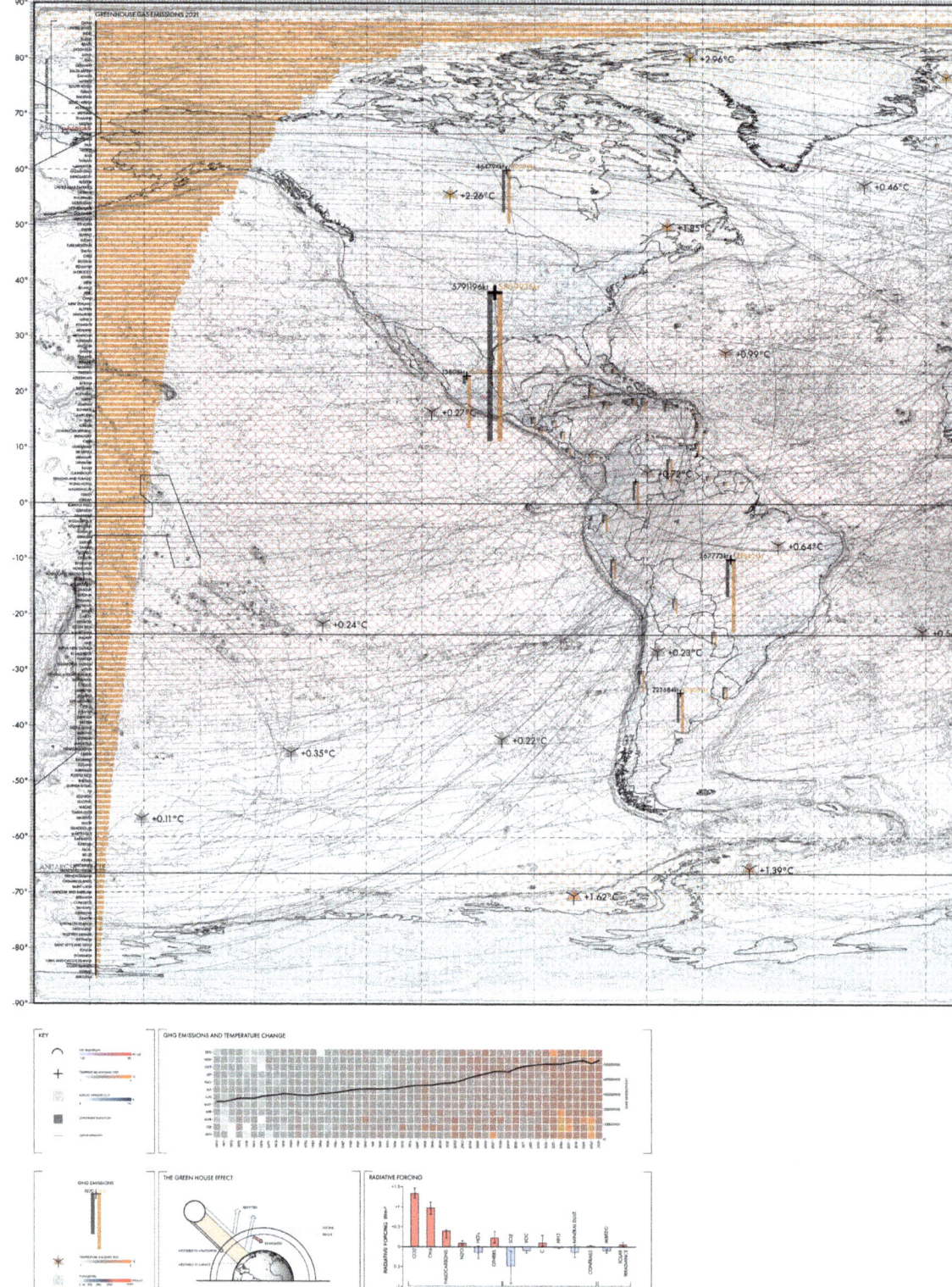

Carl Fletcher. Landfill Methan Repurposing. Global Map of Greenhouse Gases (GHG) Global Emissions (2023).

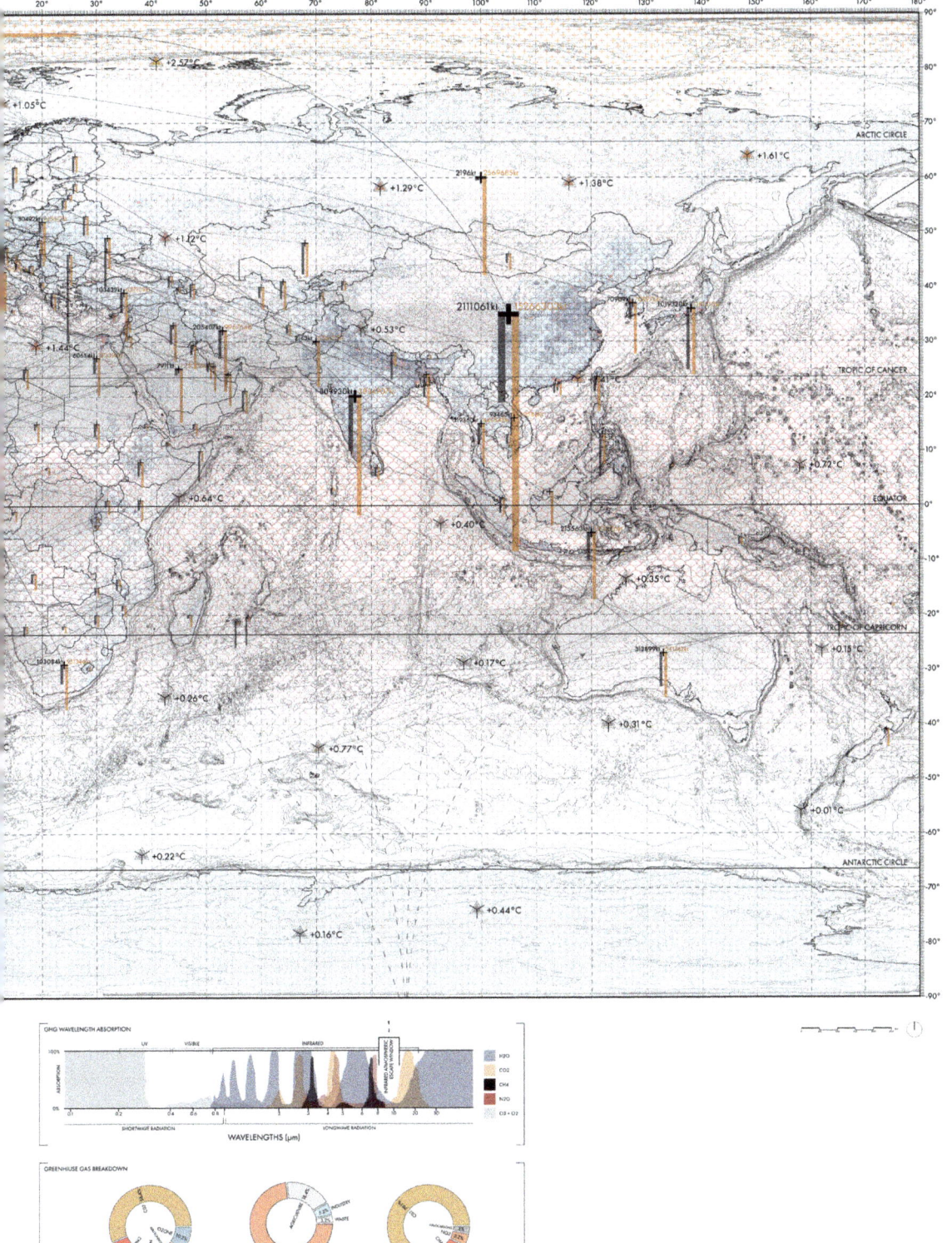

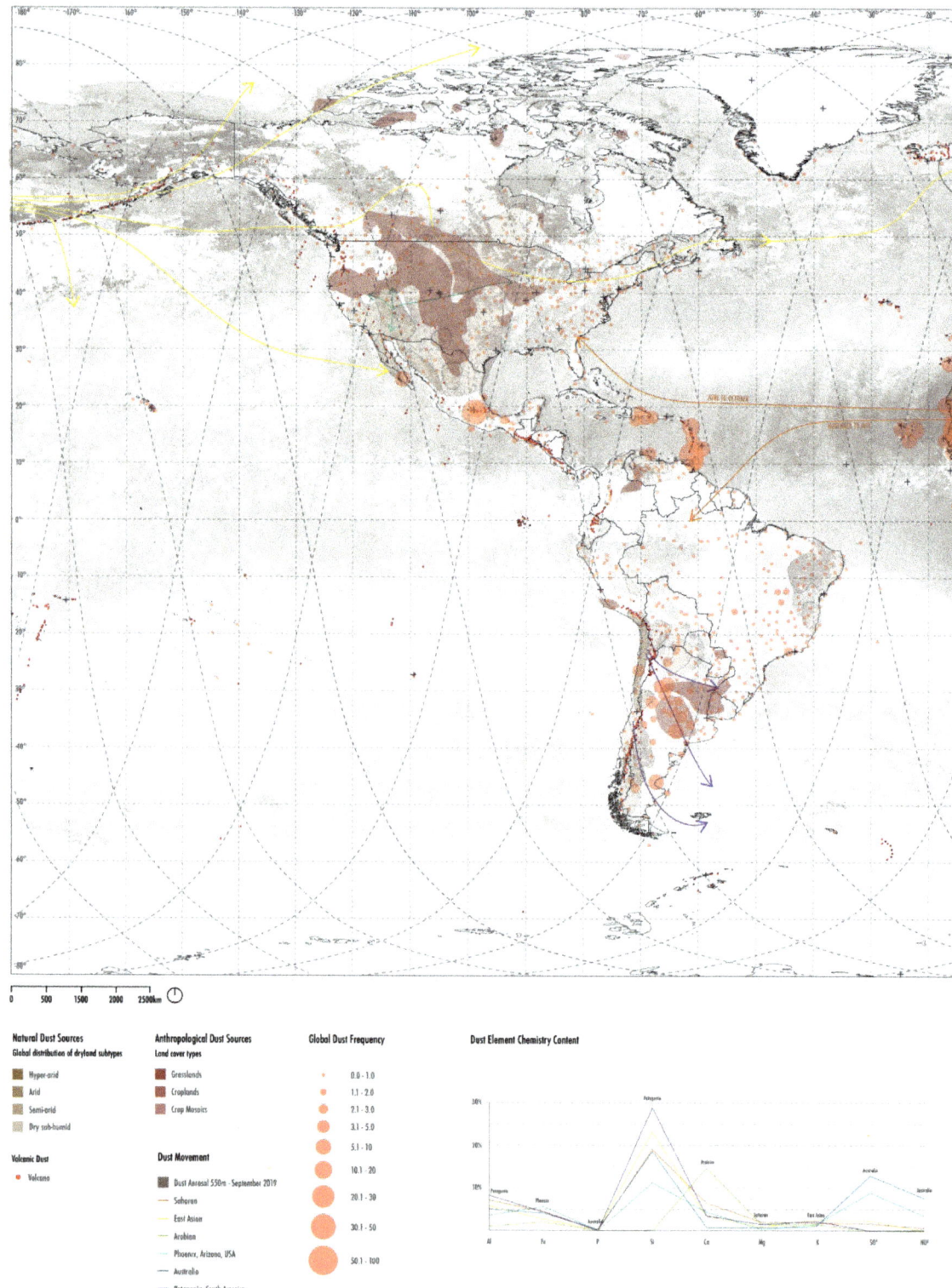

Sara Kosanovic. The Nordkapp Dust Research Station. The World Dust Map (2020).

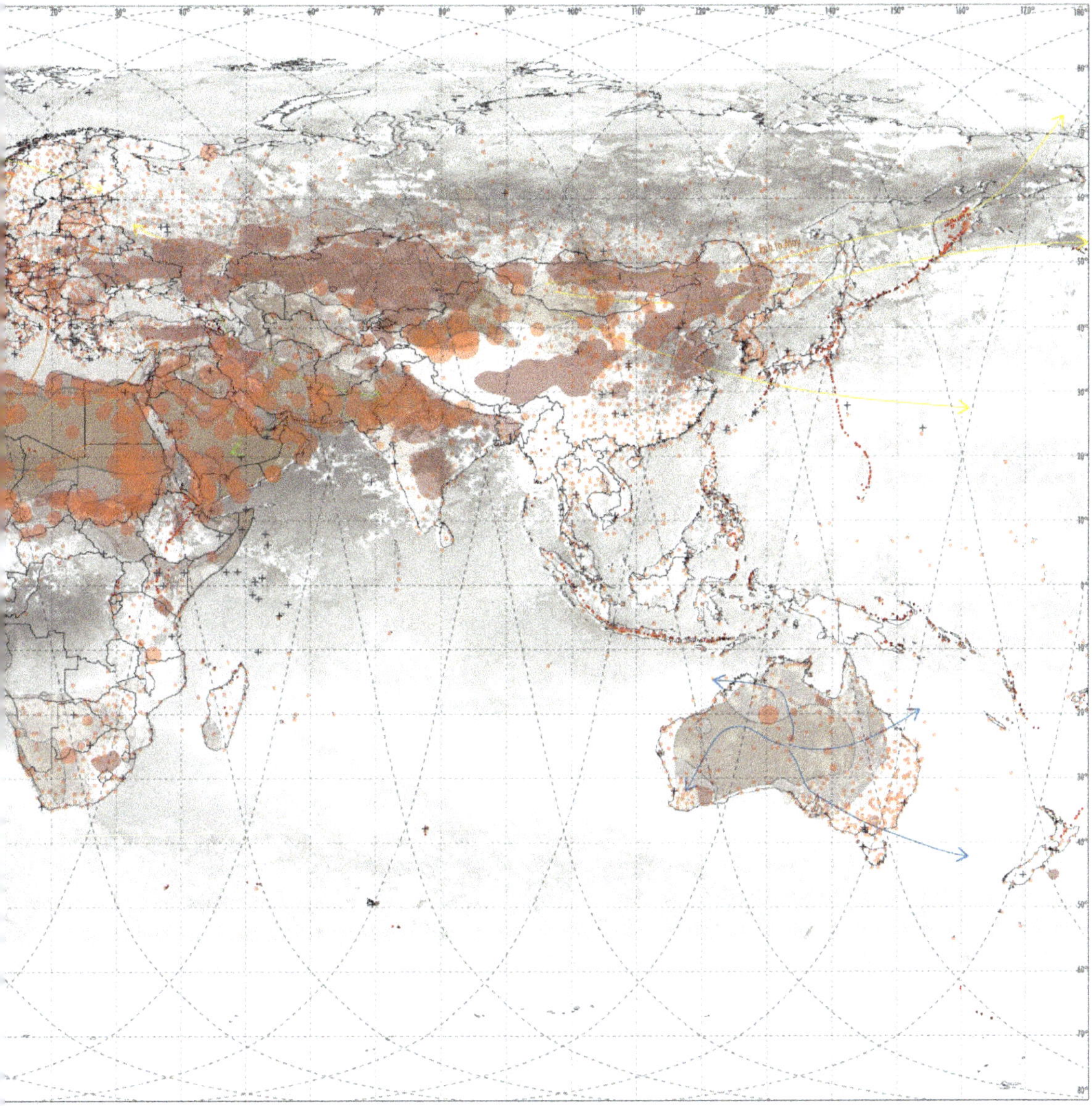

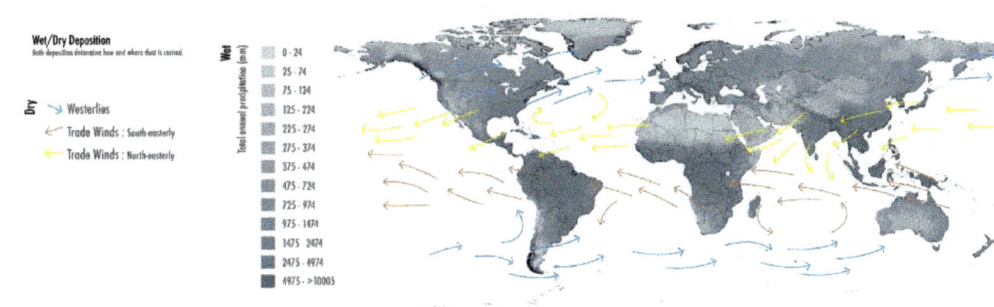

Hannah Pinsent. Fashioning the Waste Climate. Tracing Fast Fashion's Impact on the Global Environment. Maps of impact of cotton, polyester and wool life-cycles (2021).

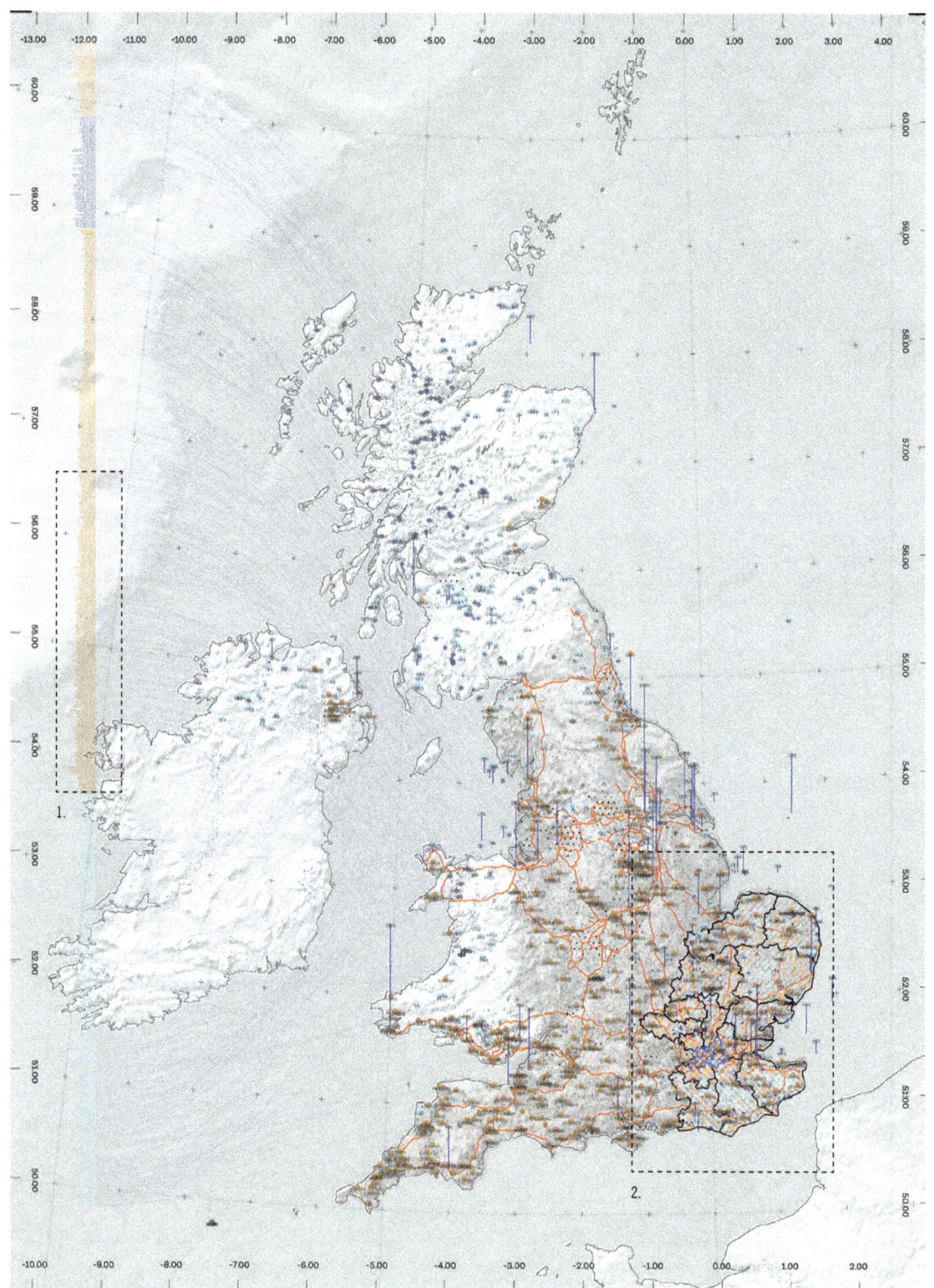

Guy Sinclair. Thermal Commons. UK Electricity Generation - Power Networks and the National Grid (2023).

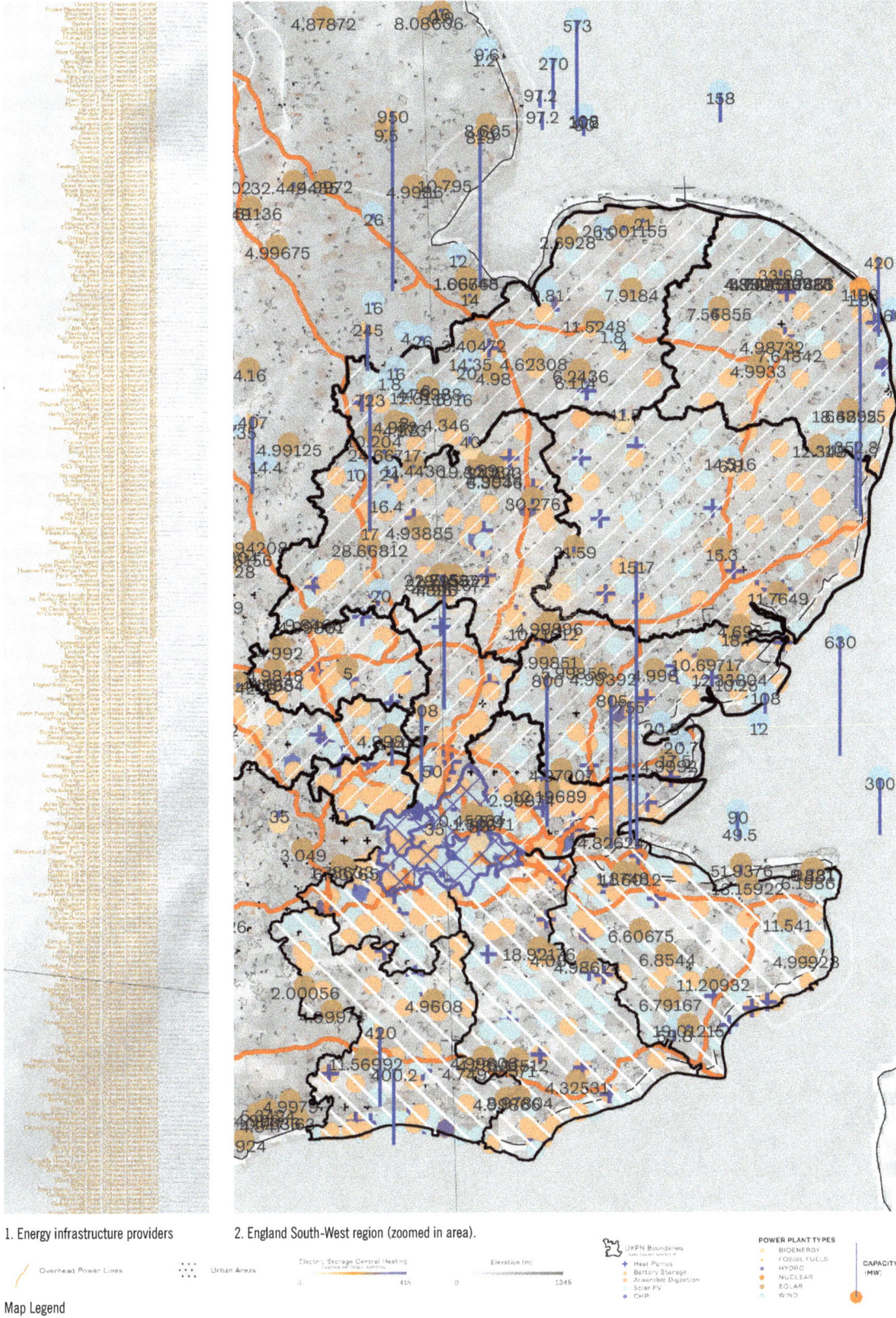

1. Energy infrastructure providers
2. England South-West region (zoomed in area).

Map Legend

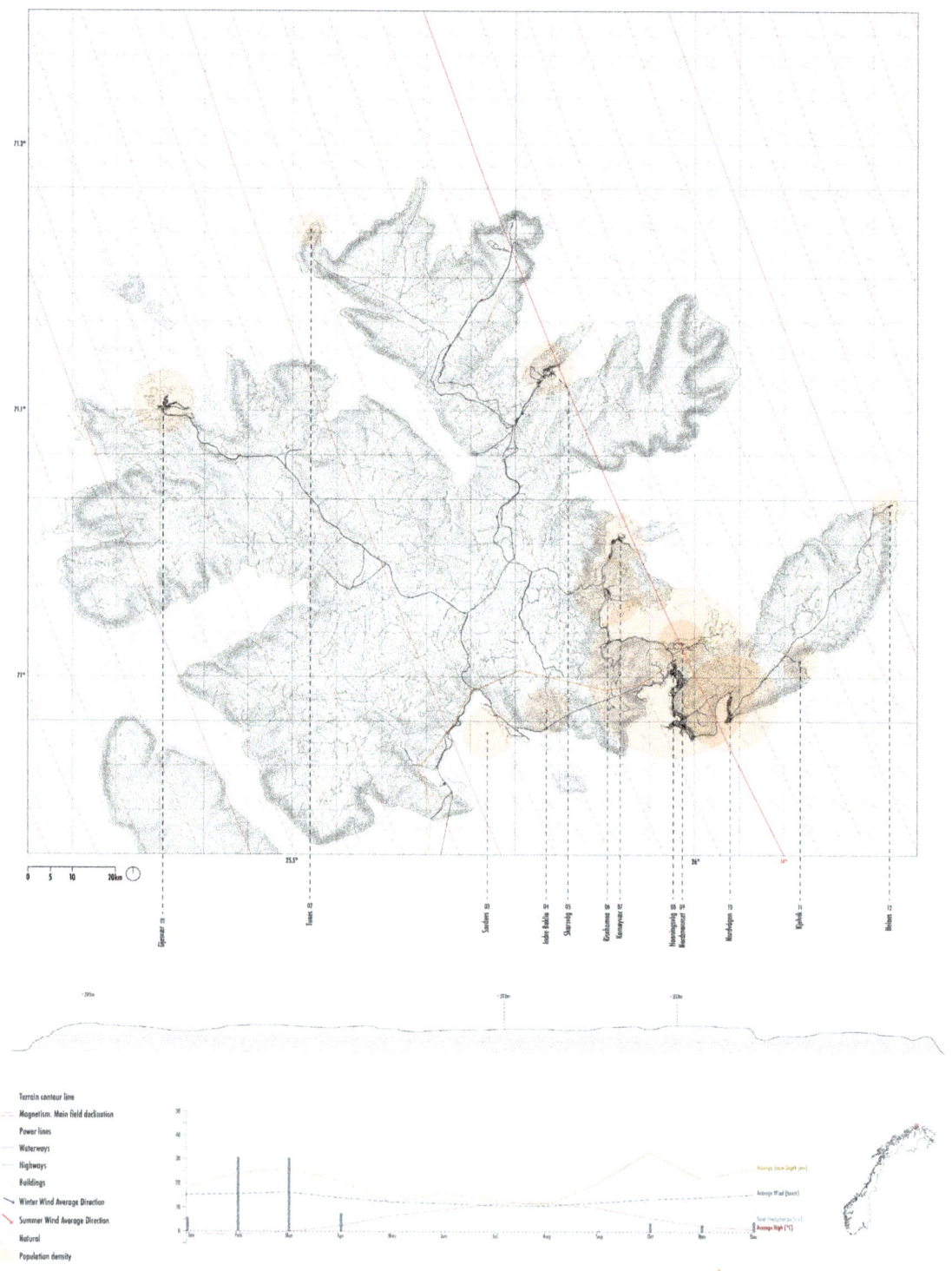

Sara Kosanovic. The Nordkapp Dust Research Station. Site Analysis (2020).

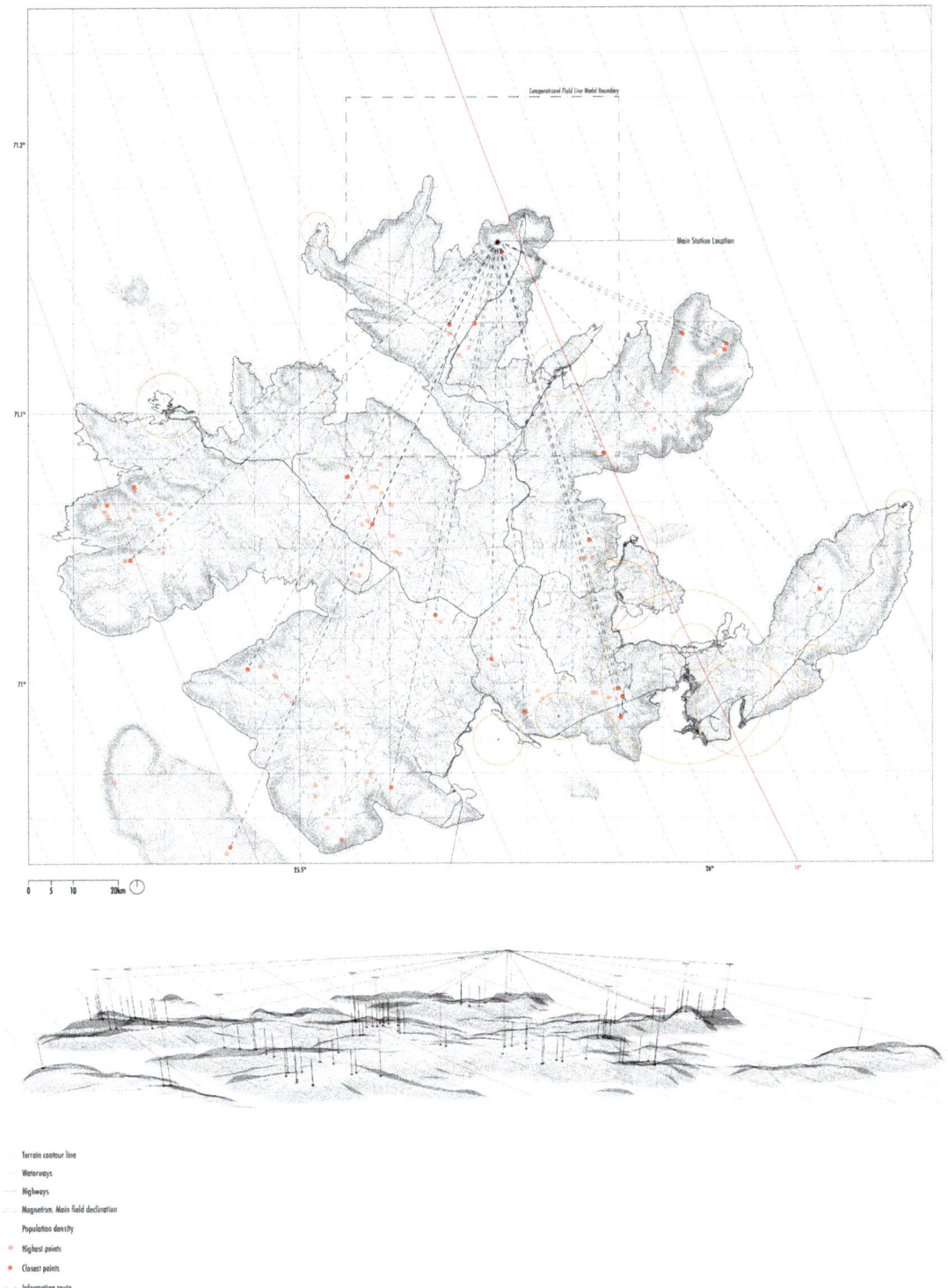

Sara Kosanovic. The Nordkapp Dust Research Station. Terrain Analysis (2020).

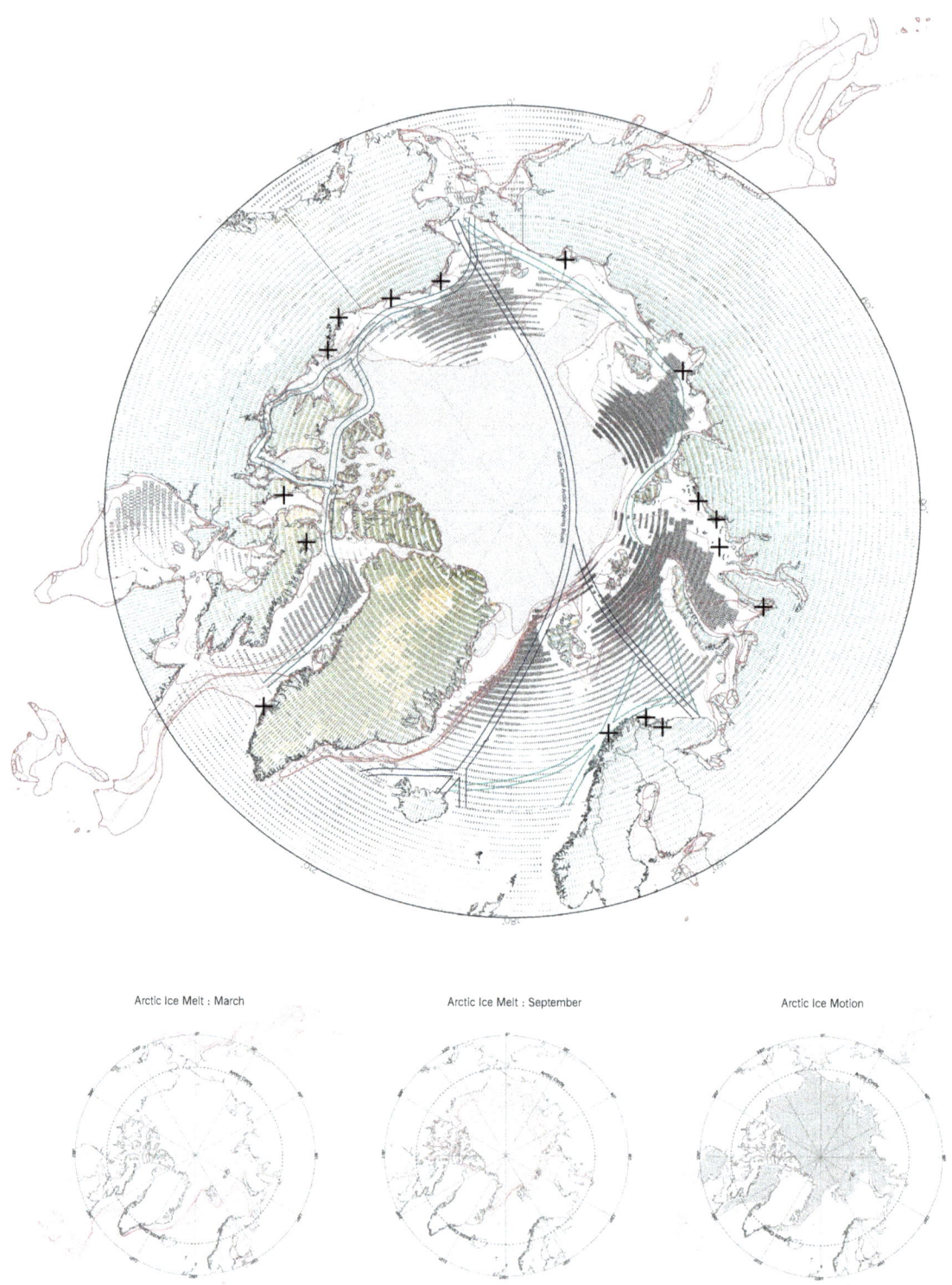

Kate Hosking. Black Ice Forum. Mapping the Melting Arctic Sea Ice (1970 - 2018) (2020).

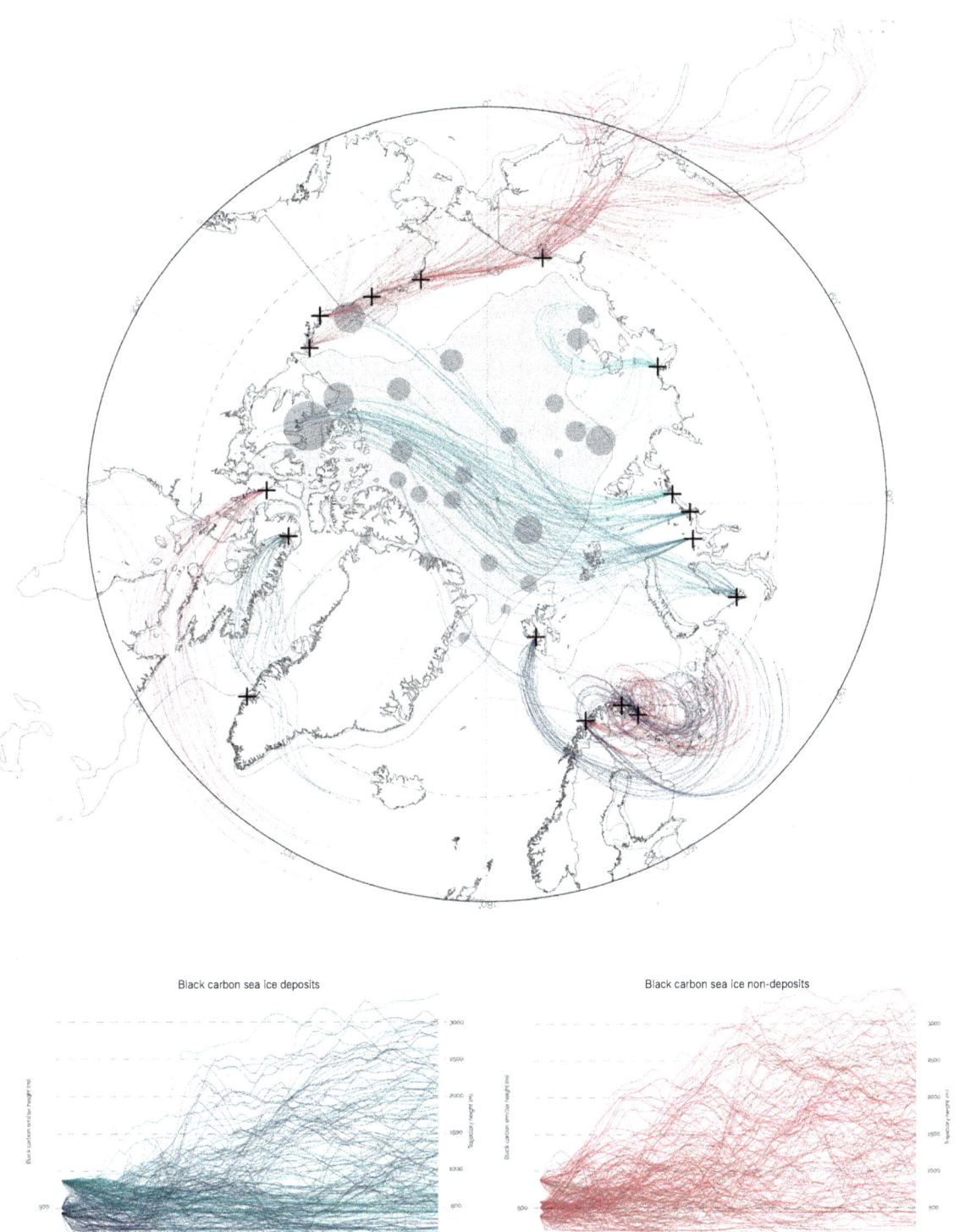

Kate Hosking. Black Ice Forum. Mapping Black Carbon Trajectory over the Arctic (2020).

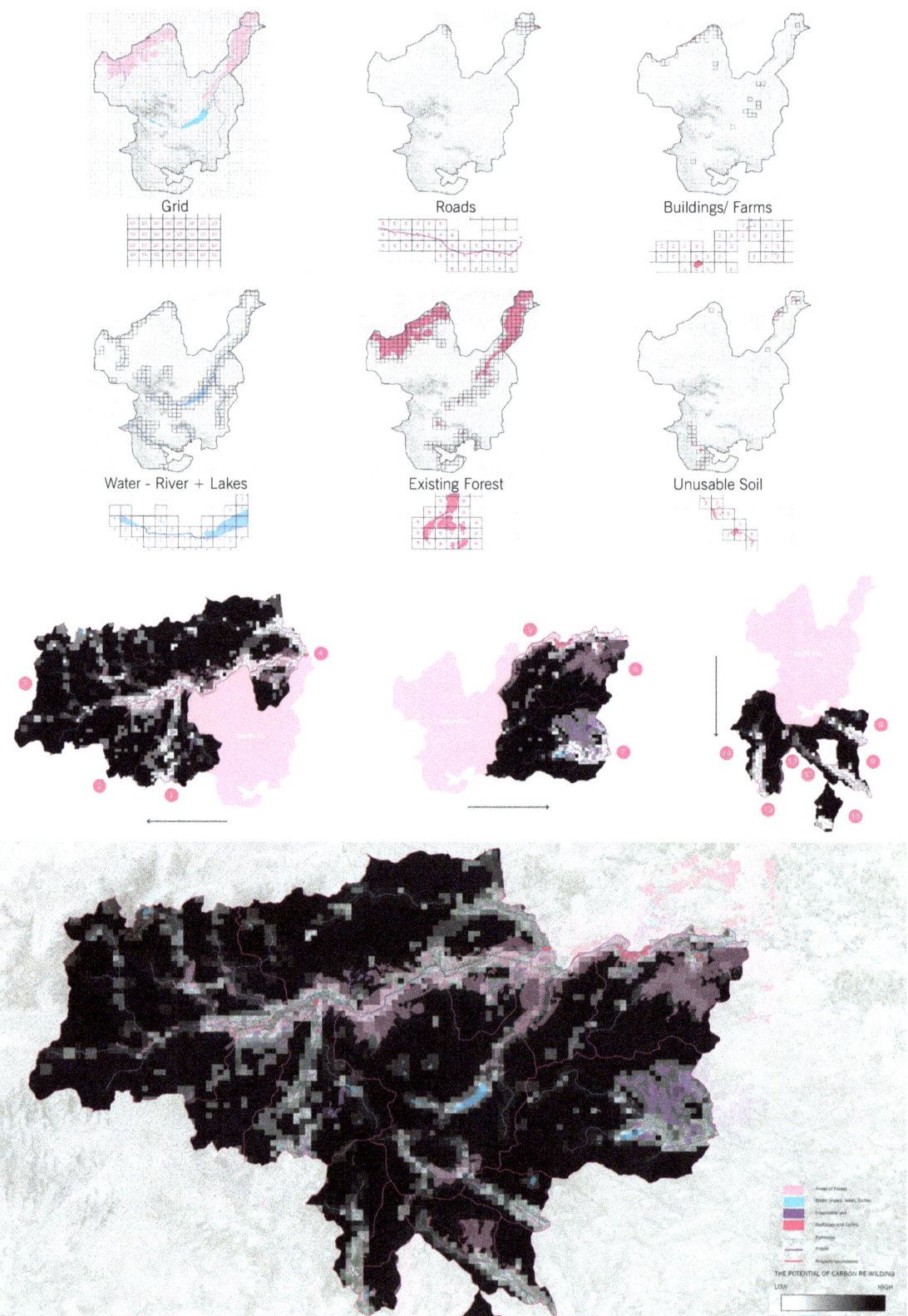

Elizabeth Terry. Balmoral Estate Re-wilding Masterplan. Existing analysis and strategic computational deployment (2021).

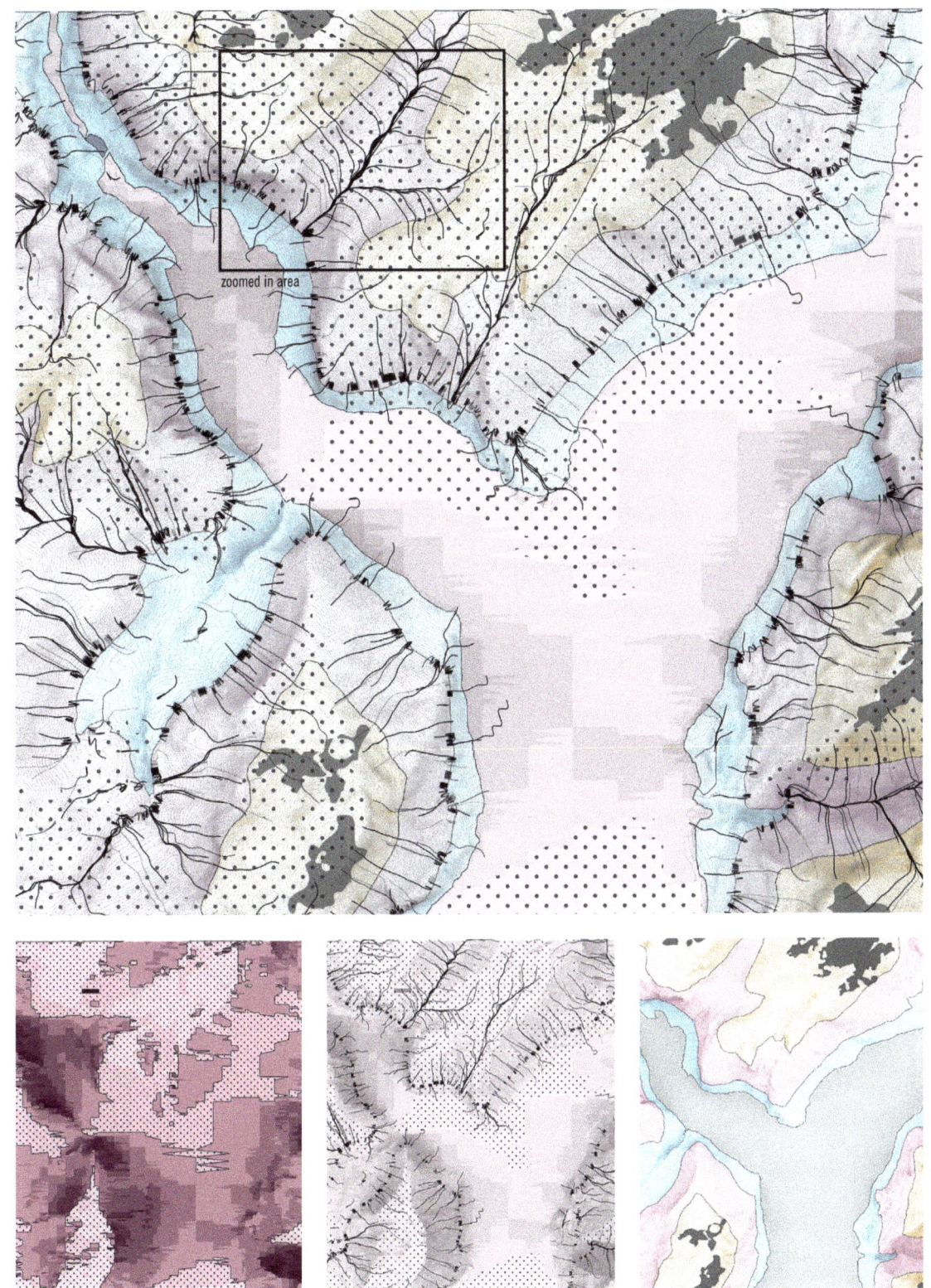

Elizabeth Terry - (top) Optimum territorial conditions for Arctic Cloudberry growth. (bottom) Zoomed in area depicting solar exposure, rainwater runoff, elevation analysis (2021).

Naomi Punnett. The Ash Arboretum. Spread of Ash Dieback in the UK. (top) Ash coverage and recorded infection. (opposite) Chronological deforestation (2023).

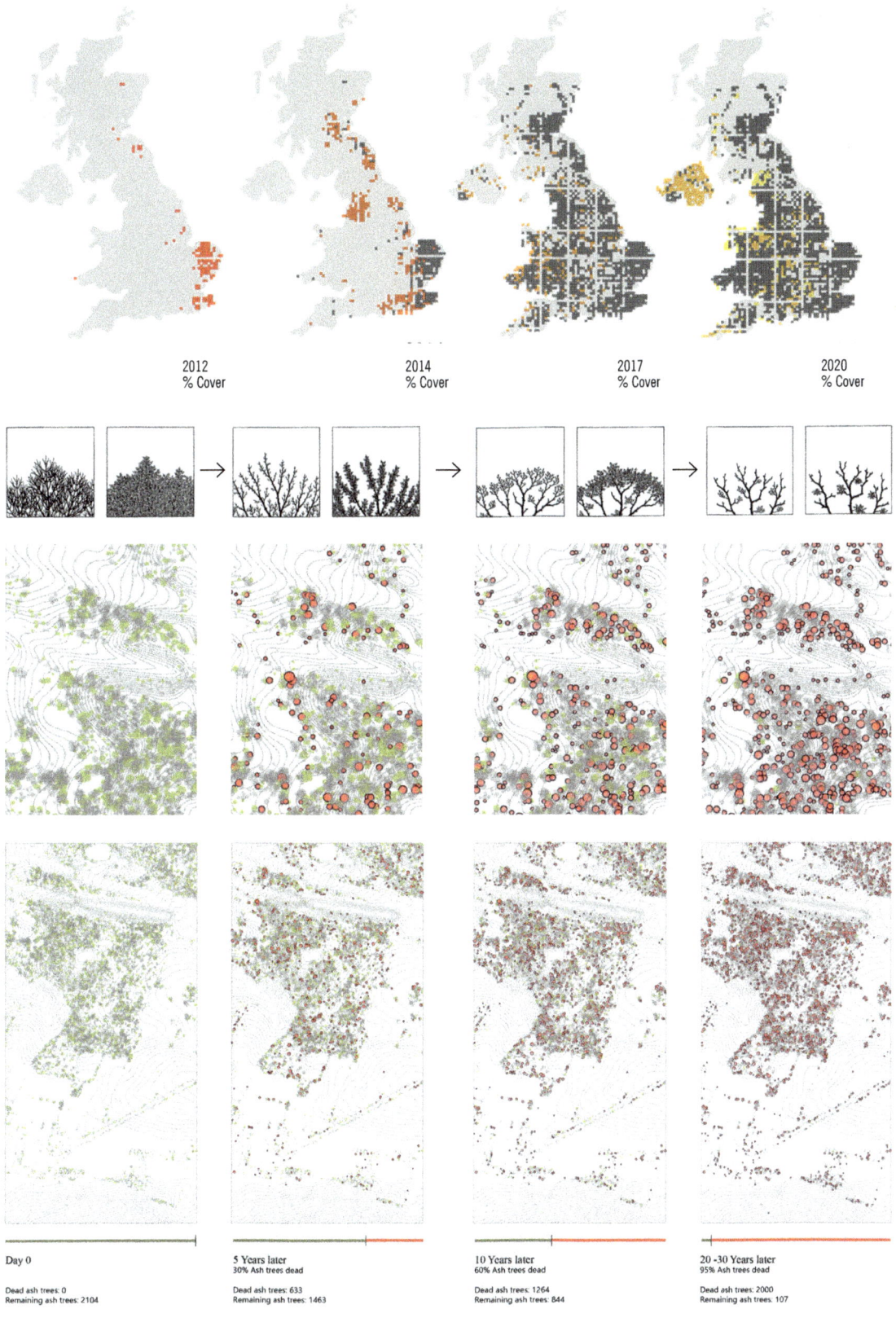

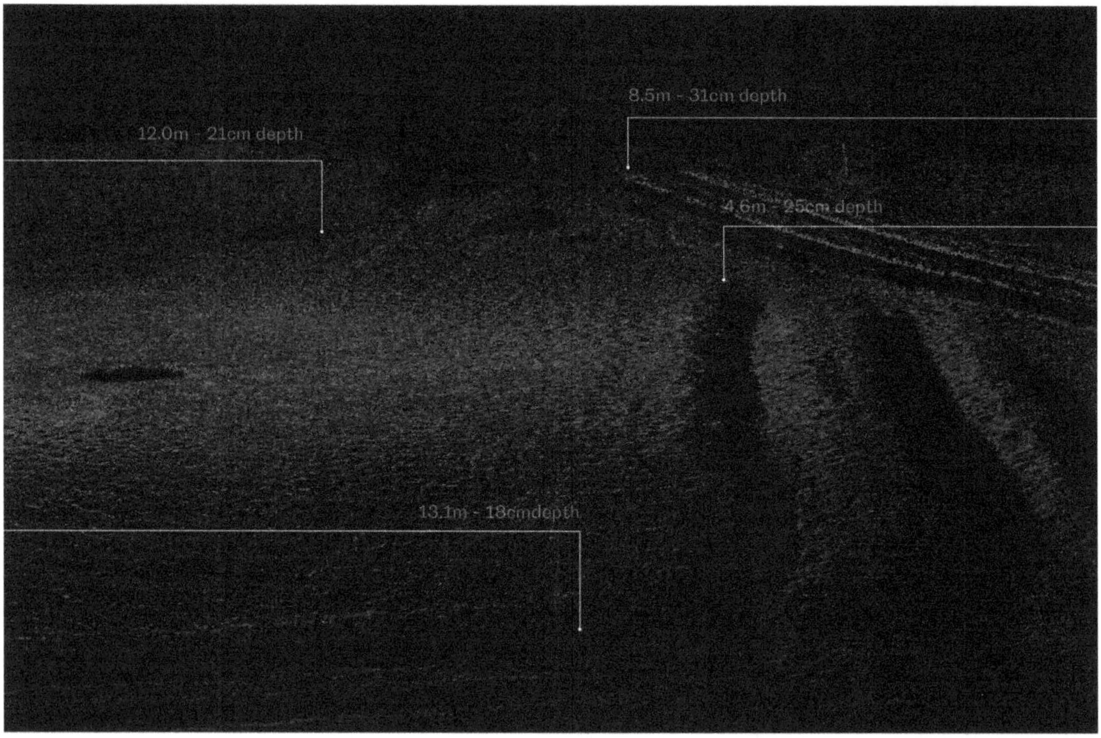

Guy Sinclair. Drift Co-operative. Institute of Superficial Geology. Lidar-survey cartographies; light detection and ranging to examine the surface of Dungeness (2022).

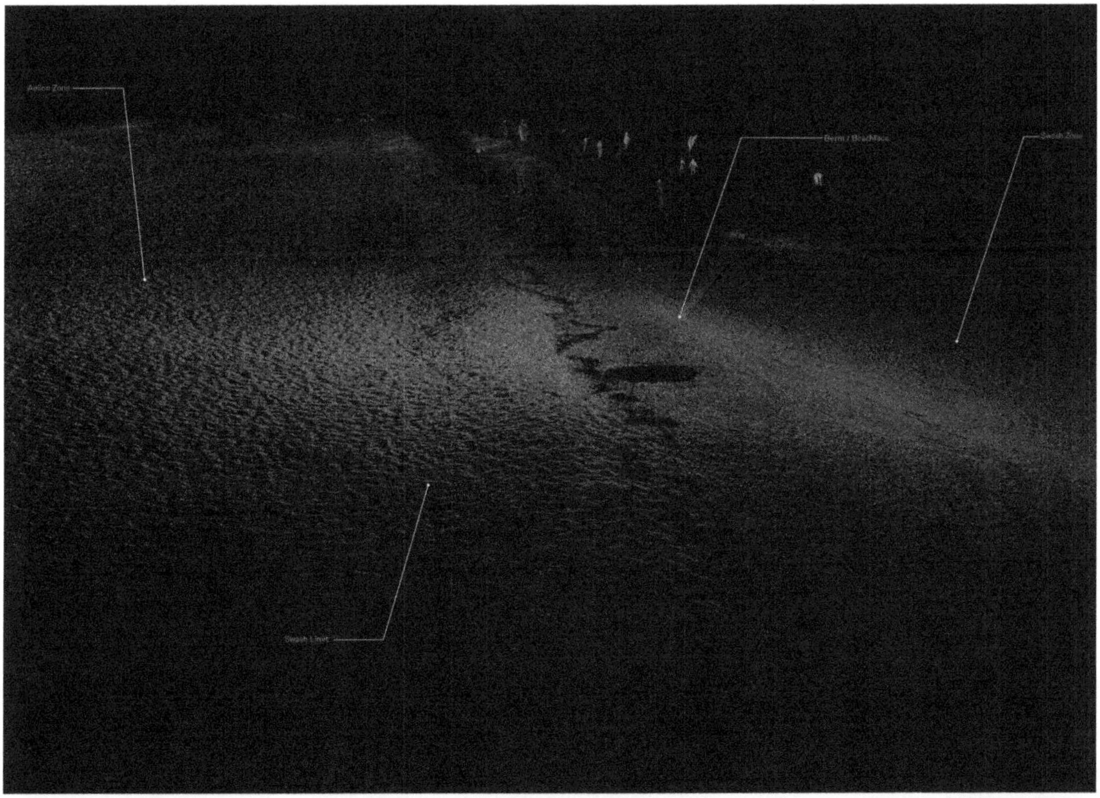

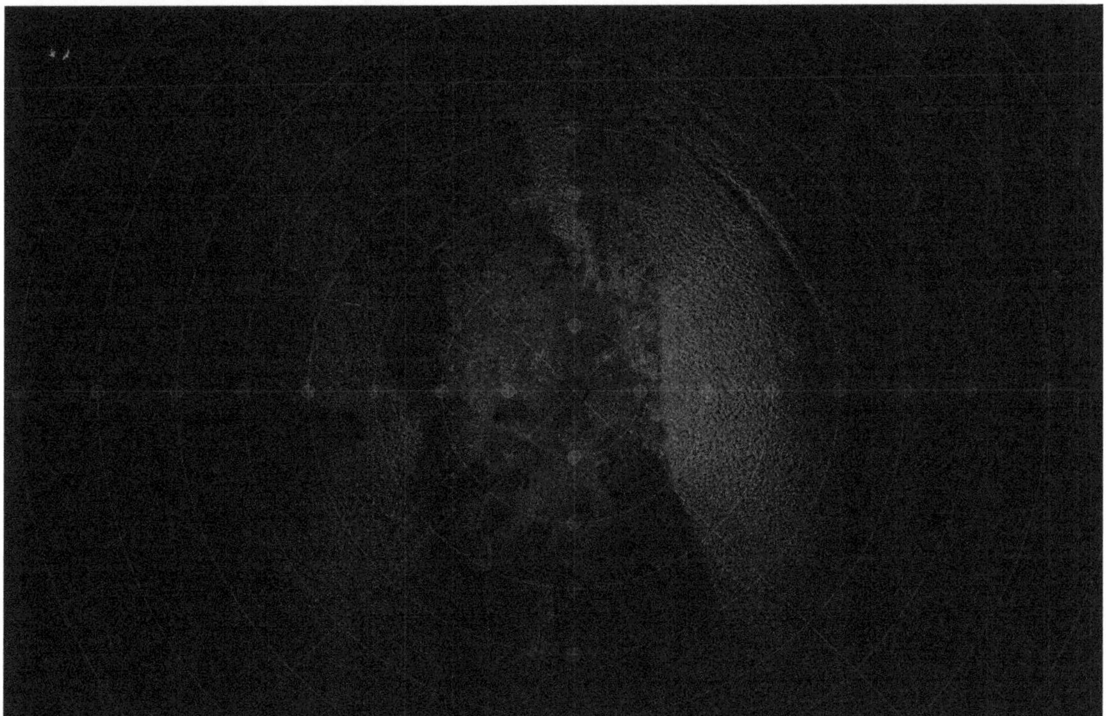

Vilde Bakkeli Sand. The Newt Sanctuary and Bio-Corridor. The Nocturnal. Device for mapping the Great Crested Newt habitat based upon tidal moon phase relations (2022).

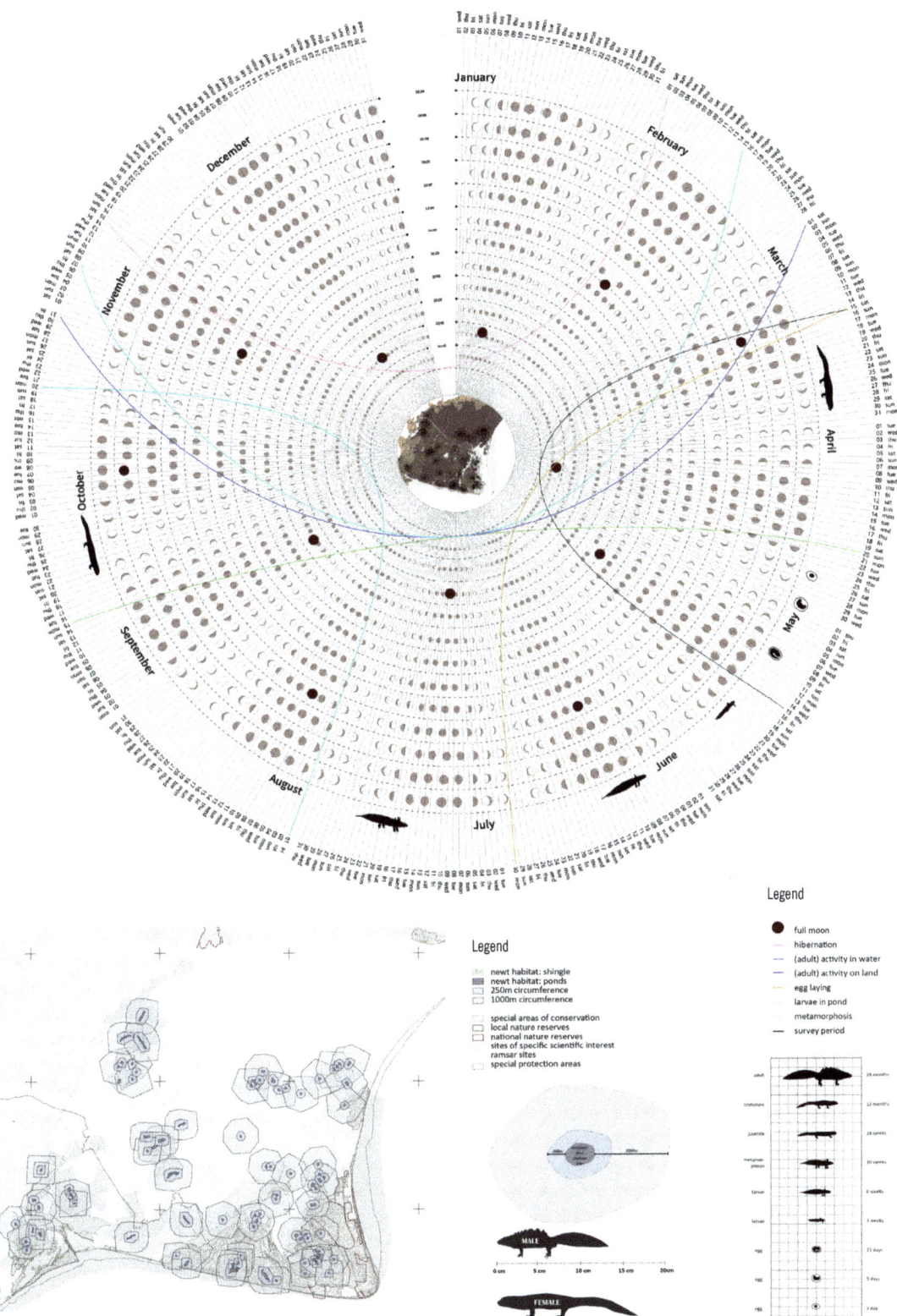

(top) Newt Life Cycle - hibernation, growth and activity. (bottom) Proposed new ponds and newt habitats.

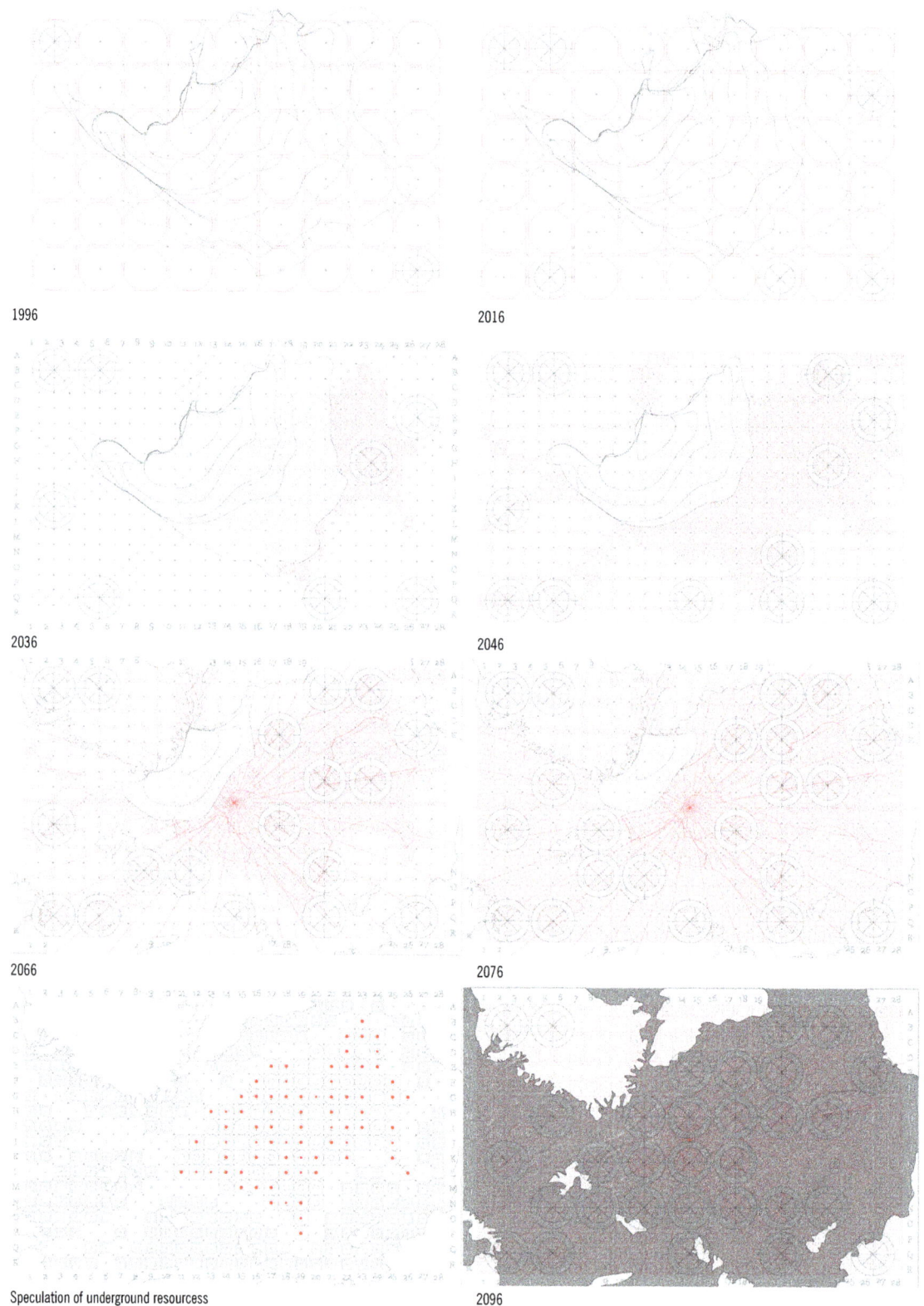

Jamie Williams. 'The Polar Silk Road' - The Grand Arctic Assets Board Game. From satellite to seabed drawings indicating the Arctic state play (2020).

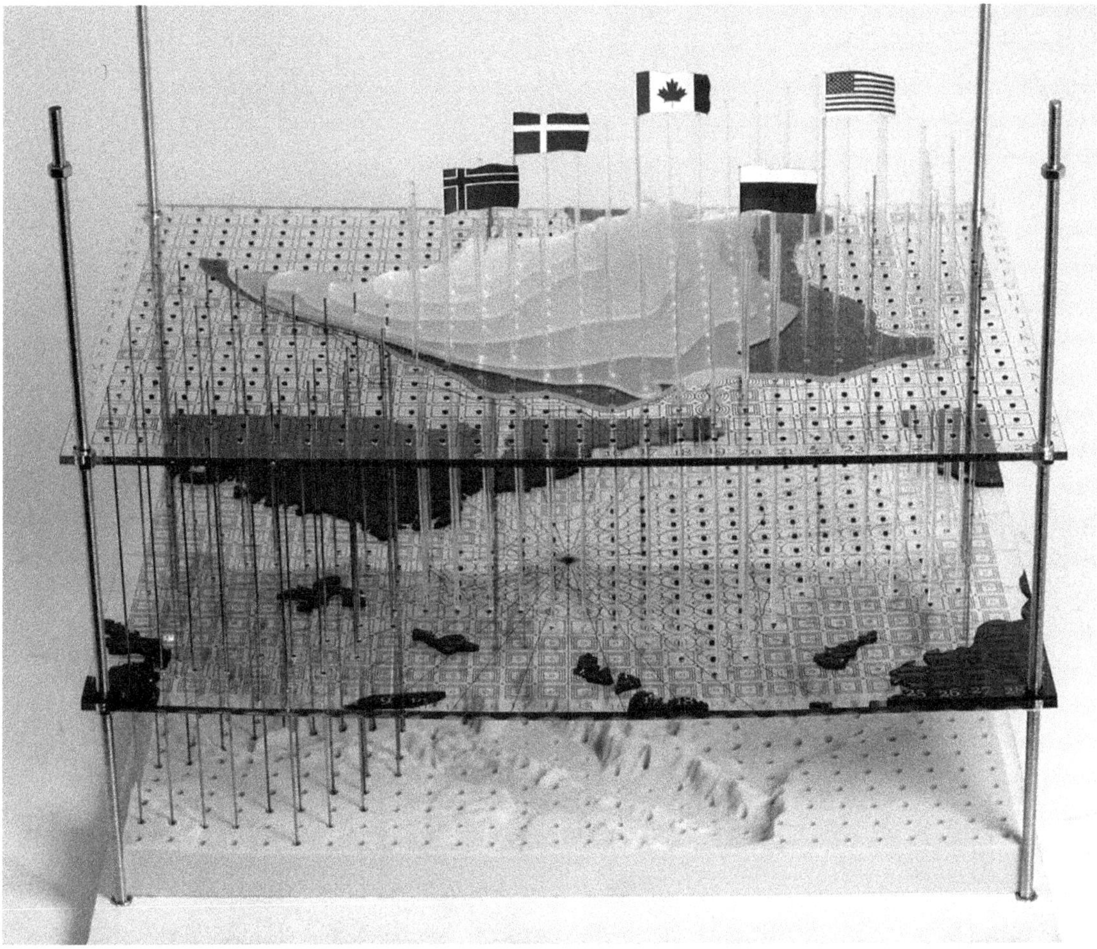

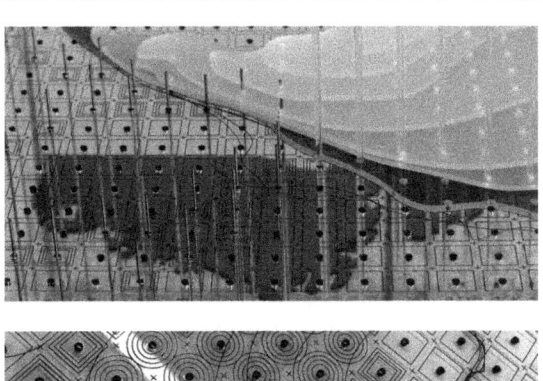
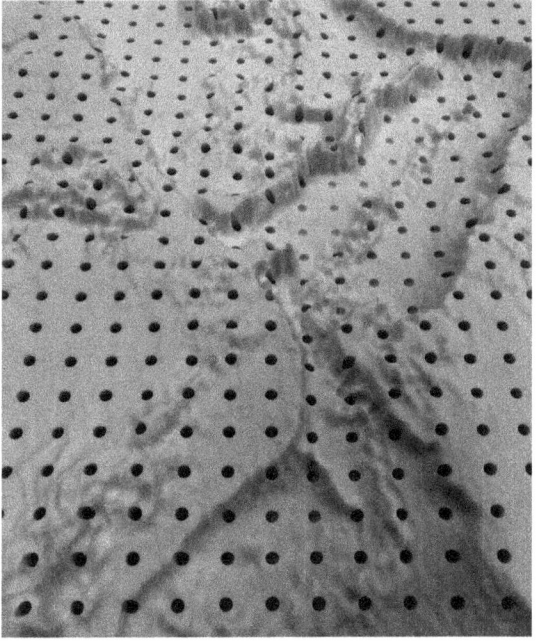
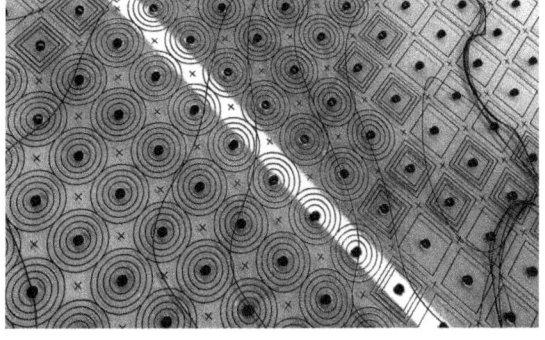

SIMULATIONS

THERMODYNAMICS AND SIMULATIONS

JOHN COOK AND LAURA NICA

Design Studio 18 has employed the use of simulation over its history through the material studies around ground and water, explored across a range of its explorative, technical and representational potentials. Computational simulation provides us with tools to engage and design amongst 'hyper-object' matters (i.e climate change), through spatial and temporal scales incomprehensible at a human level understanding, and inaccessible via traditional architectural methods.[01]

On a practical level, the evolution to the material of air required us to seek out alternative tools of simulation. The studio had previously made use of Nextlimit's *Realflow*, a fluid and multi-physics simulation software aimed primarily at the visual effects industry, and more suited to the emulation of material physics of the liquid state. This software lead to a focus centred around the motion of particles and matter through space, as well as its physical interactions with the containers and objects that held it. Autodesk's *CFD* (Computational Fluid Dynamics) however, is geared towards the technical engineering market to emulate real world fluid and thermal interactions, and more directly equipped for the studies of gaseous interactions. This software operates and presents itself more closely to its underlying mechanics - as the transferral of thermodynamic properties across volumes of linked grid cells in space. Alike the meteorological climate models CFD calculations enable, this required a conceptual shift in thinking from moving matter, weight and mass, to the transfer of invisible energies and properties (temperatures, pressures, humidities) across fluid volumes and materials.

Whilst both are built upon complex physics engines attempting to replicate real world interactions, the transferral of software from one aimed towards animated visual impact, to one of technical engineering and testing, posed new challenges and opportunities. From a representational point of view, this required new techniques in the handling of its outputted data. It demanded new skills and artistry in its conversion of gridded numerical data points to become the dynamic, material and physical representations the studio is known for. In this way, particle paths and fluid mesh forms become gridded point fields, planar gradients and threshold derived isovolumes. In addition, the practice based 'technical' application of this software, rightly or wrongly, promoted more opportunities for its usage through latter stage project development, via performance testing and optimisation of architectural proposals. Iterative testing handled through the software confronted us with *chicken-and-egg* questions, as we negotiated between imposed and generated forms, and the pre-existing and resulting energy flows they were developed within.

Importantly for our approach to architectural design, simulation provides a dynamic changing and unpredictable environment. It forces us as designers to think through design processes that are inherently parametric, ones that must be adaptable to ranging conditions and evolving circumstances, calling for architectures that are fully encompassing of, or even responsive to, a range of projected and uncertain outcomes.

These contrasts, from linear projections to gridded particle masses, between technical validation and creative exploration, are presented through the following discussions and essays of this chapter. Over the next sequence of pages we have compiled a visual glossary of terms, drawn from the themes that emerged of the years we explored this software, and one we hope provides a foundation and reference for the content that follows and beyond.

Notes

(01) R. Bottazzi, (2016). 'On Computer Simulations in the Age of Hyperobjects.', in L. Bremner and R. Bottazzi (eds.), *Architecture, Energy, Matter*, London: Department of Architecture, p. 16-22.

(right) Seni Agunpopo. The Cloud Sanctuary. Cloud simulation (2020).

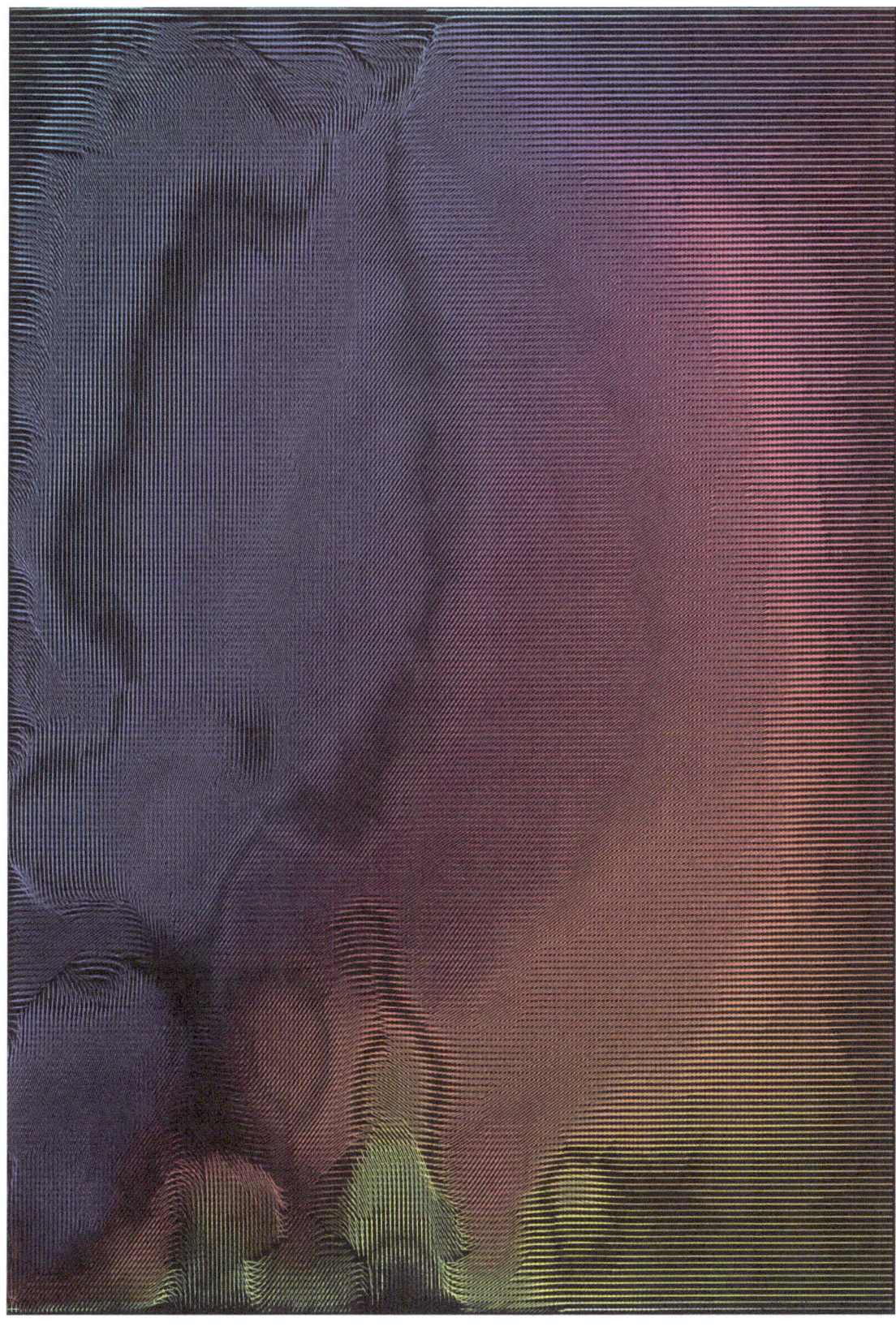

SIMULATION

Terms related to the set-up, inputs and outputs around computational simulation.

Environment
The simulated domain where fluid interactions occur, defined by spatial and temporal parameters. It provides the framework for analysing flow behaviour and energy dynamics.

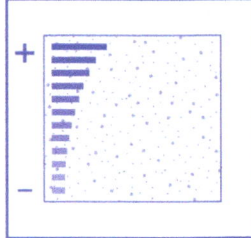

Variables
Quantities such as velocity, pressure, or temperature that change over time and space within the simulation. Variables define the state of the fluid system.

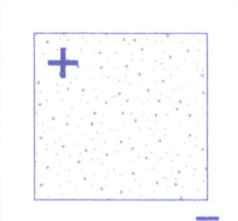

Conditions
The specific initial and boundary values applied to a simulation, such as pressure or temperature. Conditions determine the starting state and constraints of the system.

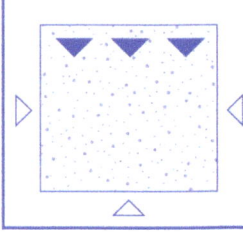

Forces
The physical influences, such as gravity or pressure gradients, applied to the fluid. Forces drive motion, deformation, and energy transfer in the simulation.

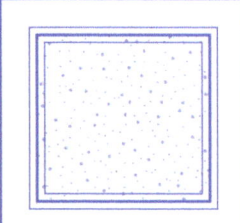

Boundaries
The limits or edges of the simulation domain where specific conditions are imposed. Boundaries govern interactions between the environment and external factors.

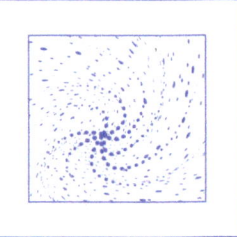

Behaviours
The dynamic or energetic responses of fluid to forces and conditions within the simulation, such as turbulence or laminar flow. Behaviours reveal key properties of fluid systems.

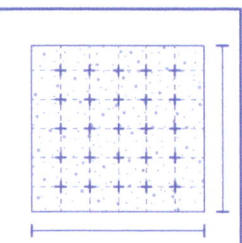

Parameters
Fixed values that define the properties or constraints of a simulation, such as fluid type or grid size. Parameters control the framework and accuracy of the model.

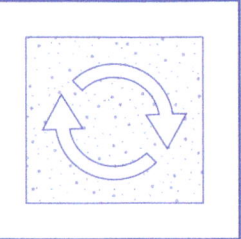

Iterations
A repeated computational step that refines the solution by solving equations for each time specified step. Iteration ensures accurate modelling of fluid behaviour over time.

NOTATION

Terms describing conceptual and visual notations for the representation of simulated outputs.

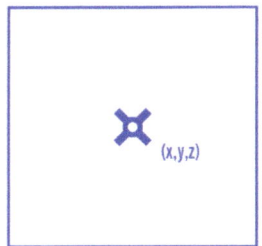

Point
A single location in space with no dimensions, used as a reference or marker. Defined by x,y,z coordinates, points describe positions and origins within a simulation environment.

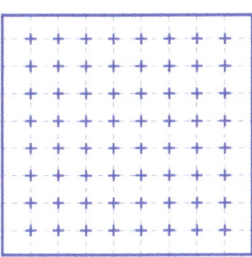

Grid
A network of intersecting lines forming cells that structure a simulation domain. Grids organize data points and enable precise calculations in computational models.

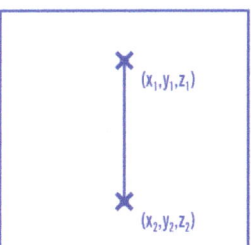

Line
A linear projection connecting two or more points in space, indicating direction, connection or boundaries. Lines are used to trace paths or define flow patterns in simulations.

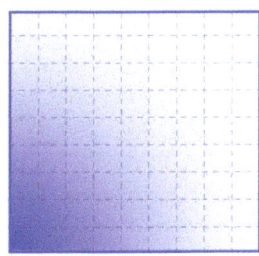

Gradient
A gradual change in a property, such as temperature or pressure, represented visually by a colour spectrum or shading. Gradients highlight spatial variations in simulations.

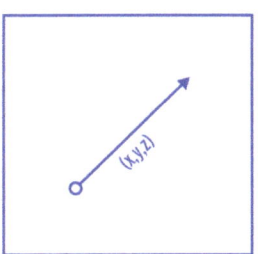

Vector
A graphical representation of magnitude and direction defined by x,y,z from a given origin point. Typically visualized as an arrow, vectors illustrate airflow, forces, or velocities in fluid dynamic simulations.

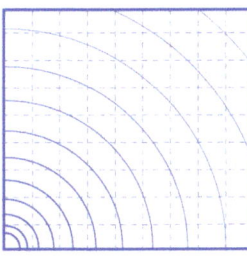

Contours
Curved lines connecting points of equal value, such as pressure or temperature. Contours illustrate spatial distributions and variations within fluid dynamics.

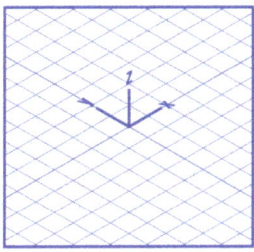

Plane
A two-dimensional flat surface extending infinitely, defined by a given origin and axis in space. Planes represent sections or boundaries in simulations and visualisations.

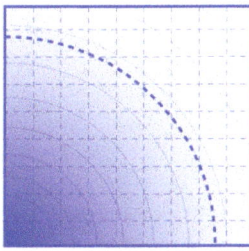

Threshold
A specified value or limit within a range of values. Thresholds are used to define, separate or filter data numerically or spatially, such as velocity magnitudes or temperature ranges.

PROPERTIES

Intrinsic characteristics of air and its physical nature, invisible variables within fluid simulations and atmospheric phenomena.

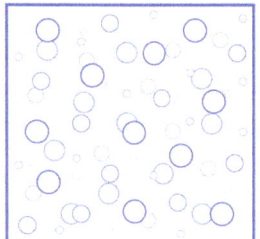

Mass
The amount of matter contained in air, measured in kilograms (kg). Mass determines density, buoyancy, and pressure variations in atmospheric systems.

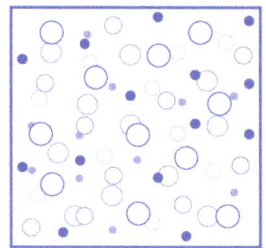

Humidity
The amount of water vapour present in air, measured as relative humidity (%). Humidity affects condensation, evaporation, and cloud formation, playing a critical role in atmospheric cycles and moisture dynamics.

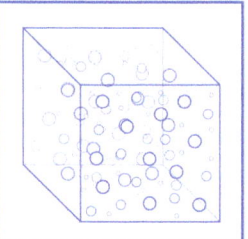

Volume
The three-dimensional space occupied by air, measured in cubic meters (m³). Volume influences density and energy distribution within atmospheric conditions.

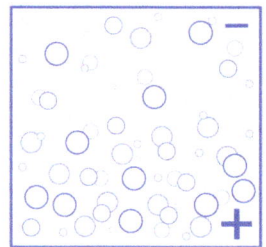

Density
The mass of air within a specific volume, measured in kilograms per cubic meter (kg/m³). Density varies with temperature and pressure, determining buoyancy, stratification, and flow behaviour in atmospheric systems.

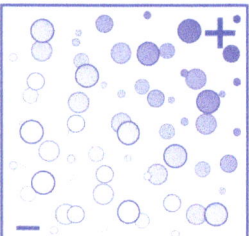

Temperature
The degree of thermal energy present in air, measured in degrees Celsius (°C) or Kelvin (K). Temperature dictates molecular motion, driving atmospheric systems and thermal energy distribution in simulations.

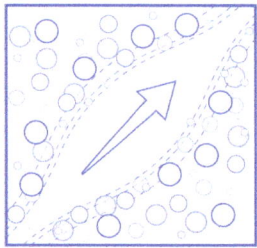

Viscosity
Air's resistance to flow or deformation under applied force, measured in Pascal-seconds (Pa·s). Viscosity impacts turbulence and smooth flow, shaping aerodynamic interactions and atmospheric dynamics.

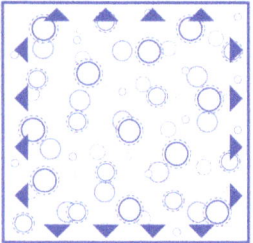

Pressure
The force exerted by air molecules on a surface per unit area, measured in Pascals (Pa) or millibars (mb). Pressure influences vertical air movement, wind patterns, and stability in atmospheric systems.

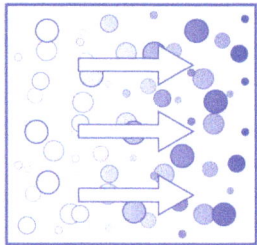

Conductivity
The ability of air to transfer heat through its particles, measured in watts per meter-Kelvin (W/m·K). Conductivity supports thermal gradients and energy exchange within atmospheric and environmental systems.

MOVEMENT

Terms describing the movement of air in space, and wider dynamic motions within atmospheric systems.

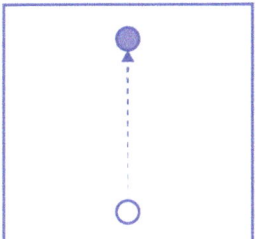

Speed
The magnitude of air movement, measured in meters per second (m/s). Speed determines the intensity of wind and contributes to flow dynamics in atmospheric systems.

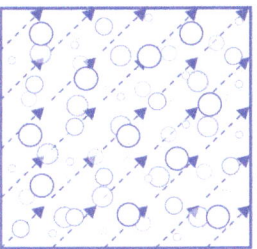

Flow
The continuous movement of air, often measured as volume per time (m^3/s). Flow patterns shape atmospheric circulation and determine energy and mass transport.

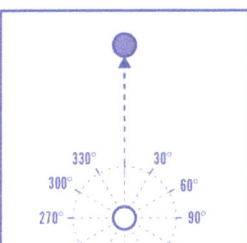

Direction
The orientation of air movement relative to a reference point, measured in degrees or cardinal points. Direction defines wind flow patterns and their impact on atmospheric behaviours.

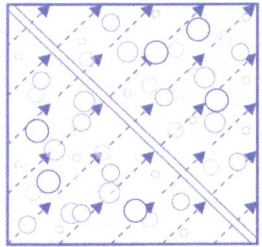

Flux
The rate of flow of air, energy, or particles through a surface, measured in units like kilograms per square meter per second (kg/$m^2 \cdot$s). Flux governs mass and energy transfer in air systems.

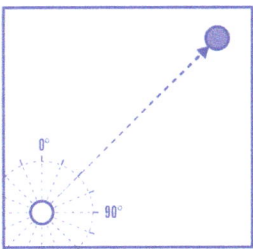

Velocity
The combination of speed and direction of air movement, measured in meters per second (m/s). Velocity determines the flow dynamics of air within atmospheric and aerodynamic systems.

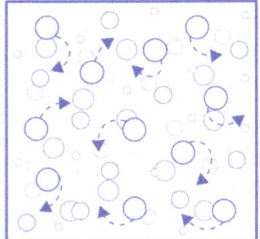

Turbulence
Irregular and chaotic air motion, involving rapid velocity and pressure changes, quantified by turbulence intensity. Turbulence affects aerodynamic behaviour and atmospheric mixing.

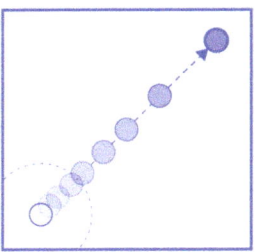

Acceleration
The rate of change of air velocity over time, measured in meters per second squared (m/s^2). Acceleration influences transitions in flow behaviour and atmospheric motion.

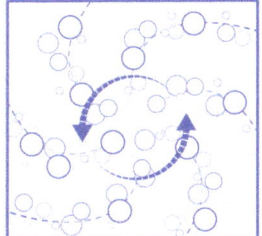

Vorticity
The rotational motion of air within a fluid, describing the local spin or circulation, measured in radians per second (rad/s). Vorticity highlights turbulence and rotational flow behaviours in atmospheric systems.

INTERACTIONS

Terms related to the natural, engineered, and dynamic processes around air and atmospheric phenomena.

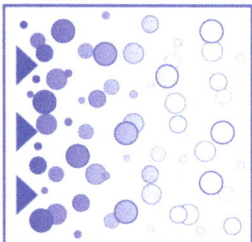

Absorption
The process by which air takes in energy or particles, reducing their transmission. Measured as a percentage, absorption influences thermal balance and energy retention in the atmosphere.

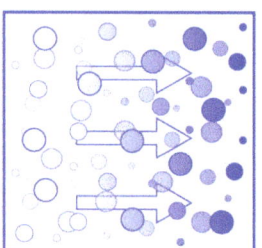

Conduction
The transfer of heat through air via molecular contact, measured in watts per meter-Kelvin (W/m·K). Conduction plays a role in energy distribution near surfaces and within atmospheric layers.

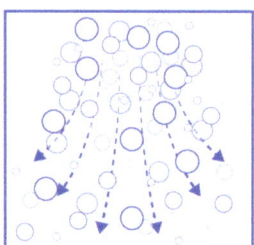

Diffusion
The movement of particles or energy within air from higher to lower concentration, measured in meters squared per second (m^2/s). Diffusion promotes mixing and uniformity in atmospheric systems.

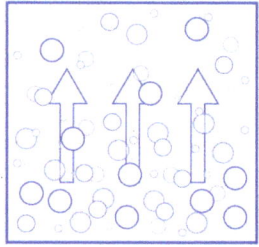

Convection
The vertical transfer of heat or mass in air due to density differences, measured in watts per square meter (W/m^2). Convection drives cloud formation and energy circulation in the atmosphere.

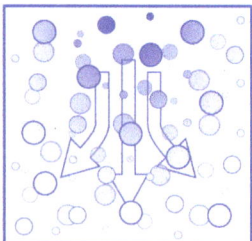

Dissipation
The loss or spreading out of energy in air, reducing intensity. Measured in watts per kilogram (W/kg), dissipation regulates turbulence and stabilizes atmospheric flows.

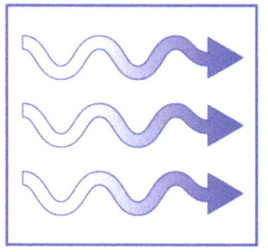

Radiation
The emission or transfer of energy through electromagnetic waves, measured in watts per square meter (W/m^2). Radiation influences atmospheric heating and energy exchange.

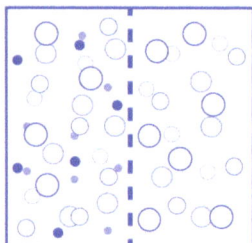

Filtration
The process of removing particles or impurities from air as it passes through a medium. Filtration is key in maintaining air quality and mitigating particulate matter in atmospheric flows.

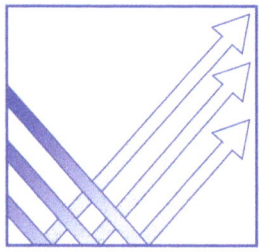

Reflection
The redirection of energy or waves upon striking a surface, measured as reflectivity or albedo. Reflection impacts solar energy distribution and atmospheric temperature regulation.

TRANSFORMATIONS

Examples of terms related to the outcomes and transformations caused by aerial processes within the atmospheric and simulated environment.

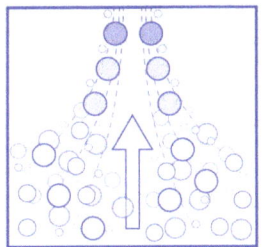

Formation
The creation or emergence of structures, patterns, or flow features within a fluid, driven by forces and conditions. Formation reveals underlying dynamics of air or fluid systems.

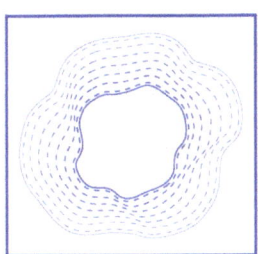

Deformation
The distortion or reshaping of airflows, fluid, or geometries under applied forces. Deformation illustrates material response to stress and flow behaviours.

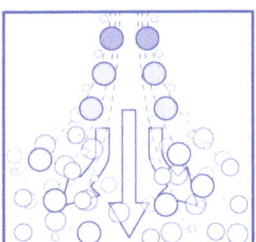

Degradation
The breakdown or loss of structural integrity in airflows, fluid properties, or geometries over time. Degradation indicates energy dissipation and system decline.

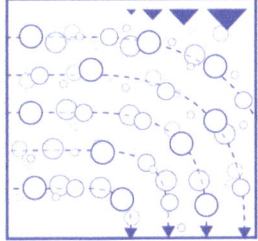

Transition
The process of change between flow states, such as from laminar to turbulent motion. Transition highlights shifts in energy and stability within the simulated system.

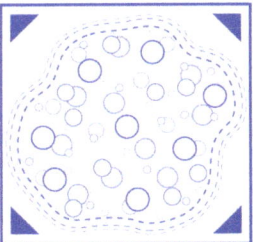

Expansion
The increase in volume or spatial extent of air or fluid, often due to pressure or temperature changes. Expansion affects flow distribution and system boundaries.

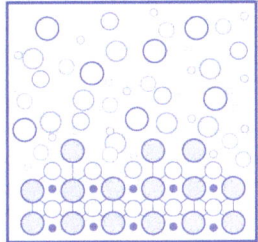

Crystallisation
The solidification process where ordered structures form from fluid particles under specific conditions. Crystallisation impacts material interactions and flow obstructions.

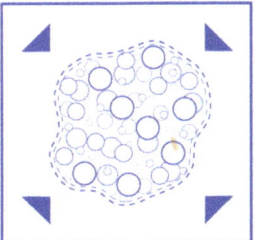

Contraction
The reduction in volume or spatial extent of air or fluid, typically from cooling or compressive forces. Contraction alters flow density and dynamic interactions.

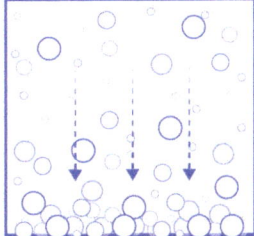

Deposition
The settling or accumulation of particles or material from a fluid onto a surface. Deposition alters surface interactions and flow characteristics in the simulated system.

Seni Agunpopo. Peat Recovery Observation. Ground simulation of compressed topographic layers and carbon within peat landscapes (2021).

MODELING AIR: ARROWS, POINT-CLOUDS AND THEIR WAYS OF KNOWING AIR

URI WEGMAN

The sciences do not try to explain, they hardly even try to interpret, they mainly make models. By a model is meant a mathematical construct which, with the addition of certain verbal interpretations, describes observed phenomena. (01)

Introduction

Architecture and geometry have been entwined for millennia. So strong is their bond that it is hard to imagine architecture without geometry's ability to furnish it with a measured, definitive and precise form. The etymological root of geometry – the measuring of the earth (or more precisely, the ground or the land), (02) points to its terrestrial cradle and its downwards looking gaze. It also alludes to what is excluded from geometry's model of knowledge: all that is non-solid, nebulous or ephemeral, everything that hovers, flows and moves above the ground. In short, all that is air. Writing about linear perspective, Hubert Damisch contests that it "[...] only needs to 'know' things that it can reduce to its own order, things that occupy a place and the contour of which can be defined by lines". (03) He then continues: "But the sky does not occupy a place, and cannot be measured; and as for clouds, nor can their outlines be fixed or their shapes analyzed in terms of surfaces". (04) Architecture's reliance on geometry is associated and confirmed by the dominance of lines in its models of representation, lines that define edges, surfaces and volumes with efficiency and precision. Yet the orthodoxy of geometric delineation as the sole arbiter of architectural space falls short if one attempts to consider air as an architectural material. Other forms of knowledge and alternative modes of drawings are needed, ones which

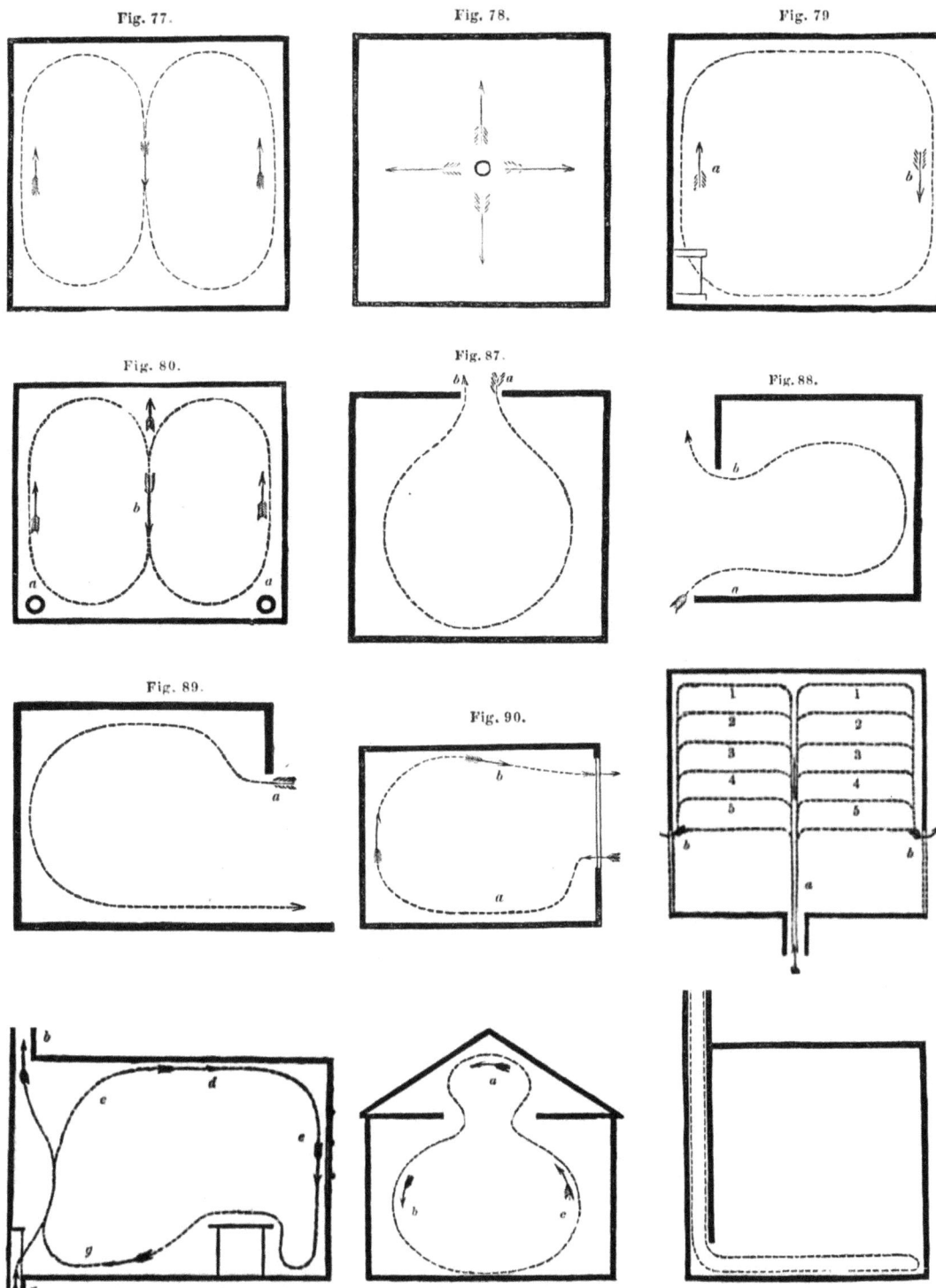

Figure 1 – David Boswell Reid
Diagrams of air circulation in chambers under different conditions and spatial configurations. From "Illustrations of the Theory and Practice of Ventilation". 1844.

Figure 2 – Otto von Guericke Magdeburg hemispheres demonstration, 1654
Engraving by Gaspar Schott.

could describe what descriptive geometry cannot.

During the 17-th century air has gradually materialized and qualified, as Robert Boyle, Joseph Black, Joseph Priestly, Antoine Lavoisier and other scientists attributed air with measurable properties such as weight, pressure, temperature, composition, consistency and conductivity. (05) The ontological transformation of air from an Aristotelian element (homogeneous, natural, steady, given) to a composed material (heterogeneous, complex, artificial, dynamic) was related to the ways in which it was observed and visualized by science. New tools such as the air pump, thermometer, barometer, hygrometer and the anemometer could precisely measure and control air, (06) thus exposing its ability to facilitate vital exchanges between living beings, plants and inorganic materials (as in photosynthesis and breathing). The process of air's materialization and qualification had its architectural consequences; by mid 18-th century, air started to appear as an active substance in the design of buildings. (07) Spaces were drawn in sections and plans, designated for the control and distribution of air by means of mechanical ventilation systems, which developed rapidly during the industrial revolution. These newly drawn spaces of aerial circulation became populated by signs that attempted to give form to a substance which projective geometry could

not describe. Architects and engineers began to visualize air, trying to describe it through many different types of annotations. Among the numerous ways in which air was architecturally drawn in the centuries following the scientific revolution, two dominant signifiers emerged; the arrow (in the late 18-th century) and the point-cloud (post World War II). Their use in drawings reflects not only an emergence of two distinct graphic conventions, but also how air was understood through two separate epistemic frameworks: empirical experiment and numerical simulation.

Arrows and Empirical Experimentation

The elaborate and inventive use of arrows in the drawings of David Boswell Reid (1805-1863) can serve as an early case study in the visualization of air as a process of empirical experimentation. Reid, a British chemist and pioneer of mechanical ventilation, tested and theorized the behavior of air in buildings by using an elaborate laboratory setup that he built at the chemistry department of Edinburgh university (**Fig. 3**). In his laboratory he was able to model and experiment with controlled flows of air inside large scale mock-ups of rooms and buildings. (08) Reid's scientific methodology was empirical, evaluating the results of the experiments by observing their direct effects

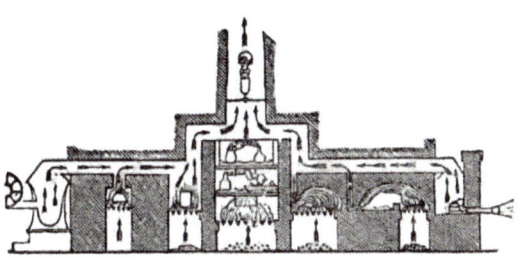
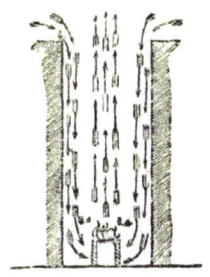
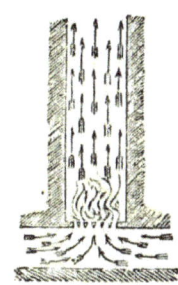
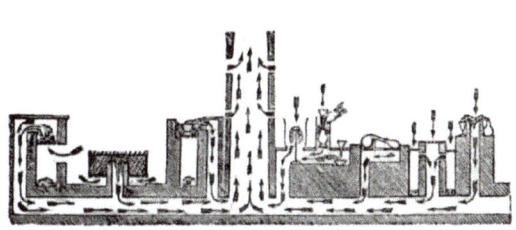
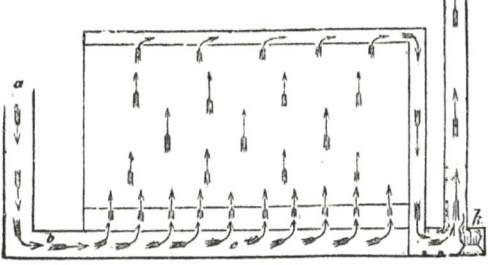

Figure 3 — David Boswell Reid. (left) Laboratory equipment for studying the dynamics of air; (right) Design for the ventilation system of the new House of Commons in London. From "Illustrations of the Theory and Practice of Ventilation" . 1844

on human participants and various scientific instruments that he equipped his lab with. (09) To make the effect of air tangible, Reid ignited gunpowder that filled the space with smoke, emitted strong odors through the ventilation apparatus, or observed the rates in which meat rot in spaces exposed to different ventilation conditions. These direct, empirical experiments often took form as spectacles or public demonstrations, where Reid gathered dignitaries, clients and peers to have a first-person experience of the ventilation experiment, sometimes having a formal dinner inside the ventilated chamber as the experiment went on. (10) The performative and demonstrative aspect of Reid's air experiments sits well within the legacy of empirical experimentation with air, from of Otto von Guericke vacuumed hemispheres demonstration (**Fig. 2**) to the asphyxiation of animals in air pumps as portrayed in Joseph Wright of Derby's painting An Experiment on a Bird in the Air Pump. In Reid's laboratory, however, the observers became the actual subjects of the experiment, placed inside what were essentially giant laboratory instruments. Reid conceived buildings as large scientific apparatus, a spatio-mechanical setup in which the interplay between machines, conduits, sensors and switches established a system of artificial climate control. (11)

One of Reid's greatest achievements was the translation of his direct empirical knowledge of air's behavior into the visual language of architectural representation, bridging the epistemological gap between the way air is experienced and the way architecture is drawn. The main semantic tool that enabled that translation was the arrow, which Reid used extensively and innovatively in his illustrations (**Fig. 1**).

Arrow as a signifier of movement and direction began to surface in architectural and engineering drawing in the mid 18-th century, appearing first in drawings of hydraulic systems. (12) By the early 19-th century, with the work of de Chabannes, Jebb, Soane and others, arrows became a standard architectural sign for notating the movement of air in buildings. The arrow is essentially a pictogram, evolving quite directly from the image of the archery arrow. It is meaningful that air was described as a projectile racing towards its target, perceived or expected to behave as arrows do once they have been launched i.e: follow a desirable and predictable path to their target. The flight of arrows create a linear, kinetic connection that could be drawn as a single trajectory between the launching point and the target. As a signifier of air, the arrow operates in a manner that is seemingly descriptive (showing what has happened) yet simultaneously prescriptive (showing what should happen). In this state of affairs, when an arrow is

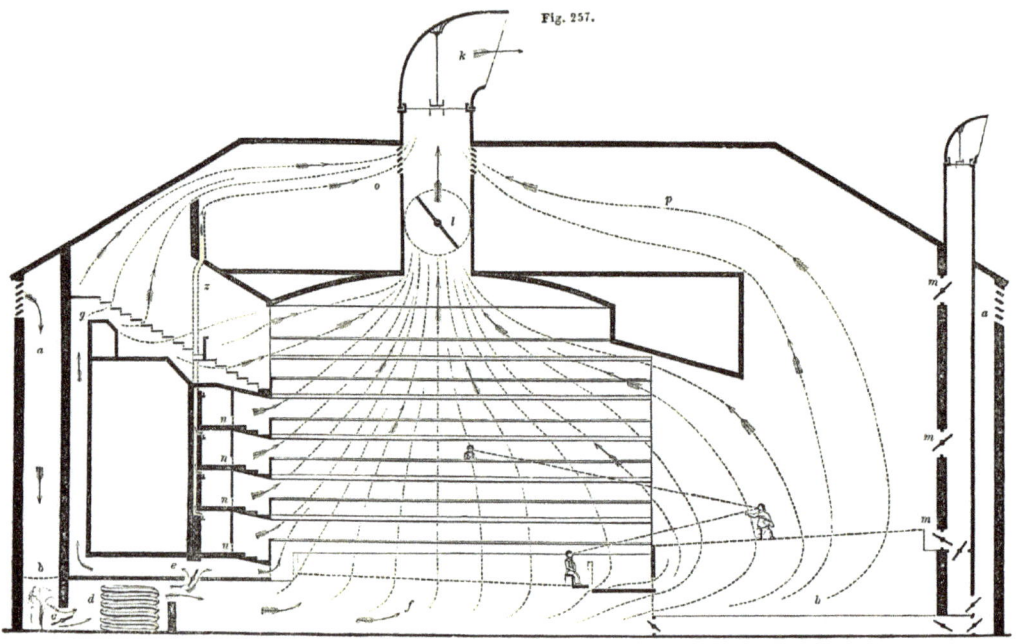

Figure 4 – David Boswell Reid
Section of a theatre showing the trajectories of mechanically - controlled air.
From "Illustrations of the Theory and Practice of Ventilation". 1844

introduced to a drawing, architecture's role is to facilitate the archer's success, ensuring that the arrow will hit its target.

In its early appearances in Reid's drawings, the signifier of air kept a strong resemblance to the archery projectile, including the feathered tail, and adhered to the general proportions of the physical object. But modifications ensued. Reid's innovative use of arrows in the diagrams that illustrate his 1844 treatise "Illustrations of the Theory and Practice of Ventilation" could be read as a set of choreographic notes, where the introduction of heat sources, ventilation, furniture and changes to the architectural space modify the arrows' form and trajectories. Some illustrations show the ways in which arrows begin to bend as they crawl inside the cavities carved in the design for the ventilation system of the new House of Commons (**Fig. 3**). The flexible arrow describes air as a malleable, plastic matter that can be shaped and deformed as viscous liquids do. The flexibility of the arrows was the first step in their transformation from a rigid pictogram to a figure that can adapt itself to the peculiar architectural and aerodynamic situations in which it operates. Another significant modification to the arrow can be observed in Reid's ventilation diagrams and sections of mechanically ventilated public buildings (**Fig. 4**). Here the arrows

shed their traditional proportions and transform into long, sinuous lines. These lines still squeeze themselves through the cavities of the ventilation system but also inscribe autonomous figures in space. Air is hence inscribed as a semi-independent spatial entity that coexists with the architectural form. Dotted, as if to preclude any confusion with the geometrical lines, the arrows have similar visual weight as that of the architectural body. A symbiotic balance emerges: it is not clear anymore if the building shapes the air or vice versa. It is similarly unclear if the behavior of the arrows explain the function of the architectural envelope or is it the other way around.

Whether rigid, short, flexible or long, Ried's arrows describe a materiality inaccessible to linear geometry. They are inserted into the drawing as what Damisch calls "epistemological emblem" [13] : symbolic figures or foreign bodies that reveal the limitation of the model into which they are inserted, creating an uneasy equilibrium between two seemingly contrasting models of representation. Reid's representation of air was an important step in establishing a grammar that can describe and explain the interdependence between architectural form and the performance of air inside it. As signs, arrows provided an explanation and an agency for air as an architectural matter, and furthermore, described architecture as an empirically designed system of

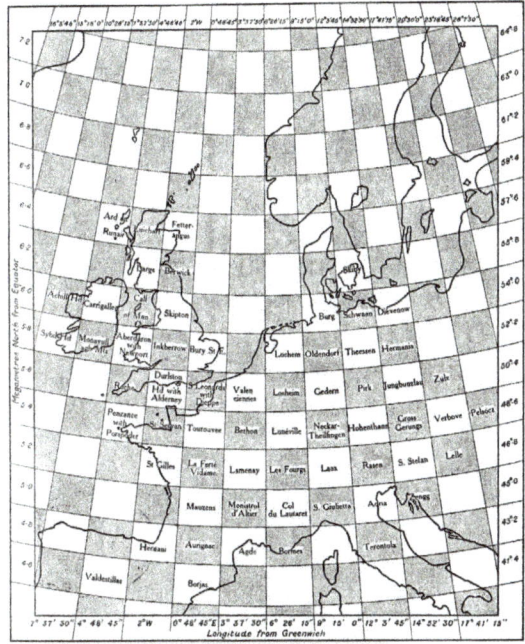
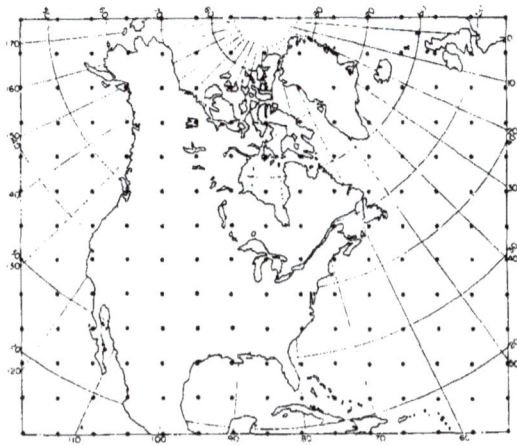

Figure 5 – Cellular space for numerical calculation
From Lewis F. Richardson, Weather Prediction by Numerical Process, 1922

Figure 6 – Cellular space for numerical calculation.
From J. G. Charney, R. Fjörtoft, and J. Neumann. "Numerical Integration of the Barotropic Vorticity Equation." Tellus 2, no. 4 (November 1950).

flows, controls and communication.

Point Clouds and Numerical Simulation

While not describing reality in the same way linear geometry does, Reid's arrows were nevertheless linear in nature, inscribing air's motion as predictable patterns, much like the inner workings of closed hydraulic systems or a mechanical clock. Empirical experimentation of the kind conducted by Reid could explain the behavior of air only by forcing it into a regulating system of ducts and pipes, yet even then, its power of prediction is limited. The larger the air control system is in terms of complexity and scale, the more it is hindered by unpredictable leaks, miscalculations and above all, the varied subjective perception of air by human inhabitants. Predicting and controlling the behavior of air in large environments, be it indoor or outdoors, remained a substantial challenge for empirical science. (14) The erratic behavior of air and the enormous amount of interdependent variables that govern its flow, made the use of large scale empirical models of prediction inefficacious.

The largest of those air environments, and therefore the hardest one to predict, is earth's atmosphere. During Reid's time, weather prediction was conducted in an empirical manner, by comparing the atmospheric readings of the present day to records of days with similar measurements, thus postulating a similar outcome in the following days. (15) Needless to say, this methodology was not sound, producing very unreliable predictions. (16) Searching for more dependable forecasting models, meteorologists began to experiment with numerical prediction in the late 19th century, using mathematical equations to describe the behavior patterns of air in the atmosphere. (17)

A key figure in the emergence of numerical weather prediction was Lewis Fry Richardson, a British mathematician and meteorologist who, in the early 20-th century developed the theoretical framework for describing and predicting weather behavior by means of calculation. In 1922 Richardson published *Weather Prediction by Numerical Process*, a book in which he laid down the basic principles of a globally interconnected weather forecasting system. The mathematical process of prediction was structured upon a spatio-temporal model in which the entire globe is subdivided into small cells that continuously collect local weather data (temperature, humidity, pressure, wind etc.) and transmit it via radio to a central "forecast factory", in which the data is calculated and a forecast is produced (**Fig. 5**). Richardson describes the architecture and the organizational structure of the "forecast factory" in

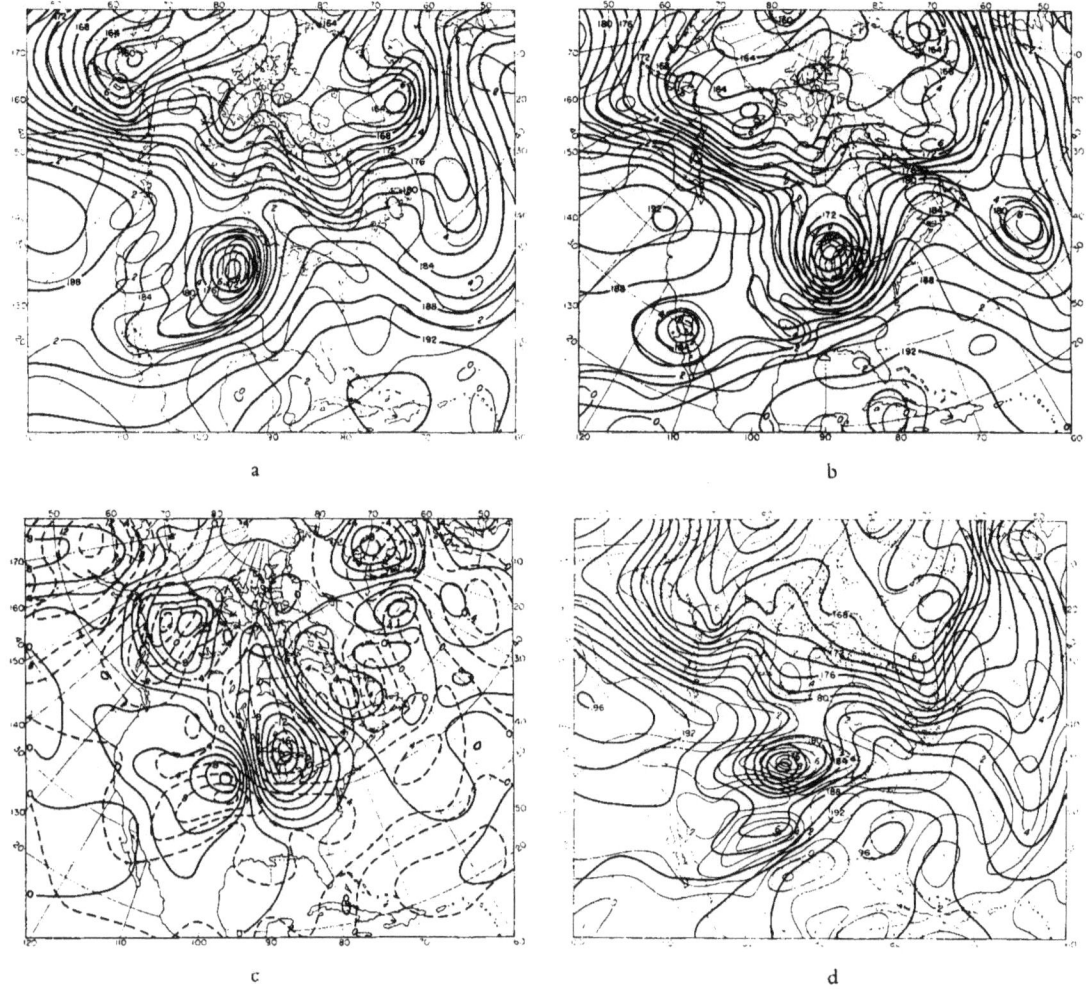

Figure 7 — Numerical forecast of January 5, 1949.
From J. G. Charney, R. Fjörtoft, and J. Neumann. "Numerical Integration of the Barotropic Vorticity Equation." Tellus 2, no. 4 (November 1950).

Figure 8 (top right) — T-3 lab numerical simulation of fluid movement.
From Francis H. Harlow and A.A. Amsden. "Fluid Dynamics; An Introductory Text."Los Alamos scientific laboratory of the university of California, 1971.

Figure 8 (bottom right) — T-3 lab numerical simulation of fluid movement.
From Francis H. Harlow and A.A. Amsden. "Fluid Dynamics; An Introductory Text." Los Alamos scientific laboratory of the university of California, 1971.

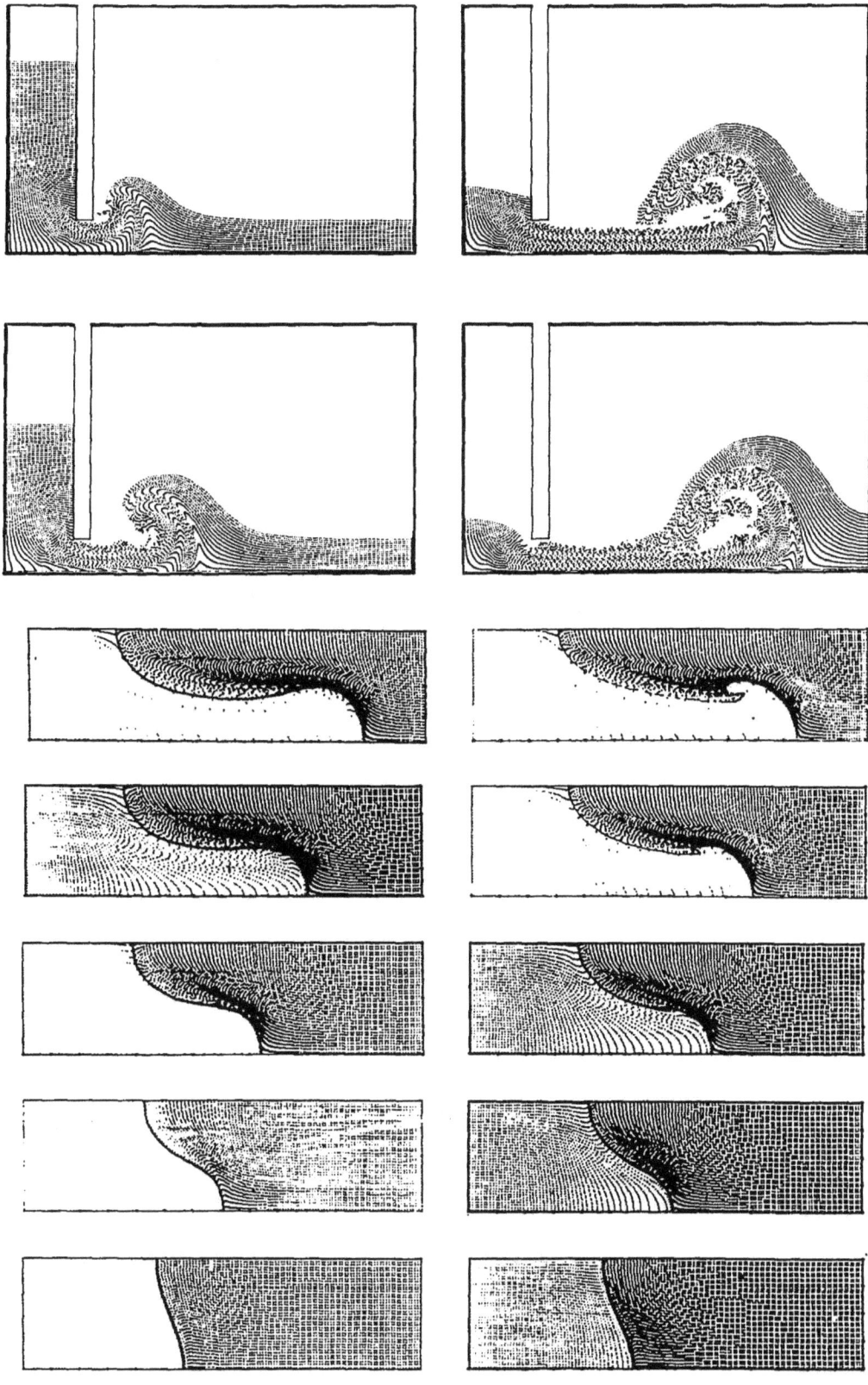

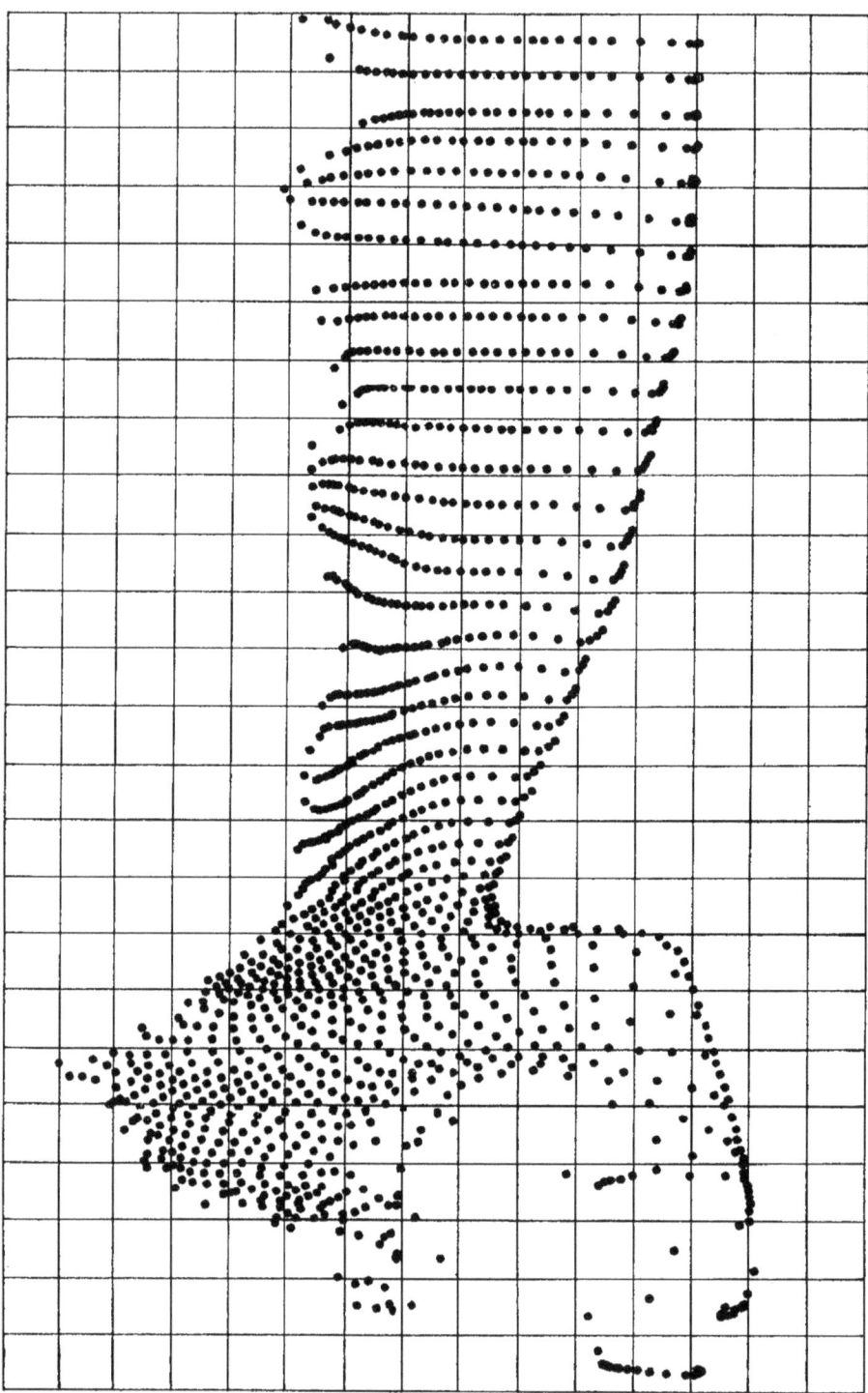

Figure 9 – T-3 lab numerical simulation of gas movement.
From Francis H. Harlow and D.O. Dickman. "Numerical Study of the Motions of Variously-Shaped Slabs Accelerated by a Hot Gas," Los Alamos scientific laboratory of the university of California. 1958

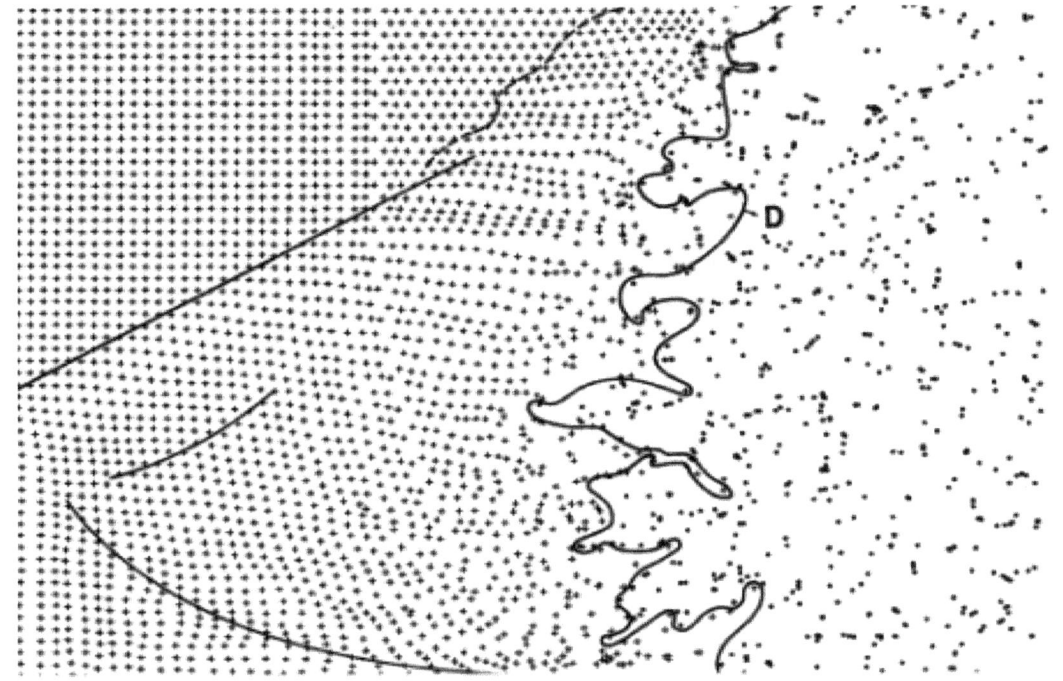

Figure 10 – T-3 lab numerical simulation of gas movement.
From Francis H. Harlow and D.O. Dickman. "Numerical Study of the Motions of Variously-Shaped Slabs Accelerated by a Hot Gas," Los Alamos scientific laboratory of the university of California. 1958

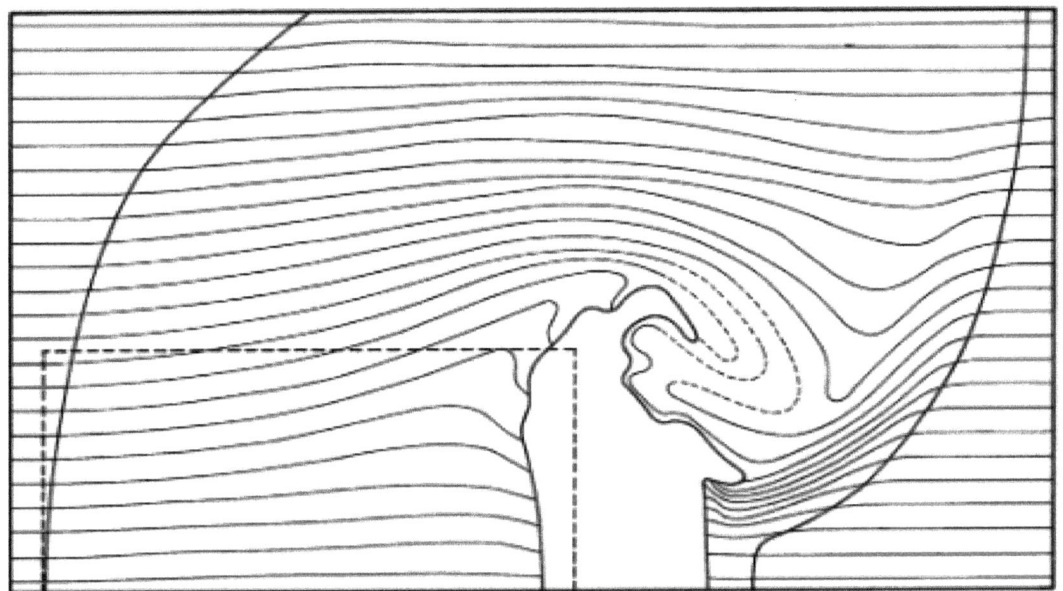

Figure 11 – T-3 lab numerical simulation of gas movement.
From Francis H. Harlow and D.O. Dickman. "Numerical Study of the Motions of Variously-Shaped Slabs Accelerated by a Hot Gas," Los Alamos scientific laboratory of the university of California. 1958

the following passage:

"Imagine a large hall like a theatre, except that the circles and galleries go right round through the space usually occupied by the stage. The walls of this chamber are painted to form a map of the globe. The ceiling represents the north polar regions, England is in the gallery, the tropics in the upper circle, Australia on the dress circle and the antarctic in the pit. A myriad computers are at work upon the weather of the part of the map where each sits, but each computer attends only to one equation or part of an equation. The work of each region is coordinated by an official of higher rank. Numerous little 'night signs' display the instantaneous values so that neighboring computers can read them. Each number is thus displayed in three adjacent zones so as to maintain communication to the North and South on the map. From the floor of the pit a tall pillar rises to half the height of the hall. It carries a large pulpit on its top. In this sits the man in charge of the whole theatre; he is surrounded by several assistants and messengers. One of his duties is to maintain a uniform speed of progress in all parts of the globe. In this respect he is like the conductor of an orchestra in which the instruments are slide-rules and calculating machines. But instead of waving a baton he turns a beam of rosy light upon any region that is running ahead of the rest, and a beam of blue light upon those who are behindhand". [18]

The "myriad computers" described above were sixty four thousand humans, toiling en masse to compute the long and tedious calculations needed to produce the forecast. Although never built in reality, the cellular architecture of the forecast factory in which each cell continuously receives, processes and transmits data to and from a central control unit became the spatial prototype for numerical gas and fluid simulations in the decades to come, laying down the foundations for computational fluid dynamics. [19]

While mathematically sound, Richardson's vision of numerical forecasting necessitated computing power that was unavailable at his time, thus lying dormant for a few decades. That changed at the end of the Second World War, when electronic computers capable of mass, rapid and precise calculation, were developed and used in the Manhattan Project for the design of the atomic bomb. Soon after the war, in 1949, those computers were used by Charney, Fjörtoff and von Neumann to produce the first numerical weather forecast, relying on Richardson's theoretical foundations. [20] Their forecast process had a similar spatial and temporal setup to Richardson's; a slice of the globe was divided into cells, each calculating the atmospheric data of its area while updating its neighboring cells (**Fig. 6**). While the techniques, capacity and applicability of numerical air visualization have significantly changed since their conception, the basic principle through which it operates remains the same; space, at any scale and size, is subdivided into myriad cells that collect and transmit data from and to its neighboring cells. The behavior of air is described, or more precisely, simulated, by a continuous process of mass calculation in which the quantified properties of the air in each individual cell is shared with its neighboring cells, creating a chain of calculations and adjustments that predict the trajectory of flow over seconds, minutes or days (**Fig. 7**). This method of predicting the behavior of air has none of the haptic, empirical sensibilities of Reid's laboratory experiments. Air is observed not through the senses but through a blind process of mass calculation inside an electronic machine. This unique epistemic framework also produced its own ways of visualizing air, introducing the numerical point-cloud.

The use of numerical simulation, performed inside a black box detached from physical reality, was a major advantage in weapon research. In the 1950's, the T-3 research group at the Los Alamos National Laboratory, working under the auspices of the U.S Atomic Energy Commission, further advanced the science of computational fluid dynamics by numerically simulating complex flows of gasses and liquids under extreme conditions of pressure and heat. In their experimentations, air, gasses and fluids were visualized as point clouds, resulting directly from the underlying cellular structure of the simulation space and the numerical drawing devices which plotted these drawings (**Fig. 8 - 11**). Point clouds emerge when each calculating cell in the simulation matrix is represented as a point. When plotted together, the large collection of cells appears as a dense, shimmering cloud. Rendered as such, air (and other fluids) does not have the same teleological, linear properties that were attributed to it by arrows. It is drawn as a statistical figure, with varied densities and gestures, devoid of sharp edges or definitive lines. Substance and movement are suggested through painterly gestures, not geometrical delineation, underscoring the nonlinearity of air both figuratively (no delineation) and ontologically (non-linear behavior). Numerical simulation casts air as a set of probabilities, as embodied in the edgeless, temporal point-cloud.

Discussing the science of Cybernetics, Norbert Wiener analyzed the difference between Newtonian, cyclical time and Bergsonian, non-linear time, describing the cybernetic condition of knowledge as a set of statistical distribution of probabilities. Using (perhaps unsurprisingly) meteorology as an example Wiener writes: "The terms 'cloud', 'temperature', 'turbulence', etc., are all terms referring not to one single physical situation but to a distribution of possible situations of which only one actual case is realized. [...] All that we can predict at any future time is a probability distribution of the constants of the system, and even this predictability fades out with the increase of time". [21] Similarly, numerical simulation of air produces a set of distribution probabilities, describing air not as a single entity but as a range of scenarios, of which some might materialize while others might not.

The Drawing of Time

Underlying the two distinct epistemological frameworks for the visualization of air discussed above is the question of the representation of movement. Looking through a temporal prism, a crucial difference between the empirical representation of air and its numerical simulation emerges. The trajectories of Reid's arrows are drawn against a background that is temporarily frozen, displaying their entire path to the observer at a single glance. The movement of air is drawn as one linear event in which the beginning of the trajectory (i.e earlier in time) and its conclusion (i.e later) are drawn together on the same page. This singular temporal structure is fundamental to Reid's empirical understanding of air, as it guarantees the arrows' ability to be descriptive (showing what happened) and prescriptive (showing what will happen) at the same time, affirming the certitude and the predictability of the empirical process.

The temporal structure of numerical simulation operates differently. Simply put, it's cinematic; depicting motion through a sequence of frames that follow each other consecutively in time. The computational fluid dynamics drawings from the T-3 lab were almost always displayed as a series of images of the same space at different time intervals. Each frame represents a reality which exists only in the present, capturing an instant in a potentially endless process of movement. Numerical simulation thus depicts motion in the same manner as the film camera does; it fragments the continuum of time into multiple frames that must be read in relation to each other, a direct mirroring of the mass calculation cycles which produced these images. Air is captured in movement by movement, [22] ascribing a model of drawing that is in itself ephemeral and ever changing.

Notes

(01) A. Taub (ed.) *John von Neumann Collected Works*, Volume VI, p. 491-498.
(02) Oxford English Dictionary, s.v. "geometry (n.), Etymology," September 2024, https://doi.org/10.1093/OED/2414415407.
(03) H. Damisch, *A Theory of Cloud: Toward a History of Painting*, Stanford University Press, 2002, p.124.
(04) Ibid.
(05) S. Johnson, *The Invention of Air: A Story of Science, Faith, Revolution, and the Birth of America,* Riverhead Books, 2014.
(06) J. Kisacky, 'Breathing Room: Calculating an Architecture of Air', in A. Gerbino (ed.) *Geometrical Objects. Archimedes*, vol 38. Springer, Cham, https://doi.org/10.1007/978-3-319-05998-3_11, 2014, p. 249.
(07) M. Gleich, *Inhabited Machines: Genealogy of an Architectural Concept,* Birkhäuser, 2022, p.72.
(08) H. Schoenefeldt, *Rebuilding the Houses of Parliament: David Boswell Reid and Disruptive Environmentalism* (1st ed.). Routledge, 2020. p.28.
(09) E.J. Gillin, *The Victorian Palace of Science: Scientific Knowledge and the Building of the Houses of Parliament*, 1st ed. Cambridge University Press, 2017. p.151.
(10) Schoenefeldt, p. 30.
(11) D.B. Reid, *Illustrations of the Theory and Practice of Ventilation : With Remarks on Warming, Exclusive Lighting, and the Communication of Sound*, Longman, Brown, Green, & Longmans, 1844. p. viii.
(12) R.J. Finkel, 'History of the Arrow', in *American Printing History Association* (blog), 1 April 2015, https://printinghistory.org/arrow/.
(13) Damisch, op.cit., p.124.
(14) Gillin, op.cit., p.131.
(15) L. F. Richardson, *Weather Prediction by Numerical Process*, Cambridge University Press, 1922. Reprinted by Dover Publications, 1965, with a new Introduction by Sydney Chapman, xvi+p. 236.
(16) P. Lynch, 'The Origins of Computer Weather Prediction and Climate Modeling', in *Journal of Computational Physics 227*, no. 7, March 2008, p.3432.
(17) ibid.
(18) Richardson, op.cit. p.219.
(19) Lynch, op.cit. p.3433.
(20) Lynch, op.cit. p.3435.
(21) N. Wiener, *Cybernetics: Or, Control and Communication in the Animal and the Machine*, 1948, 2nd edition, 2019 reissue. The MIT Press, 2019, p.47.
(22) See discussion about 'life-in-movement' in S. Papapetros, *On the Animation of the Inorganic: Art, Architecture, and the Extension of Life*, University of Chicago Press, 2016, p.62.

MANUFACTURING ATMOSPHERE A DIALOGUE ON CALIBRATION

LAURA NICA IN CONVERSATION WITH ARUP (OLIVIA EWING, SHAHID PADHANI AND DIMPLE RANA)

DS18 has been collaborating with ARUP since 2019. This crossover and dialogue provided an alternative perspective to students, on how simulations are used in practice, by the built environment industry.

ARUP is a global multidisciplinary consultancy that provides engineering and design services for the built environment; with a vast expertise including Advanced Digital Engineering, Wind specialists, Environmental Physics, Computational Fluid Dynamics, and others.

Calibration refers to the estimation and adjustment of a (digital or physical) model of a simulation parameters to improve the agreement between model output and a data set. In the context of extreme weather events of our warming world and the energy transition that are challenging the way we design for comfort and resilience, this discussion will aim to address on one hand, themes of simulations (and their set-up) and on the other hand modes of visualisation to inform and anticipate how designs can evolve. By interrogating the models - their set-up, data insights, context and results – the conversation will challenge the notion of calibration to inform the dynamical systems and our notions of thermodynamics.

Figure 1 (top right) – Visualisation of 'streamlines' of selected computed paths of air movement around a modelled urban environment.
Figure 2 (bottom right) – Plot of instantaneous air velocities from a model of directional wind through an urban environment.

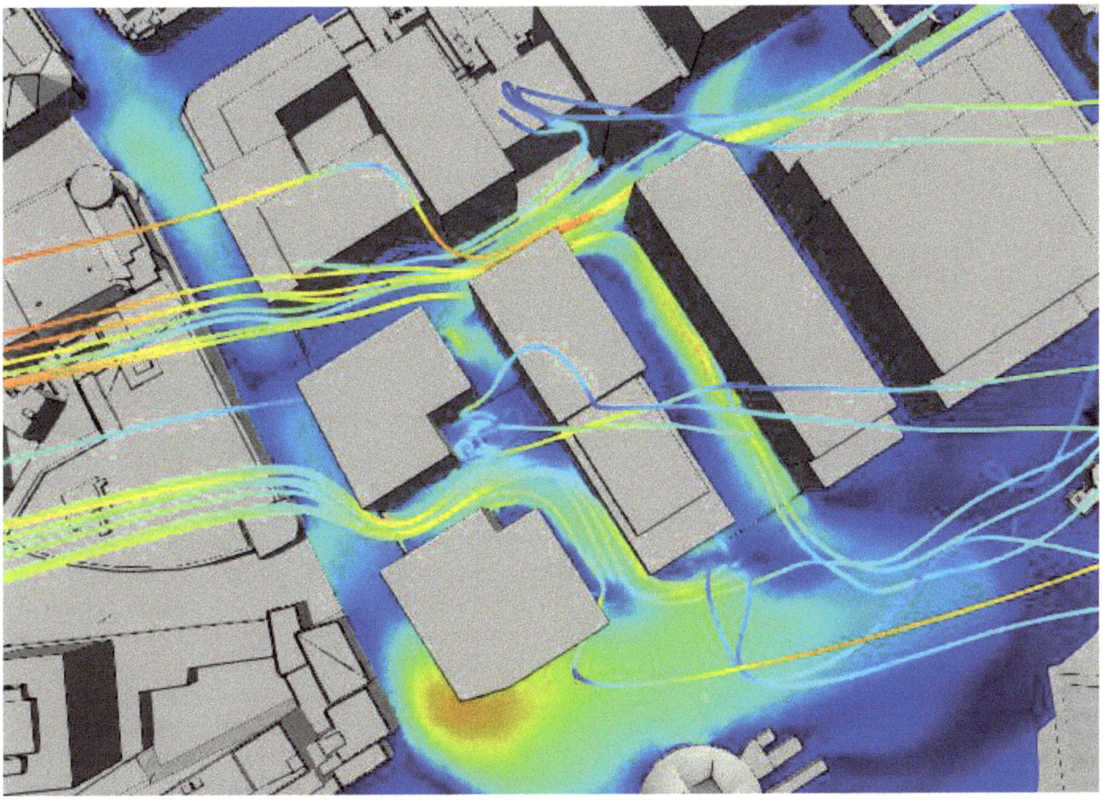

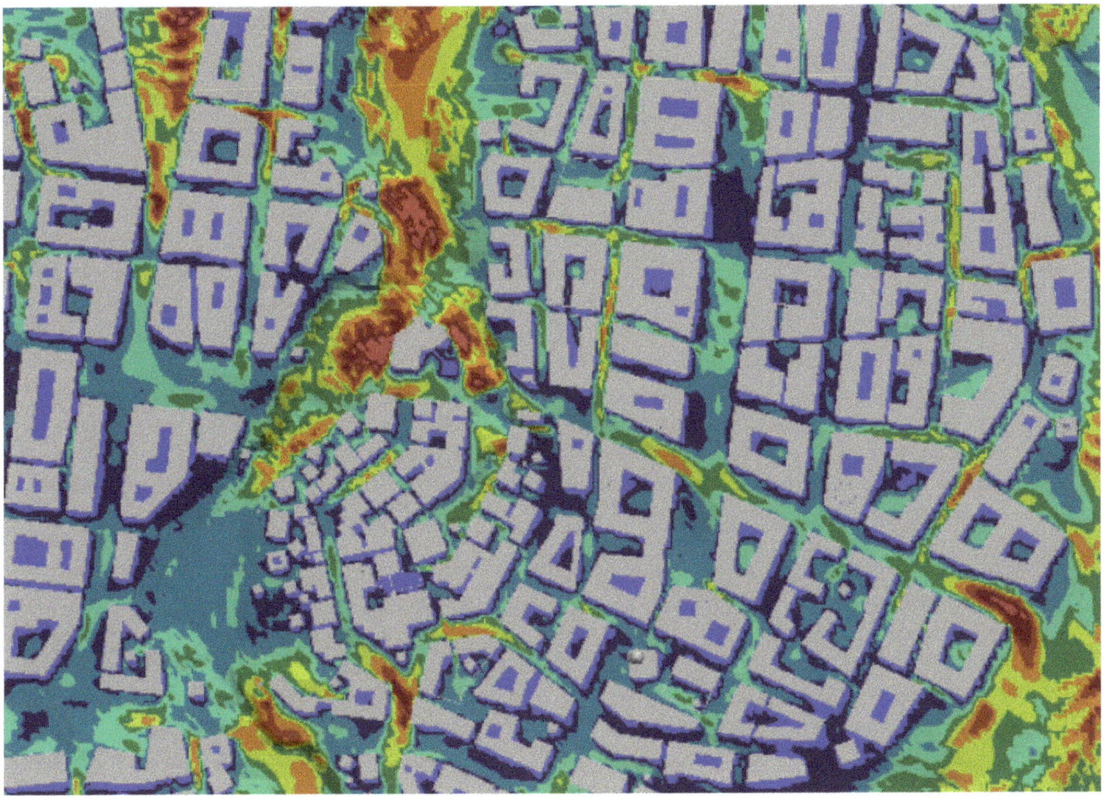

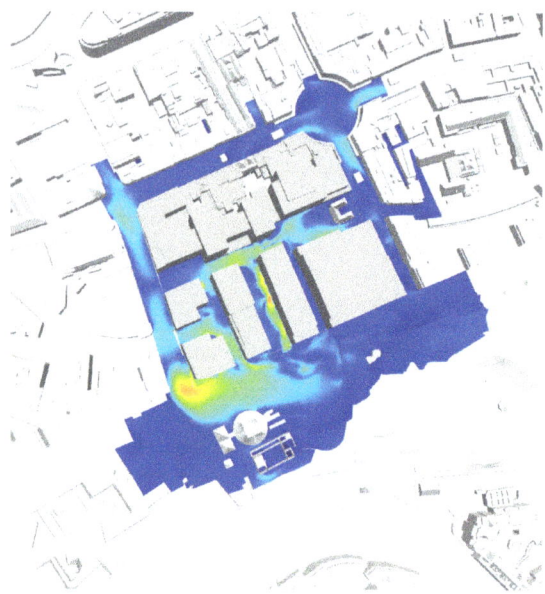

Figure 3 – Plot of averaged speed ups from a model of directional wind through an urban environment and nearby park.

Laura Nica: Could you give us a brief introduction to yourself, your role within ARUP and how you became interested in addressing matters of the environment and climate?

Olivia Ewing: I am Olivia Ewing. I am Wind Microclimate specialist, working around challenges on how wind and humans interact with the built environment – with concerns around questions of comfort and safety. The fact that wind mechanisms change around taller buildings and cities is becoming increasingly important to local governments who want to create safe and inviting places for people to live and visit.

Shahid Padhani: I am Shahid Padhani. I started being interested in physics at school, in particular fluids, which evolved into the role I currently do at ARUP in the Environmental Physics and Wind team. My role involves the use of analytical and numerical methods to model complex problems, such as those posed by air flow in and around the urban environment, and answer critical questions, help inform and verify designs. To this end I work on projects at a range of scales and across multiple topics, from electromagnetic interference within a building to wind and thermal comfort across a masterplan.

Dimple Rana: I am Dimple Rana, I work in the Environmental Physics and Wind, as a Senior Engineer. I have a background in architecture, and I have studied physics before. I provide consulting in areas which includes both external and internal environments and the interaction between the two. I would say that sustainability and climatic aspects are increasingly becoming embedded within pretty much all the work that we do. We do try to take a 'first principal' approach when it comes to climate variables, where we break down issues into more basic parts and we can then, build them up to the relevant bits, to meet the project needs.

LN: What sort of digital tools do you use within your day-to-day role? Do you use more tools for assessment or visualisation?

OE: From my side, I do a lot of wind tunnelling testing; I also collaborate with Shahid and rest of the team to carry out Computational Fluid Dynamics (CFD). Wind testing is a well-known, established and well-respected method of simulation; but it does leave a lot to the imagination because you can only measure in finite points, and it takes a lot of time to set up; there is a lot of upfront work that you have to do beforehand (such as coordinating and building the scale model and negotiating where to place your limited number of sensors); whereas with CFD, it is becoming more popular. You can get a lot of high quality visuals of flow paths and you can capture whole planes of wind results at any level. Other types of computational modelling have been around for a while for other specialists such as fire or structures, but it is now being used more in my line of work as computation limits have expanded. We can better estimate the impacts of turbulence and interacting flow patterns in our CFD models. Not 100% accurate, but it fills a lot of the gaps.

SP: I have been mainly focusing on the simulation aspects of work. The primary role of a simulation is to answer questions and help guide the design. It is important to define our problem. We cannot simulate everything. It is computationally quite expensive. You must pick an element that you are trying to resolve, or to answer the questions you are trying to answer for a project. We currently use different types of simulations tools including CFD tools such as OPENFOAM and CFX, inhouse dynamic thermal modelling tools. Depending on the project we decide what modelling method is appropriate for each case.

DR: CFD is one of the key tools I use, for dynamic thermal modelling; but it is worth mentioning that we do use a lot of the existing software and modelling available, but ARUP also spends time creating several different scripts and developing its own tools. In the case of dynamic thermal modelling, we have our own tool that has been created by ARUP that helps increase the capability; and I have been heavily involved in creating a tool that brings

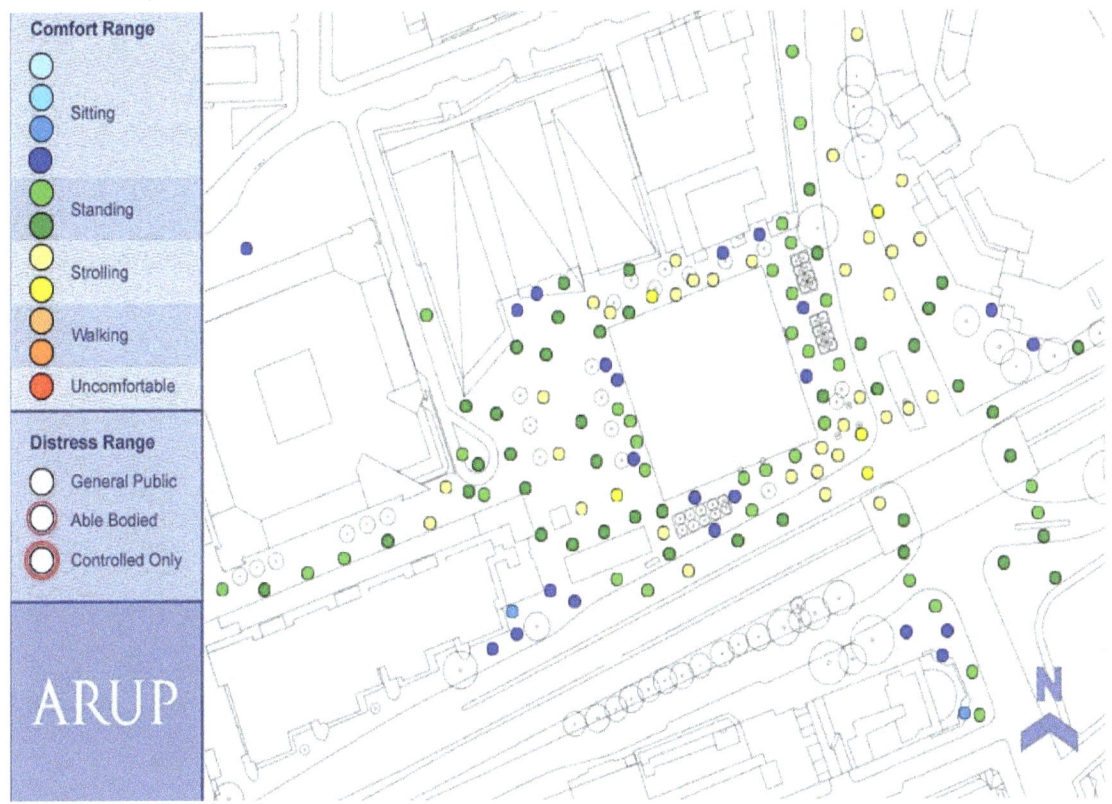

Figure 4 – Plot showing Lawson based wind comfort results at receptors from a boundary layer wind tunnel test.

together satellite data and events of climate simulation to understand the urban heat island in cities. The tool can produce plots or 'Urban Heat Snapshots' for major cities so hot spots can be clearly identified as well as the corresponding land used, facilitating conversations about where and how to make improvements.

LN: What would be a particular situation when you require a digital simulation and how is that affecting the design workflow?

SP: In most of the cases, the problems we are tackling, are quite hard to model. There are a lot of inputs and quite complex physics which results in non-linear interactions and complicated behaviours. For example, to model flows inside a building, we may have to consider the geometry, the climate, the material build ups, the sources of heat, and the dynamics of the entire system. Depending on the question we want to answer, it may not be possible to provide answers using design guidance or hand calculations and thus, this would drive us towards digital simulations.

LN: What sort of criteria or parameters are you relying on when setting up a simulation?

SP: It depends on the project. For example, to model wind flow around a building you start with a city scape and context, which is full of different geometrical forms. Then you would consider the wind which can come from different directions at different speeds. If you are doing a study on outdoor thermal comfort, you would also consider temperature and humidity. For any given study you could keep increasing the number of inputs and detail of the modelling procedure, but the difficulty and time required would increase, so you need to think about what questions you are answering. Usually, we start with desktop study using engineering judgement, design guides and hand calculations to begin forming a general understanding of what is happening, and to understand what the important physics is driven by, and this can help inform what you need to capture in the simulation.

OE: In many cases, I see it as a validation tool or a visualisation tool. This helps communicate to clients where the risks and opportunities are; and in many cases the visual, helps the client accept the information a lot more easily. In terms of data, there are regulations, especially for winds; you must prove using these verified modelling

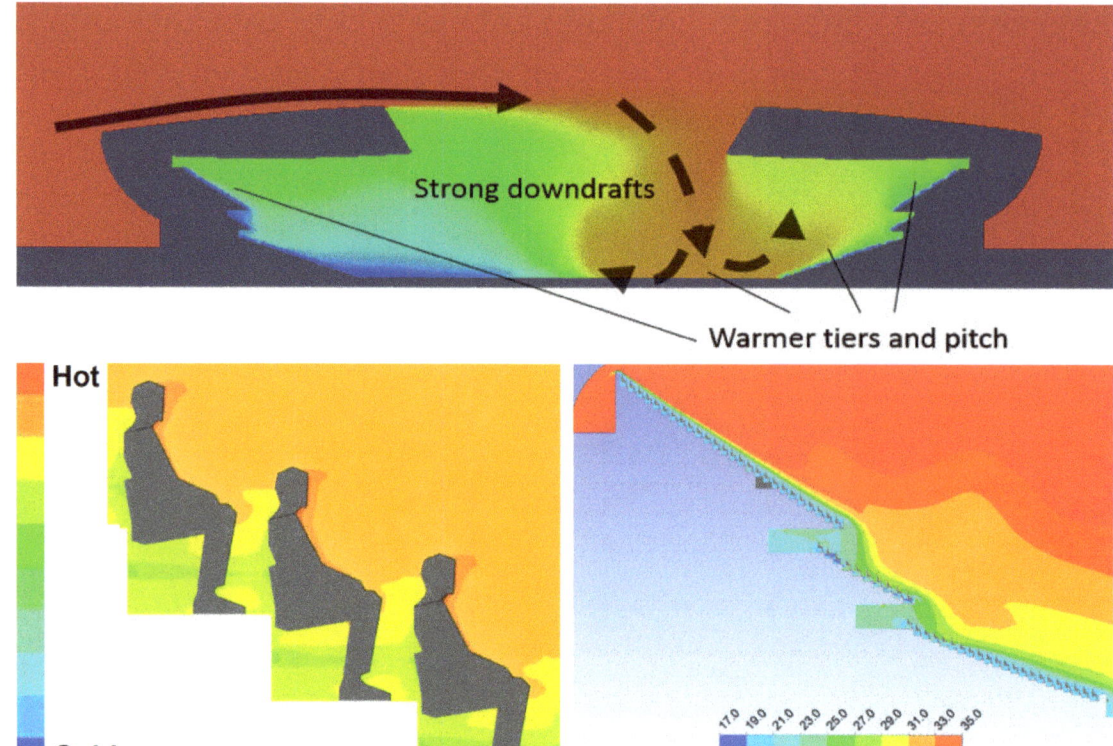

Figure 5 (top) – CFD models showing the impact of hot winds on mechanically conditioned areas of the stadium.
Figure 6 (bottom) – Under-seat cooling system performance assessment.

methods, used to back up your advice – what you say it is going to do. I would say that we need it at all stages of the design process.

DR: We work on very broad types of projects and across different sectors, industries and scales. From masterplans projects to zooming into a pipe that is going to be part of a large infrastructure project. We would look at air, water and others. All the tools that we plan to use – on what problems we are trying to solve, who are we solving it for, how much budget is there, and how much time we have - and it is trying to balance all those things out.

LN: Constraints are really important, and it is something we are trying to get our students to reflect on. To define and observe a phenomena, to question presumptions and potentially think of setting up simulation models that have a dual characteristic: where both the input and the model set-up influence the results. What sort of data do you use to feed your simulation with and how important is to filter or select certain datasets for the model?

OE: There are a lot of open sources of data where you can get years' worth of historical data from airports or other locations like National Oceanic and Atmospheric Administration (NOAA) in the USA. But when we talk about using it, there is certain amount that is going to be purged, to be cleaned (e.g.: maybe you have years of data that were formatted wrongly or have weird inputs - all this is sometimes very important when interrogating why a model behaved the way it did. There is a bit of "detective" work that can go into the historical wind aspects.

SP: For thermodynamic simulations you also need weather data. You can find weather data curated by various institutions that monitor a 'typical year' or 'heatwaves'; you could look at the raw weather data from a weather station to create your own dataset. It is important to check the data you will be using that makes sense for your problem, and that it is correct. There are different types of weather files for different problems (e.g. comfort vs energy load). Sometimes you will need to search the internet for the right value of to use. For example, when you are modelling a pipe and you might want to include the roughness of the inner walls; but you do not have any measurements because it has not been built yet; you will be looking through other sources (like technical documents) to try to find out that data or compensate for the missing information. I think it is important to make sure that what is going in the model is realistic and you can communicate any sort of assumptions you have made.

OE: There are also regulatory frameworks such as the British Standards, Eurocodes that deal and reference wind and speeds. So, if you start to get something like double the references, then you know there is something you need to check. There are some things that you can pinpoint to guide you in the right direction; we try to use those publications as much as possibly, although they can be quite broad.

SP: Yes, it is true. In places like the City of London you have got wind guides, in some situation a clear guide on what to use when.

LN: In the context of climate change, with more uncertainty or disrupted weathering patterns across the globe, I was wondering how do you plan the model or work with predicted data (say in the next 100 years' time)?

DR: I think the industry does not use as much climate change projection data as it should. A lot of projects are still based on current data and it is a challenge to balance between being overly conservative and actually having something realistic that we can build with. But increasingly, we are starting to look at projections, in particular at the lifespan of a project. It really depends on the context and what is our particular role within the proposal development. For example if you are a structural engineer, you tend to be on the conservative side and there are standards and clear bounds. But in our domain, if you work more with a mechanical system, we tend to use things like 'peak values' for summertime, 'winter temperature', and even less conservative values. The main point is that you need to take a bit of a judgement on what data you use, the uncertainty surrounding that data and make sure you record the assumptions, you are explaining those. Everything that we do is going to have a level of uncertainty, it is a prediction, it is not real life, it is a simulation; and it is our job to make sure that clients understand that information so that they can make the right decisions; but there is not just one answer.

OE: We know there is a lot of unpredictability with wind. There have been some studies, including UK Climate projections (UKCP18 Factsheet: Wind) by the Met Office, which is suggesting that there is so much variability already within the historic wind data that all the projections are still within the existing bounds of recorded wind speeds. So, we are still using the assumption that the current projections will stay within that variability.

LN: Would you be able to give an example of a project or situation where you used a specific workflow to formulate or plan a simulation and how the simulation results have been used to inform a design decision?

OE: So, a typical project for me, would start with someone approaching us to say 'we need to get through planning and we need to verify this from a wind-performance perspective.' But then, it would normally evolve into a much deeper understanding of the site (specific wind conditions), thresholds that we are trying to meet, how do we alter the local wind mechanisms – now that we know the specific conditions; there is a lot of validating, and we use a wind test to get those initial results. And probably some CFD to try to communicate these. This is because with wind tunnels simulations, you cannot see much. The air is invisible, and the air is blowing upon a model – you cannot see what is happening. All the measurements are taken using pressure taps, so you have to view these afterwards as best as you can. But with CFD, you can use streamlines and other 3D visuals, which are much more 'digestible', you can get much more detail in a CFD plot, so you can identify immediately the extend of the area that you need to be worried about. And then you can, isolate it, test and iterate relatively quickly. The architects would send us the 3D model, we would plug that into the simplified 3D surroundings, fine tune the mesh resolution and get that to run for a couple of hours to days with a calibrated wind environment (i.e. set velocity profiles and turbulence models) in order to provide feedback. There is a lot of going back and forwards in the design process. And, in the end, we would run a final wind tunnel simulation, just to get that final 'tick box' validation.

LN: How do you cater your model to working and addressing various challenges at different scales?

OE: The model stays consistent through the process. You may need to simplify the model – there will be a point where the amount of detail becomes less relevant and it would just slow things down. There is a bit of judgement there based on experience and just trying things over the past years on various projects. For example, in the case of a tall building, anything modelled under a meter, leads to diminishing returns. We have to keep an eye on what is happening at larger scale, especially since architects deal with a lot of changes and so many factors that influence the design; a small detail might seem insignificant but could actually have large impacts, especially when it comes to human safety. For example, if a tower had round or chamfered corners, this would mean fast oncoming winds can easily flow around the tower at high above, reducing downdraft. If the tower corners change to become more square in plan, more down drafing will be promoted and could result in acute local corner accelerations that are uncomfortable or unsafe. So, it is good to keep an eye on the larger scale, even when looking at a narrow and specific area.

SP: From a thermal modelling perspective, often a mechanical engineer designing a non-typical space will get us to check that their design works. The system is meant to operate the whole year around; we cannot simulate a whole year with CFD, but we can simulate that with a dynamic thermal model (which does not capture the smaller scales). So, we often use a combination of different modelling techniques to capture smaller scales and time. Based on the results of the dynamic thermal mode, you might either look at a specific moment and simulate that moment in time using CFD. Or, you might decide that the focus on the smaller scale behaviour of a particular feature, and use CFD modelling and accept losing the temporal aspect of it. And then, using your results look at comfort, e.g. using temperature, humidity, and comfort metrics, and check if they are acceptable and if not, propose mitigation measures.

LN: How do you work around preparing a simulation when there is no sufficient data available or the levels of publicly-available information are limiting? Do you have to use alternative methods to simulate?

SP: The weather data is global. For context, we use Open Street Map and Google Earth to build up the city or topography, and sometimes we use third-body providers who own that data.

OE: There have been a couple of projects where we took wind readings and data that we knew were not detailed for our specific location, but were valid for that wider area. The data was taken from a few kilometres away; and we modelled the greater terrain to see how that initial input could change the site – and make some assumptions about that.
There is a lot of data out there but not all of it provides valuable information. For example, there are lots of amateur weather stations but they might not be calibrated, for anything from true north to poor readings or bad positioning. We have to discard a lot of data because it is not useful or cannot be validated.

LN: At what point, would you consider building up your own tools?

DR: We cannot answer every question with the tools that we have; especially if we are trying to increase the sustainability aspects and the response to climate change – all of those things are usually driven by the clients needs, but some are driven by our own curiosity when we have certain problems and we want to understand them better – but we do not have the tools for that. Urban Heat Island or the thermal comfort and heat stress in cities is just something that people are becoming more and more interested in and it is becoming an increasing global problem, a problem which we did not fully understand previously.

SP: Another example is some work with MSF which we did as a community engagement project. MSF were trying to use more solar power, be more sustainable, and needed a tool that would help them assess if it was worth investing in solar panels for a particular site. We got involved in creating a tool using a dynamic thermal model to assess the solar system they would need (e.g. number of panels), tell them the return on investment and carbon savings, and visualise the results in an easy to understand way. The front end had to be clear, easily understandable and to easy to navigate. The users were not engineers, and the underlying model involves technical inputs - so a lot of the discussions were around what assumptions we could use, and how to simplify the inputs to make them understandable but still provide them with useful results. For example, they probably do not know the U-Values of their bricks that they are putting up and there would not be able to find out; so, we made assumptions on the types of materials they could select in their tool. For this, we had to engage with some of the users and they helped translate our technical inputs into the inputs that the users would understand.

LN: The accessibility and visualisation capacity of the results of a simulation are important. How are the results of a simulation being formatted and represented to be easily read or understood? How do you calibrate your representation to suit different audiences?

SP: We had research projects looking at 3D visualisation – e.g 3D PDFs, web viewers, dashboard etc. These are not really in demand and are quite expensive to develop. Clients tend to expect standard reports and slides and static images. Occasionally, we would develop a unique feature for bespoke projects. But really, our idea was to make something general that could apply to multiple projects.

OE: In some areas, such as describing the regulations and report-writing, it has to be a static 2D image (PNG, PDF etc.), which does take away a lot of

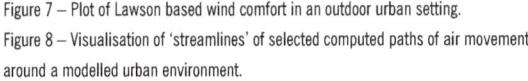
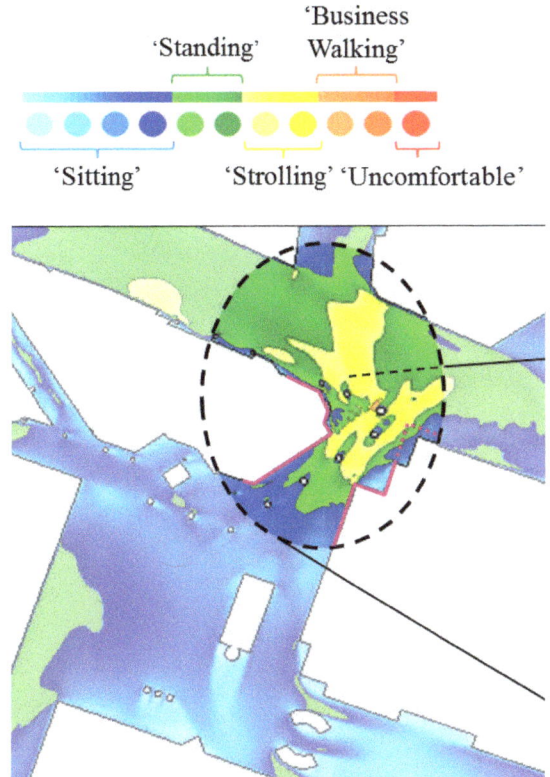
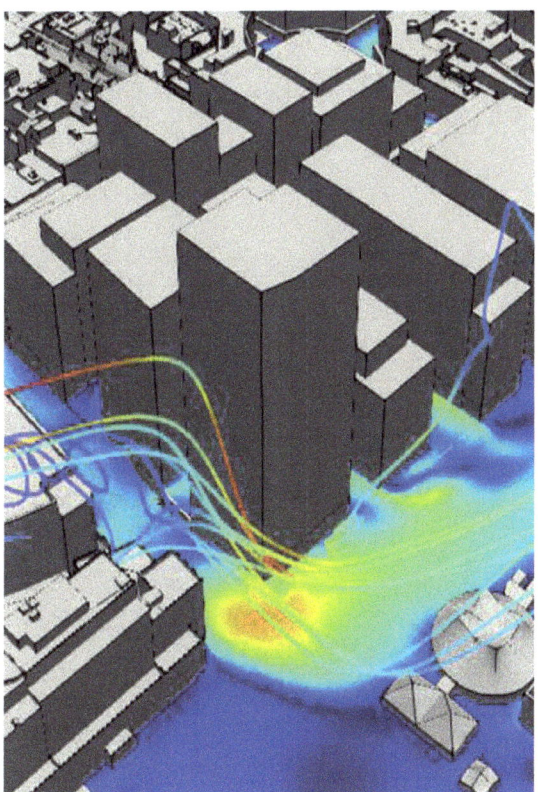

Figure 7 – Plot of Lawson based wind comfort in an outdoor urban setting.
Figure 8 – Visualisation of 'streamlines' of selected computed paths of air movement around a modelled urban environment.

information that explains the 'what', 'why', and 'how' behind the result. E.g. How far beyond a threshold is the result? What is causing the result? Why is the result different or better to other solutions? - so we could find a way to incorporate more interactive models, then it would help to better document and explain the design solutions.

LN: I was thinking in the case of BIM models, with the desire to incorporate as much information as possible - would there be scope to apply analysis or results from an analysis inside, as validation and certification information?

OE: It would be great to have more information and have a more dynamic way of engaging with these sorts of simulations. For example, the wind tunnel testing, we actually have again, an in-house software which is very interactive – final results are presented with a colour coded scheme for each measurement point overlaying a 2D plan of the development and surroundings. You can hover over each receptor, and it shows you the direction of the wind in which it cames through, the speed-up ratios and the calculated maximum speed condition at that point. This interaction allows you to have conversations regarding data really easy; but, as soon as it is coming to documenting that, in an official capacity, it has to be broken into these static, standalone images.

SP: Another thing, when you have a fixed format, it is easier to tell a narrative; if the system is more interactive, you get people to go through the information in a way that you might not had the intention.

LN: What is the future development or potential integration with machine learning/AI for using, preparing and displaying simulations?

SP: We do use automation quite a lot – as it allows us to do more (e.g. run a greater number of wind directions in a wind simulation). The value in our services would lie in looking at the results and understanding what is happening, or in suggesting solutions and less so in setting up simulations (but that is just a necessary step). With regards to ML, it has been very useful to help us synthesise inputs for downstream simulations, although its use in simulations themselves is currently limited. What is exciting is the potential to use it for early stage assessments where we need to iterate through designs, parametrically.

FLUID SURFACES AND SATURATED SUBSTRATES

ANDREAS KÖRNER

Fluids are ambiguous, especially in architecture. There are manifold meanings of this term. Fluid architecture is often associated with smooth, curvilinear forms as those popularised by the late Zaha Hadid; the two publications summarising her fifteen years (2000-15) of teaching at the University of Applied Arts in Vienna were titled *Total Fluidity* (2011) and *Fluid Totality* (2015). According to the *Oxford English Dictionary* (OED), 'fluid' has several meanings. As a noun, it refers to a substance 'that has no fixed shape and gives way'. [01] As an adjective, it means either 'able to flow easily', 'not stable', or 'graceful'. Fluid forms, therefore, are turbulent yet aesthetically pleasing. In the case of Hadid, as mentioned above, fluidity is derived from the fluid appearance of the shapes, which are designed using advanced parametric modelling tools and digital fabrication techniques. She writes: "Total Fluidity is the slogan that most succinctly describes the objectives and the character of the work of Zaha Hadid Architects". [02] It refers to a specific formal agenda that became synonymous with the digital project in architecture in the two decades between 1990 and 2010: smooth, curvilinear, white, glossy, and plain. However, inspired by aero-/fluid-dynamic, smooth, and monochrome references from nature, the resulting shapes are what I would rather call 'fluid-morphic': they possess fluid qualities while not directly informed by fluid dynamics. Contrary to the dictionary, such fluid shapes are stable and quite solid. They are fixed shapes but are conceived through fluid considerations.

> *Movement creates pattern and form. Moving water arranges itself into eddies, and sometimes places these in strict array, where they become baroque and orderly conduits for unceasing flow.* [03]

Over the past decade, DS18 has explored the negotiations between climate change, computation, and design. Intensive and extensive design parameters are distinctively non-hierarchical, allowing students to investigate the complex relationships between the built and the natural environment through architectural design. The results are sometimes concrete and material, in other cases, ephemeral and fluid. The term fluid is surprisingly absent when reviewing DS18's design briefs of the past five

Figure 1 – The sculptures of the Trevi Fountain in Rome, designed by Nicola Salvi in the mid-18th century, are a highly controlled mix of textures, fluid, and refined form: naturalism and abstraction. Photo by Andreas Körner, 2020.

Figure 2 – The Kollegienkirche in Salzburg, designed by Johann Bernhard Fischer von Erlach in the early-18th century, combines fluid shapes with excessive transitions and intricate weatherings. Photo by Andreas Körner, 2023.

years. However, another familiar term is mentioned yearly: "flow". In various combinations such as "air flow" (2019-20), "object flow" (2020-21), "material flow" (2021-22 and 2022-23), and in the case of the 2023-24 brief's title: "Flows, Forms & Functions". If we consult the OED again, we learn that flows are continuous like currents or streams and move steadily. However, 'flow' also has a second meaning: like 'fluid', it has an aesthetically pleasing second connotation of hanging 'loosely' and 'elegantly' (**Fig. 1-2**). Flows are fluid, and fluids flow.

Fluids

In engineering, design, and architecture, fluid dynamics are often used to understand – and consequently optimise – a shape's performance within a fluid, for example, air or water. When done as numerical operations, this is called computational fluid dynamics, commonly abbreviated as CFD. While the use cases, impact, and methodologies of using CFD simulations are covered in other parts of this book, this essay will look at the surface dynamics that appear at the permeable boundary between substance and atmosphere. CFD is a tool that helps us understand those interfaces better, simulating the motion of fluids and their interaction with solids. In the last part of the essay, I will investigate aspects of materialising fluid considerations and the material, weathering, and biological negotiations along those boundaries that turn a substance into a substrate (**Fig. 3 and 7**). Those boundaries themselves are realms of mediation, oscillating between firm datum and dynamic interface. In his influential book *Interface*, Branden Hookway writes:

"Taken together, the interface and the fluid were essential to nineteenth-century conceptions of dynamic form. Dynamic form is less a form than a forming, a process active across space and time, and elusive to formal analysis unless captured in some way. Such capture may occur when dynamic form is fixed in time and place as static form; of greater interest is the capture of dynamic form in another important nineteenth-century concept: that of work." [04]

During the 19th-century, both the scientific

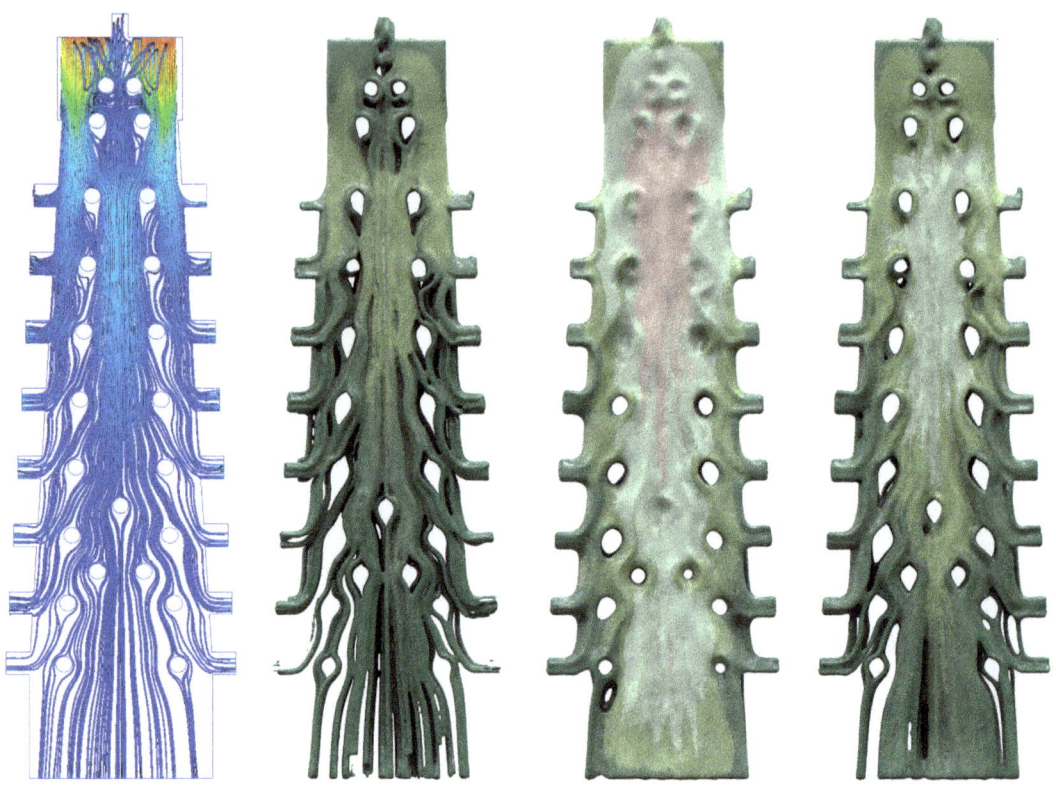

Figure 3 – Digital simulations and analysis can be used to translate intensive parameters to extensive form through computational means. The results are intricate shapes with fluid qualities. Renderings of Integrated Sequestration by Andreas Körner and Anete Krista Salmane, 2024.

understanding of fluids and the role of fluid morphologies in Baroque architecture were advancing. At the end of the 20th-century, the influence of Baroque thought, style, and visual language on digital architecture cannot be dismissed. This is especially true for the notion of the surface – or hypersurface – as a generative force. Andrew Benjamin excellently traces this emergence of the surface from Borromini to Gottfried Semper to Adolf Loos. [05] On the other hand, the combination of numerical design methods and fluid shapes underpinned by the writings of Gilles Deleuze – particularly *The Fold* – formed the theoretical underbelly of much of the digital architecture between 1990 and 2010. Anthony Vidler [06] traces Deleuze's baroque analogies to Heinrich Wölfflin's 19th-century writings on Baroque form:

"Wölfflin noted that the Baroque is marked by a certain number of material traits: horizontal widening of the lower floor, flattening of the pediment, low and curved stairs that push into space; matter handled in masses or aggregates, with the rounding of angles and avoidance of perpendiculars; the circular acanthus replacing the jagged acanthus, use of limestone to produce spongy, cavernous shapes, or to constitute a vortical form always put in motion by renewed turbulence, which ends only in the manner of a horse's mane or the foam of a wave; matter tends to sill over in space, to be reconciled with fluidity at the same time fluids themselves are divided into masses." [07]

Without diving unnecessarily deep into philosophy, it is important to understand the emergence and consequences of this aspect of the digital project in architecture. The focus on topology – the continuity of a surface – is a fluid, unstable base on which to build. Outside the virtual realm, such surfaces are incredibly hard to conceive. Simultaneously to the software used for the fluid shapes, computer numerical control (CNC) fabrication and 3D printing were established as a smart, scalable, and cost-effective way to materialise digital information directly. However, the materials were often synthetic; homogeneous, and smart, contradicting the otherwise highly biomorphic and biomimetic agenda. In *Animate Form* and *The Structure of Ornament*, Greg Lynn outlined the impact of such new technologies on the generation of virtual form and its translation into the material world. [08]

A quarter century later, materials are in the

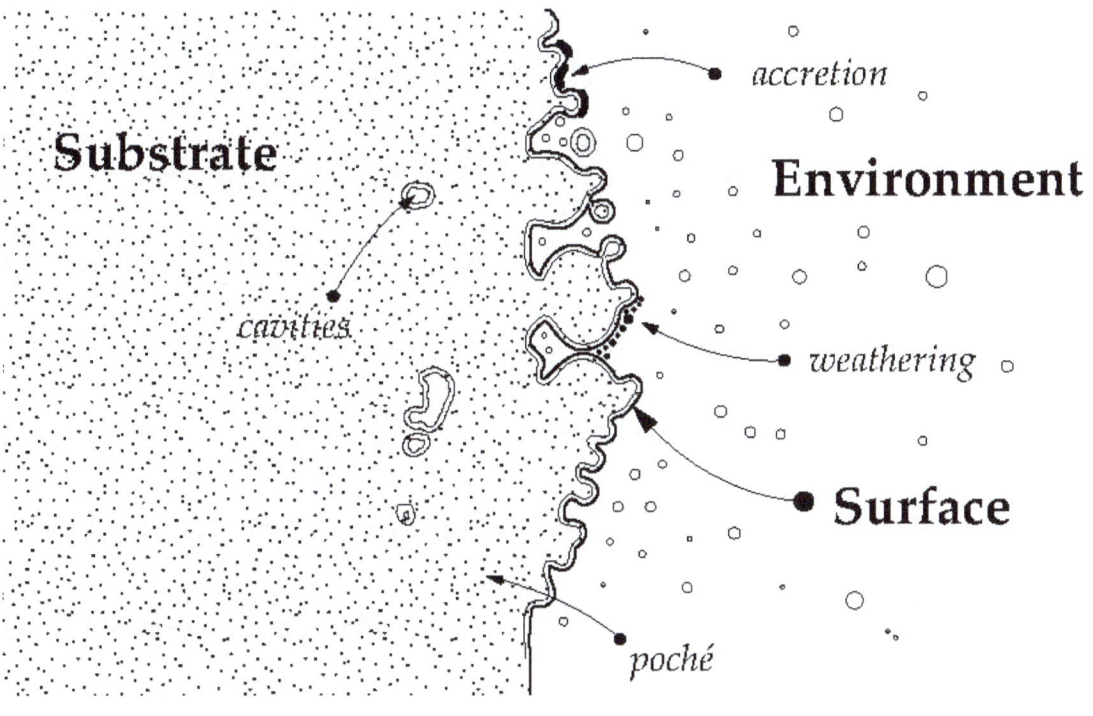

Figure 4 – Investigating how materials, shapes, and environmental parameters impact each other means understanding body-surface-environment relationships. Drawing for Variegated Poché by Andreas Körner, 2023.

foreground, driven by ecological concerns. The 2007-8 financial crisis and the urgency of global warming shifted the focus of academic curricula away from technological innovation towards climate response and, more recently, climate justice. With this comes stronger considerations of architecture's ecological responsibilities, the interaction between buildings and their environment, the carbon footprint of materials, and sustainable construction.

The use of CFD simulations – like many other digital tools, both software and hardware – shifted from generative to analytical, helping to assess the performance of shapes better. At the same time, modern procedural and parametric design tools and advanced additive manufacturing allow digital morphologies with unprecedented intricacy. [09] Unlike the earlier smooth and continuous – impermeable – topologies, the surface has been broken up, and its pores and cracks have been exposed. Designing with environmental flows of matter and atmosphere – like in DS18 – is a productive mode of co-designing with nature. Therefore, it partially aligns with 19th-century romanticism and 20th-century organicism and naturalism.

Flows

The interaction between a fluid and a solid is usually not to the benefit of the latter's integrity. It is a corrosive, abrasive, and erosive interaction. Consequently, a fluid form weathers the surrounding flows most efficiently. A generative fluid, therefore, is a contradiction. However, this is limited to the mechanical level. On a chemical and biological level, this interaction creates pockets and niches, porous areas where life can thrive. Through accretion, a substance is added, and a substrate is formed. Airflow brings nutrients, fertilisers, dust, spores, and seeds. The fluid is generative to both form and ecology:

Over time the natural environment acts upon the outer surface of a building in such a way that its underlying materials are broken down. [10]

When considering flows and fluid dynamics as generative agents in design processes, we can differentiate between two morphological operations: erosion and

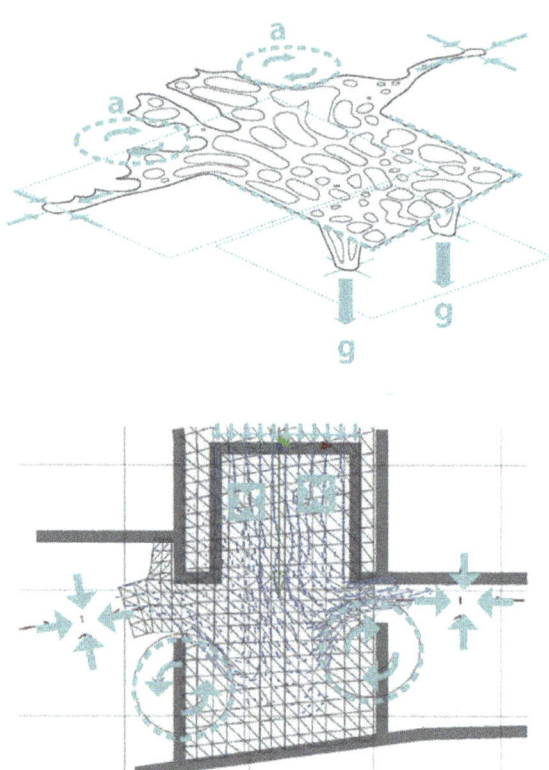

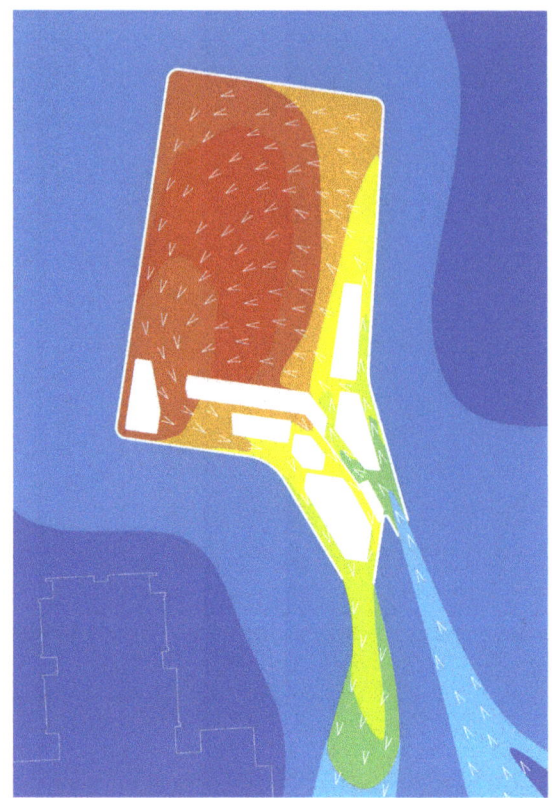

Figure 5 – Viscous Affiliation in Salzburg, designed by MOA-Architekten/soma-architecture (Martin Oberascher and Alexander Matl) in 2012, explores the direct translation of digital fluid dynamics simulations into tectonic structures. Image courtesy of MOA.

Figure 6 – Windtrap, designed by Philippe Rahm Architects in 2009, utilises understanding air flows to shape the massing of a building; tectonics become climate. Image courtesy of Philippe Rahm Architects.

accretion. The former is a subtractive process, carving a shape from inert mass over time. The latter accretion refers to a gradual build-up of layers in biology. In both cases, the flowing fluid is the carrier of matter, either adding or taking away (**Fig. 4 and 8**). Both are weathering processes that change and alter the shape of matter over time in correspondence with the ambient climatic conditions. David Leatherbarrow and Mohsen Mostafavi highlighted the mathematical dualism of weathering in their seminal book *On Weathering*. However, they juxtapose its subtractive nature with the potential addition of meaning by making ageing processes visible. [11] Christoph F. E. Holzhey goes further, telling us that 'to weather' is an enantiosemic verb: "Usually signifying a deteriorating change, it can also mean, on the one hand, successfully opposing such change and, on the other hand, undergoing a beneficial change." [12]

In the context of designing with flows, this small excursion into what happens after a structure is built can help better understand the dynamic correlations between time and matter in the ambitious endeavour of co-designing with nature. However, abstraction and metaphor are powerful tools in architecture. Both are required to translate spatial and tectonic concepts into buildings. Two selected examples – one built and one unbuilt – from practice illustrate ways of forming with flows.

The new foyer for the Building Academy Salzburg, titled Viscous Affiliation (2012), by MOA-Architekten (formerly a part of soma-architecture), is a particle flow simulation that is frozen in time, generating a three-dimensional mesh later in situ cast in concrete (**Fig. 5**). The roof structure above the entrance creates a "fluid space", according to the architects. [13] Visitors experience a space surrounded by fluid motion, calculated by the software and directly materialised using CNC milling for formwork.

Windtrap (2009), by Philippe Rahm Architects, is a competition entry for a sports hall in Slovenia (**Fig. 6**). The architects used wind flow analysis to understand better the movement of warm and cold air in the building. The architects describe their proposal as "architecture as weather", using tectonics to manage airflow. [14] The

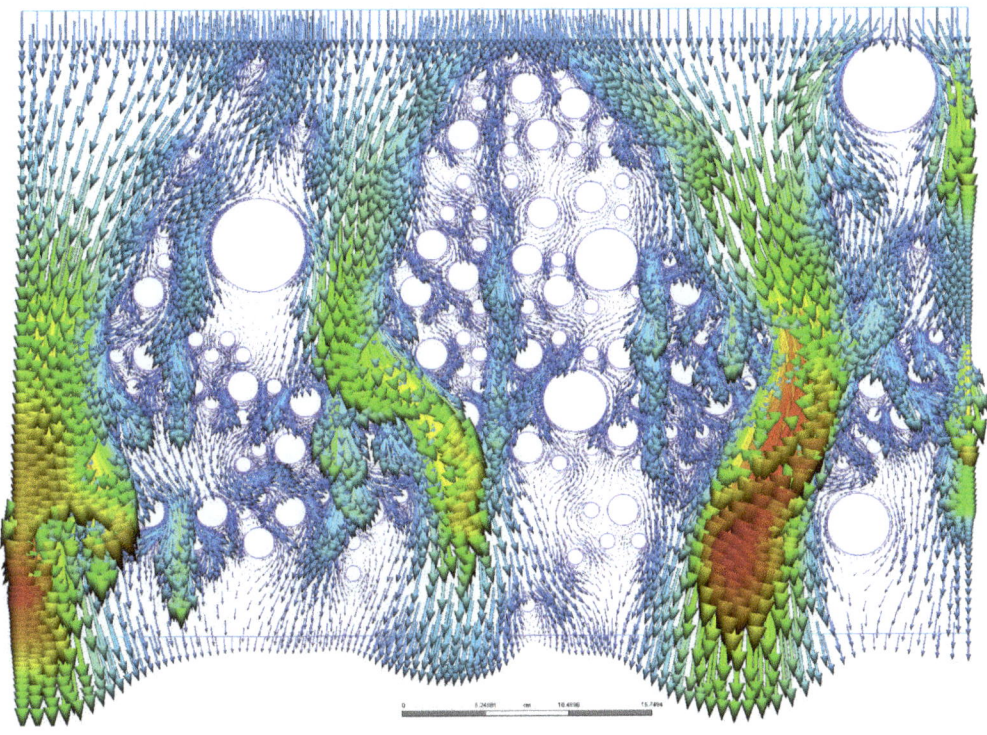

Figure 7 – Understanding flows as analytical and generative tools can help designing with climatic conditions and embedding this information into materialised form. CFD simulation for Integrated Sequestration by Andreas Körner and Anete Krista Salmane, 2024.

building is essentially a ventilation device – "double flow heat exchange air removal system" – upscaled into the size of a building. Surfaces are lined with different materials to absorb or release heat to the passing air. Although following modernist functionalism – a typology of climate – one wonders if this is "a building that breathes in unison with its landscape?" [15]

While Viscous Affiliation sophisticatedly translates a frozen fluid simulation literally into a load-bearing structure for a building entrance, Windtrap operates both on extensive and intensive levels. Massing and programme are subordinate to the control of energies and flows. Differently materialised functions are strategically placed to use hot and cold air as it passes by, interacting with surfaces. In the first case study, the function of the fluid is generative yet restricted to the design phase. In the second case, the shaping flows remain relevant during operation. However, neither of the two projects considers how the flows shape and interact with the building surfaces over time.

Substrates

A substrate is the base for something and lies beneath the surface. In the context of weathering and the generation of form through corrosive and erosive flows, this substrate is revealed and covered repeatedly. The substrate's composition – if heterogeneous – influences the carved-out form depending on varying densities. Examples are riverbeds and canyons. When exposed to wind and weather, buildings turn into ruins. Architecture – as in a building – is the balance between 'nature' and human 'spirit', according to the German philosopher Georg Simmel (1858-1918). Accordingly, the roles are reversed, and buildings become nature's material:

"The same forces that give the mountain its shape through weathering, erosion, collapse and the growth of vegetation have proved effective here on the masonry." [16]

When visiting, for example, Tintagel Castle on the north coast of Cornwall, one can experience an area formed by flows over time (**Fig. 9**). The meandering coast with the

Figure 8 – CFD simulation materialised as CNC-milled relief, turning flow into landscape, fluid into terrain. Photo for Threshold Occupation by Andreas Körner and Biophile, 2017.

Figure 9 – The ruins of Tintagel Castle (13th century) in Cornwall, UK, showing lichen and moss growth, weathering and erosion. Photo by Andreas Körner, 2024.

peninsula jutting, crowned by the 13th-century structure. The wind blows away the soft parts first, and the seeping of water does the rest. The results are jagged columns, exposing the natural stone slabs stripped of the binding mortar. In exposed areas, the ruin becomes overgrown by lichen and moss, colourising the otherwise dark grey stone. Over time, wind and weather round all corners and grind away the features. They strip the structure, taking away dust, powders, and spores.

Flows and fluids can be powerful, generative tools. However, they can be detrimental to a structure's integrity. Flows are patient and beautiful, but they may also turn into brutal torrents. With the increasingly relevant integration of environmental and ecological considerations into digital design processes comes an acceptance and, at least partial, appreciation of the transient nature of designing with flows. As design concepts focus more on material flows and ecological interactions, the surface must be considered an interface. In CFD software, intensive parameters are given as so-called boundary conditions. They specify what physically happens at those locations: temperature, fluid velocity, pressure, heat flux, et cetera. From this, ideal scenarios are created and solved as transient or steady-state calculations. Such simulations help us better understand a fluid flow's impact on a solid surface. The results are interpreted numerically or graphically and coded as colours and tables (**Fig. 7**). While conventionally used to assess a form's performance given the defined environmental conditions, they can also directly feed into a design process to generate form (**Fig. 5-6**).

By using additive or subtractive operations, the flow data can be translated into meshes, volumes, swirls, patterned surfaces, reliefs, caverns, tunnels, spaces, voids, and terrains (**Fig. 10-11**). Far from reducing flows to fluidity – selecting appealing features and omitting troublesome ones – such approaches result in grimier and wilder flow shapes. While they are equally form frozen in time, this approach operates on multiple scales and invites change over time. As in the case of Tintagel Castle, flows smooth features over time. However, on a smaller scale, surface, substrate, and flow interaction provides rich ground for life. Acknowledging the material consequences of a building 'weathering the storm', the thermodynamic interactions between mass and space – surface/substrate and flow – can overcome established functionalism and create open landscapes that host humans and non-humans.

Expanding on these observations, integrating flow-driven design strategies into architectural practice represents an opportunity to rethink the interface between the built and natural environments fundamentally. By embracing the dynamic interplay of erosion and accretion, architects can develop forms that respond to immediate environmental forces and anticipate their evolution over time. This approach demands a shift from static, impermeable structures to designs that celebrate change, adaptability, and ecological integration. It involves crafting porous and textured surfaces that foster biodiversity and sustain ecological networks, effectively transforming buildings into living systems within urban landscapes.

Furthermore, coupling CFD with digital fabrication enables architects to move beyond performance optimisation, using simulations as generative tools for imaginative and expressive design (**Fig. 10**). The marriage of analytical rigour and creative exploration unlocks the potential for architecture to operate as a mediator between human habitation and environmental processes. This synthesis challenges the traditional boundaries of architecture, positioning it as an active participant in broader ecological cycles.

Ultimately, the study of fluid surfaces and saturated substrates calls for a paradigm shift in architectural thinking that recognises the inherent impermanence and interconnectivity of all forms. By designing with flows, we can cultivate built environments that are not only resilient but also regenerative, fostering a harmonious coexistence between nature, culture, and the constructed world. This vision heralds a future where architecture thrives as an adaptive and inclusive practice, bridging the temporal and spatial scales of human and non-human interactions.

Notes

(01) M. Waite, ed., *Paperback Oxford English Dictionary*, 7th ed., Oxford: Oxford University Press, 2012, p. 276.
(02) Z. Hadid, 'Foreword', in *Total Fluidity: Studio Zaha Hadid*, ed. Zaha Hadid, Patrik Schumacher and Institute of Architecture, Wien: Springer, 2011, p. 6.
(03) P. Ball, *Flow: Nature's Patterns*, Oxford, New York: Oxford University Press, 2011, A tapestry in three parts.
(04) B. Hookway, *Interface*, Cambridge, MA: The MIT Press, 2014, p. 63.
(05) A. Benjamin, 'Surface Effects: Borromini, Semper, Loos' in *The Journal of Architecture 11*, no. 1 (2006).
(06) A. Vidler, *Warped Space: Art, Architecture, and Anxiety in Modern Culture*, Cambridge: The MIT Press, 2001, p. 220.
(07) G. Deleuze, *The Fold: Leibniz and the Baroque*, Continuum impacts, London: Continuum, 1993, p. 4.
(08) G. Lynn, *Animate Form*, New York: Princeton Architectural Press, 1999; Greg Lynn, 'The Structure of Ornament' in *Digital Tectonics*, ed. N. Leach, D. Turnbull and C. Williams, Chichester: Wiley-Academy, 2004.
(09) M. Carpo, *The Second Digital Turn: Design Beyond Intelligence*, Writing architecture, Cambridge: The MIT Press, 2017.
(10) M. Mostafavi and D. Leatherbarrow, *On Weathering: Life of Buildings in Time*, Cambridge: The MIT Press, 1993, p. 5.
(11) Mostafavi and Leatherbarrow, *On Weathering*, p. 6.
(12) C. F. E. Holzhey, 'Weathering Ambivalences: Between Language and Physics', in *Weathering: Ecologies of Exposure*, ed. C. F. E. Holzhey and A. Wedemeyer, Berlin: Institute for Cultural Inquiry, 2020, p. 15.
(13) MOA, 'Viscous Affiliation: New Foyer and Adaption of the Building Academy', moa-architecture.eu, accessed November 22, 2024 https://www.moa-architecture.eu/en/portfolio/en-neues-foyer-und-mehrzweckhalle-bauakademie-salzburg/.
(14) Philippe Rahm architects, "Wintrap", accessed November 22, 2024, http://www.philipperahm.com/data/projects/windtrap/index.html.
(15) C. Girot, 'Forword' in *Atmosphere Anatomies: On Design, Weather, and Sensation*, S. Benedito (Zürich: Lars Müller Publishers, 2021), p. 7.
(16) G. Simmel, 'Ein Ästhetischer Versuch', in *Materialästhetik: Quellentexte Zu Kunst*, Design Und Architektur, ed. Dietmar Rübel, M. Wagner and V. Wolff, 2nd ed. (Berlin: Reimer, 2017), p. 247.

Figure 10 – CFD simulation materialised as a 3D-printed (binder-jet) relief, creating pockets of higher intricacy and Art Nouveau-esque formal langauges. Photo of Allostatic Arabesque by Andreas Körner, 2021.

Figure 11 – CFD simulation materialised as a spatial proposal for an inhabitable wall. How can we live in such a weather world? By building weathering structures. Rendering of Hypertrophic Poché by Andreas Körner, 2023.

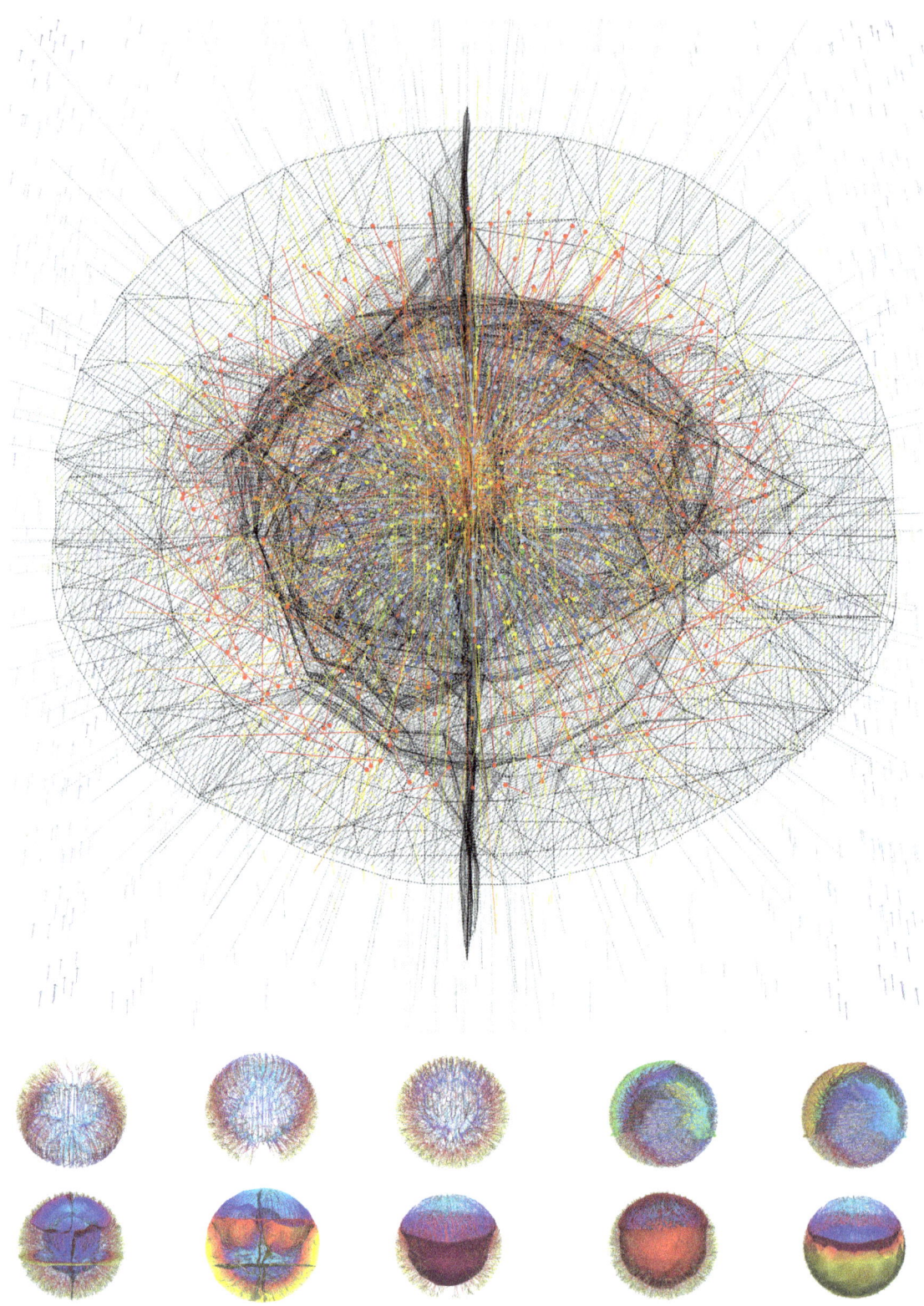

Denise Carcangiu. Platform P2413.2
Petrol and oil particles. Experimental combustion of oil particles, under extreme heat and pressure (2021).

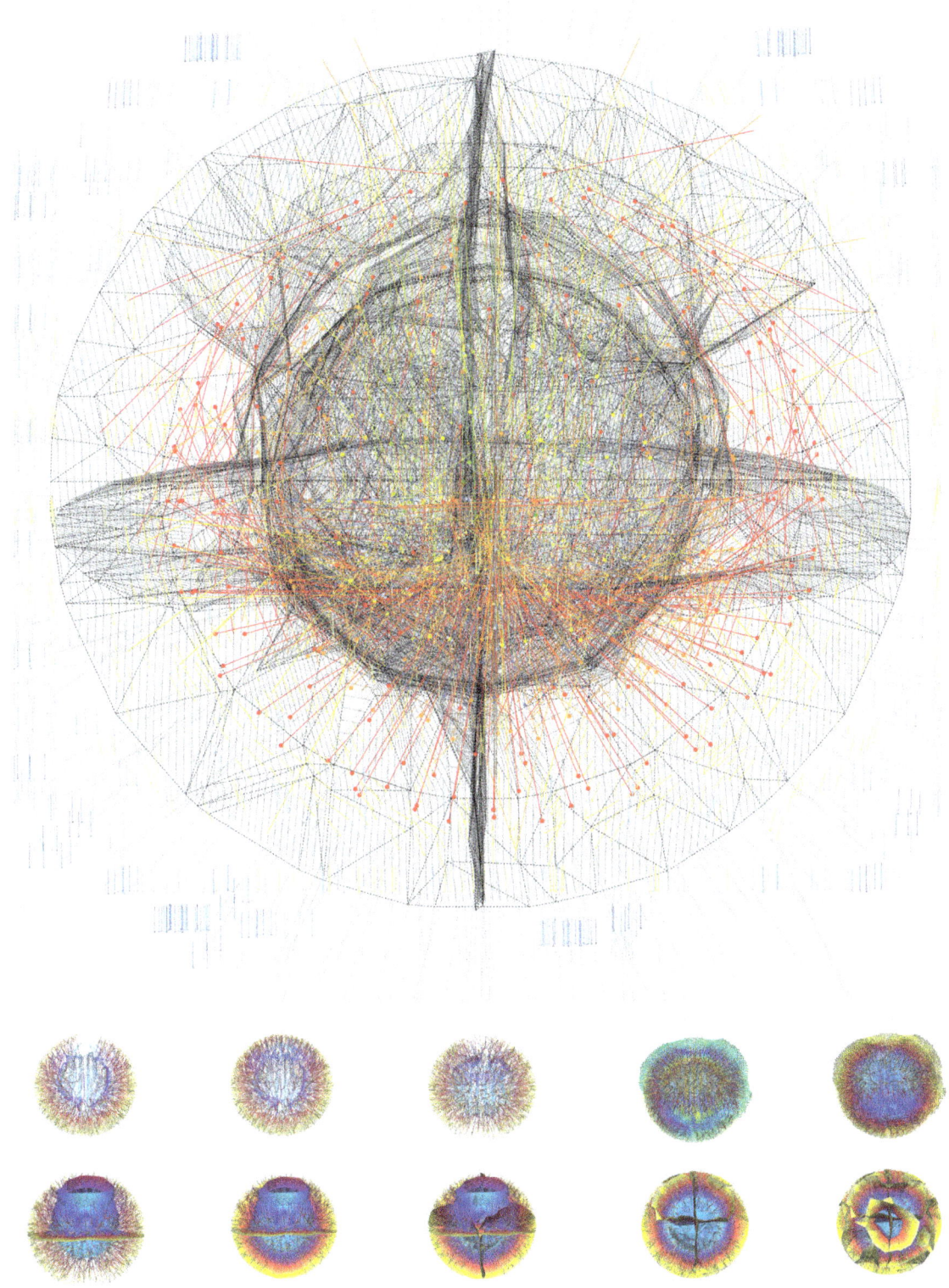

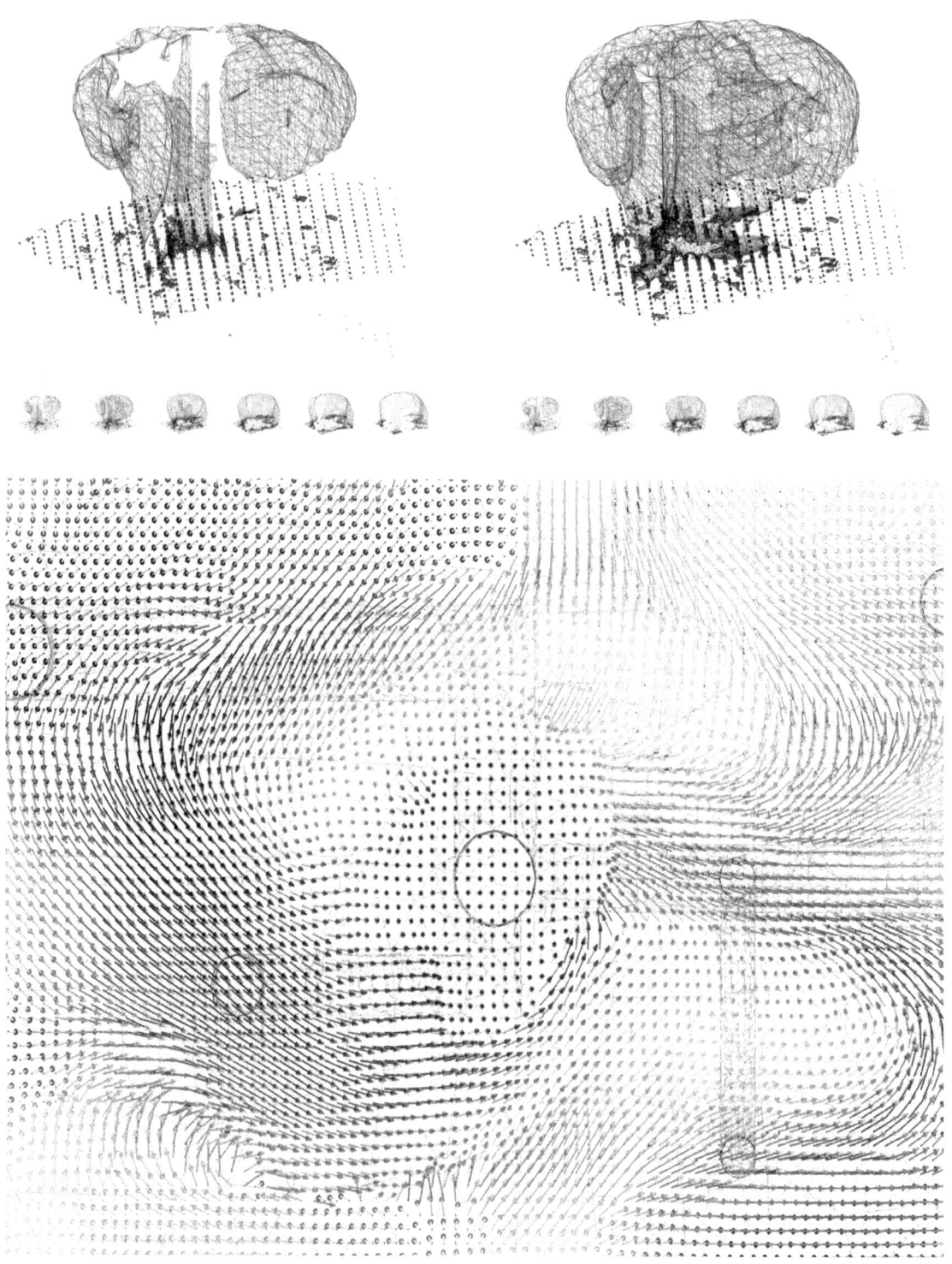

Seni Agunpopo. The Cloud Sanctuary.
(top and right) Cloud formation and fragments. (bottom left) Atmospheric geothermal space simulation (2020).

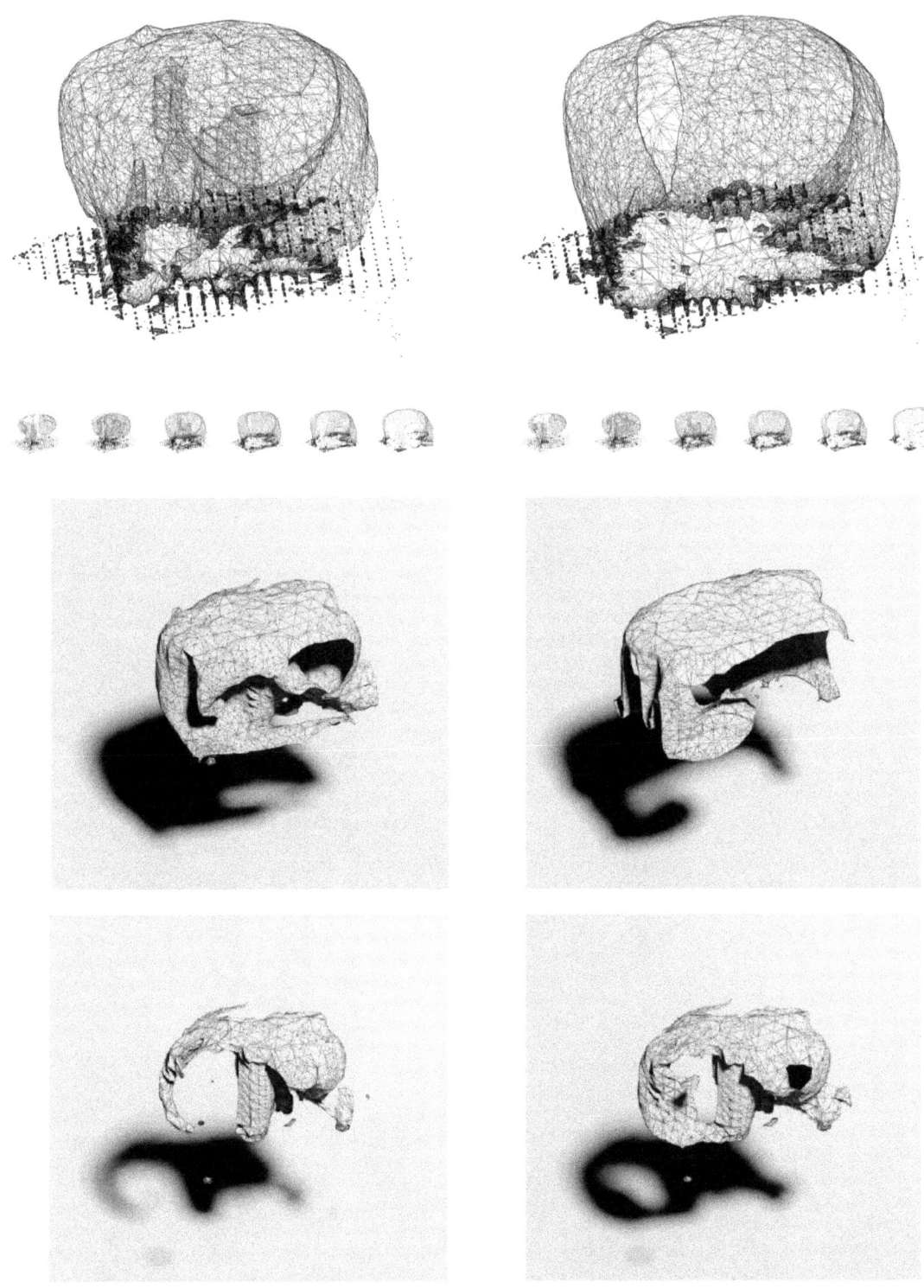

Seni Agunpopo. Peat Recovery Observation.
(top) Pressure prints of geological peat slices. (right) A slice of the biosphere, illustrating the flow of air and carbon particles within a soil probe of peat.

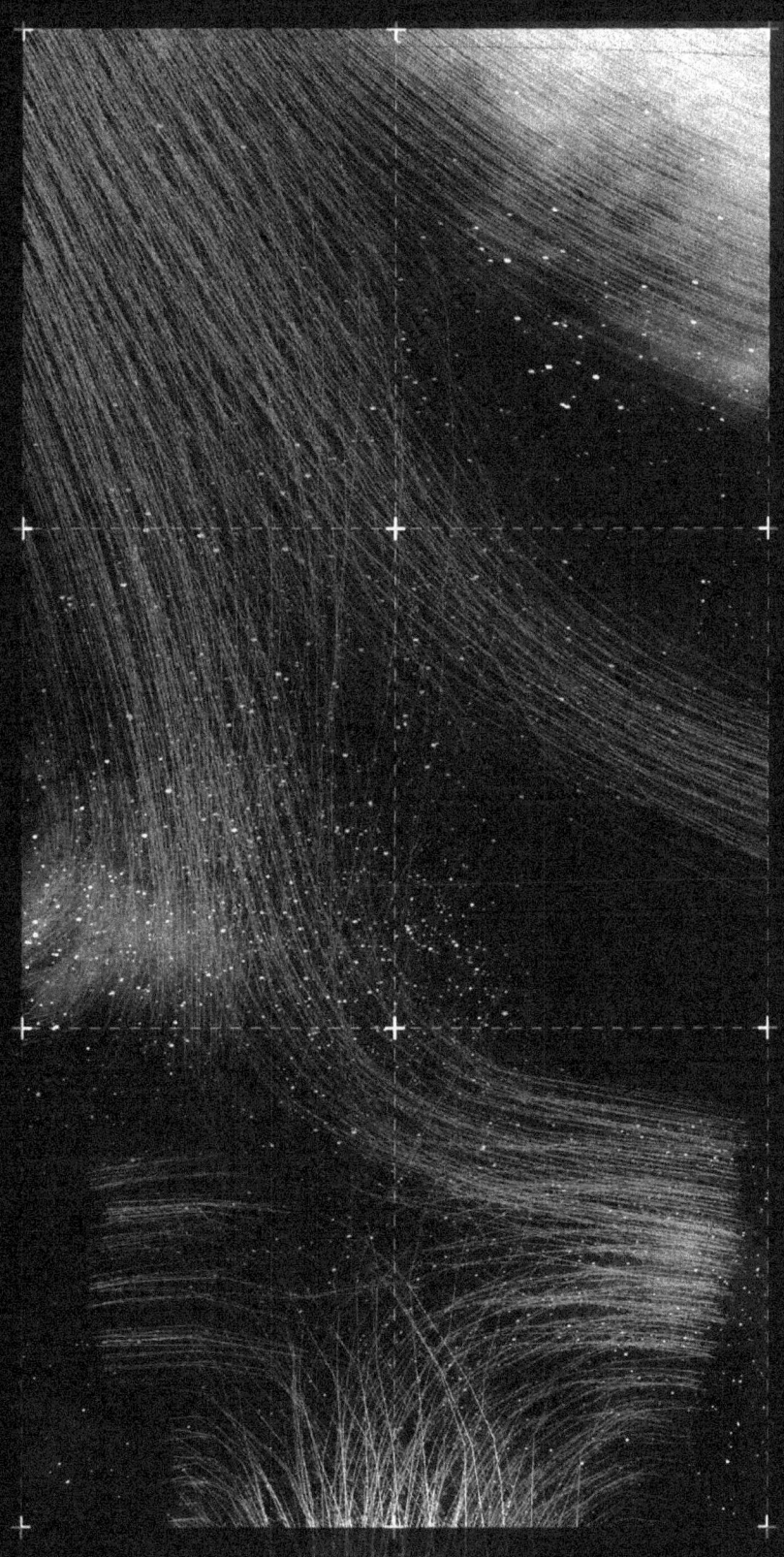

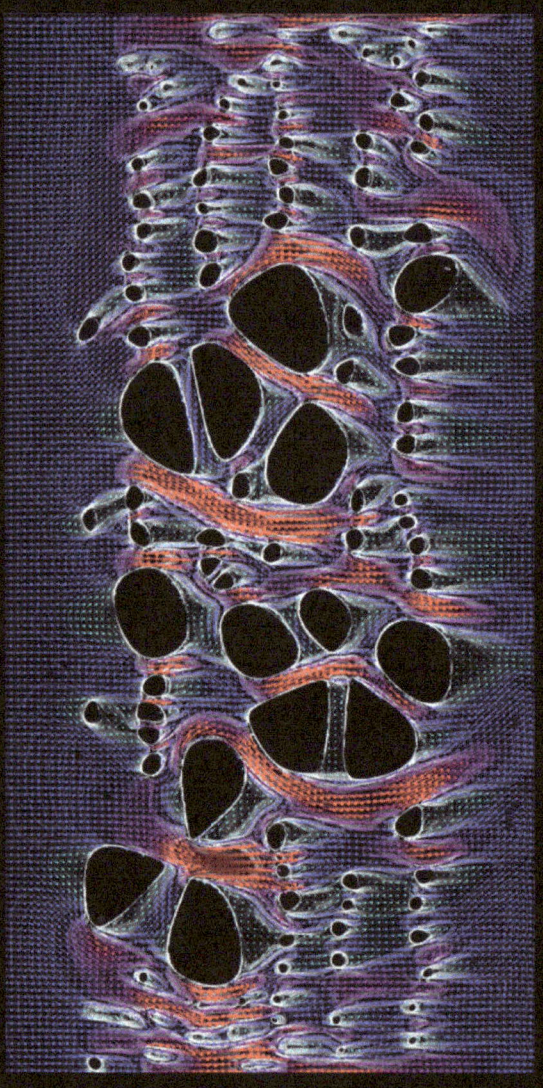
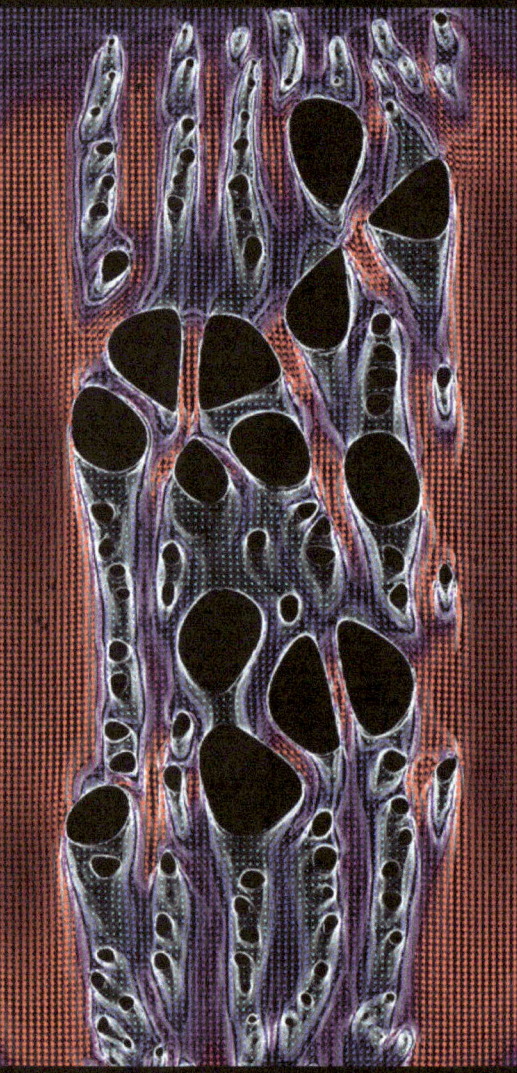

Jamie Williams. The Atlas of The Carbon Economy. Carbon Sink Experiment: Absorption of 'One Carbon Credit' in hard wood (forests) (2021).
"A carbon credit is a tradable permit or certificate that provides the holder of the credit the right to emit one ton of carbon dioxide or an equivalent of another greenhouse gas."

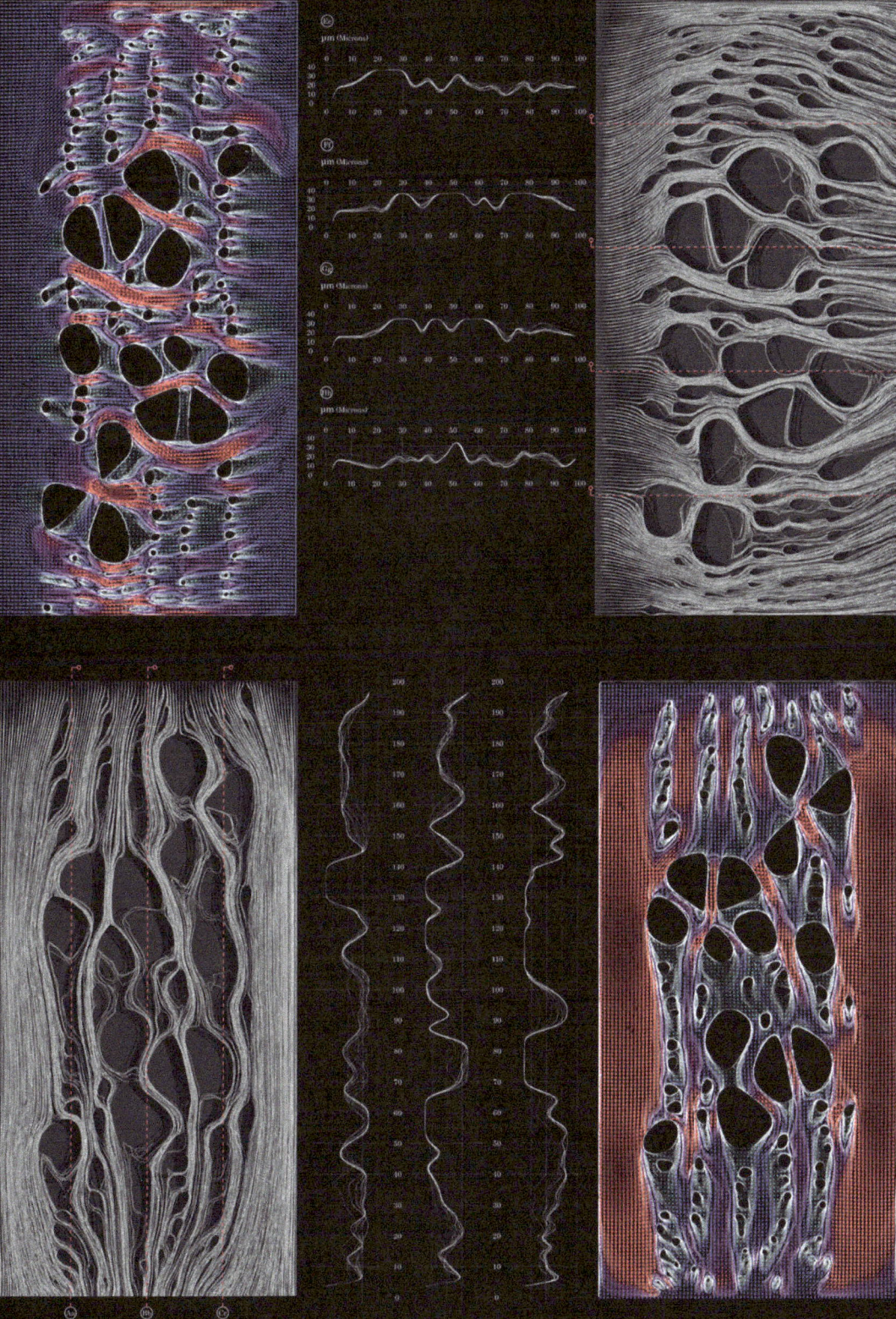

Chada Elalami. Smouldering Interface. Fire dynamics (2023).
Simulating wild fires - (top) through external wind patterns, (top right) heat intrusion for vegetation structures and (bottom right) flammability of ground studies.

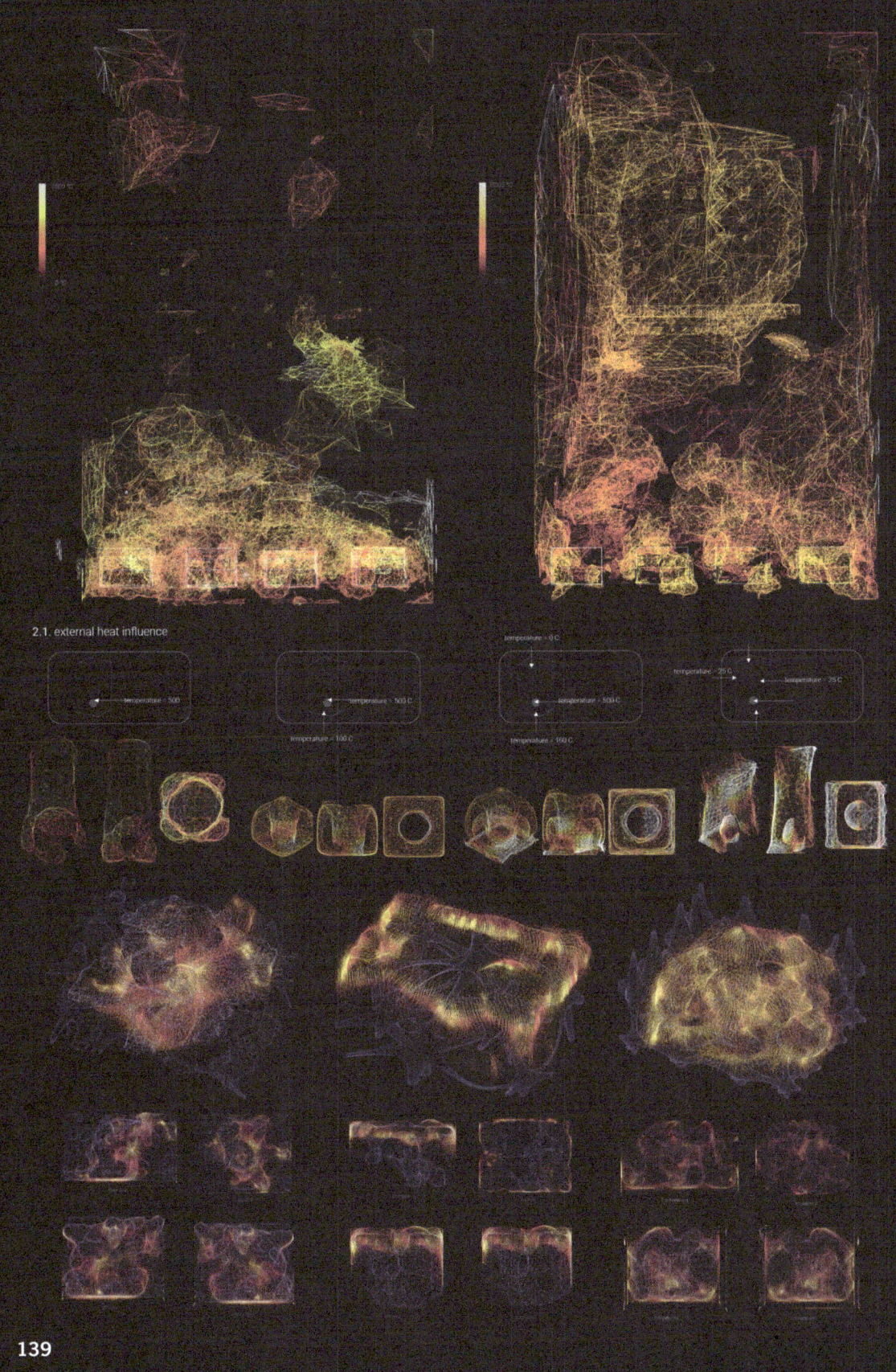

2.1. external heat influence

Muhtasim Mojnu. Landscape Conduits. The Water Cycle - Precipitation, Evaporation, Moisture and Humidity (2021).
(top) Canal Energy - Fluid and Sediment Interaction. (right) Energy through canal iterations.

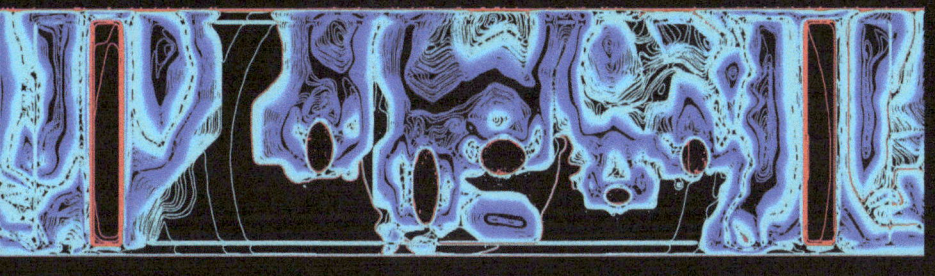

Test 1
Energy exchange from precipitation on artificial waterways.
Low — Intermediate — High

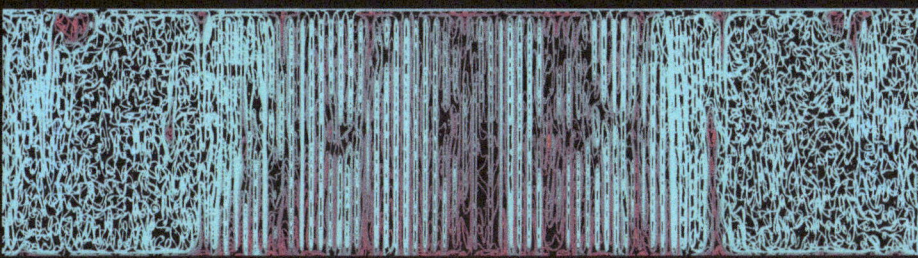

Test 2
Canal energy
Low — Intermediate — High

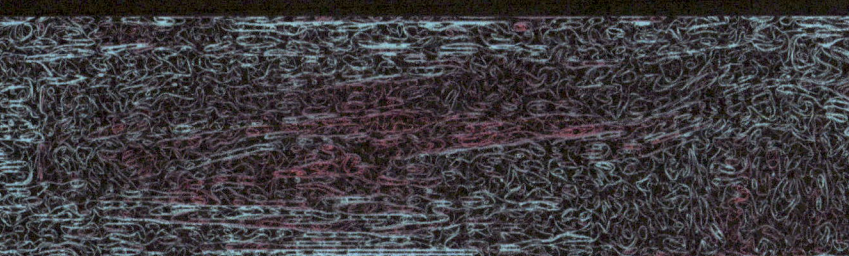

Test 3
Energy transfer when canal meets river.
Low — Intermediate — High

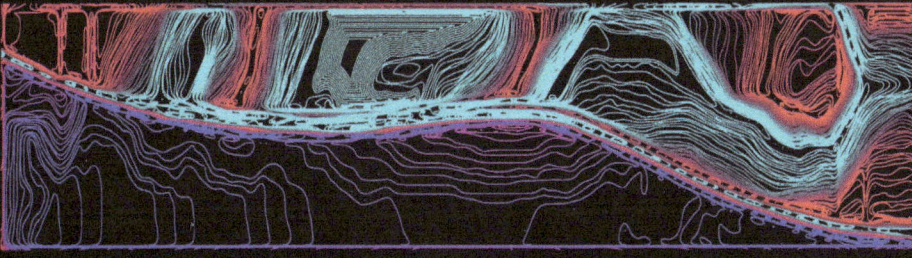

Test 4
River Energy
Low — Intermediate — High

	VELOCITY MAGNITUDE	VELOCITY MAGNITUDE	THERMAL TRACE	THERMAL CONTOUR
HIGH — LOW			HIGH — LOW	

01

	Pressure (Pa)	Temperature (°C)
Methane	150	0
Soil	100	0
Air	10	0

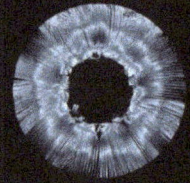  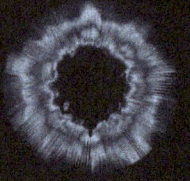 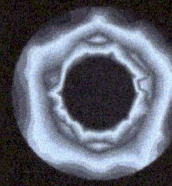

02

	Pressure (Pa)	Temperature (°C)
Methane	200	0
Soil	10	0
Air	10	0

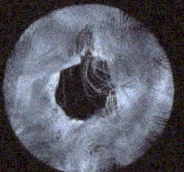 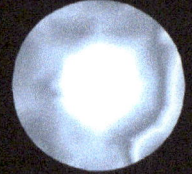 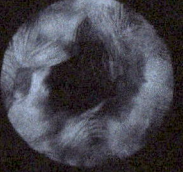 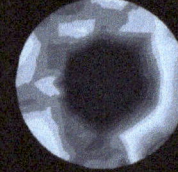

03

	Pressure (Pa)	Temperature (°C)
Methane	10	-100
Soil	10	100
Air	1	10

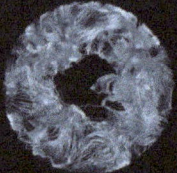 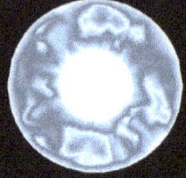  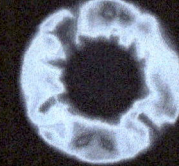

04

	Pressure (Pa)	Temperature (°C)
Methane	150	25
Soil	-	-
Air	-5	-50

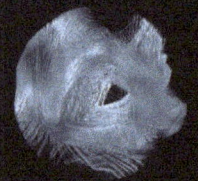  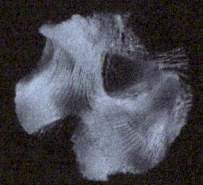 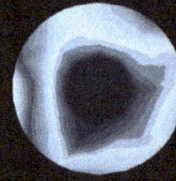

05

	Pressure (Pa)	Temperature (°C)
Methane	100	1000
Soil	100	1000
Air	10	100

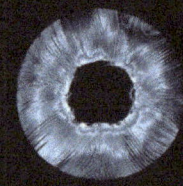  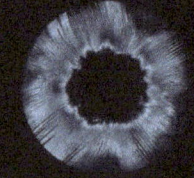 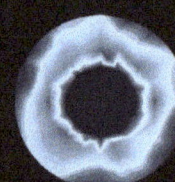

06

	Pressure (Pa)	Temperature (°C)
Methane	100	-10
Soil	100	-15
Air	10	0

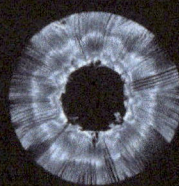  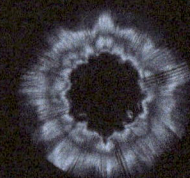 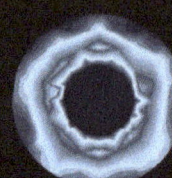

Helen Windsor. The Seeping City. Simulating methane release from permafrost (2020).

The experiment explores the microscopical movement of methane particles through frozen soil into the atmosphere.

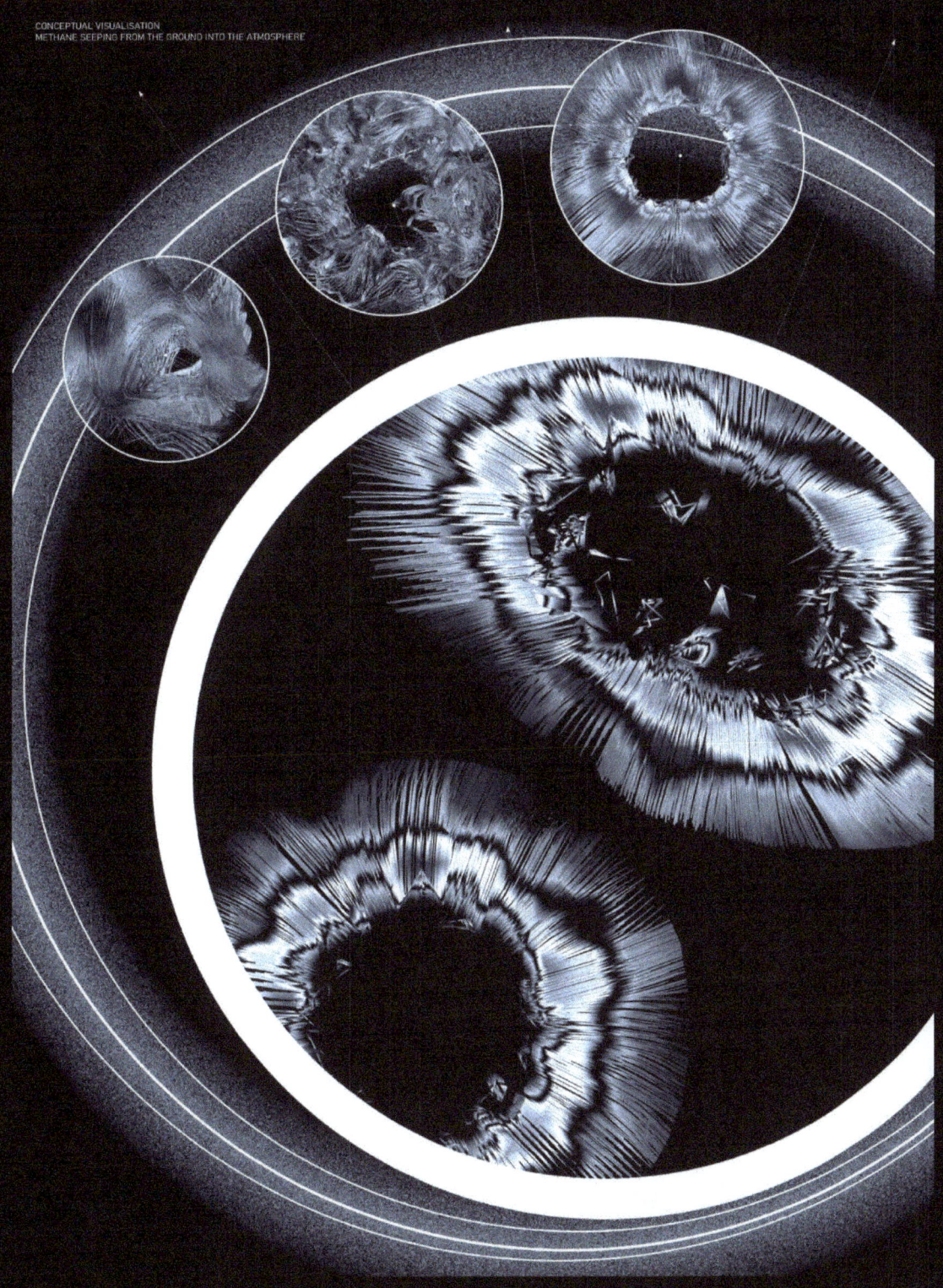

CONCEPTUAL VISUALISATION
METHANE SEEPING FROM THE GROUND INTO THE ATMOSPHERE

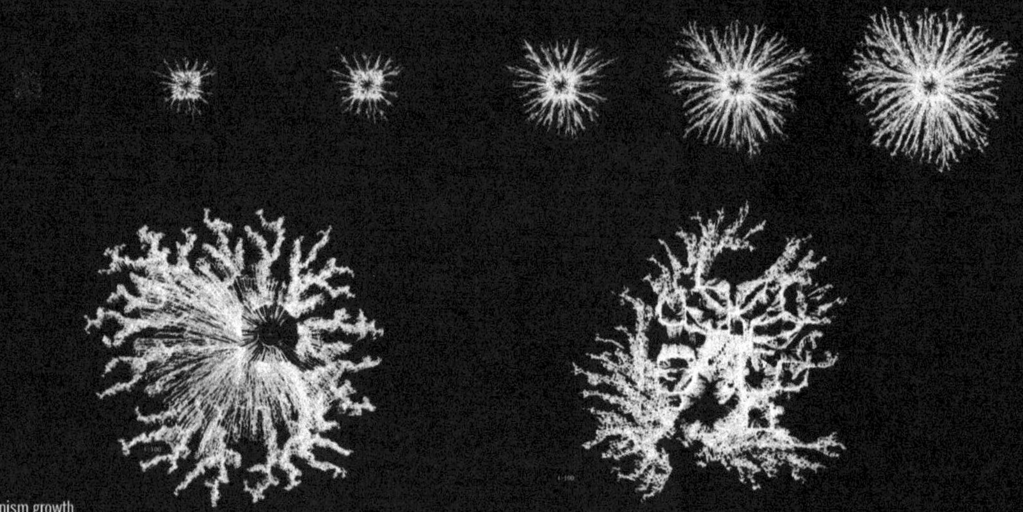

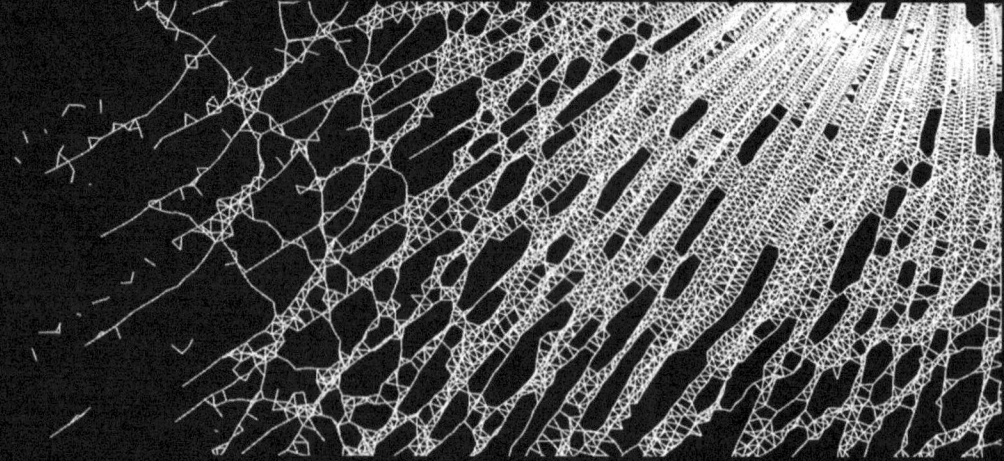

Micro-organism growth

Repel and attract algorithm

Carl Fletcher. Landfill Methan Repurposing (2023). Microbial Remediation. Methanogens, thriving in the anaerobic conditions of landfills, produce methane as a by product of their metabolism. Biological simulations of growth, digital, natural and combined.

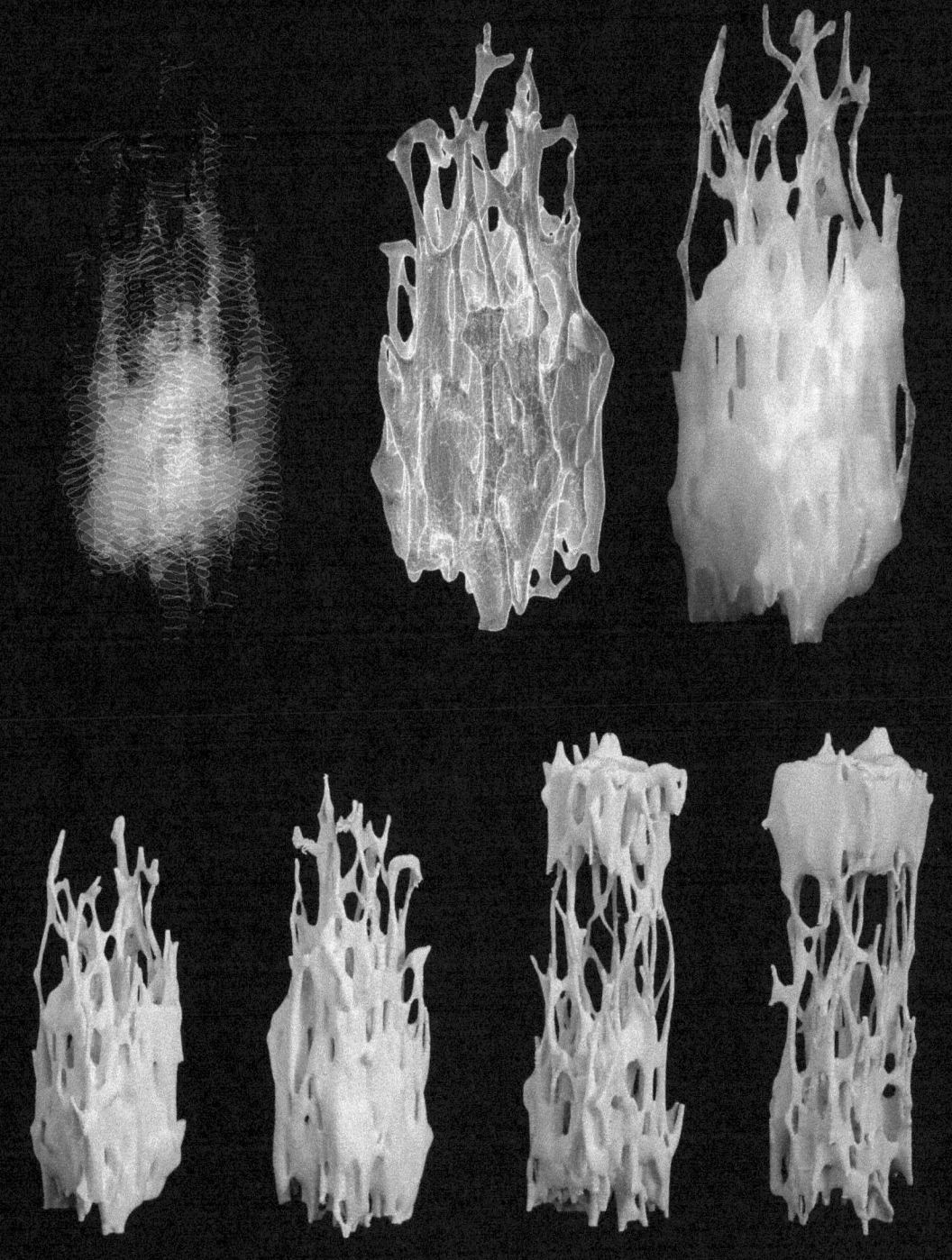

Carl Fletcher. Landfill Methan Repurposing (2023).
Bacterial topographies. (top left) Digital/ Analogue growth comparison. (top right) Predicted growth pathways. (right) Three types of territorial densities and spread patterns.

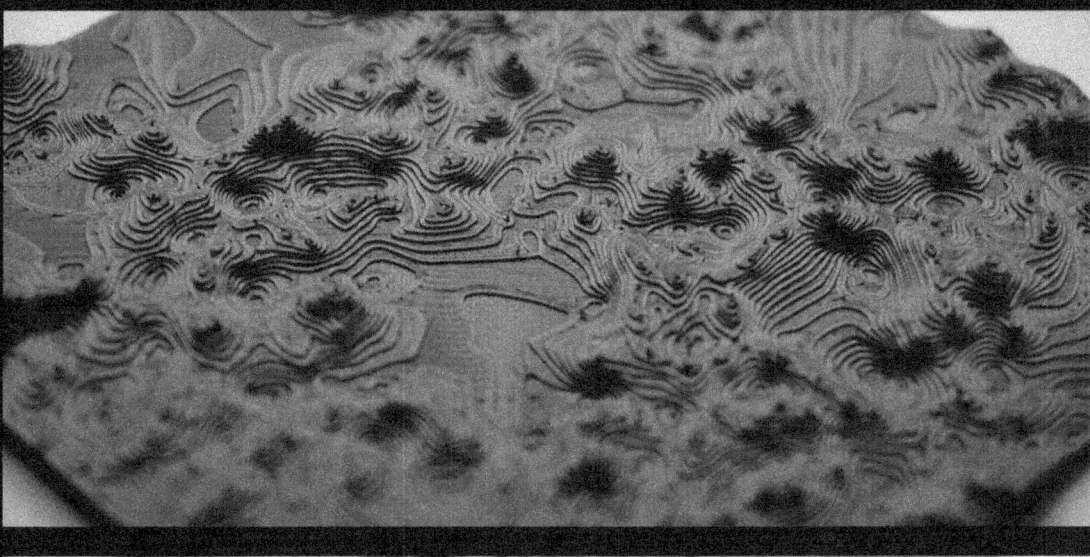
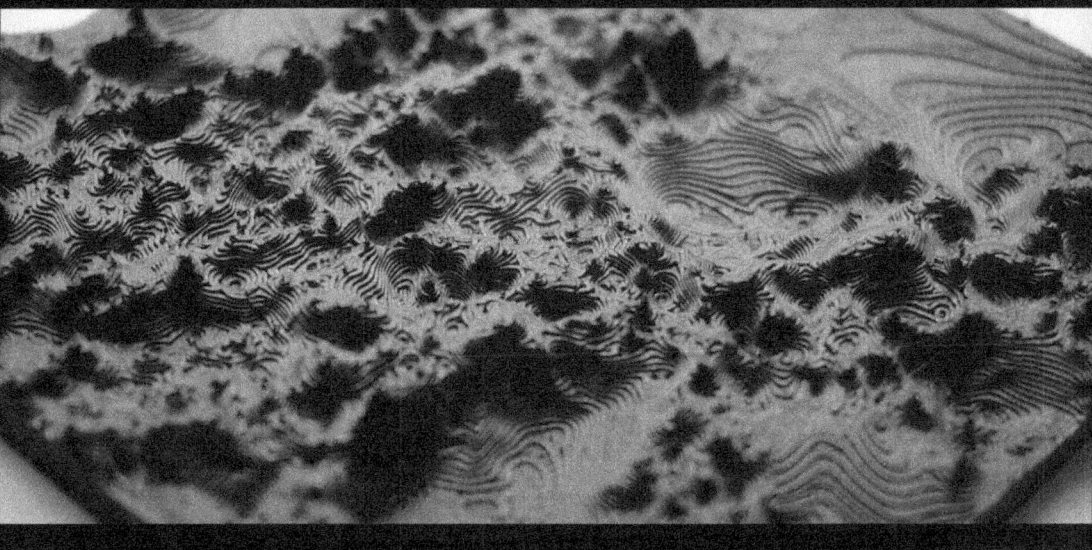
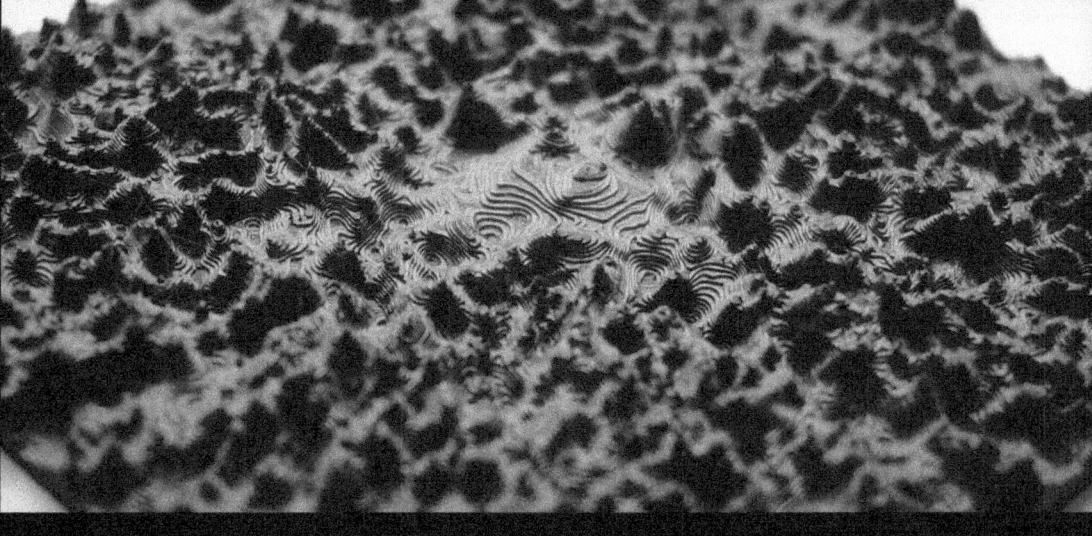

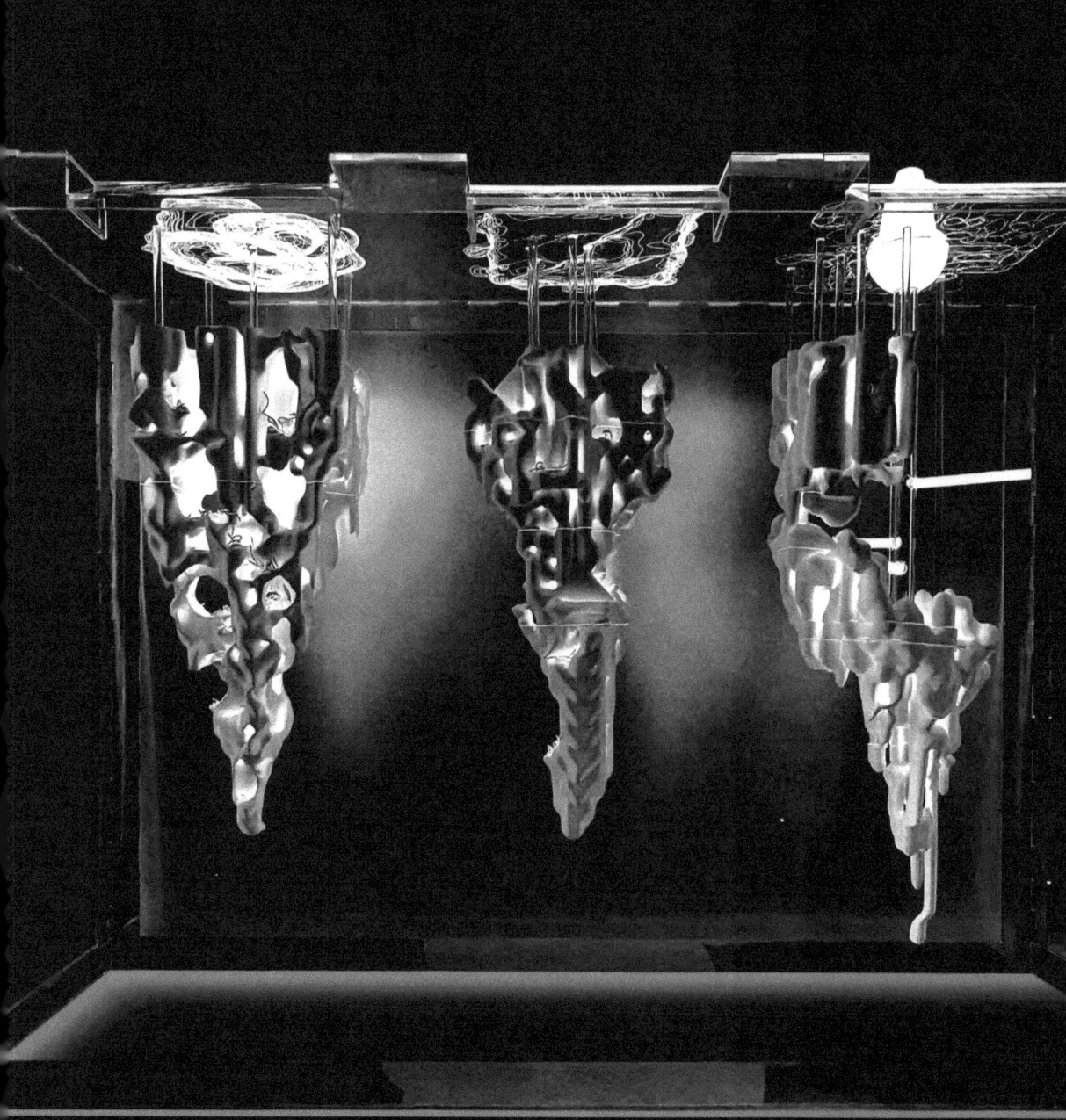

Sian Sliwinska. The Brew Laboratories. River Algae Bloom Growth Studies (2023).
(left) 3D printed 'states' of algae blooms. (right) Digital simulation matrix of various atmospheric factors impacting blooms.

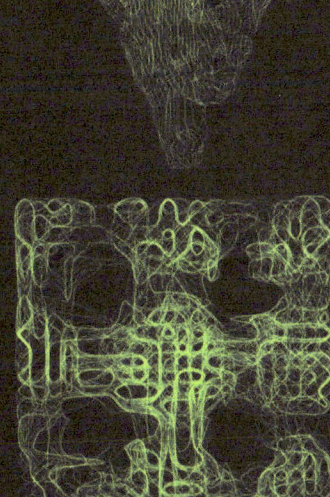

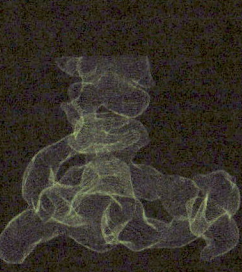
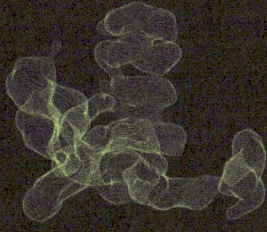

Average Winter Cold, Low Wind.   Average Summer Heat, Low Wind.   Heatwave, Low Wind.

Average Winter Cold, Medium Wind.   Average Summer Heat, Medium Wind.   Heatwave, Medium Wind.

Heat fluctuation morphologies

+0.4⁰ C

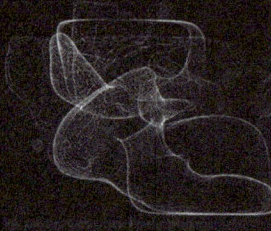
+0.8⁰ C

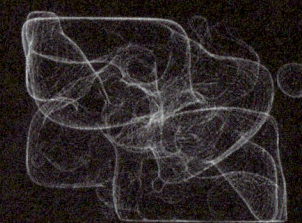
+1.2⁰ C

Solar energy morphologies

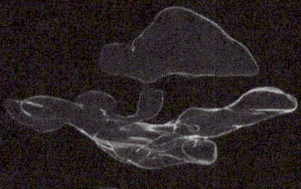
+0.4⁰ C

+0.8⁰ C

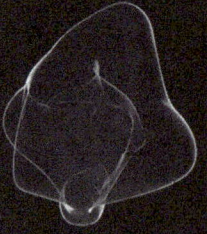
+1.2⁰ C

Thermal Pendulum

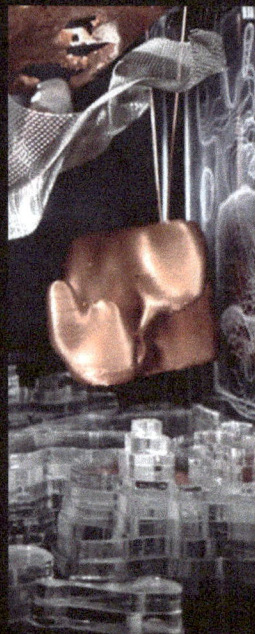

Georgios Malliaropoulos. Lochness Lake Heat Exchange (2023).
(right) Volumetric heat studies, describing temperature fluctuations (emissivity, absorption and heat transmission) and ecological disruption impacts due to rising temperatures.

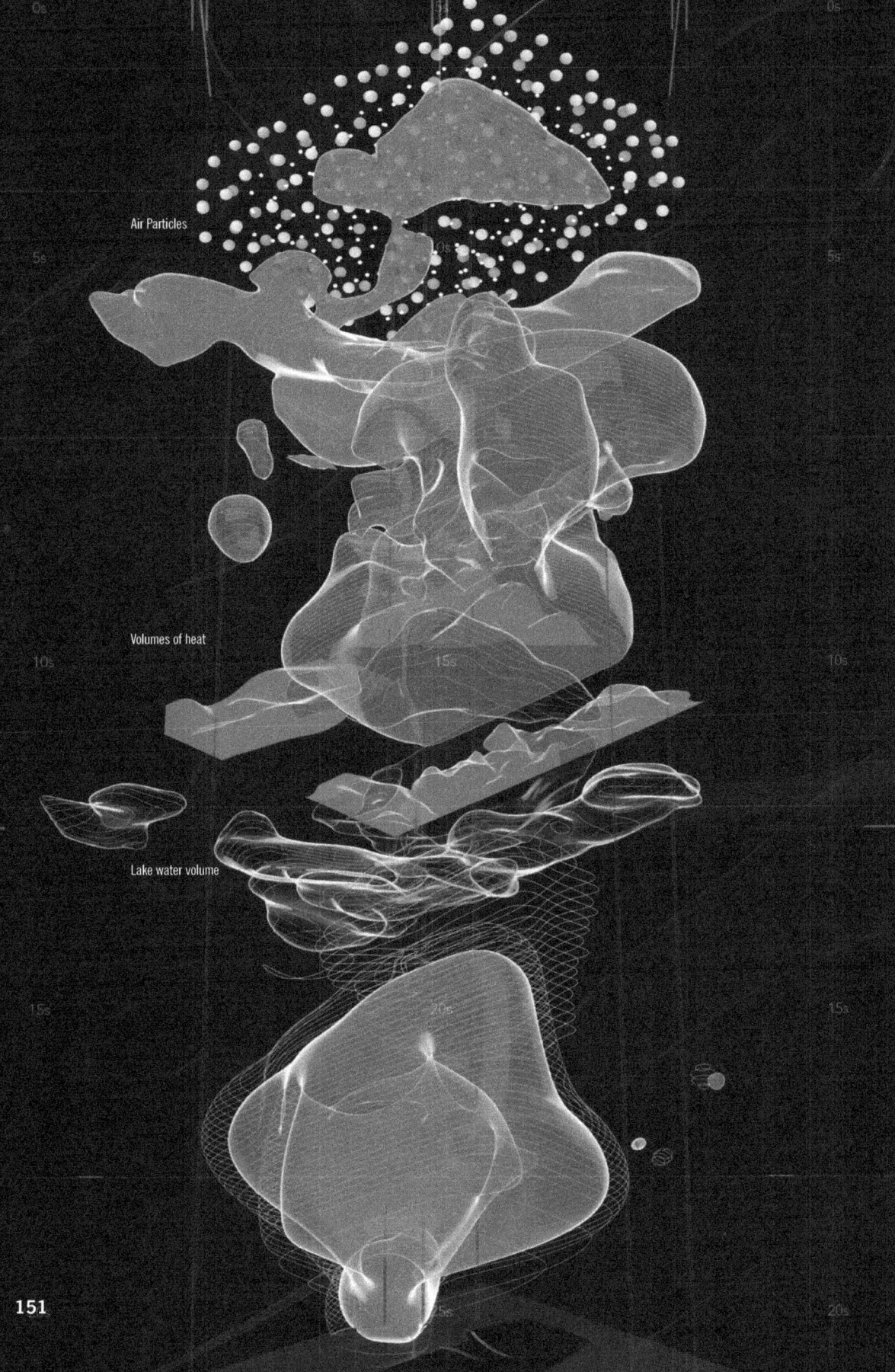

Georgios Malliaropoulos. Lochness Lake Heat Exchange (2023). (left) Territorial simulation, exposed to different heat levels to study the fluidity, melting points and dispersion.
Georgios Malliaropoulos. Institute of Ground Tectonics (2022). (right) Storm simulation, extreme water and air erosion of sandy soil and resulting deformation morphologies.

Air flow concentrations through soil - terraforming through wind and rain.

Air strip passage - 0.6m.

Air strip passage - 0.4m.

Air strip passage - 0.2m.

Air flow concentrations through soil - terraforming through wind and rain.

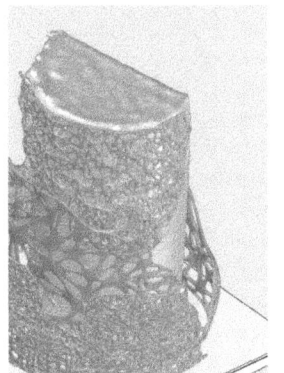

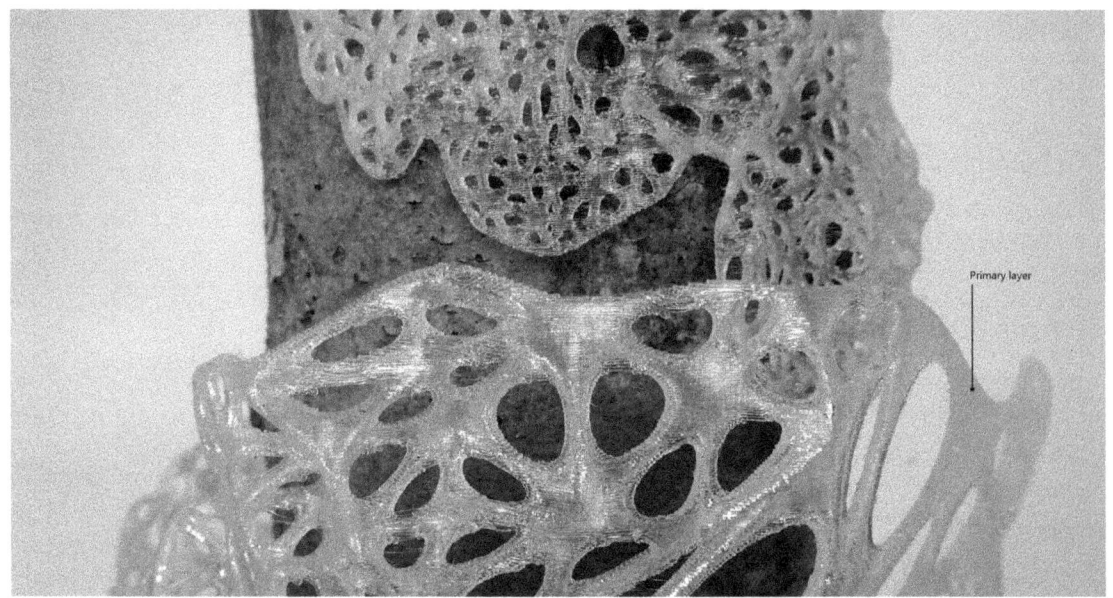
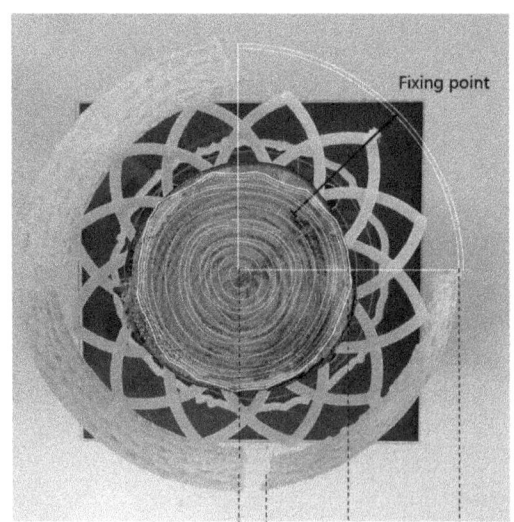
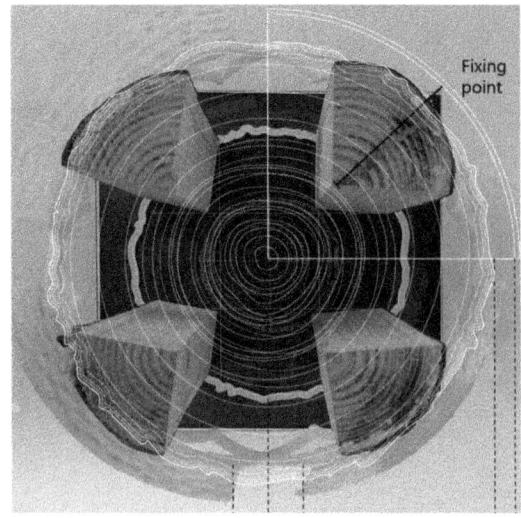

Naomi Punnett. The Ash Arboretum. Ash Dieback Protection Skin Prototype. A prosthetic biopolymer device attached to a tree bark, offers protection against diseases and pests. The skin was developed using LiDAR scanning, AI, and 3D printing and inspired by Hoberman sphere mechanisms (2023).

Kirsten Davis. Saline Landscapes (2022).
Sal(t)-arium. Device for sodium chloride crystal growth with drip-feeding salty water, saturated solution and strings.

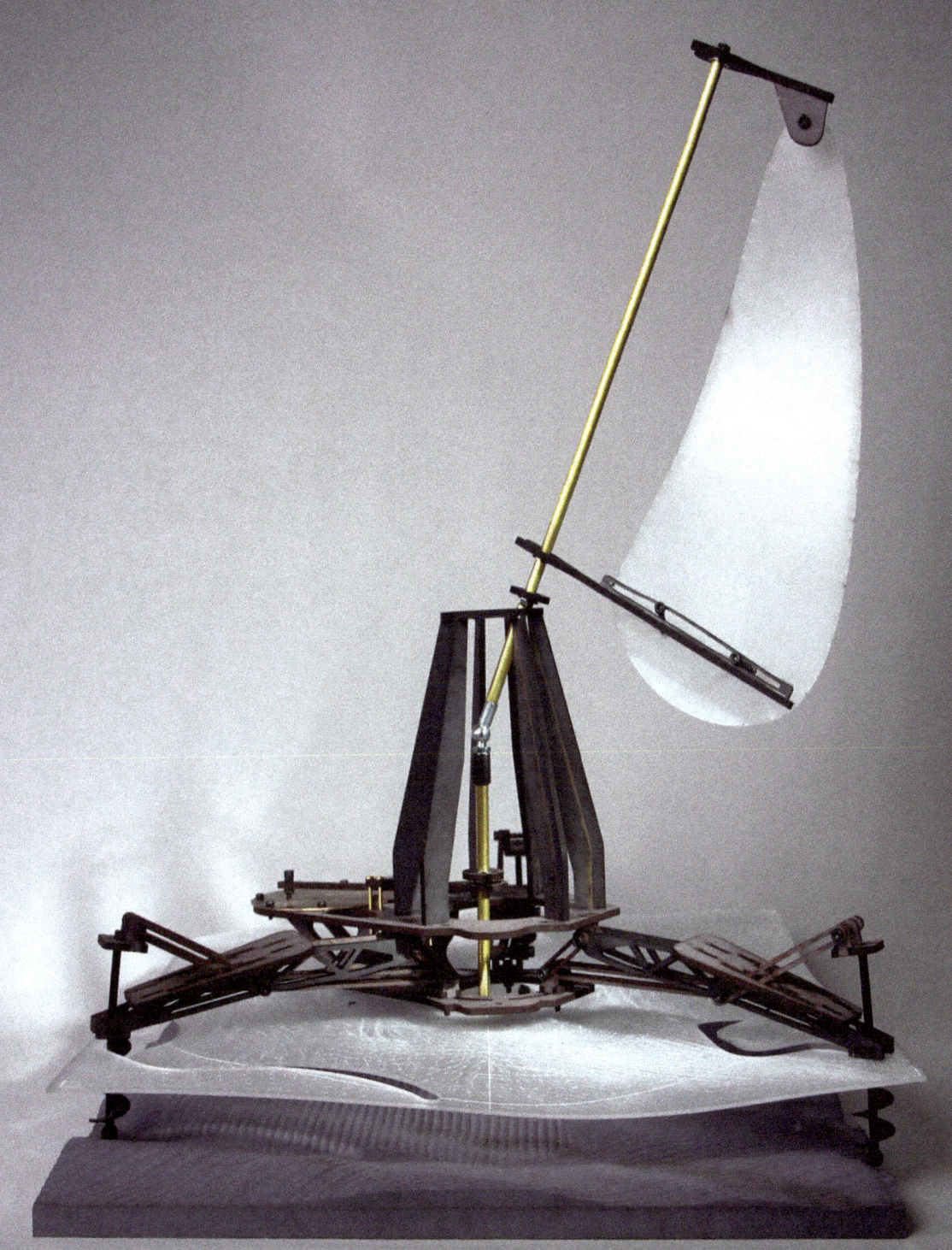

Guy Sinclair, Drift Co-operative, Institute of Superficial Geology (2022).
Shingle Mass Radial Seismograph. Prototype for transferring translational movement of shifting grounds and inscribed forces to an engraved plate.

Yuechuan Xi. Dungeness Solar Park (2022).
Solar Voltaic Prototype - deployable and motorised solar capturing device.

Muhtasim Mojnu. Wind Community Hub (2022).
The Oscillating Wind Turbine Prototype. An elastic sail and mast prototype, low-tech device for wind capture and local energy production.

ARCHIVES

THE EARTH AS AN ARCHIVE DIGITAL ASSEMBLAGE AND EMBODIMENT OF AIR

LAURA NICA

The Earth Archive Initiative

Launched at the end of 2019, the *Earth Archive Initiative* promised to be an unprecedented scientific effort that aspired to create a high-resolution record of the earth's entire surface and everything on it. [01] Every rock, crevasse and vegetation species, every tree (with its size, width, biomass, carbon content, etc.), each settlement type, natural or man-made geo-morphologies, a register of various levels, datums in material strata, displaying densities, associated geology and ecological habitats, were to be scanned, digitised and compiled to create a true three-dimensional digital twin of the world. The urgency behind this undertaking was driven by the idea that the shapes of the continents will soon become unrecognisable due to the rise of sea levels, vast areas of the planet will become desertified, pockets of forest will turn to grasslands, urban settlements will continue to expand, and the entire frozen territories will change in character and properties in the next century, accelerated by climate change.

This gargantuan ambition and scientific effort to create a permanent digital record that is high in resolution and does not degrade, that can be kept, curated and used in perpetuity by various disciplines, poses cultural, technological and spatial challenges. Despite promises to aid environmental monitoring systems, facilitate disaster preparedness, track changes over time, preserve cultural heritage sites that are at risk of being lost due to natural disasters, help reveal lost landscapes, forgotten histories of life, hidden cities, cultures and material traces in remote corners of the planet, the project is controversial. On one hand, the initiative brings to light potential limitations in data-gathering techniques from various sources, the design of adequate algorithms for recording, and issues of authorship or public control (who maps versus who/what is mapped). On the other hand is the ephemeral nature of digital data, which is constantly subject to obsolescence and upgrade, material that is prone to deletion and duplication, the overwhelming amount of information and the dependency on digital stewardship.

This essay seeks to conduct a critique of this initiative, emphasising its disproportionately ambitious scope, its heavy dependence on digital technologies and

Figure 1 — A potential Atlas of Ecological Tectonics and planometric matrix of annexact geometries (various models of student's project proposals), 2025.

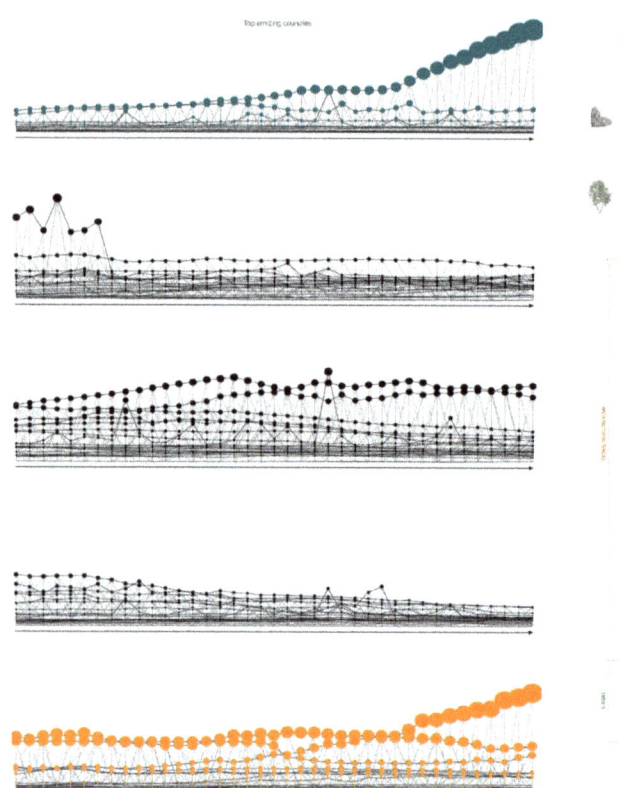
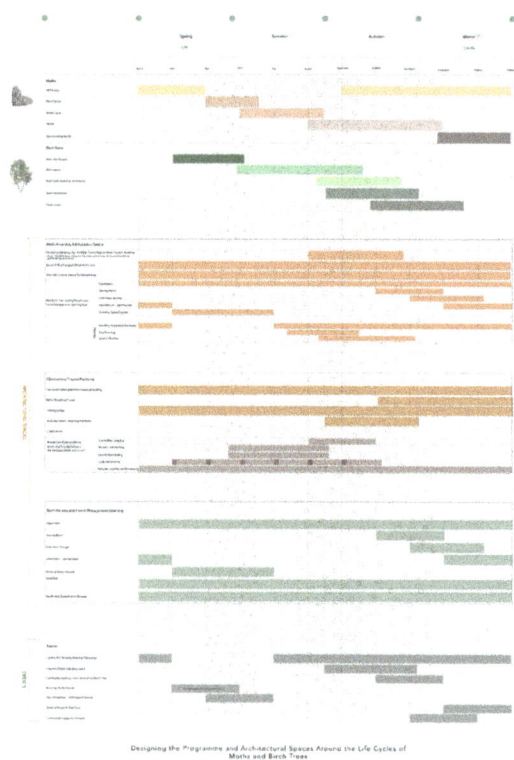

Figure 2 – Kate Hosking. Black Ice Forum. Methane, Nitrous Oxide and Black Carbon emitters graph, main greenhouse gases in the Arctic (2020).

Figure 3 – Gabrielle Bucknall. Moth Assembly. Life Cycle of Moths and Birch Tree, seasonal rhythms and data sampling (2020).

its characterisation as a repository rather than an authentic archive. The paper introduces two design methodologies used in Design Studio 18 (DS18) to record, preserve and manage climatic information. The project invites a broader dialogue on how to archive climate change, encouraging discussions on time (archives that need to transcend generations), space (types of records describing fluid matter) and formats of climatic records (repositories of both digital and physical commons). Without attempting to comprehensively cover scientific or cultural archives, this essay explores the creative dimensions of data archiving, stimulating archival imagination in both prospective and retrospective directions. It includes the (im)possibility of creating an Atlas of Ecological Tectonics and explores architecture's potential role as an organiser of the earth's amorphous matter (air), recording various layers in flux to create a physical mark of memory and visualise a new condition of space (**Fig. 1**).

Climatic Heritage

In architecture, nature and human sciences, archives of the most diverse forms – the herbaria of botanists, the observational records of astronomers, the data banks of geneticists, the fossil compendia of geologists, the microfiches of anthropologists, the digital silos of meteorologists and the libraries of tables, papyrus rolls, parchment manuscripts, printed books, e-books and digital files – make the collection of cumulative knowledge possible (**Fig. 2-5**). Humanity has long been committed to preserving these archives, including the earth's heritage. Since the 1970s, this preservation effort has expanded to the digital realm, to include many initiatives like the Seed Vault, the Microbiota Vault Trust, the UK Met Office and the Protein Data Bank, and the CyArk organisation is leading an effort to collect three-dimensional information and computerised data.

Creating a climatic heritage database involves constantly collecting, analysing and shaping a wide range of data including historical climate data, [02] environmental records, cultural heritage (documenting traditional knowledge and practices related to climate adaptation and mitigation), geospatial data, ecological data, socio-economic, policy and legal documents (**Fig. 6**), and digital records (including photographs, videos and digital documents) to name a few. [03] However, not all of

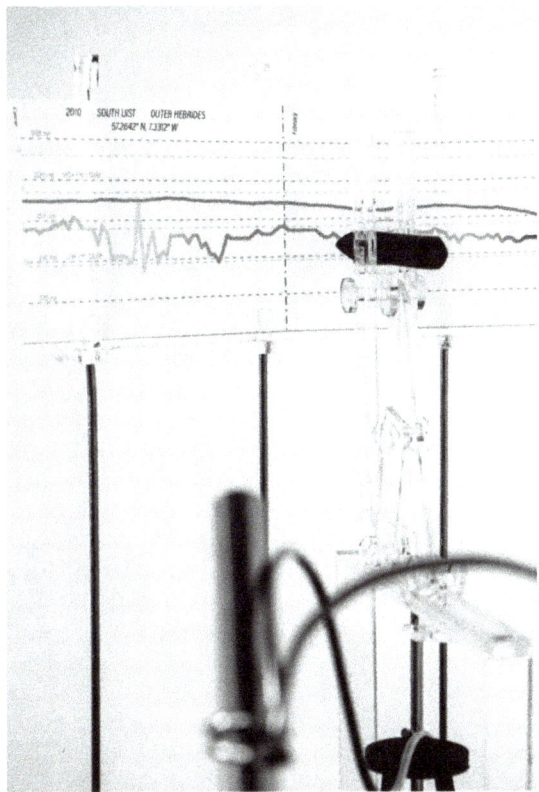

Figure 4 – Guy Sinclair. Shingle Mass Radial Seismograph. Tracing shifts in material movement on a plaque (2022).

Figure 5 – Kirsten Davis. Ferrel Periphery. The Jet Stream Drawing Machine, a visual transcript of recorded climate data (2023).

this information results in an archive. The term 'heritage' when used in relation to climate-related phenomena usually refers to their historical and cultural significance and their impact on human societies and natural environments. It encompasses the ways in which climate has shaped cultural practices, architectural designs and the preservation of historical sites. [04] Unlike cultural archives, scientific archives demand a timescale of observation and preservation that is *longue durée*: a human super-endeavour that could motivate generations across millennia to study continuous phenomena. [05]

These diverse data sets provide a holistic view of climate and life. In *Science in the Archives*, Daston and her co-authors offer multiple examples of how historical records advance further knowledge from various fields of study. [06] Historical climatic data can assist scientists in refining their models, which is crucial for identifying long-term changes, and reveal the natural variability of climate systems, thereby distinguishing between human-induced changes and natural fluctuations. Furthermore, reconstructing recent and past climatic variability in the context of human-induced atmospheric processes and their economic implications can inform future research and policy decisions. [07]

Atmospheric Archives

Archiving air presents unique challenges due to its perpetual state of flux, and the difficulty of capturing irreducible reality and preserving its essence or durable principle. [08] Atmospheric archives have their own inner metabolism, transforming raw observational data into verified records that may morph into different forms over time. Their content can and does change. Morphing implies working with a continuous unpredictable phenomenon, leading to 'improved data', raw observational data (patchy and subject to error and physical biases), artefact-free data (revised and adjusted to render the 'raw data' free from biases and errors), algorithmically compressed data (products of elaborate modelling and simulation) and synthetic data (statistical proxies that await further montage, e.g. Soil Moisture Index, Degree Days, Drought Index, etc.). [09] Regardless of its types, data needs a material support to exist, as it cannot remain as simple raw, unprocessed information. [10] Janković challenges the traditional view that climate archives are often imagined as an information 'warehouse' in which raw data, having been harvested from the natural environment, remains deposited

LEGISLATIVE DATA VISUALISATION - "CHANGES IN THE ARCTIC BACKGROUND AND ISSUES FOR CONGRESS"

Sea(44) : Air(12) : Borders(222) : Dispute(69) : Territory(20) : Minerals(72) : Oil(75) : Regulations(4) : Control(5) : Legal(0) : Activities(36) : Conduct(10) : Passage(10) : Traffic(12) :

Rights(11) : Russia(44) : America(3) : Canada(35) : Norway(22) : Denmark+Greenland(37) :

Total word count: 31328

Figure 6 — Jamie Williams. The Atlas of the Carbon Economy. Creation of legislative playing cards for studio board game to analyse common occurrences of conflictual worlds in Arctic, air and sea legal documents. Managing and visualising large data sets (2021).

LEGISLATION DATA VISUALISATIONS - "UNITED NATIONS CONVENTION ON THE LAW OF THE SEA"

Sea(110) : ■ Borders(184) : ■ Dispute(192) : ■ Territory(68) : ■ Exploitation(39) : ■ Provisions(64) : ■ Regulations(121) : ■ Control(39) : ■ Legal(25) : ■ Activities(109) : ■ Dispute(75) : ■
Conduct(20) : ■ Passage(33) : ■ Traffic(20) : ■ Parties(78) : ■ Rights(63) : ■

Total word count: 41006

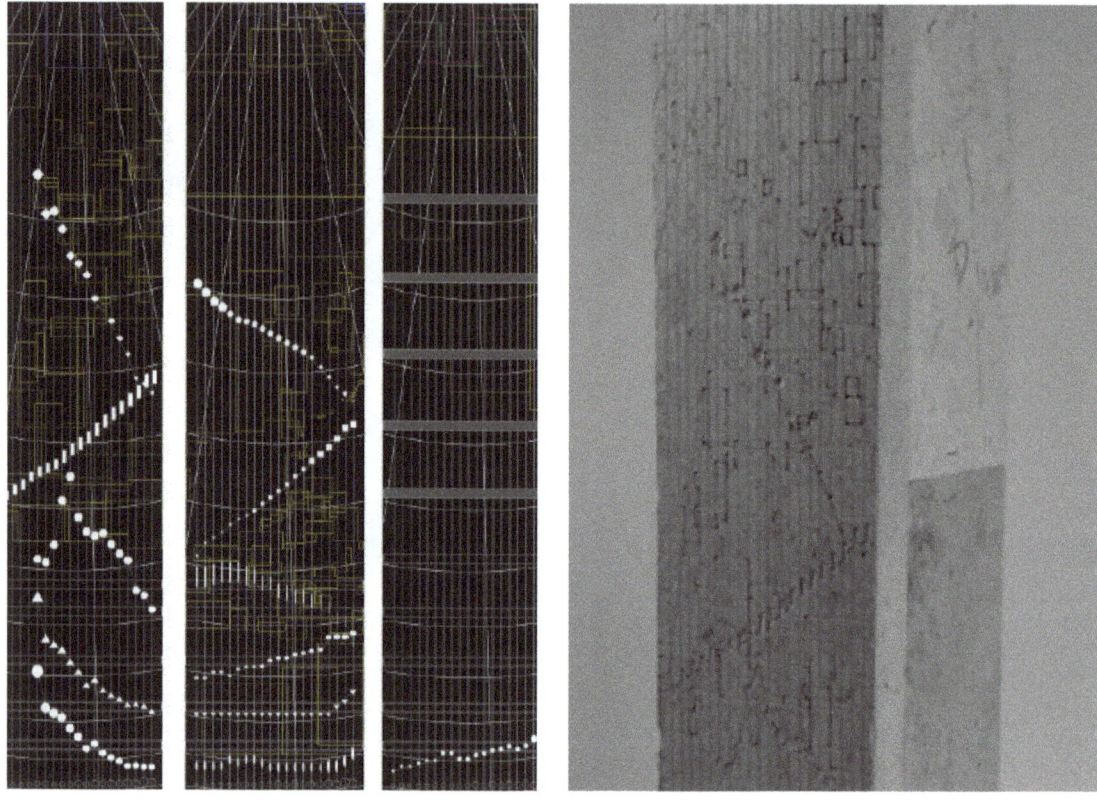

Figure 7 – Rishi Mistry. Offshore Oil tanker board. An innovative atmospheric gauge, visually indicating air acidity changes with litmus paint. This part-digital part-physical totem provides real-time air quality updates, relevant to the Arctic region's major shipping routes air monitoring system (2020).

in a secure space until it is retrieved for 'higher' theoretical or modelling purposes, and explains that climatological data archiving should be seen as *a process* and *a practice* rather than a 'repository', and that such a process should relate to specific objectives of climate research. [11] For this material to withstand a vast chronology, it must be designed, together with its details, including the system workflows of maintenance, the accessibility strategies and policies of ownership.

The *Earth Archive Initiative* is an extensive record of collected information; however, not all that is collected is archivable. For it to become an archive, the data must be embedded and preserved with its context – cultural, temporal, ecological, structural and spatial contingencies (i.e. atmospheric and climatic events). The success of embedding information depends on the scientific framework, the narration (and its bias), political constraints and abstract criteria used for engaging with databases. Databases differ from archives, collections, lists and the like, as the term precisely identifies a structured collection of data stored digitally. [12] As Manovich has argued, "databases and narratives are natural enemies since a database represents the world as a list of items and refuses to order this list, while a narrative creates a *cause-and-effect* trajectory of unordered items (events)".[13] Databases are simpler than historical records and are designed to support efficient querying, reporting and analytics. In computational archives, their retrieval and visualisation protocols change, [14] as the same dataset can be rendered in several ways, via different workflows, tools/instruments used and 'secondary artefacts' produced. Data processing allows the same data structure to inform various kinds of media and requires conceptual notation or spatial images that could be geometrical, statistical or topological.[15]

Climate is a complex system resulting from multiple variables that unfold over long periods of time, and is the result of statistical calculations that average empirical data. [16] This vast accumulation of information and large-scale databases plays a role in revealing patterns. For example, the World Meteorological Organization defines climate as the mean values of environmental parameters over a minimum of thirty years, so that the recent climatological 'normal' derived from datasets prepared for the period from 1961 to 1990 was replaced in 2020 by a new normal based on the 1991 to 2020 corpus. [17] In this case, statistics become a tool for the creation and application of

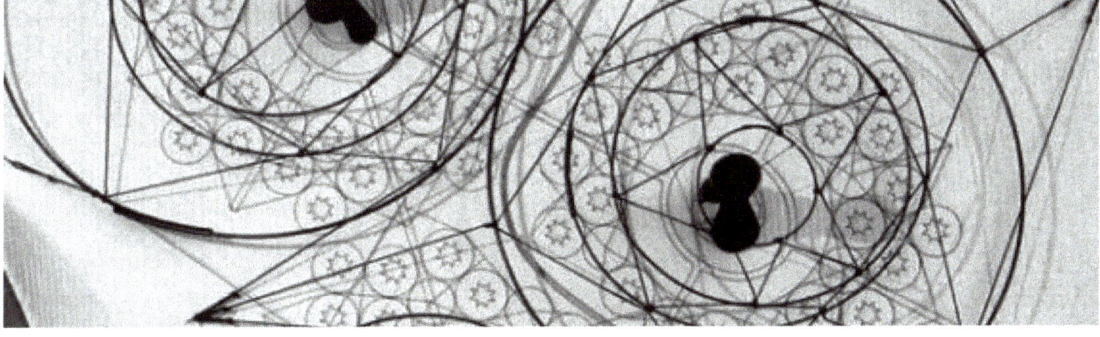

Figure 8 – AG (Tomas Garcia de la Huerta, Bruno Ganem, Zack Bryson). Generic Artifact (2020) Physical models. Devices that visualise energy.

mathematical theories to transform raw information into meaningful insights. However, 'to predict does not equate to explanations'. [18]

This dynamic nature of engaging with atmospheric phenomena requires creative approaches to ensure the continuity of the earth archives amid constant change, which in turn leads to emergent practices for narration. In this context, the following paragraphs will present two potential creative dimensions of climatic data: a pictorial (two-dimensional) method and a volumetric (three-dimensional) method for aiding the transition from a data recording to a design manual and architectural representation.

Archival Two-Dimensional Engravings

The way we record, organise and store information collected in the field is a crucial factor in the process of knowledge production. Today, the instruments that may be employed to record design evidence and interaction over a two-dimensional surface (a computer screen, a piece of paper, posters, drawings, murals, facades, floorplans, etc.), as well as the typology of database, provide many options for recording material culture. [19]

Tapestries, as a form of archival transcription or mapping, imply creating images, rather than patterns. Often flat, abstract translations, two-dimensional inscriptions, or surface notations, they represent visual chronicles that weave together artistic decisions and local or global identities, as well as documenting collective memory and power relationships. Together with diagrams, tapestries are narrative summaries of data. [20] They serve as dynamic artefacts that interact with atmospheric elements (**Fig. 7-9**), revealing impending climatic events or other significant phenomena, and reimagine markers as active participants in the preservation and transmission of knowledge. One historical example of a physical tapestry of information are the Hunger Stones, hydrological landmarks found along the Elbe River in Central Europe. Erected in Germany from the 15th to 19th centuries, these stones marked water levels during droughts, warning future generations of famine-related hardships if the water sank to that level again. [21] Serving as famine memorials and warnings, these physical markers imagine a range of affective and aesthetic registers in their poetic and artistic warnings to future readers. [22]

To record and imprint air in any physical material

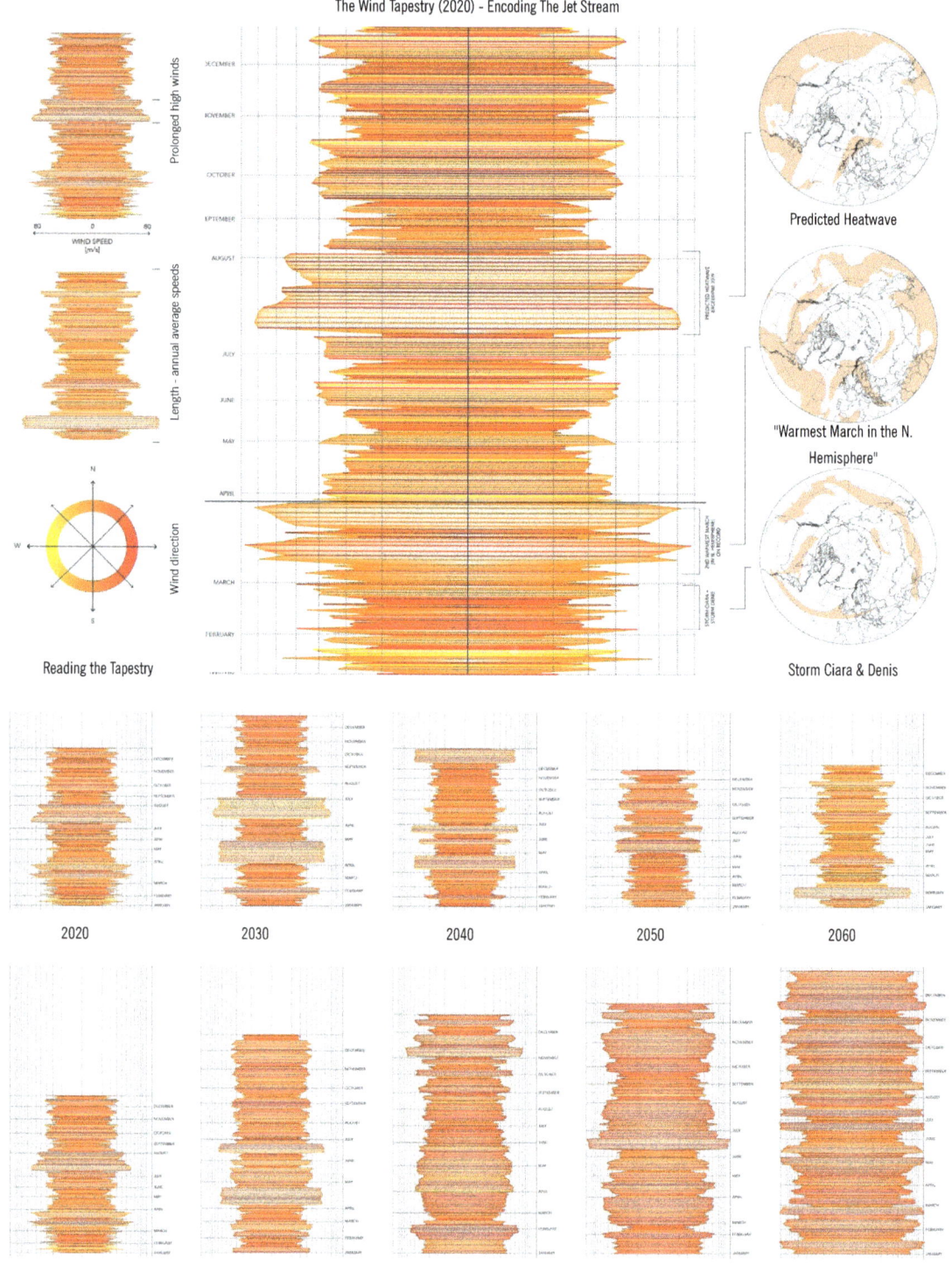

Figure 9 – Charlotte Grasselli. The Polar Wind Park. This project explores the Polar Jet Stream's changing path, by introducing a network of Tropospheric Kites along the Arctic Circle which fly high into the atmosphere, monitoring the high winds. The focal point is the Archival Wind Tapestry, formed by a circular knitting machine loaded with 12 coloured yarn, controlled by the Tropospheric Kite through its direction and velocity, and produces a continuous archive of climatic conditions experienced directly over the site (2020).

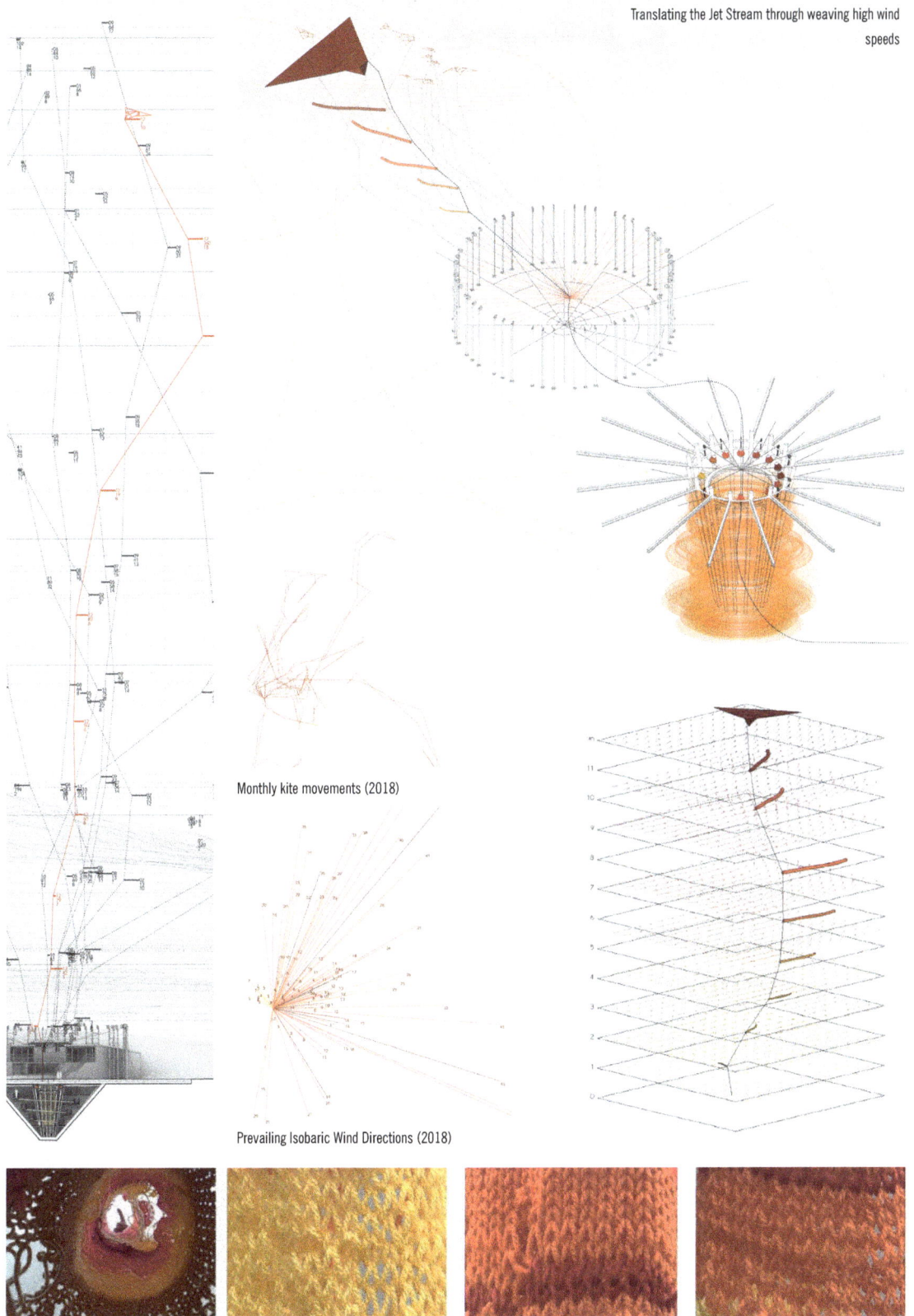

Translating the Jet Stream through weaving high wind speeds

Monthly kite movements (2018)

Prevailing Isobaric Wind Directions (2018)

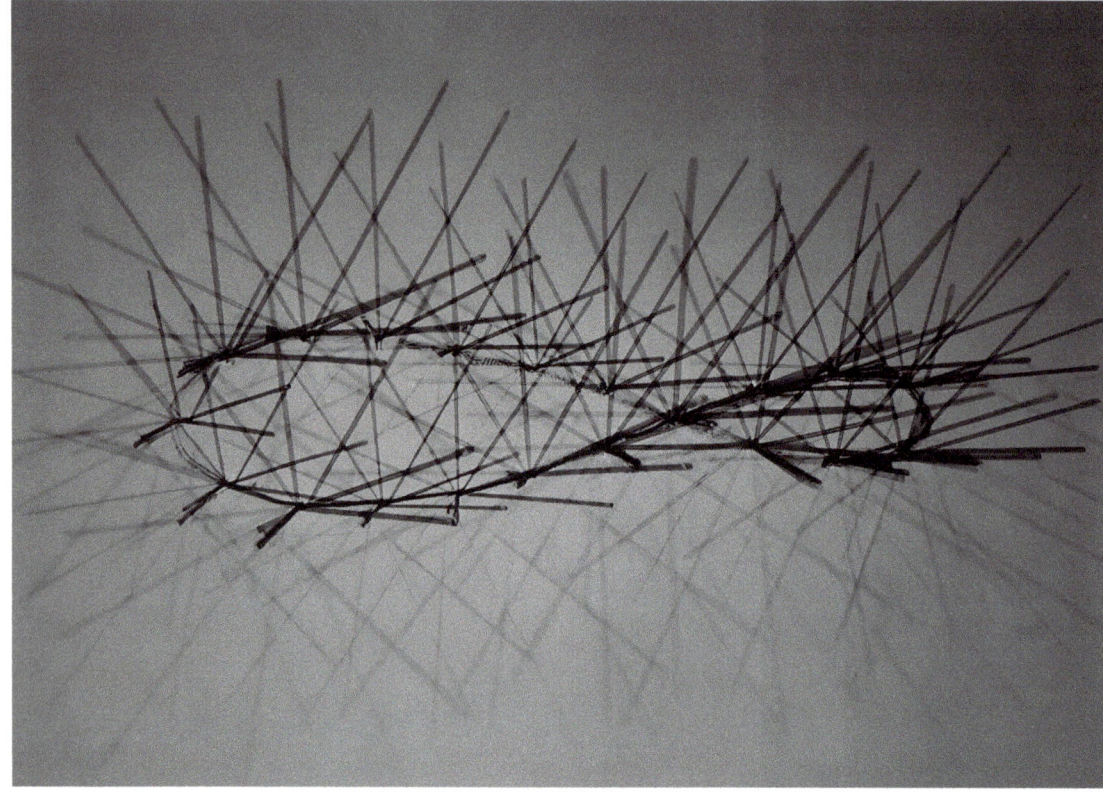

Figure 10 – Helen Windsor. Mission Astraea - Trawling for Treasure in the Celestial Seas. Orbital and sun paths study; a pin shadow model, marking geosynchronous orbital pathways via architectural boundaries (2021).

implies creating a stable, fixed indicator. This safeguards the continuity of narration, promising to withstand temporal deterioration, provides a static reminder of significant moments of the past and imagines new modes of visibility. Materiality starts aiding encryption of the actions performed by a physical phenomenon. [23] This involves on one hand 'immobilising' an occurrence and on the other hand developing a mediator, an abstract 'reader' that translates energy to a two-dimensional surface.

By capturing and preserving a specific moment, a 'time-capsule' or 'deep freeze' layer is created. These elements of stratification, layering and variations in sequence register the momentary direction, speed, pressure and angle of markers and their numerous subtle variations, carrying meaning by tracking, tracing and imprinting a visible index, a planimetric matrix or computable compendium. [24] This is similar to the way that the earth's natural 'data freeze' archives, intertwined in ice cores (in which air bubbles are trapped), pollen, corals (containing oxygen isotopes), sediments, tree rings and more, can reveal a wealth of information about past climatic conditions and environmental changes.

To solidify such phenomena is to reduce their scientific reality: 'Scientific objects [...] are unstable concatenations of representations. To record the transformation – from nature to second nature (abstraction or scientific empiricism), under the carefully controlled conditions [...] the tangled complexity of nature is slowed down or speeded up, winnowed or enriched, measured and modelled, probed by instruments, and translated into graphics.' [25]

Translating these stagnated moments into interpretations and abstract notation, such as drawings or graphical inscriptions, is a crucial step in creating a comprehensive and meaningful archive. Drawings serve as containers of information, abstract devices conveying convoluted data 'incompletely, yet in one image'. [26] The reduction of the complex system to a single layer (or a combination, or stratification) requires the reduction of concrete, lived experience of reality into a form of 'certainty' of data. By creating a drawing, the ultimate purpose is to reduce every element of the phenomenon to a measurable entity, [27] a legible image to think with, to operate with, to analyse with and to use for descriptive purposes. These types of inscriptions – whether visible at all times, hidden, partially dormant, or triggered by

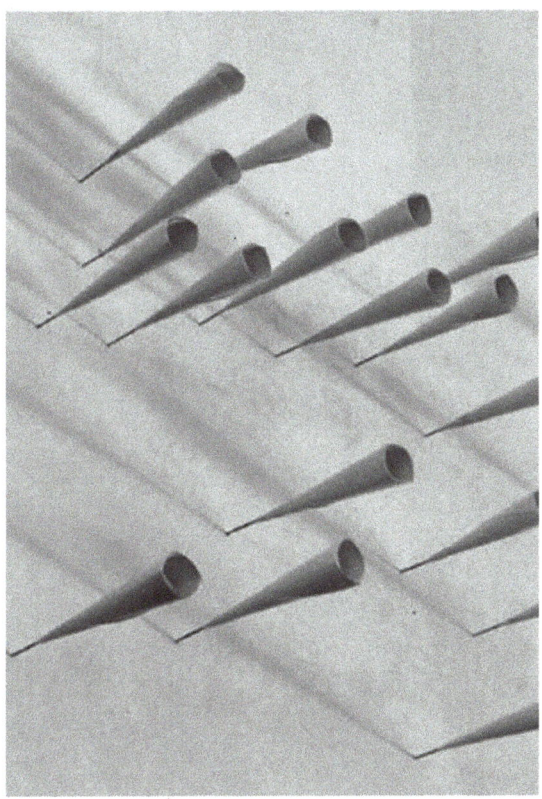

Figure 11 — AG (Tomas Garcia de la Huerta). Generic Artifact (2021)
Blowing. Empowering the fragility. Paper, needles, glue, copper tube (blowgun), air.

Figure 12 — AG (Tomas Garcia de la Huerta). Generic Artifact (2018)
The gravity of memory. Rope, bronze, cord, wire, stone cobblestone.

specific changes – represent design tactics and memory mechanisms that combine digital and physical formations. The relationship between permanence and temporality in creating such tapestries and two-dimensional engravings for encapsulating knowledge of climatic heritage reimagines architecture as an active participant. Within the DS18 context, the creative and design agency of working with archival climatic data implies the ability to synthesise data into culturally relevant or humanly meaningful 'secondary artefacts' built around a specific climate or novel weather event.

Anexact Three-Dimensional Geometries

Architecture has the potential to become the material organiser for archival information. Because of its predilection for fixity and stasis, **(Fig. 11 & 12)** in opposition to weather and meteorology, it represents a privileged site for the elision of eidetic geometry and holistic organisation. [28] A physical space for memory and records, it brings legibility and aesthetical dimension and rethinks the ideas of mnemonics. On one hand, structures construct and envelop their own microclimates, containing amorphous material and invisible atmospheres; and on the other hand, they preserve external (and internal) climatic influences through their envelope indentations, by balancing the record of form and its generation over time (parameters and nested information).

Usually, architecture is strategically positioned at crucial junctions within landscapes (**Fig. 10**), acting as a channel between the atmosphere and the earth's crust, where the surroundings interact with solid, gas and liquid components, catalysing the exchange of energy, matter and life. The horizontal datum of the ground, a critical threshold, becomes the absolute line where the main transactions occur. The active relationship between site conditions and building design proves to be a continuous evolution with the environment through, for example, resilience, relinquishment, restoration, amplification, amelioration and reconciliation. As such, 'buildings breath in unison with their landscape', [29] and they have the potential to become real-time recorders of climatic schedules and conditions, to offer a 'bio-climatic diagnosis' and to embody various forms of life. [30]

The environment gives rise to complex, hardly simplifiable shapes. [31] Its amorphousness of entity,

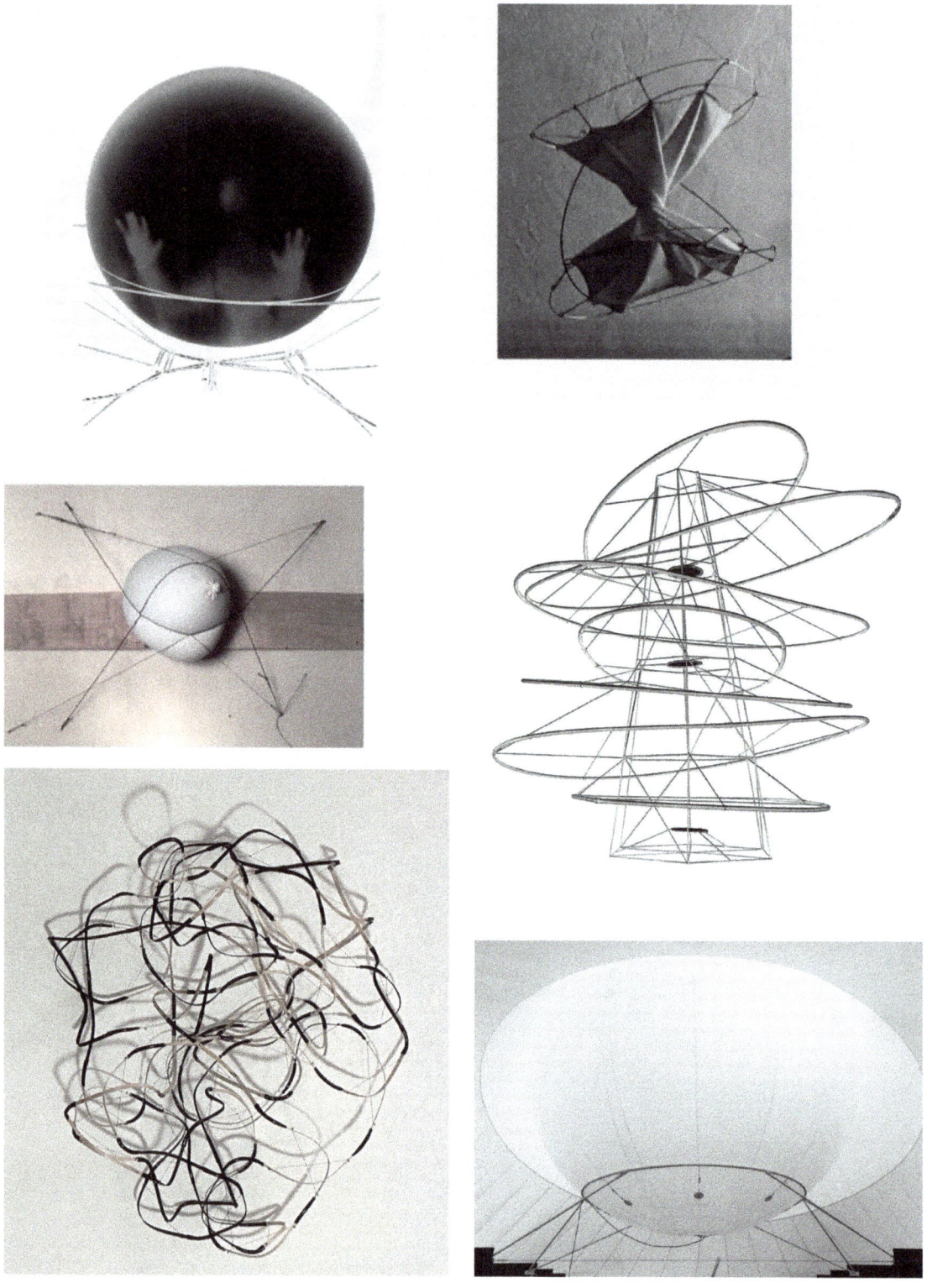

Figure 13 – GA Studio (Tomas Garcia de la Huerta and Xaviera Gleixner) - Generic Artifact / AG (Tomas Garcia de la Huerta) – Generic Artifact (2017–2024). Artifacts of various kinds. They express tension, surface tension, compression, gravity, fragility, and virtuality. The dialogue between stable and unstable elements, physical and virtual.

Figure 14 – Georgios Malliaropulous. Heat Exchange (2023-2050). Adaptable melting wax amphitheatre, morphing according to extreme weather conditions in Scotland.

characterised by its lack of a defined structure or form, requires innovative methodologies to quantify its fluidity (**Fig. 13**) and delimit things that are whole. Air requires a form, with an enclosed envelope that defines various degrees of stability. (**Fig. 14**) The logic of curvilinearity argues for an active involvement with external events in the folding, bending and curving of the form. [32] Life sciences and disciplines dedicated to the study of vital matter (embryology, virology, biology and geology to name a few) begin with studies of formlessness and the intention of describing these vague entities via geometric descriptions. The analysis of biometric shape changes often utilises flexible, adaptable geometries to illustrate how unforeseen external forces are integrated into the ongoing morphogenetic evolution of form. [33]

In *Probable Geometries*, Lynn proposes an adequate description of amorphous matter through 'anexact yet rigorous' [34] geometries, as opposed to relying on exact or inexact forms. On one hand, he argues that traditional, rigid geometries, 'exact' forms – those that can be reduced eidetically, precise in measure and contour, visually fixed and identically repeatable (i.e. a sphere) – are structures that only offer pure and ideal proportions. In line with the etymology of the word 'geometry', which translates to 'earth measurement', it reflects the power of linking spatial relationships, land and air matter (such as astronomy). On the other hand, Lynn claims that 'inexact' forms – those figures that cannot be fixed or reduced because their contours cannot be described – are insufficient for capturing the complexities of vital fluids and substances. Irreducible but precise anexact geometries are typically associated with disciplines that are forced to develop models that must remain incomplete. For example, the geologic sciences of the earth cannot develop a single fixed model for the continuous transformation of matter. Therefore geologists employ anexact geometries to measure various contours before they are reduced to clear statements. (**Fig. 15**) These statements are rigorous, describing local effects with a precision not possible in alternative global systems, yet many resist being reduced to exact forms and lack completion.

If these geometries allow for the incorporation of unpredictable external forces and continuous morphogenetic developments, architectural spaces become 'continuous registries'. These contain large bodies of information, 'time-capsules' of their own evolution of design and material usage in relation to their engagement with the earth's resources, climatic archives that describe fluid, flexible, open, provisional, incomplete, indefinite and irreducible effects of climate over its envelope, as well as instruments of interaction and archival gauge. The three-dimensional models become tools for archiving, instruments of knowledge production and distribution. 'Architecture form' becomes a cognitive tool to investigate, analyse and understand situations and to speculatively reassemble them at a range of scales, [35] linking information and design, immaterial and material flows, energetic conversations and human activities, and ultimately providing air with an anatomy. Defined primarily by the envelope, architecture form and its threshold gives tactility, programme and materiality to climatic archives.

Conclusion

Archives serve as roadmaps, dictionaries, and card indexes, [36] simply awaiting new queries and doubts and new hypotheses. [37] In its origins, knowing started to be understood as a matter of creating relationships and classifying impossible paradoxes. [38] In a productive archive, this requires a forensic view of collected fragments, a critical eye for managing information, and imagination to stimulate new narratives and methods of thinking about the relationship between climate, computation and culture.

Items become worthy of archiving, only when they cease to act as stable markers of climate 'reality' and when, through calibrations, moves and transformations (through design), they become creations fit for future and outside use. The variety and heterogeneity of climate archives could be defined by form, location, content or proprietor, yet the boundaries between archives and collections (including museums, libraries and data banks) continue to be historically fluid.

Climatic archives maintain a fine balance between rational classification and imaginary meandering. They are architectural, in the sense that they enable the flow of communication between data and their ordering, curation, ease of access and montage – creating a pictorial (two-dimensional) and a volumetric (three-dimensional) assemblage. These are reflections, rather than perfect containers of information. The case studies for the creation of tapestries and 'probable geometries' move architecture's fixed orthogonality through scientific disciplines and closer to the behaviour of vital matter, while retaining a rigorous system of measure.

Today's archival urgency is determined by the speed at which we are losing digital media, which is much faster than ever before. The famous term 'Digital Dark Ages', [39] coined by Vint Cerf, indicates fear that 'little or no record' of the twenty-first century will survive for future generations because of the lack of clear technological digital preservation strategies. Here, spatial practices, at various scales, invite an alternative solution: one of creating physical imprints, encodings in tactile materiality, or formulating physical encryptions and tectonic assemblies of atmospheric systems.

Future archives, informed by multi-scalar thinking and (proto)-ecological sensibility, will need access to data on the earth's energy flows in order to maintain the overall energetic balance. The fact that we design archives as sites to hold historical records of atmospheric events reflects not only our wish to preserve the past, but also our expectation that such a record may serve a future – not in the sense of random serendipity, but by virtue of the archive's diachronic growth.

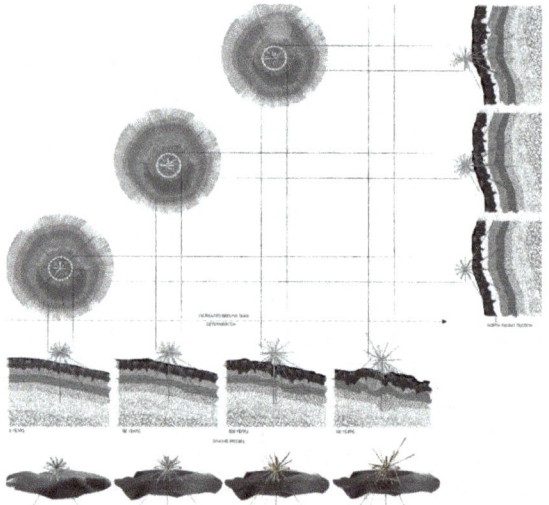

Figure 15 – Helen Windsor. The Seeping City. Monument to Permafrost thaws over time.

Notes

(01) C. Fisher and S. Leisz, 'Introduction to the Earth Archive Congress', *Youtube - Earth Archive channel*, 22 June 2021, https://youtu.be/c2_d8th945g?si=PvZpoaGGjn99XaPA.

(02) Press Office, 'Victorian rainfall data rescued', *MetOffice.gov.uk*, 25 March 2022, https://www.metoffice.gov.uk/about-us/news-and-media/media-centre/weather-and-climate-news/2022/rescued-victorian-rainfall-data-released.

(03) Historical climate data, environmental records, cultural heritage, geospatial data, legal documents, and digital records encompass temperature and precipitation records, sea level changes, glacier movements, biodiversity metrics, demographics, and multimedia documentation etc.

(04) M. P. Nastou, S.C. Zerefos, 'Effects of climate change on open air heritage: a review and the situation in the region of Mediterranean' in *Heritage Science 12*, 367 (2024). https://doi.org/10.1186/s40494-024-01484-y.

(05) L. Daston, 'Sciences of the Archives explained by Lorraine Daston', *YouTube – Latest Thinking*, 09 March 2017, https://www.youtube.com/watch?v=iPSa4Ub8FU8&ab_channel=LatestThinking.

(06) L. Daston, 'Introduction: Third Nature', in L. Daston (ed.) *Science in the Archives. Past, Presents, Futures.* The University Chicago Press, 2017, p. 6.

(07) V. Jankovic, 'Montage and Metamorphosis: Climatological Data Archiving and the US National Climate Program', in L. Daston (ed) *Science in the Archives. Past, Presents, Futures*, The University Chicago Press, 2017, p. 228.

(08) One of a few examples of uncertainty and political agency include the *NOAA Climate Change* website suspended in 2018-2019 due to federal shutdown around budget. NOAA Climate Chnage Website Suspended During Government Shutdown, *Columbia Law School, Columbia Climate School*, 23 January 2018, https://climate.law.columbia.edu/content/noaa-climate-change-website-suspended-during-government-shutdown.

(09) V. Jankovic, p. 234.

(10) R. Bottazzi, *Digital Architecture beyond computers: Fragments of a Cultural History of Computational Design*, London, New York: Bloomsbury Publishing, 2018, Preface, p. X.

(11) V. Jankovic, p. 228.

(12) Ibid., p. 13.

(13) L. Manovich, 'Database as Symbolic Form', in V. Vesna (ed), *Database Aesthetics: Art in the Age of Information Overflow*, Minneapolis: University of Minnesota Press. 2007), p.44.

(14) R. Bottazzi, p. 13.

(15) Ibid., p. 80.

(16) Ibid., p. 190.

(17) V. Jankovic, p. 225.

(18) Thom, R., 1975. Structural Stability and Morphogenesis. Translated by D.H. Fowler. Reading, MA: Addison-Wesley.

(19) N. Dell' Unto, '3D models and knowledge production', in I. Huvila (ed) *Archaeology and Archaeological Information in the Digital Society*, Routledge, 2018, p. 54.

(20) D. Sepkoski, 'The Earth as Archive: Contingency, Narrative and the History of Life', in L. Daston (ed) *Science in the Archives. Past, Presents, Futures*, The University Chicago Press, 2017, p. 75.

(21) C. Damonoske, 'Drought In Central Europe Reveals Cautionary 'Hunger Stones' In Czech River', in *NPR.org*, 24 August 2018, https://www.npr.org/2018/08/24/641331544/drought-in-central-europe-reveals-cautionary-hunger-stones-in-czech-river.

(22) Similar global examples include Japan's Tsunami Stones, the Nazca lines in Peru, the Equatorial and Prime Meridian Markers, NASA's Golden Record, 10,000 Year Clock, etc.

(23) R. Bottazzi, p. 97.

(24) W. Mitchell, 'Improvisations, Instruments and Algorithms', in S. Piedmont-Palladino (ed) *Tools of the Imagination: Drawing Tools and Technologies from the Eighteenth Century to the Present*, Princeton Architectural Press, New York, 2007, p. 117.

(25) Rheinberger, H-J., 2017. Montage and Metamorphosis: Climatological Data Archiving and the US National Climate Program. In: L. Daston, ed. *Science in the Archives: Past, Presents, Futures*, Chicago: The University of Chicago Press, p. 225.

(26) E. Panofsky, *Meaning in the Visual Arts*, Chicago, 1955.

(27) P. V. Aureli, *Architecture and Abstraction*, The MIT Press, 2023, p.53.

(28) G. Lynn, *Folds, Bodies & Blobs Collected Essay*, Lettre volée (2nd ed), 2004, p. 41.

(29) C, Girot, 'Forward: Breathing Shades of Design', in S. Benedito (ed), *Atmosphere Anatomies. On Design, Weather, and Sensation*, Zurich, Lars Müller Publishers, 2021, p. 7.

(30) P. V. Aureli, p. 22.

(31) R. Bottazzi, p. 39.

(32) The logic of curvilinearity that can be characterised by the involvement of outside forces in the development of form. This concept was developed by Leibniz and many resonances with S. Kwinter's discussions of biological space.

(33) [...] such examples include stereology, random sectioning, tubular anisotropic elements etc. In G. Lynn, *Folds, Bodies & Blobs Collected Essay*, Lettre volée (2nd ed), 2004, p. 85.

(34) Derrida, J., 1989. *Edmund Husserl's Origin of Geometry: An Introduction*. Translated by J. Leavey Jr. Lincoln, NE: University of Nebraska Press.

(35) H. Sarkis, R.S. Barrio and G. Kozlowski, 'Architecture and the World Scale', in H. Sarkis, R.S. Barrio and G. Kozlowski (eds.), *The World as an Architecture Project*, Cambridge, MA: MIT Press, 2020, p.10.

(36) H. U. Obrist, E. de Waal, 'Archives as Places of Memory and Encounter', in E.de Diego and H.U Obrist (ed), *Future Archives*, Norman Foster Foundation Press, 2023, p. 46.

(37) L. Daston, p. 6.

(38) J-P. Chupin and C. Cucuzzella, '108 Embodiments of Potential Architecture. On Sisyphean Digital Libraries of Projects', in F. Goffi (ed.) *The Routledge Companion to Architectural Drawings and Models. From Translating to Archiving, Collecting and Displaying*, 1st ed. London: Routledge, 2022, p. 371.

(39) P. Ghosh, 'Google's Vint Cerf Warns of 'digital Dark Age', *BBC News Science and Environment*, 13 February 2015, https://www.bbc.co.uk/news/science-environment-31450389.

DIGITAL REPOSITORIES

LAURA NICA AND BEN POLLOCK

The primary aim of these brief case studies is to reflect on the impact of three types of digital repositories, that Design Studio 18 experimented with in the past years.

Digital repositories serve are platforms or containers designed to aggregate, store, preserve, disseminate, and provide access to digital content. Users of these platforms not only can explore but also comment on, critique, popularise architectural and experimental projects. The studio's type of work demanded the digital, as fine-line representations and rich 3D assets would display higher resolution properties; rather than physical bound, paper-based catalogues such as *Open Studio* or physical exhibitions.

Building a small virtual museum exhibition (using *Sketch Fab 3D*), logging and utilising in real-time a vast series of collected material (using *Miro Board*), as well as archiving the everyday (using *Instagram*), provided the studio with multiple versions of digital twins. While all three types deal with representations, these contain various gradients of interactivity, curation authorship and hierarchical information display. As virtual replicas of physical entities, systems and processes (whether these are drawings, models and sketches, crit panel, tutorial tables etc), they embody a holistic and constructivist approach, unlocking new possibilities of activating historical information and formulations of 'data banks'.

Accelerated by the context of the global emergency which started in March 2020 (the novel coronavirus pandemic), traditional methods such as live final crits, portfolio-paper assessments, and end-of-year exhibitions physical material were removed, as the phatic and spatial elements of the design process changed.

As amateur archivists and digital designers, the primary aim on creating DS18 website, was to encourage exchanges of architectural thinking (for alumni, current and future students), activate conversations not bound by geographical constraints (with distant audiences) and pose questions of digital artefacts - what concept of the archive can be pursued by a design studio that is appropriate and explores the digital forms to engage with the radical transformation of the database experience and memory?

The three examples provided will illustrate, on one hand, an uncontrollable, intuitive, intertwined, and multifaceted process, and on the other hand, present an artistic strategy for preserving memory. As digital media is an ever-increasing archive in which no piece of data is lost, the vast repository of objects, constantly changing and recombining into new formulations, embodies the dynamic interplay of diverse forces that shape an evolving database condition, ultimately defining the studio's identity, through categorisation and classification of its documentation.

Archiving Studio Chapters

In response to the pandemic constraints in 2020, the studio transitioned to a new website to share student work. Initially a substitute for the traditional end-of-year physical exhibition, the website evolved into an annually updated archive showcasing each cohort's thematic explorations and theoretical frameworks. Each academic year is documented with dedicated studio pages detailing the studio's brief, thematic ideas, and theoretical framing, followed by a tile index of student pages. In alignment with the studio's ethos, all students select and showcase work of their choosing, ensuring equal representation of all students and their year's collective efforts and accomplishments.

Since its launch, the DS18 website has garnered significant global attention, with 43,000 page views from over 100 countries. Notably, 60% of this traffic originates from organic searches related to specific students work and its associated research teams. This widespread visibility has led to international opportunities, including guest critiques from Australia, conference invitations in Germany, and further publication prospects for student projects (from the UK, US/MIT, Spain and the Netherlands).

The DS18 website exemplifies how digital platforms can effectively archive and disseminate academic work, extending its reach beyond geographical limitations and fostering global engagement. It serves as a testament to the adaptability and resilience of the studio in the face of unprecedented challenges, ensuring the continuity and evolution of its educational mission.

2013/14 Fracked Urbanism

2014/15 Energy Economies

2015/16 Emergent Energies in a Coral Archipelago

2016/17 Monsoon Assemblies: Chennai

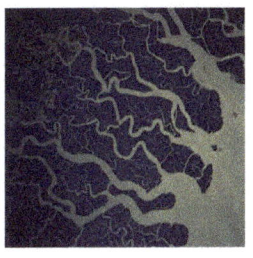
2017/18 Monsoon Assemblies: Dhaka

2018/19 Monsoon Assemblies: Myanmar

2019/20 Jet Stream: Norway

2020/21 Carbon Transitions: UK

2021/22 Climate Futures: Dungeness

2022/23 Thermal Domains: UK

2023/24 Flows, Forms & Functions

2024/25 Actions, Intra-actions & Uncertainties

Screenshot of DS18 main website. Available at: designstudio18.com.

Archiving the Everyday

Images are data, and all imaging is, knowingly or not, an act of data processing. The quantity of images and visual representations produced by DS18 students throughout the academic year is extensive. Working with data-intensive models, complex computational morphologies of various resolutions and diverse digital file-formats – pose a question of extraction, of capturing and of selecting an indexing method that would allow on one hand for consistency, legibility, but also a more accessible and casual platform.

Within the commodified realm of social media, the studio's Instagram page operates as a collective 'brand' composed of an annually changing cohort of contributors. Given that it does not market design services or directly sell a product for financial gain, we effectively capitalise on the platform's algorithmic structures for fleeting moments of influence. In playing this game, we are deeply a wear of its limitations and pit falls, however in conjunction with the website's formality, we see the studios profile as a space to casually archive work-in-progress, ideas, field trip photographs, and spontaneous studio snapshots. This real-time documentation fosters a culture of transparency and continuous feedback, indirectly encouraging and promoting individual work to a wider audience beyond the studio. It allows designers to reflect on their past work and engage with a broader audience. Additionally, Instagram's visual and interactive nature fosters a sense of 'artificial community' among design enthusiasts who share common values with the studio, be it climate-emergency and ecological principles or spatial and representational research. Pedagogically, it serves as a valuable educational resource, providing students with a visual matrix of the studio's representation, creating a slow, cumulative bank of captured material.

A relative quick process, of posting a series of standardised representations in a certain format (squared display, or short GIFs/animations and time-restrained 'stories') contrast however with the carefully curated descriptions that go alongside the images. Through precise labelling and semantic tagging, these photos can be categorised and contextualised, making them more accessible and searchable for users. The metadata that goes along the visuality of the post, helps convey the architectural intent, the style, the historical context, the research references, as well as the design intent, using certain "#"; thereby enriching the viewer's understanding and engagement.

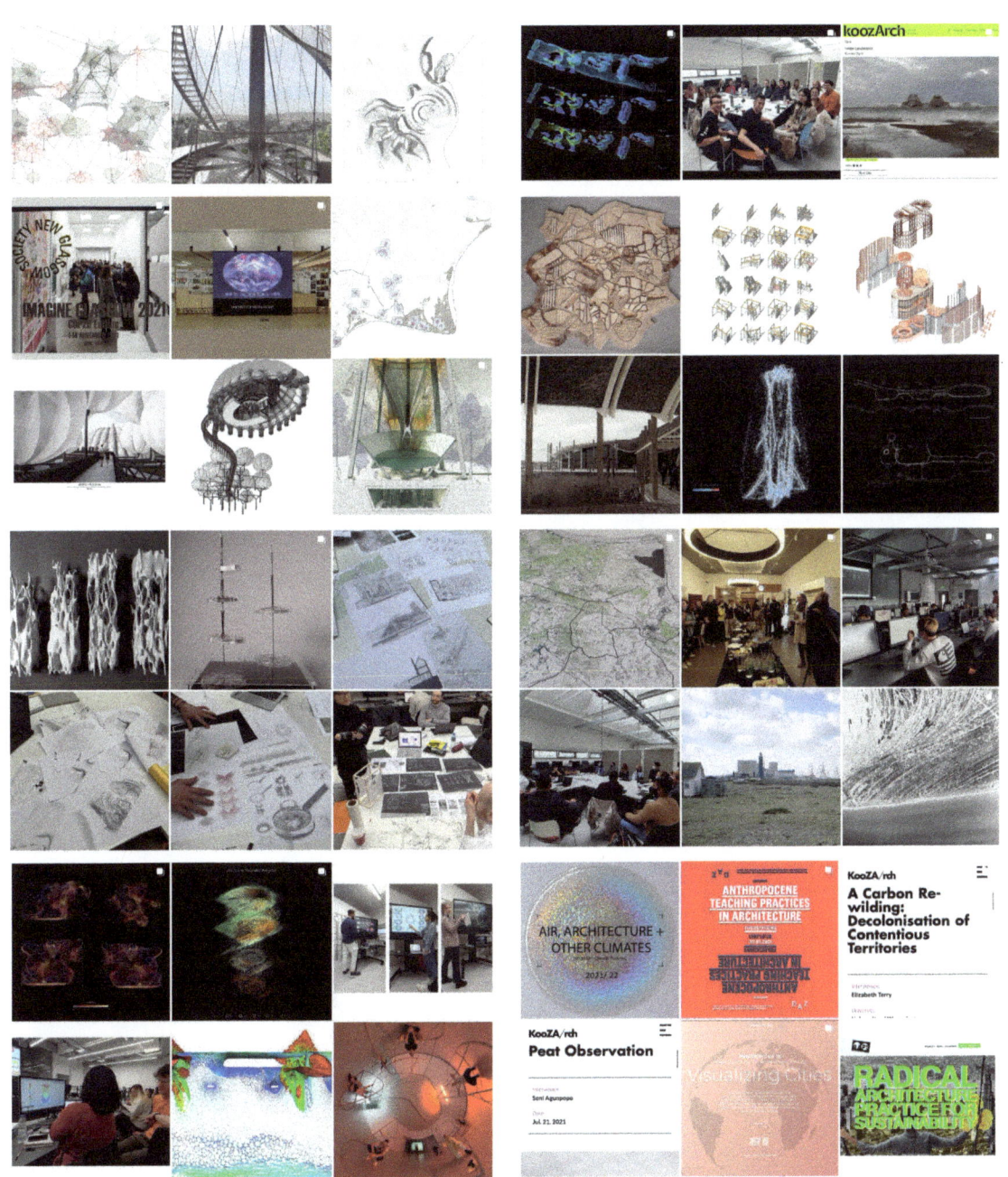

Screenshot of DS18 instagram. Available at: @ds18_westminster.

Digital Totem: A Curated Virtual Exhibition

The idea of a virtual museum is not entirely new in the digital age, but it is derived from the early twentieth century. As Erkki Huhtamo (2002) has illuminated in his media-archaeological study, such pioneers as Laszlo Moholy-Nagy, El Lissitzky and Frederick Kiesler in this era attempted to transform the exhibition space of the traditional museum in way that render the artworks to be "integral elements of a total environment that envelops the visitors and encourages them into a dynamic relationship with the space and all its dimensions and elements". (01)

The *Arctic Ecologies: An Atmospheric Assemblage* is a virtual model, prepared by DS18 students for the 2020 exhibition, part of an alternative to *Open*, the University organised end-of-year student show. Containing 18 different students 'layers'. These levels are abstract interpretations, conceptual synthesis of each proposal, including a hyperlink to more details of each project.

The model is rendered through temperature extremes, with tones of blue and red corresponding to low and elevated temperature anomalies within the Norwegian context. These tones change through time and perspective with each orbit rendered, alluding to the complex dynamics of atmospheric temperature change, and the uneven stresses it exerts on these delicately balanced systems. The project layers are arranged according to their geographical spatial references and distributed from the ground to the air.

A monument for 'future memory', this digital tectonic unit allows objects and layers to be adjusted, replaced, juxtaposed in a continuous curatorial process by the platform' user, in real-time. By spinning around the model, panning, and zooming into selected areas, certain details are rendered to unpack unexpected overlaps, densities of data and new representational compositions.

As a prototypical three-dimensional virtual environment, designed as a small virtual space, did more than just propose a new museum model. It raised questions about storage, capacity, erasure, time, latency, memory, resolution and framing because it changed both the objects on display and how visitors interacted with them.

(01) P. Bogner and G. Zillner, 'Vienna 1924. Hotspot of the Avant-garde. Frederick Kiesler's International Exhibition of New Theater Technique, 2018, https://worldartfoundations.com/kiesler-foundation-vienna-1924-hotspot-avantgarde/.

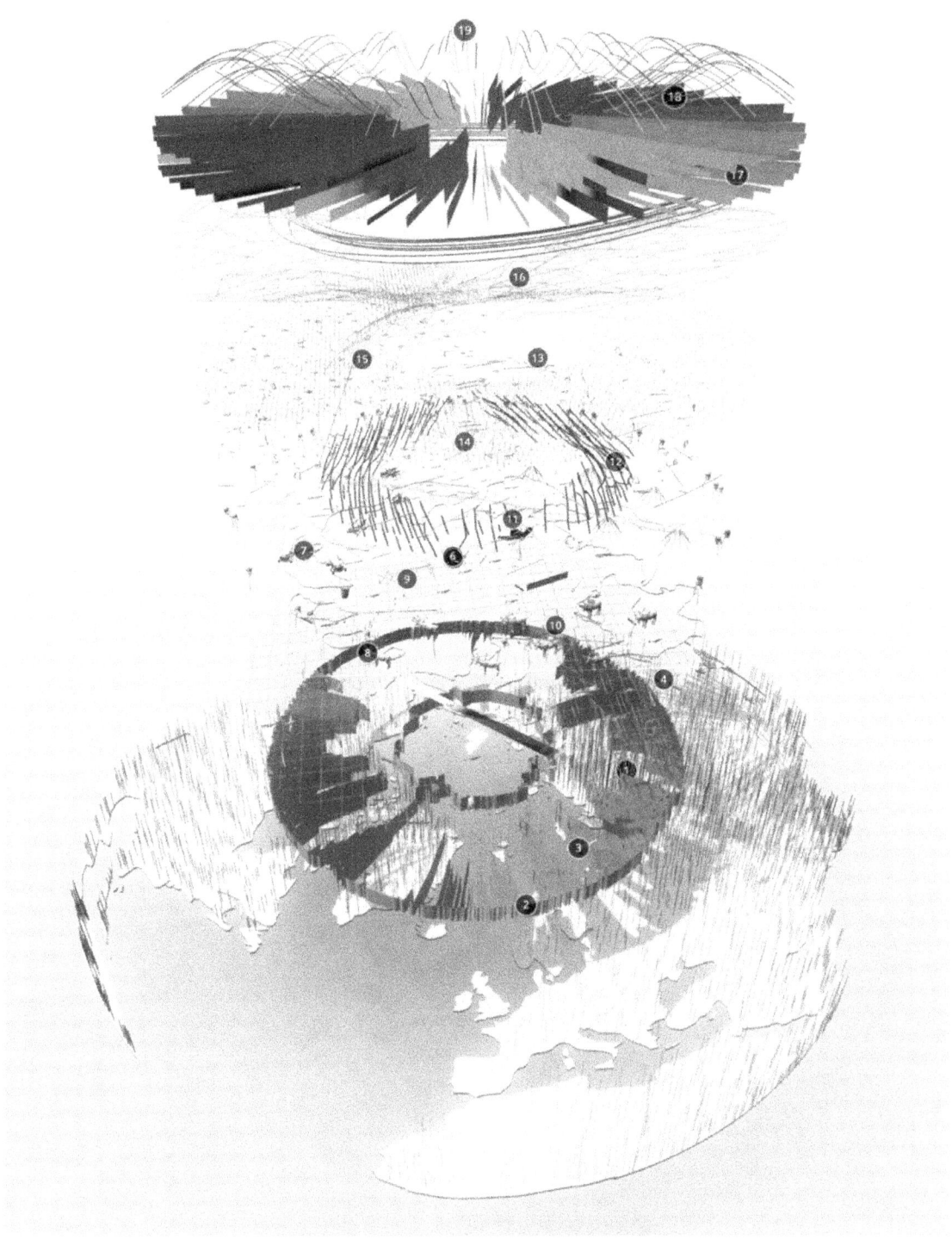

Screenshot of Digital Totem. Available at: https://designstudio18.com/Arctic-Ecologies-An-Atmospheric-Assemblage (SketchFab).

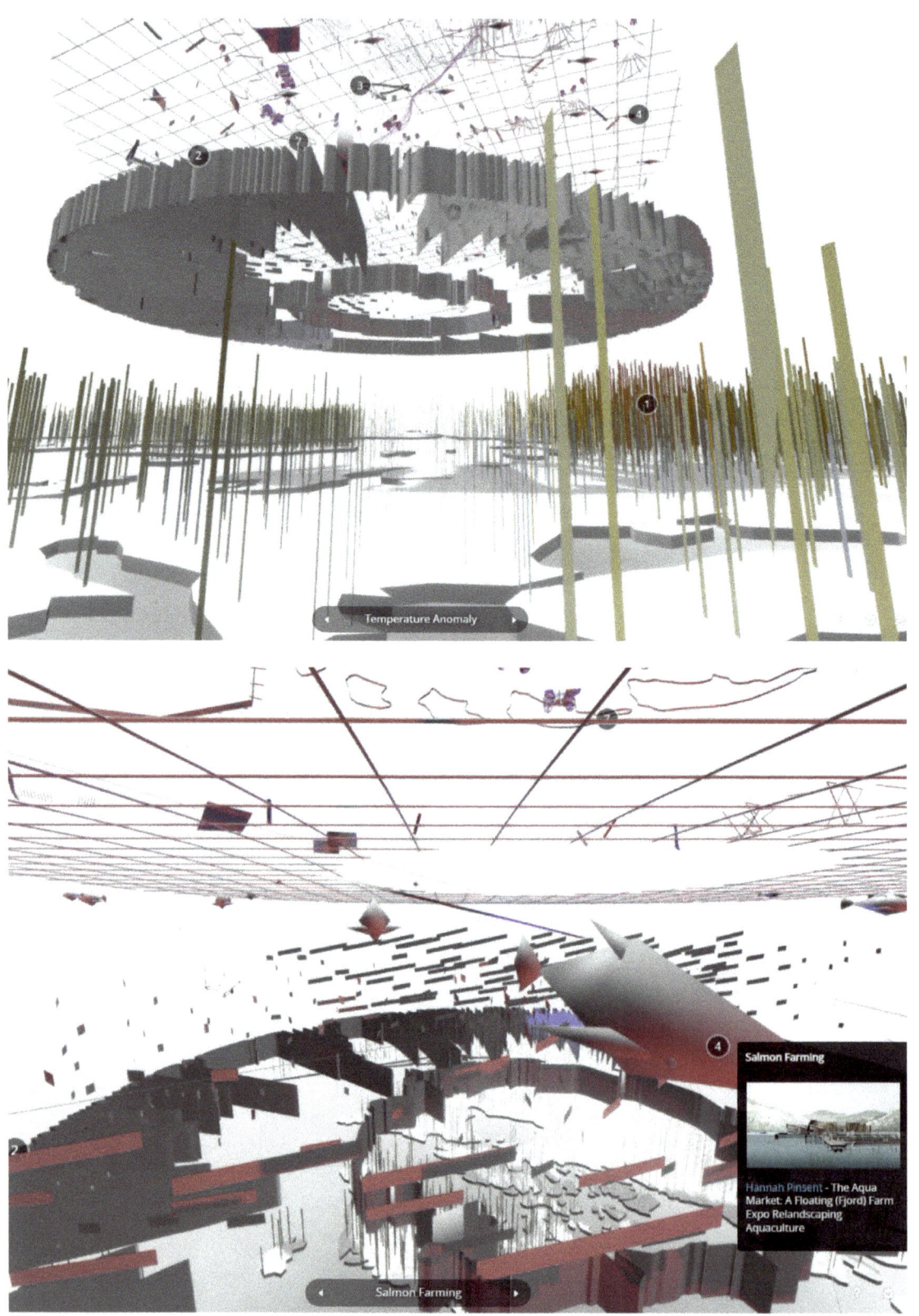

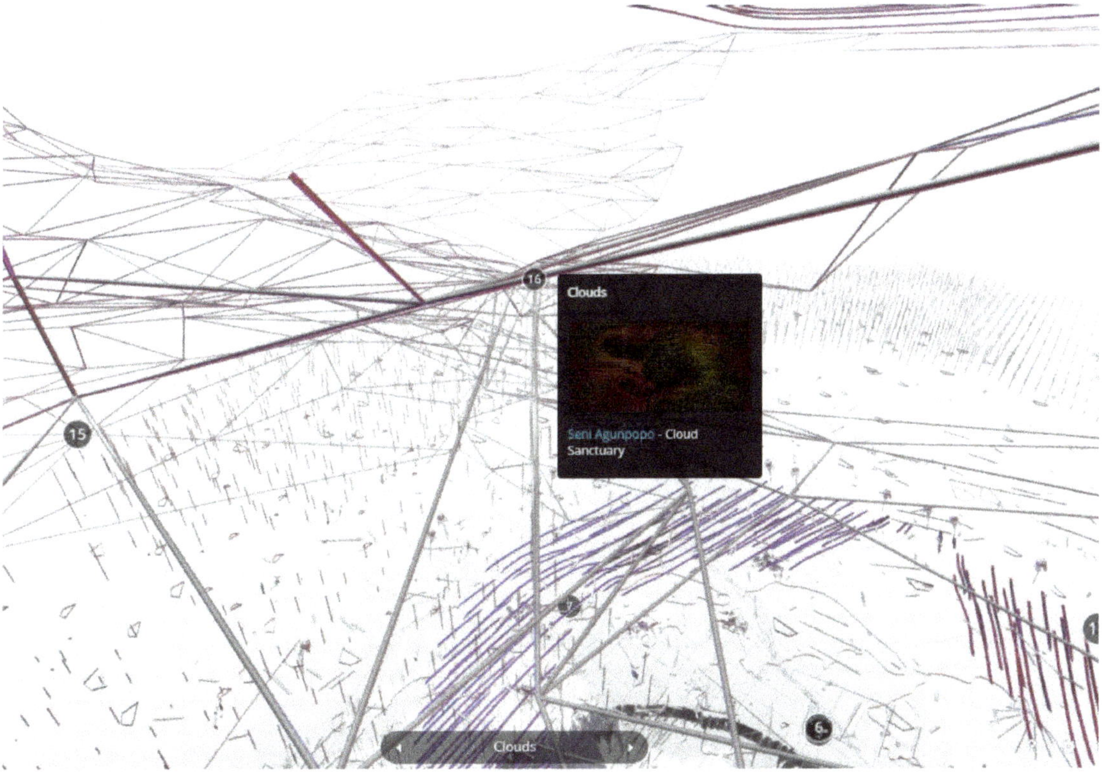

185

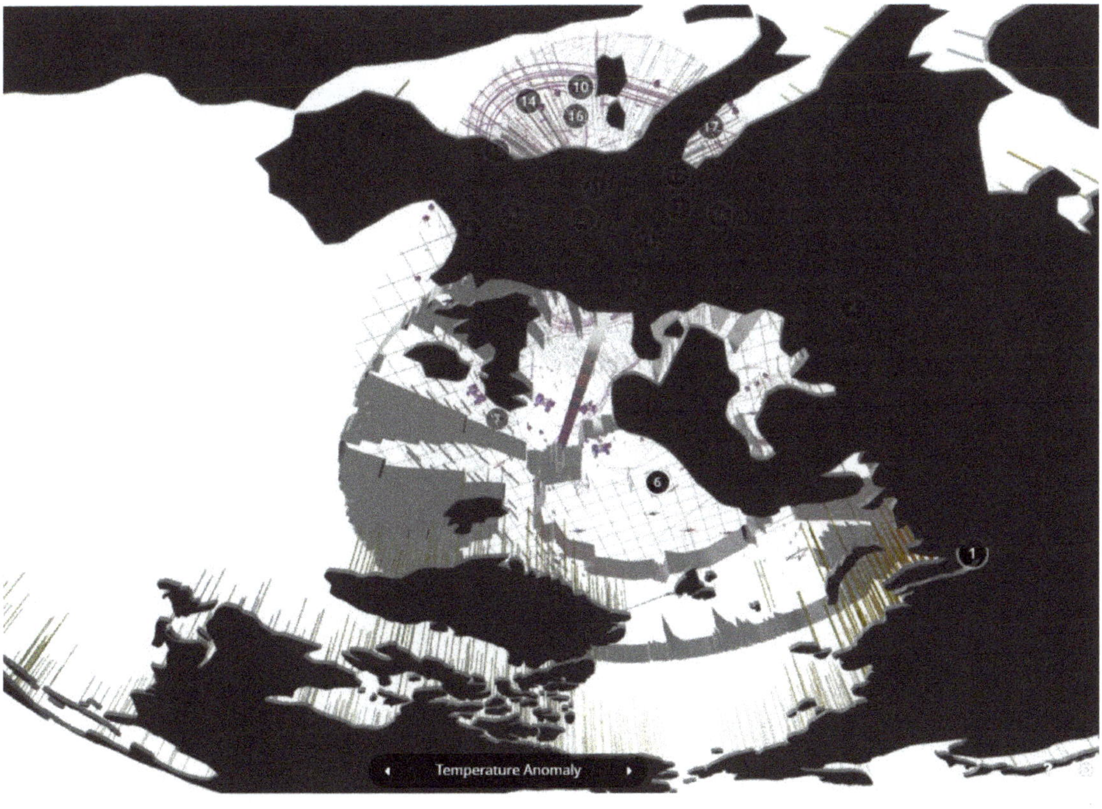

Interactive Repository (Miro)

Miro is an online whiteboard platform that enables users to collaborate in real-time on a virtual canvas. While Miro is now ubiquitous in both academia and practice, DS18 was one of the first design studios to implement, popularise its use and experiment with it. Primarily used during design tutorials, students were encouraged to use this as a digital log to record both the production of material (either as brainstorming sheets or final portfolio evaluations) and feedback during design studio tutorials.

The virtual space became a highly graphical 'interactive tableau'. The permutability of the virtual allows for open-ended deposition, repositioning, arranging and clustering of an exponential volume of data, including information searching, design precedents, images, text fragments, links, sketches, tectonic assemblies, screenshots or renders of 3D-assets and drawings.

The *Digital Charette*, which took place during a 3-hour long session in January 2021, involved over 23 people, simultaneously producing, sketching and uploading ideas for each other's projects. Based on the *Double Diamond* process, [01] which emphasised divergent and convergent thinking as well as methods to explore problems and design solutions effectively, the studio's aspirations focused on evolving ideas through iterative cycles.

Starting from a tabulated framework, containing a list of student's names and a brief descriptions of projects and research ideas, the *Sketched Matrix* maintained clarity and order. It served as an experimental 'playground', facilitating a real-time exchange of ideas, and constant reformulation of information management. This involved layering and creating palimpsests, where sketches were drawn on top of existing ones and continuously redrawn. This approach encourages participation beyond the traditional critique, which was often too passive, fostering a more dynamic and interactive pedagogy.

In contrast to the traditional studio, which engages in solitary coach-and-student problem solving with the help of a sketch; designers work with virtual assets in a fluid way, mobilising these new digital sources. Certain inactive digital repository assets become activated (unexpectedly or to contrast an idea), with fragments and components used in the design process. The connections in the web of questions, positions and arguments define by qualified relations like content, temporal evolvement, and hierarchical order. This interactive synthetic register, formulated concepts, provoked thought and augmented design as a participatory critical enquiry. Overall, this involved a different mode of communication with materials and shapes, with hierarchy of digital content, leading to a different type of cognitive research based practice.

(01) Design Council. 'The Double Diamond', Design Council, https://www.designcouncil.org.uk/our-resources/the-double-diamond/.

(top) Screenshot of DS18 Miro board during student charrette session and (middle and bottom) Portfolio preparation and reviews.

SELECTED STUDENT PROJECTS

MICRO-PLASTIC PARLIAMENT

KATHERINE DECHOW

Plastic is an ever increasing global issue and one of this generation's key environmental challenges. As a product, it has been engineered to last a lifetime. The consequence of this, is that every piece of plastic ever produced still exists today.

Micro-plastics are present everywhere and have received recent attention due to their persistent nature and detrimental impact on humans and the environment. The movement and distribution of micro-plastics is an under-researched topic. The studies which have been completed suggest that microplastics can reach and affect remote, sparsely inhabited areas through atmospheric transport.

This research seeks to develop an alternative discourse, exploring the political and aesthetic properties of micro-plastic (MP) in the atmosphere, by visualising the continuously shifting territories of air-borne micro-plastic (ABMP) pollution and making visible, the invisible consequences of urban life. By making ABMP pollution visible the project aims to encourage discussion and policy formation on micro-plastics in our atmosphere and will create a space for continuous public awareness of their huge prevalence and persistent nature.

Architecture is usually seen as an act of mediation- a process of blocking or absorbing various forms of energy. These same energy variables can become the subject of design, and the architecture, an act of amplification, used for strengthening and augmenting the energy flows in the environment. Boundary edges, which are usually defined by lines, points and surfaces are called into question when talking about energy flows and are perhaps better communicated by gradients of different intensities. Realising this shift towards a gradient boundary will have fundamental implications for how we design, represent and organise spaces. Throughout research, computational fluid dynamic tools are used to conduct extensive analysis of these shifting territories of wind velocity zones.

Located south-east and within 95km of Bergen, Norway, the site is downwind within the micro-plastic geographical limits of the city. The master plan of the site is defined by shifting wind patterns with high and low velocity areas helping to define programmatic function. In the low velocity spaces, and based on the process flow of Norwegian policy formation, the breakout space leads into the learning, discussion then decision spaces. The envelope of these spaces aims to actively accelerate the collection of MP, building up over time to conceal the building yet draw increased attention to the issue being discussed within. This is achieved through an envelope of statically charged rods, varying in length to correspond with openings and spaces for human interaction. These specialist components remain the central focus of the project. In the high velocity spaces, the surrounding landscape will engage the public and encourage participation in pushing political leaders to create policies for cleaner air. The high velocity zones will house wind stalks, which generate the electrical power for the site and the static charge of the micro-plastic envelope.

(right) Micro-Plastic Pathways. Overview of open-source data on average wind velocity and anthropogenic aerosol optical thickness collated and presented to capture the continually shifting energies of ABMP viewed across the site.

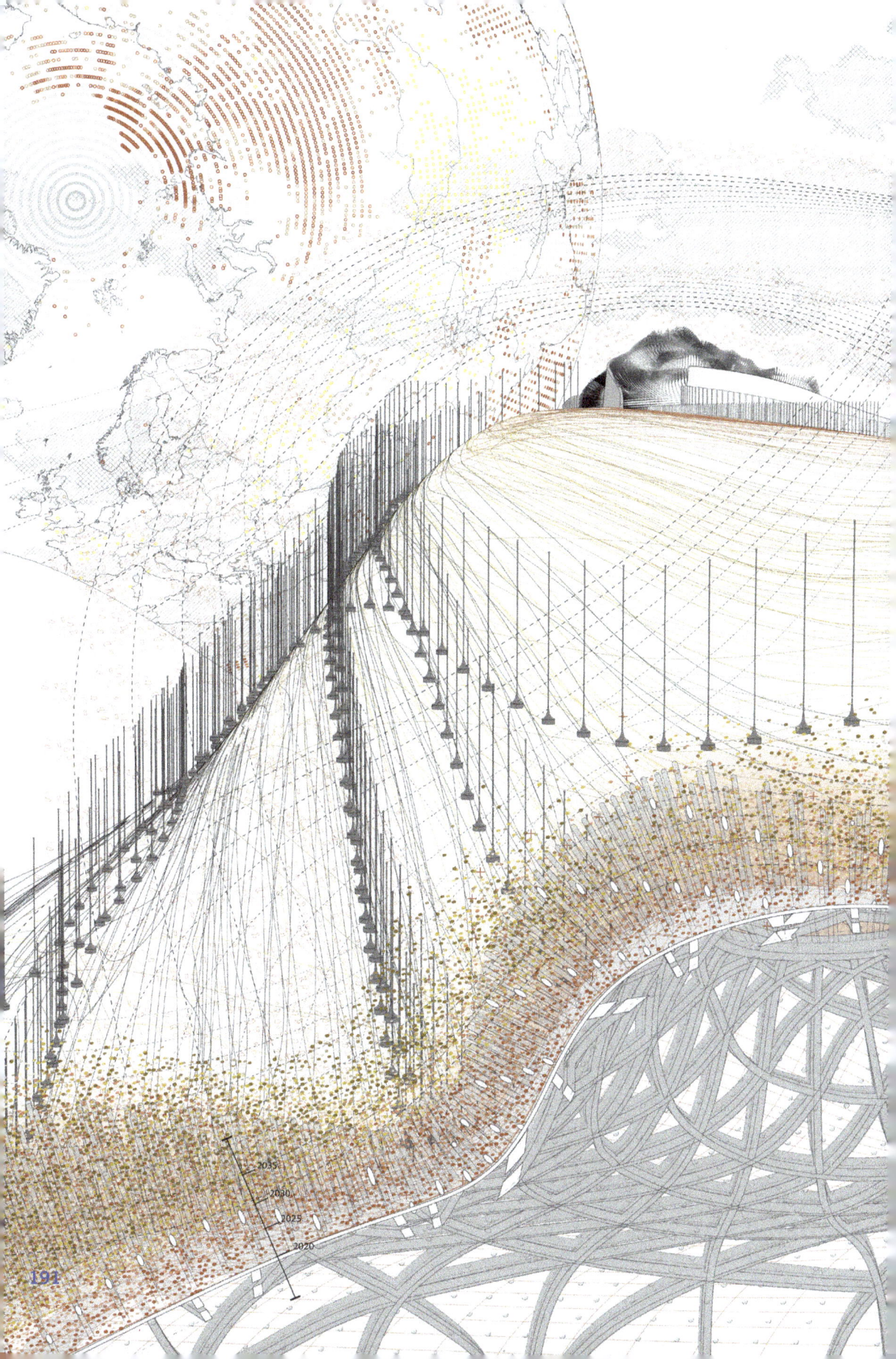

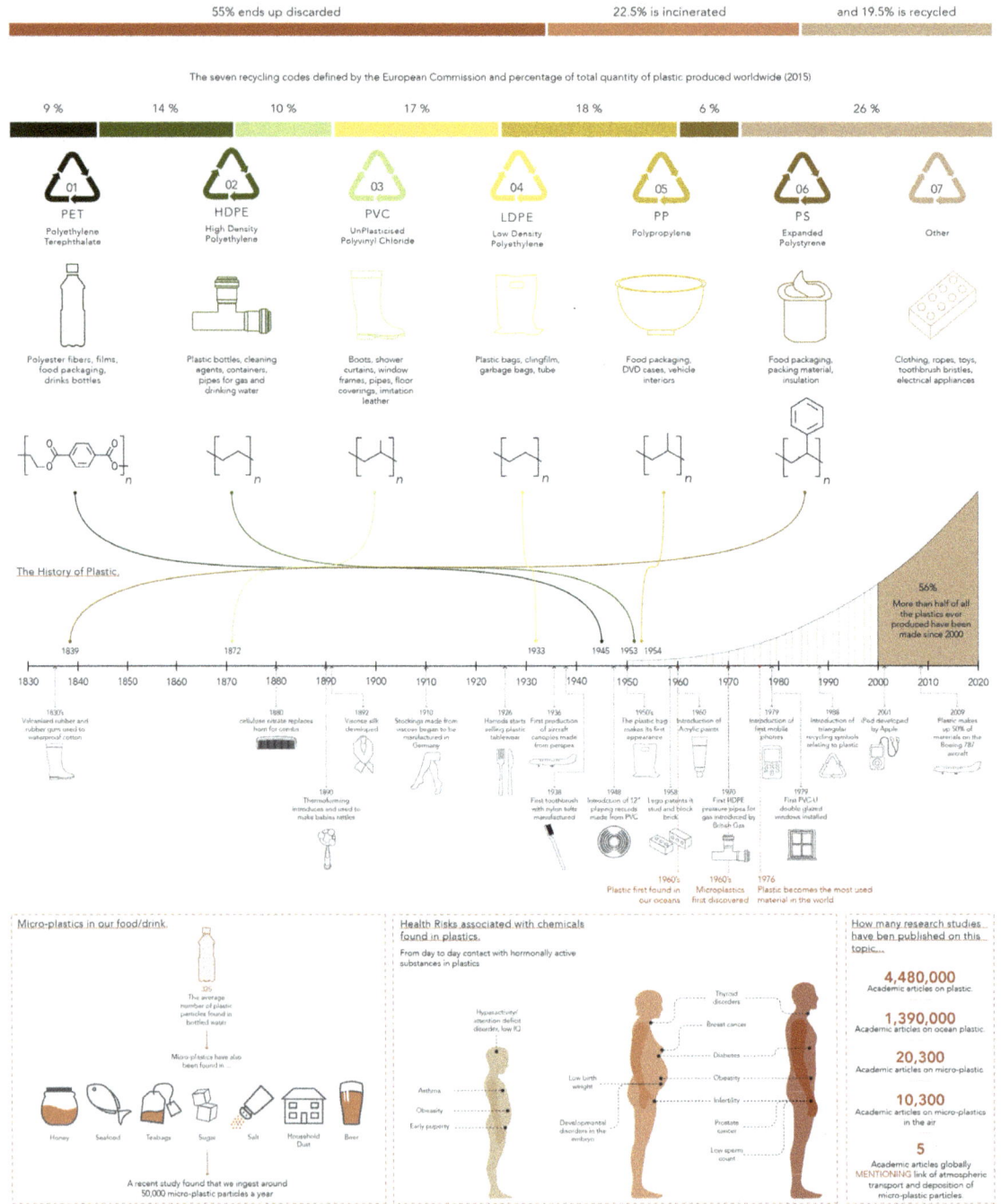

(top) Understanding Plastic. History, chemical properties, products and health risks.
(right) Spatial configuration under low velocity zones. Initial massing and arrangement.

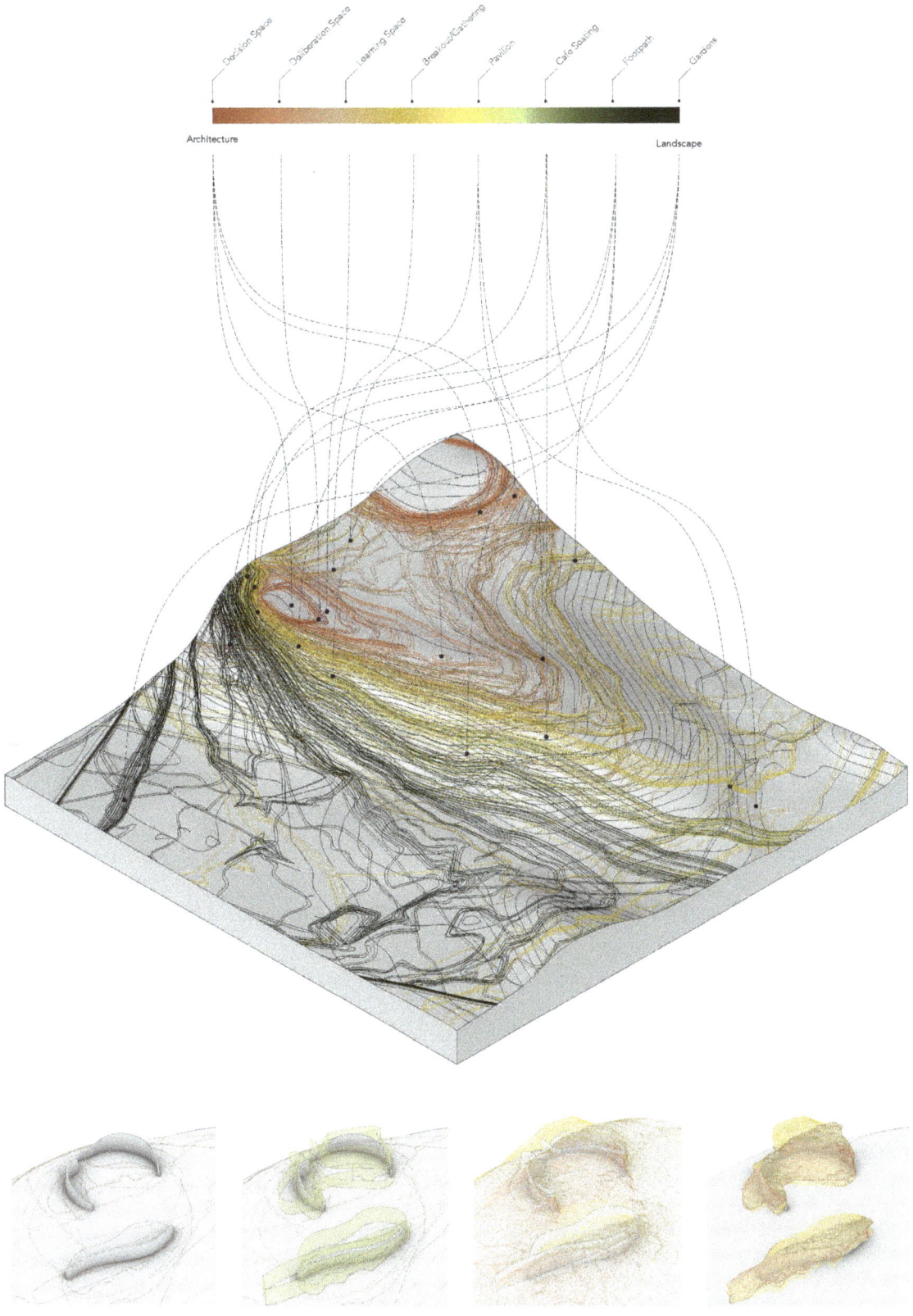

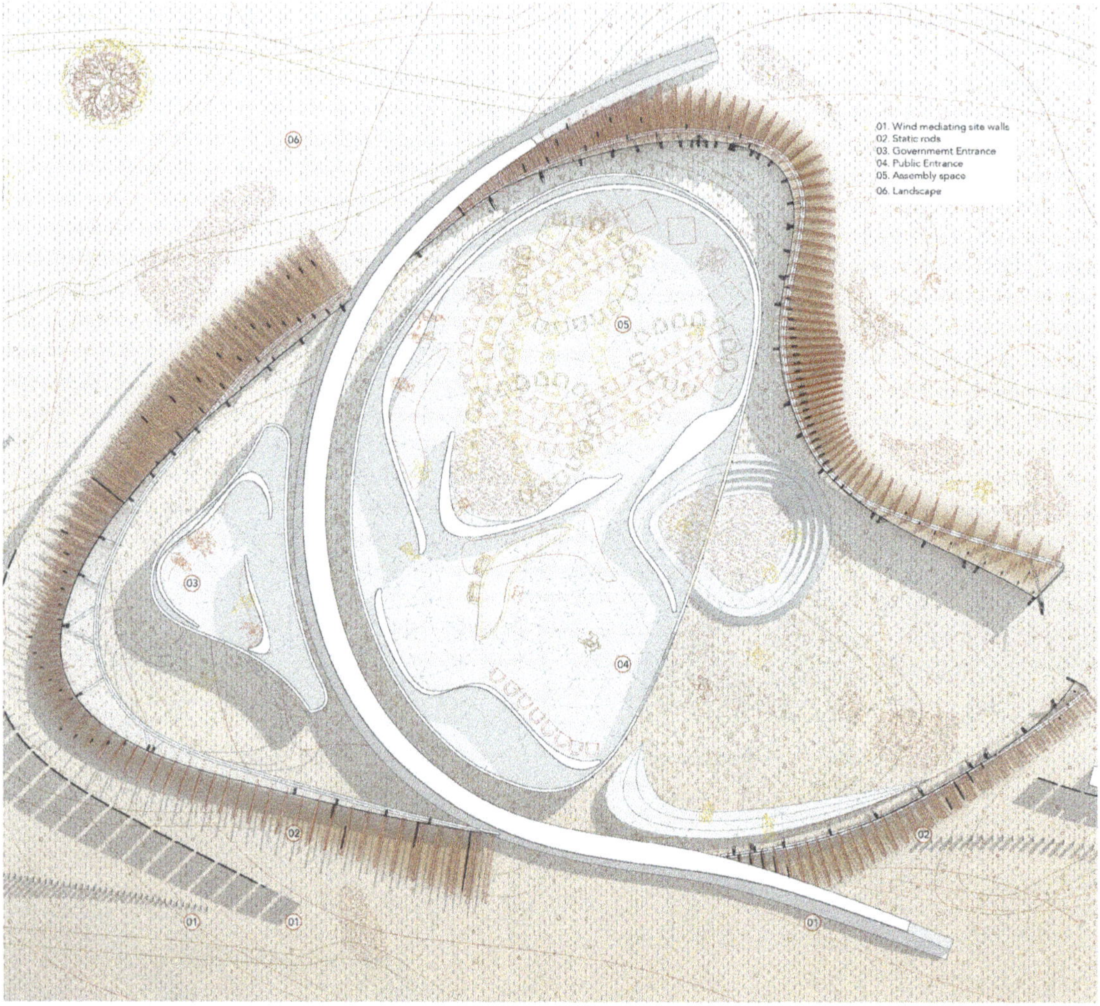

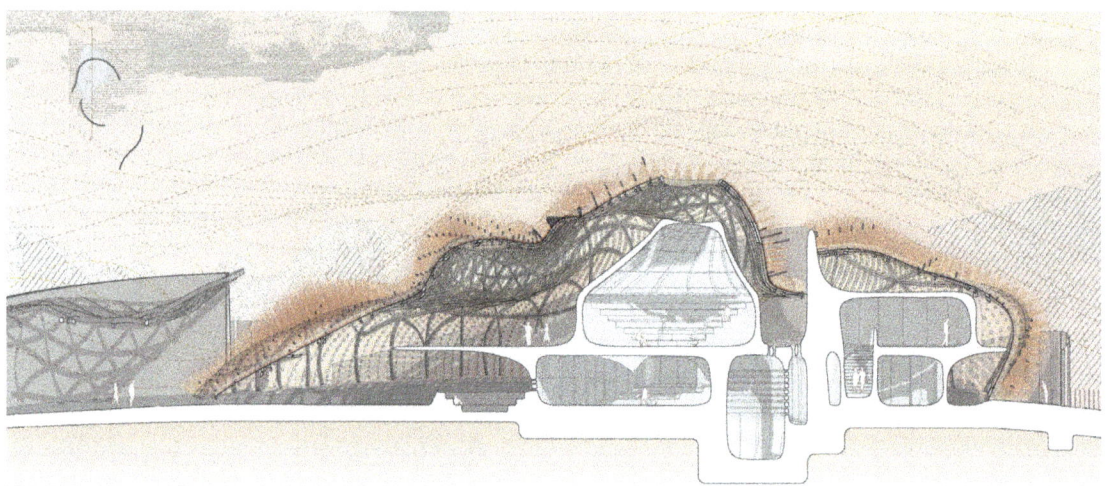

(top) Internal configuration of Parliament Chamber. (bottom) Zoomed in section.
(right) Seasonal site plan gradients of accumulated micro-plastic and air pollutants.

Internal render, under the envelope.

(top) Electrostatic episodes. (middle) Facade cycle. (bottom) A dusty envelope. Detailed view of performative electrostatic rod facade.

BLACK ICE FORUM

KATE HOSKING

Black carbon, commonly known as 'soot', is a particle produced from incomplete combustion, shipping traffic and burning fires. It is also one of the biggest contributors to climate change. With shipping traffic increasing in the Arctic region, more black carbon is being released into the atmosphere and subsequently falling on the Arctic ice, reducing the reflectivity of the ice and increasing its rate of melting. This has a profound effect on the receding Arctic ice mass.

It is predicted that by 2090 85% of the sea ice will remain in winter whilst only 10% will remain in the summer. [01] This further reduces the surface reflectivity in the region allowing further absorption of solar energy, affecting a range of delicately balanced Arctic systems from ocean temperatures, air temperatures, animal migration patterns and political interests.

Recent lower summer sea ice extents in the High North have led to more Arctic shipping as new routes become feasible and attractive to operators as they are shorter and cheaper to run. For this reason, it is widely speculated that shipping routes across the Arctic are only going to increase and become more heavily trafficked with global trade and the movement of goods, particularly from Asia to Europe. This is creating a deadly feedback loop of increasing shipping opportunity, black carbon emissions and ever increasing rates of melting sea ice.

Black carbon is not recognised by the Intergovernmental Panel on Climate Change due to being classified as a "short-lived atmospheric particle" - unlike Carbon Dioxide and other air based anthropogenic pollutants. Until black carbon is fully recognised within global climate change policies and legislation, its contribution to the environmental destruction of the Arctic ice will continue at unprecedented rates. This is more significant along Arctic shipping routes along Russia and towards Europe where the sea ice extents has declined significantly.

The Black Ice Forum is a master plan that addresses the issue of black carbon emissions and its detrimental effects on the melting Arctic ice and consequently global warming. The purpose of the master plan is to use architecture as a climatic marker within the shifting landscape of sea ice, whilst bringing the overwhelming scales and effects of global warming to an experiential human scale. This is done through a blurring of boundaries between architecture and landscape, by using the changing climatic conditions to expose, conceal and manipulate both the structure and its surroundings. As part of the project, sea ice groynes are implemented as large pieces of infrastructure to capture the shifting sea ice masses. By capturing the sea ice, the structure encourages fragments of sea ice to fuse together, preventing the sea ice from thinning and dissipating. The building hosts a 'Black Ice Forum', an international assembly space to bring black carbon to the forefront of climate summits and discourse, through the implementation of policies, a new measure of GDP (based on environmental factors) and black carbon credits.

(01) T.S. Rogers, J.E. Walsh, T.S. Rupp, L.W. Brigham, M. Sfraga, "Future Arctic marine access: analysis and evaluation of observations, models and projections of sea ice", (2013-02-25).

(right) Black Ice Forum, masterplan.

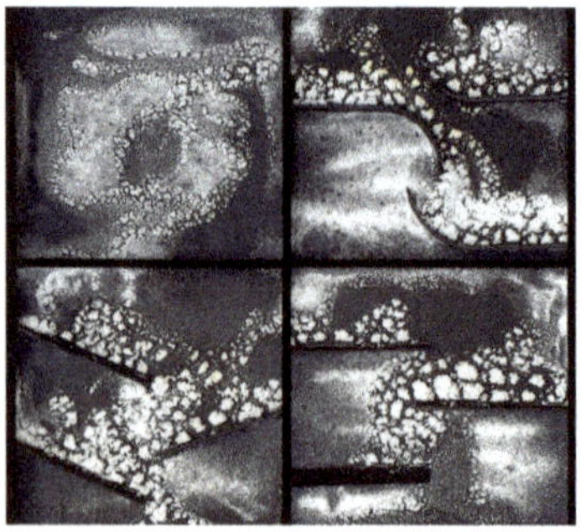

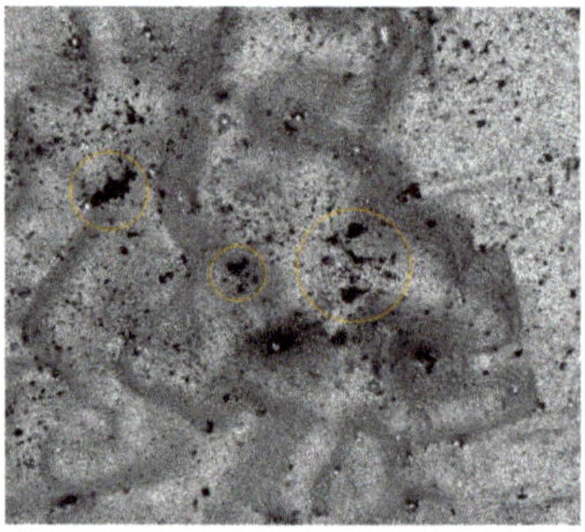

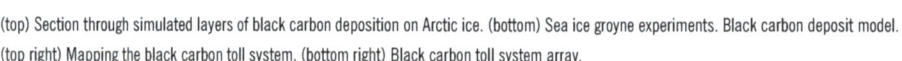

(top) Section through simulated layers of black carbon deposition on Arctic ice. (bottom) Sea ice groyne experiments. Black carbon deposit model.
(top right) Mapping the black carbon toll system. (bottom right) Black carbon toll system array.

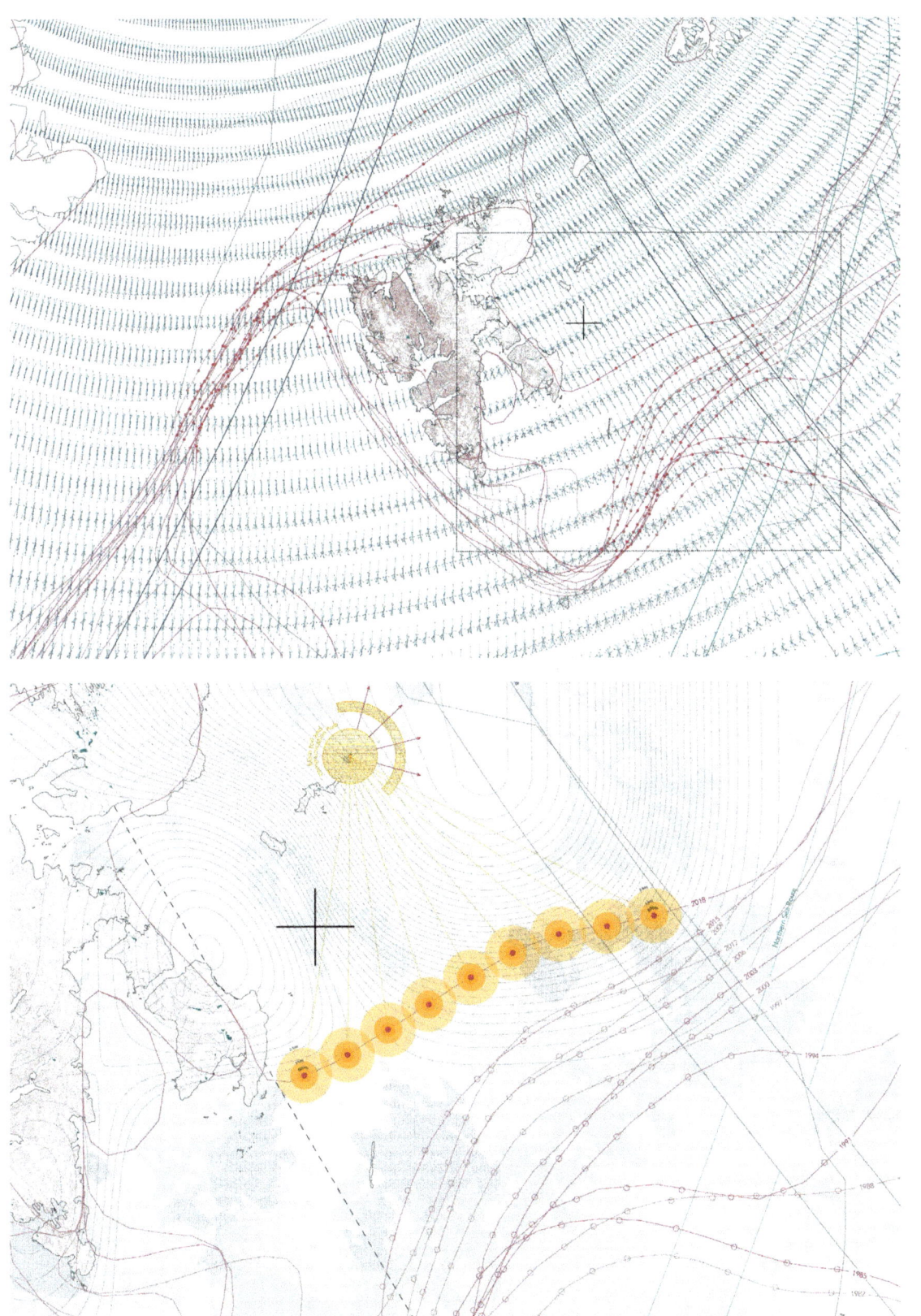

Overview of the Black Ice Forum; sea ice and black carbon movement flows.

Seasonal sea ice growth from summer to winter - overall section

Chamber Hall, main space of the Black Ice Forum - overall floorplan.

MOTH ASSEMBLY

GABRIELLE BUCKNALL

The project focuses on a region in the far north of Norway, where birch trees are perishing due to an invasive moth species, triggered by increasing temperatures and climate change. Moths and larvae, dispersed by the wind, eat birch leaves, preventing photosynthesis and ultimately destroying the trees. The future is bleak for these forests, as rising temperatures will encourage moth populations to thrive and increase in numbers.

Society often regards moths as pests, leading to interventions aimed at eradicating them. However, this project questions that stance, highlighting that the insect migration problem in Norway is ultimately a result of human actions, and the moths' behaviour is a natural response. The project imagines an alternative ideal that balances the needs of humans, trees, and moths, promoting the recovery of the forest ecosystem.
A new Hiking Reforestation Route is proposed, featuring a series of architectural pavilions that allow visitors to engage with the forest and this little-known phenomenon, while encouraging the planting and replenishment of the damaged forest. These interventions enable interactions between humans, birch trees, and moths at different scales.

One intervention, "The Tower," offers visitors the opportunity to stand above the tree canopy and marvel at the forest beneath. This allows them to appreciate the extent of the moth and birch habitat, witnessing first-hand the damage the scheme aims to repair and bring harmony to. Another pavilion, the Moth Inspection Chamber, allows humans to climb into the tree canopy layer and observe the moths and trees as they change with the seasons. This platform also provides a base for local scientists and researchers to monitor the moths and birch trees. The cage-like timber form of the interventions provides a mediating surface and structure between tree, moth, and human. Additionally, there is a birch tree nursery and education centre where visitors can collect saplings to carry with them on the reforestation hiking trail.

The pinnacle of the route is The Moth Assembly and Reforestation Forum, which, along with the pavilions, responds in its design and program to the lifecycles of the forest, particularly the intertwined life cycles of the moth and birch trees—of growth and decay throughout the seasons.

The forum is a publicly accessible, external space that celebrates the seasonality of these ecosystems and the cycle of birth, death, and regrowth through the replenishment of the architecture itself. It also serves as a host for the moth and its lifecycle. Timber from the surrounding forest is used in the construction of the structure, while smaller birch leaves and twigs are collected and woven into the frame throughout the year, creating a layered framework to attract the moths. The moths lay their eggs, and the pupae lie in the depths of the framework during the quieter winter period until late spring and summer when they start to emerge, erupting into the assembling space. This stage of their life coincides with the yearly forum and the human pilgrimage to the assembly site, allowing all entities to be involved in conversations around forest management and future strategies. The space acts as a pivotal location to discuss and share future strategies for methods of living together and retaining the forests for future generations and the local Sami community.

(right) Moth Assembly - The Forest Forum Meeting

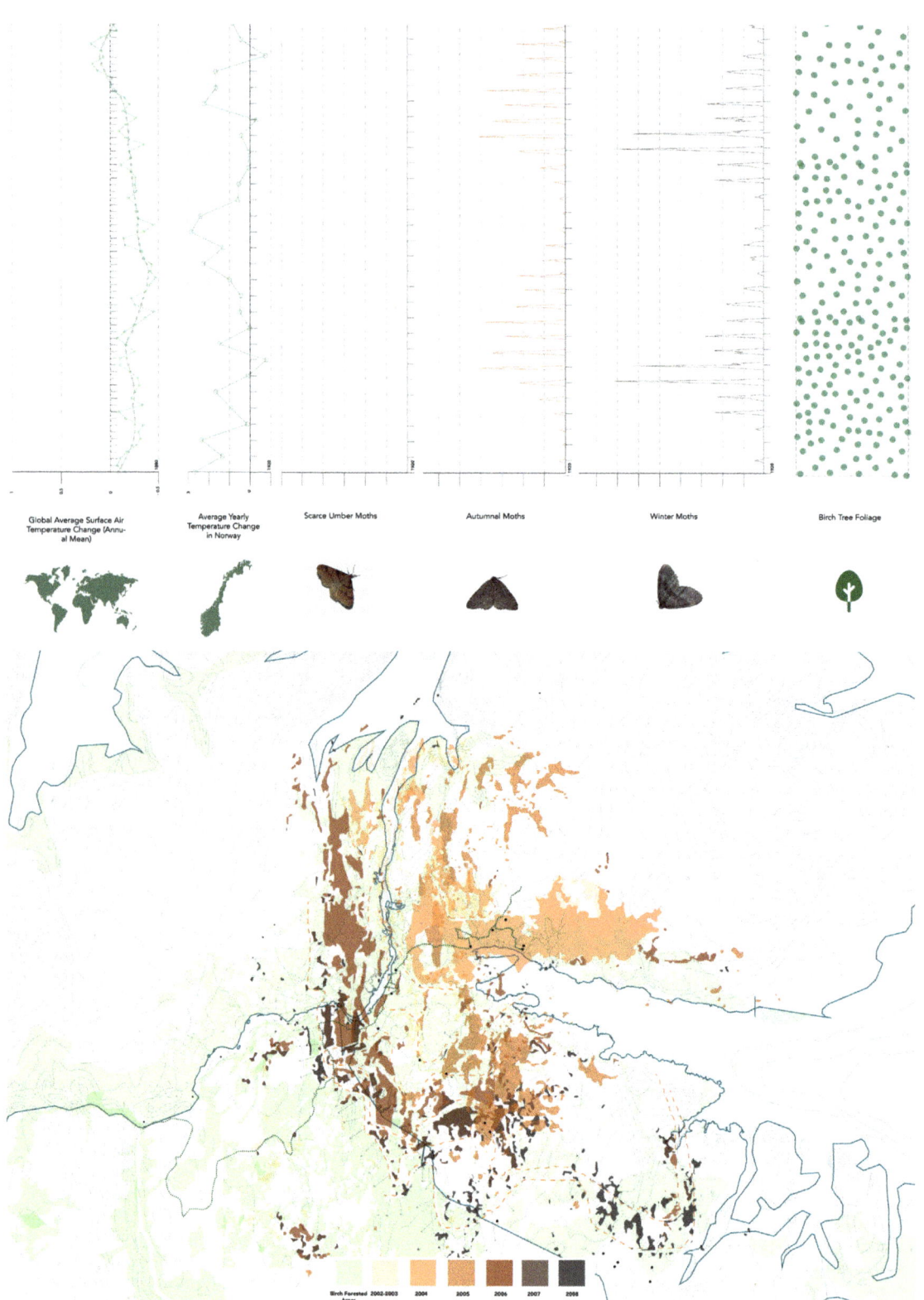

(top) Moth Climatic Sensitivity and Outbreaks Chart. (bottom) Defoliation in Varranger. Locations of last monitored moth defoliation outbreaks.

Cycle of Life, Death and Replenishment.

Moth Assembly - Site section.

Moth Assembly - Overview.

AIR ARCHIVE

AIMÉE DANIELS

The Arctic is experiencing climate warming at twice the rate of the rest of the world, and is therefore simultaneously the best place to identify changes in climate and most at risk from climate change. Lying halfway between mainland Norway and the North Pole, Svalbard is over 60% glaciated and has established itself as an international centre for climate science. Impending climatic breakdown threatens to alter Svalbard's arctic landscape entirely.

Glacial ice was selected as the research focus for this project, enticed by its capacity to record atmospheric information through deep time. It is formed from the gradual accumulation of snow over long periods of time. Air trapped in annual snowfall is compressed into bubbles under the mass of new snow. These bubbles contain information about past atmospheric conditions. Through analysing air bubbles from ice cores, information about yearly temperature, levels of greenhouse gases like carbon dioxide, methane, and nitrogen, concentrations of dust, volcanic ash, and sea salt, and more can be discerned. Paleo-climatologists use this information to reconstruct the Earth's climate through time as well as to predict the effects of a warming future. The increased pace of glacial melt associated with human industrial activity precipitates the increased loss of Earth's climate archive and connection to our planet's past.

This project proposes an archive of the atmosphere since the Industrial Revolution sited inside of a retreating glacier on the Norwegian archipelago of Svalbard. Several large tidewater glaciers terminate in the bay of Kongsfjord. They have already notably retreated, and will eventually be gone altogether, as a result of anthropogenic led temperature rise, representing the significant loss of embedded climatic data capturing the history of the Earth.

The Arctic Air Archive is a monument to human imposed climate change. The project is centred around a vertical 'carving' mechanism that simultaneously harvests ice cores, spatially translating the climatic data they contain through excavation down into the glacier according to four chosen atmospheric parameters: carbon dioxide (CO_2), methane (CH_4), nitrous oxide (N_2O), black carbon (BC). The archive is supported by a research station for Svalbard's scientific community.

At first, the archive is a void in the glacier. It is eventually solidified using rock aggregate from the ground below in advance of the glacier's total retreat, when it reveals itself as a free-standing tower. The excavation of the archive takes place over five years and is theoretically powered by the momentum generated by the glacier's own retreat. The glacier's gradual disappearance works to preserve the atmospheric archive contained within its ice. The project is primarily a speculative building, an ecological artefact, that aims to reframe humans' relationship to climate change and serve as a record of climatic decline for future civilisations.

(right) Glaciers as Atmospheric Archives - Section through the Earth's crust depicting air bubbles.

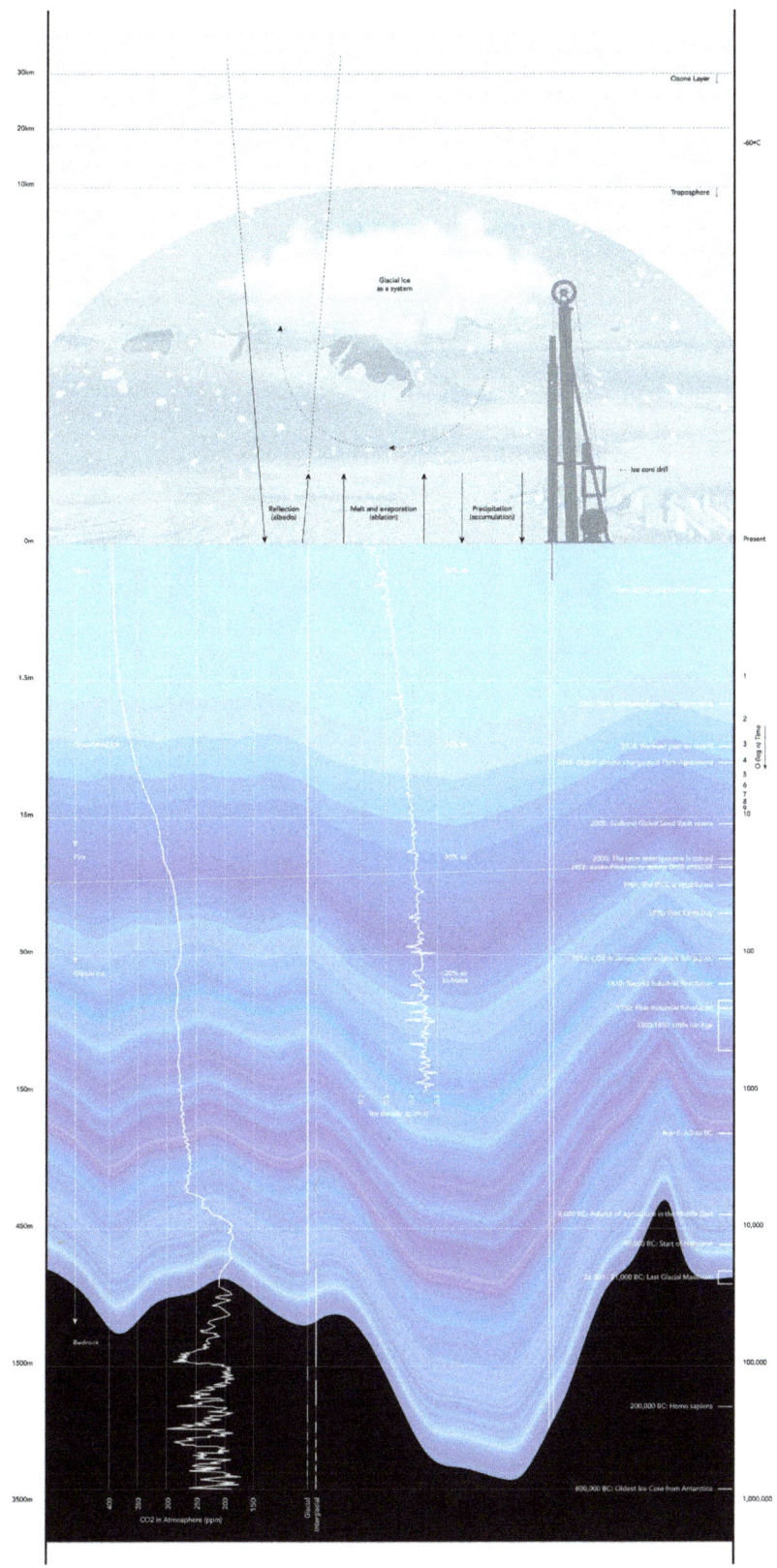

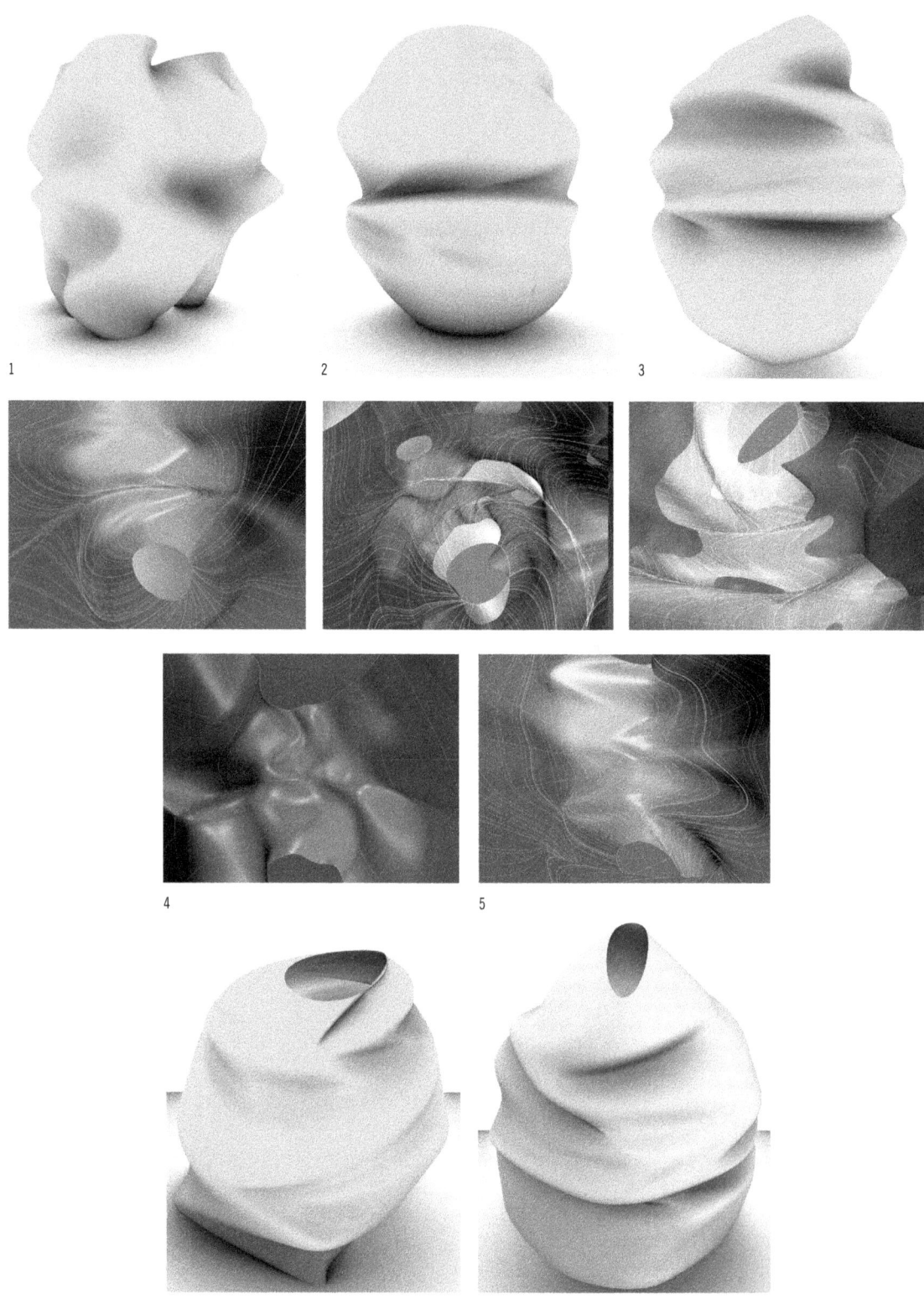

Morphological reconstructions of air bubble experiments (1-5), CFD & Grasshopper.

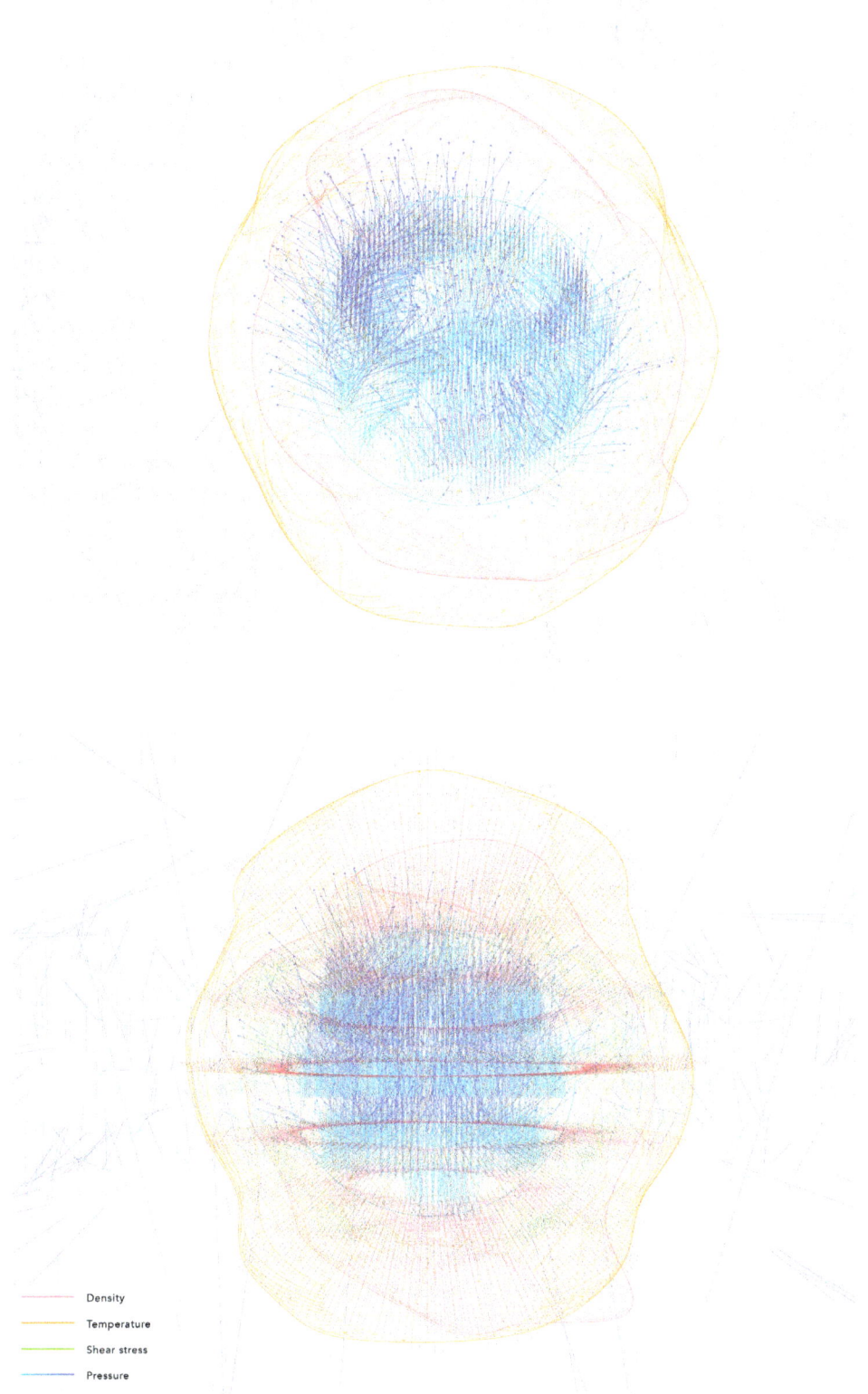

Microscale simulation of a glacial air bubble at different pressures.

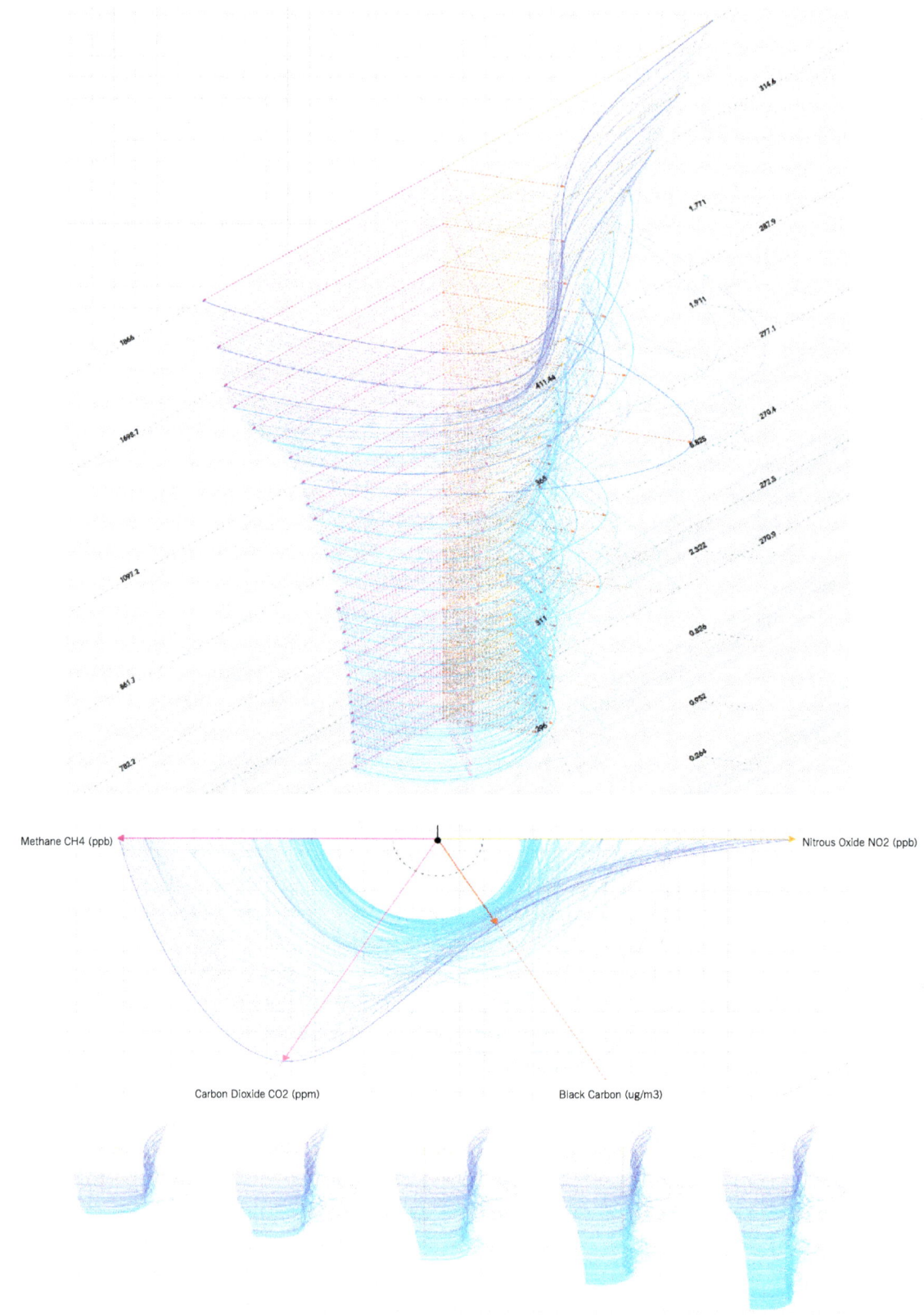

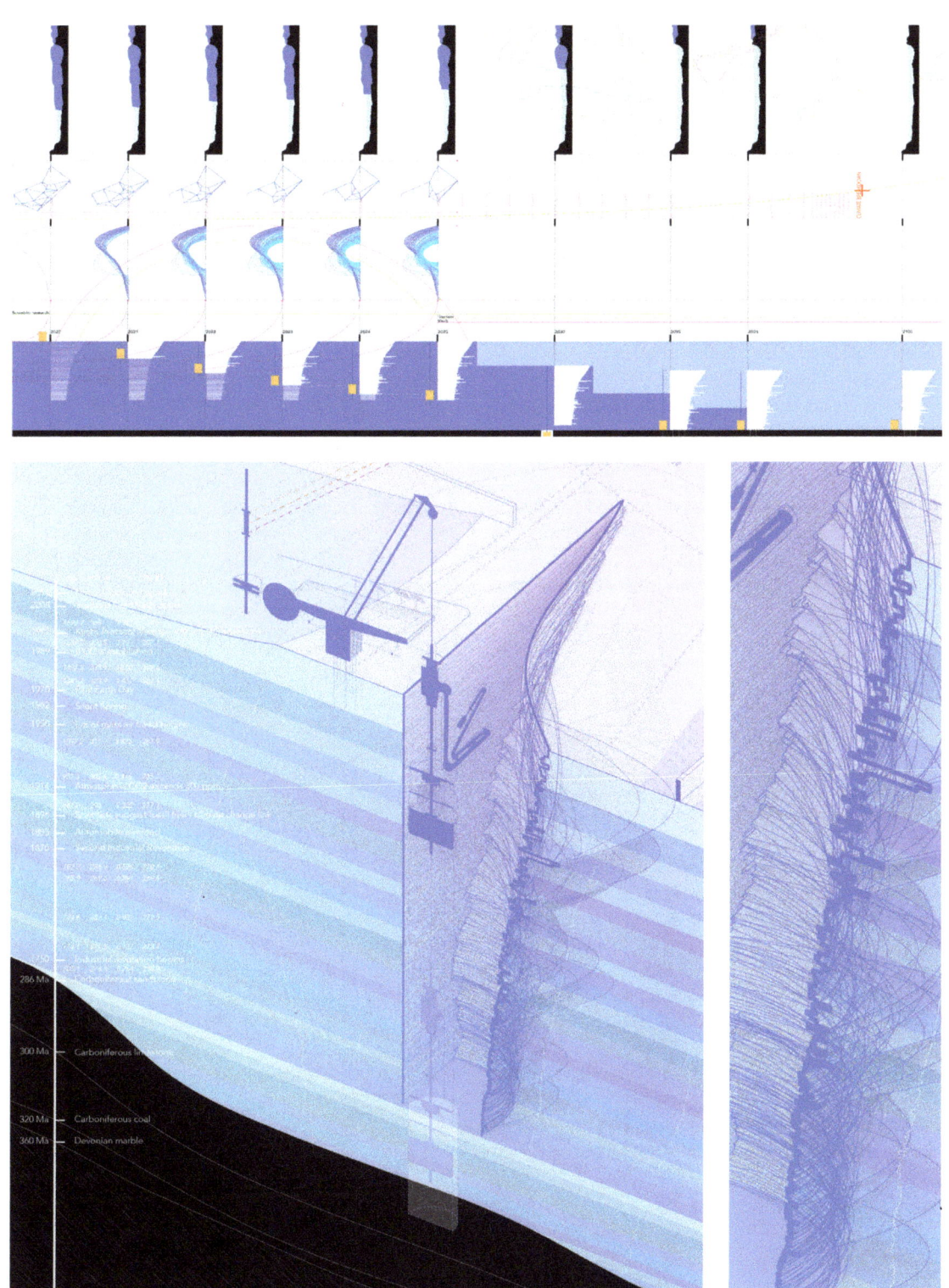

(left) Ice Core Archive - 274 years of climatic data and excavation layers.
(top) Conceptual timeline of archival readings. (bottom left) The Carver Rig and the Grinder. (bottom right) The Anthropocene Air Marks - zoomed in area.

OCEANIC RESEARCH AND DIATOMIC HUB

ZIXIN (TIFFANY) YAO

The "Diatom" project reimagines an existing oil rig into an Interactive Oceanic Research and Adventure Hub, setting a new precedent for sustainable tourism and marine research. Situated in the North Sea, this innovative retrofit bridges environmental science, tourism, and architectural ingenuity, turning an industrial relic into a living laboratory for the cultivation of diatoms—microscopic algae critical for restoring marine ecosystems and combating climate change.

The project addresses the urgent need for climate resilience and ocean health. Oceans currently absorb 40% of global CO_2 emissions, yet rising carbon levels are causing acidification, endangering marine biodiversity. Diatoms, responsible for producing 50% of the world's oxygen, offer an organic solution to counter ocean acidification and carbon imbalances. By cultivating diatoms at scale, this project contributes directly to carbon sequestration while raising public awareness of oceanic ecosystems and their role in the global fight against climate change.

Inspired by regenerative design principles, the rig undergoes a transformative architectural process, integrating both formal and functional requirements. A state-of-the-art thermal tensile facade wraps around the structure, optimizing natural ventilation and light. The facade system utilises high-tensile steel wires to allow seamless movement of tensile fabric, dynamically responding to weather conditions and enhancing energy efficiency. Complementing the exterior, the interior incorporates lightweight sail fabric, ensuring structural flexibility, thermal comfort, and a nod to the rig's maritime legacy.

Central to the hub is the diatom ocean farm, where seawater is drawn from the ocean depths via a liquid spiral transfer system and circulated throughout the rig, sustaining diatom growth and purifying the water. This self-sustaining ecosystem creates a mesmerising educational experience for visitors, fostering a deeper understanding of oceanic health and marine biodiversity. A multi-tiered organisational layout integrates research labs, observation platforms, and an interactive ocean bar, allowing visitors to immerse themselves in the beauty and scientific significance of diatoms.

The "Diatom" project transforms a dormant oil rig into a beacon of innovation, sustainability, and tourism. By merging environmental stewardship with economic potential, it creates a model for repurposing industrial infrastructure while empowering communities to explore and protect our oceans. This project stands as a symbol of forward-thinking design, a celebration of marine life, and a vital step toward a resilient, low-carbon future.

(right) Repurposed Oil Rig and Phytoplankton Farm overview.

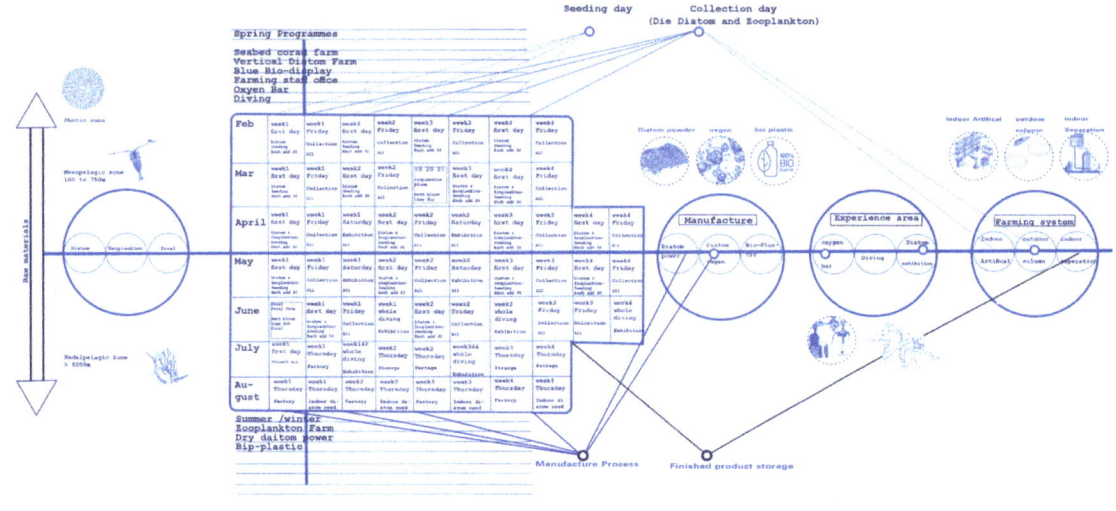

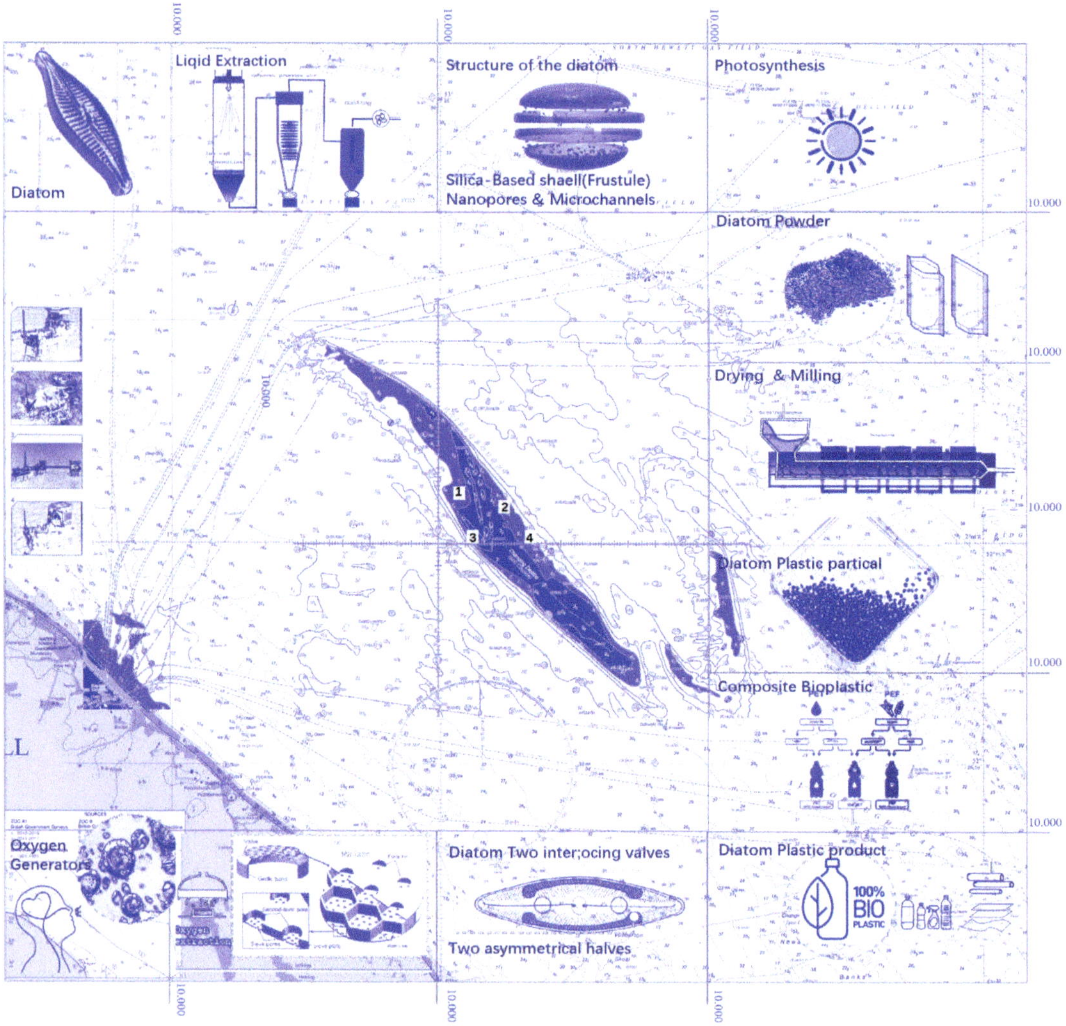

(top) Proposed decommissioning activities. (bottom) Bacton Village North Sea masterplan.

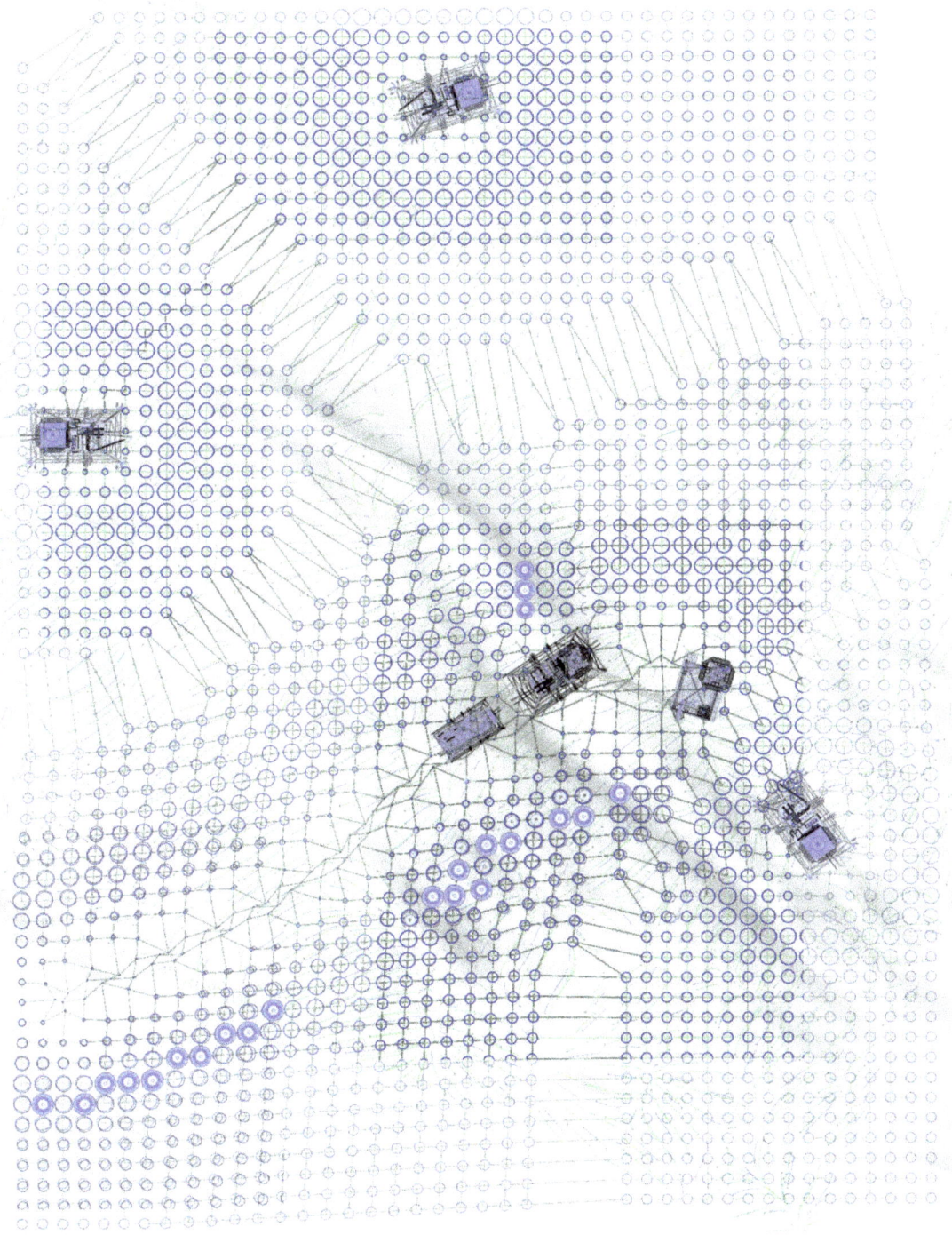

Proposed masterplan highlighting integration of six oil rigs and diatom farming.

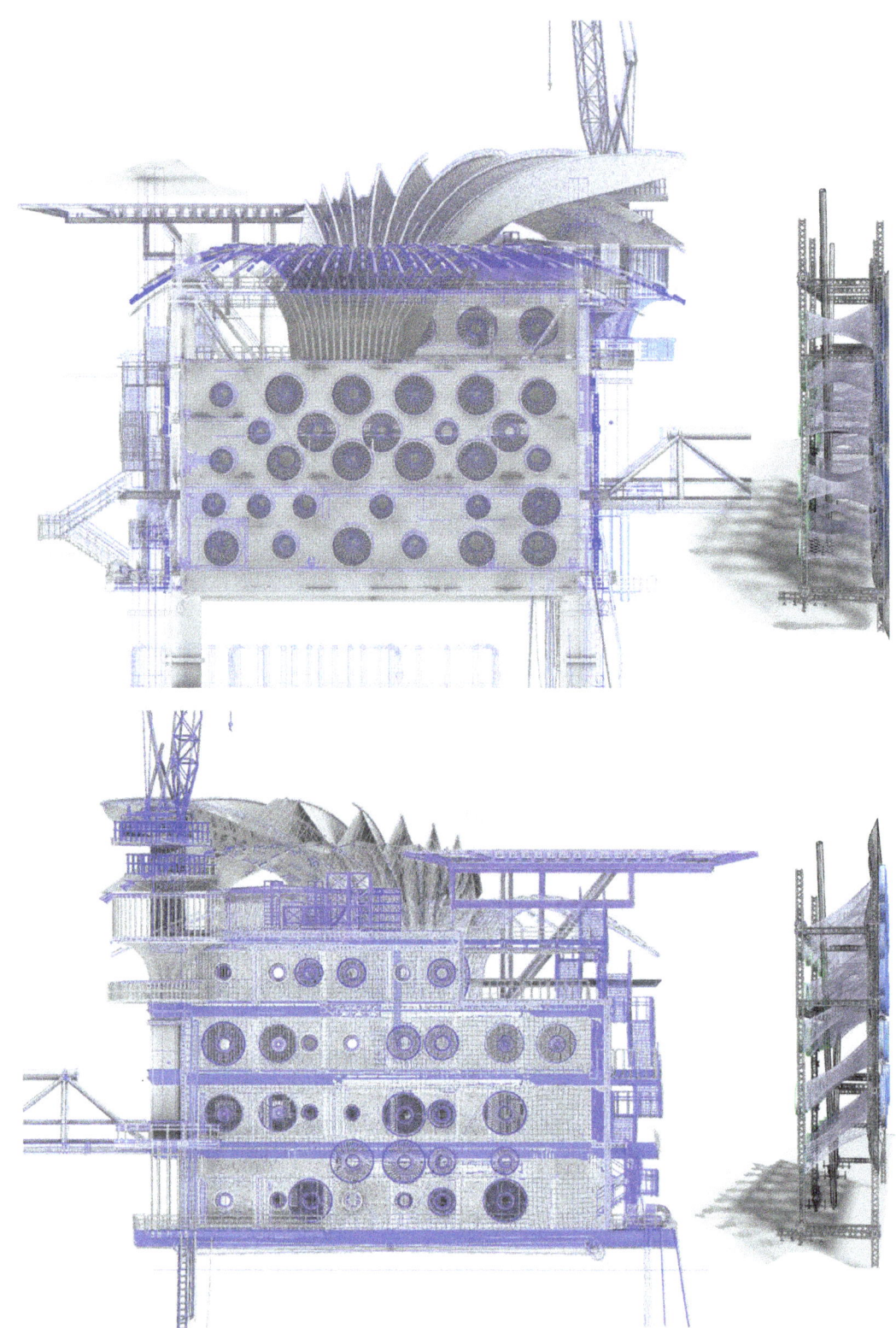

(top left) Proposed east and west elevations. (top right) Thermal bio-facade.
(right) Proposed oil rig retro-fit and technical details.

SEEPING CITY: A VISION FOR PERMA-POWER

HELEN WINDSOR

The Seeping City is a power plant that harnesses the methane released from thawing permafrost to produce energy in the world's first 'Perma-power Plant'. The Perma-power Plant reimagines the oil platform city, Neft Daşları, Azerbaijan, as a resourceful hypothetical response to the effects of global warming on permafrost in Norway. Permafrost is a vast carbon sink which has compacted and stored crystallised methane from the ice age. As it thaws, the methane is released into the atmosphere.

Methane capture from landfills has proven to be an effective method of slow-energy generation. It is crucial to mitigating climate change, as methane's warming potential is 28–34 times greater than carbon dioxide. Methane from biogas has an electrical conversion efficiency of 35%; therefore, 1 cubic metre of methane will yield 10kWh. The project translates this proven method of energy generation into a unique hypothetical vision where seeping methane is captured, generated and valued nationally.

Thawing permafrost transforms vast landscapes into a watery geometric pattern of wetlands and lakes, known as Thermokarst terrain. The nature of permafrost thaw is undetectable to the human eye as it occurs beneath the earth and, therefore, is unpredictable, causing landslides, sinkholes and flammable bubbling methane. The project is designed to have flexible, adaptable infrastructure to evolve with the uncertain landscape. Every functional space is flexible and uses recycled low-carbon materials. Staff are housed in connected recycled telegraph pole 'raft' homes and cultivate food in the 'CH4 Good' Greenhouse. Scientists cultivate seeds discovered in thawing permafrost in the botanical garden. The local high street and public realm address the day-to-day challenges of the scheme and enhance community spirit and place-making.

The Perma-Power plant is the focal point. To collect methane, a network of expandable funnels covers the thermokarst lakes to harvest the seeping methane as it escapes from the ground. The collected gas is drawn toward the power plant, which converts it into energy through combustion. The energy generated is used to power the city, and all excess power is transferred to the national grid. The bi-products from methane combustion, such as water, are utilised by households and plant cultivation. Using this process, the consequences of permafrost thaw from global warming are minimised, to an extent, as a reduced volume of methane will be released into the atmosphere.

Thawing permafrost poses a catastrophic threat to our planet. If global CO2 emissions continue at current rates, the remaining carbon budget for keeping warming to 1.5°C will likely be exhausted before 2030. [01] An alarming 3,640 gigatons of carbon currently stored in the frozen ground could be released by permafrost thaw, pushing atmospheric carbon dioxide to unprecedented levels. The water released from permafrost alone could raise sea levels by an estimated 3 to 10 meters. This process also unleashes mercury into waterways and food chains, methane from bog bacteria and ice-bound crystals, and nitrous oxides as the tundra's nutrient absorption capacity collapses. These are irreversible consequences of permafrost thaw. Once a vital carbon sink, permafrost is now teetering on the edge of becoming a destructive carbon source, amplifying the impacts of global warming.

The Seeping City offers an innovative approach to capturing methane and transforming it into energy while addressing some of the profound challenges of a warming world.

(01) Dhakal, S., J.C. Minx, F.L. Toth, A. Abdel-Aziz, M.J. Figueroa Meza, K. Hubacek, I.G.C. Jonckheere, Yong-Gun Kim, G.F. Nemet, S. Pachauri, X.C. Tan, T. Wiedmann, 2022: Emissions Trends and Drivers. In IPCC, 2022: Climate Change 2022: Mitigation of Climate Change. Contribution of Working Group III to the Sixth Assessment Report of the Intergovernmental Panel on Climate Change [P.R. Shukla, J. Skea, R. Slade, A. Al Khourdajie, R. van Diemen, D. McCollum, M. Pathak, S. Some, P. Vyas, R. Fradera, M. Belkacemi, A. Hasija, G. Lisboa, S. Luz, J. Malley, (eds.)]. Cambridge University Press, Cambridge, UK and New York, NY, USA. doi: 10.1017/9781009157926.004.

(right) The Seeping City - Manifesto for the World's Perma-Frost Power Plant.

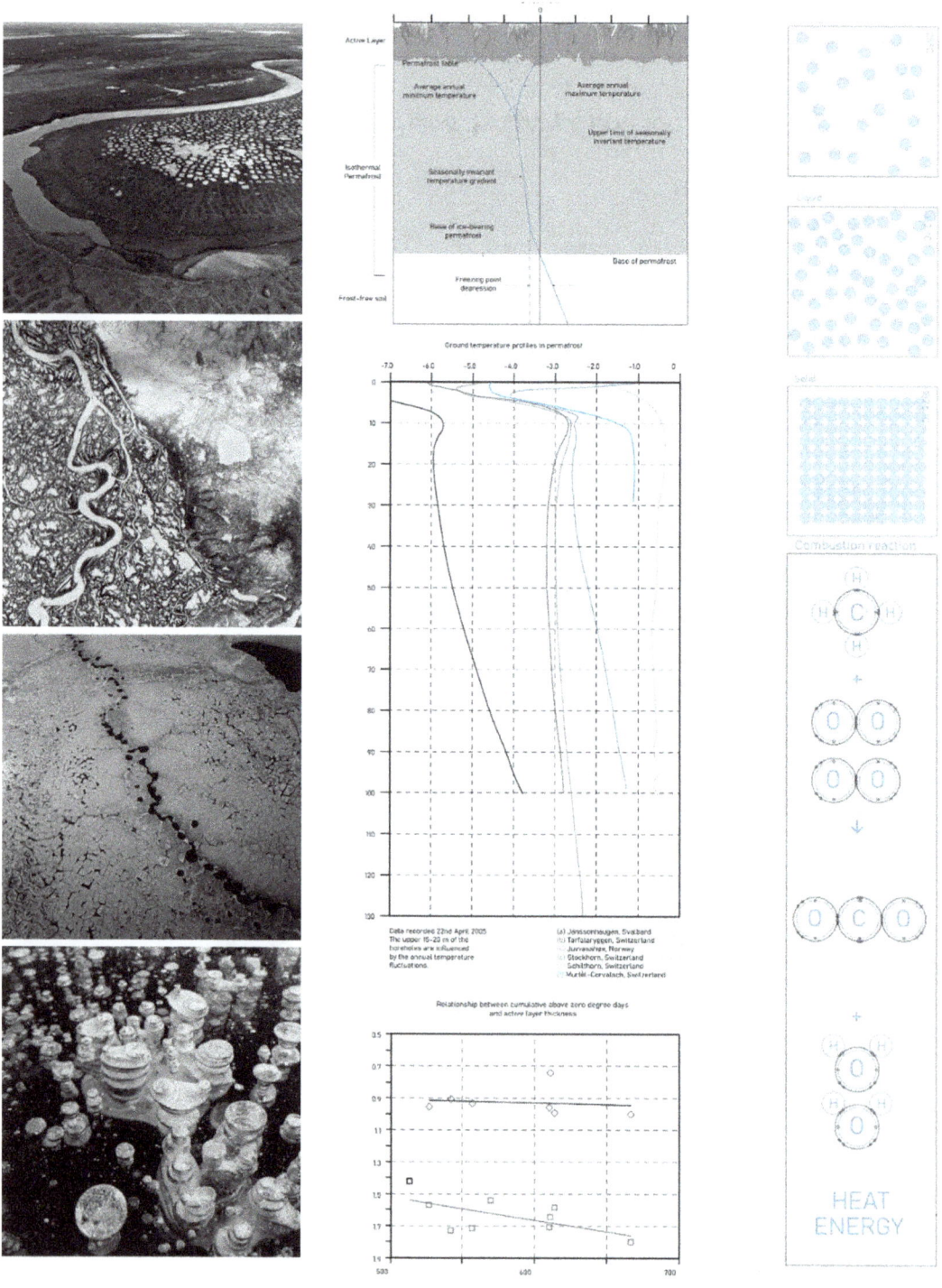

(left) Photographs of permafrost and thermokarst landscapes; (middle) Permafrost temperature profiles; (right) Converting greenhouse gas into renewable energy.

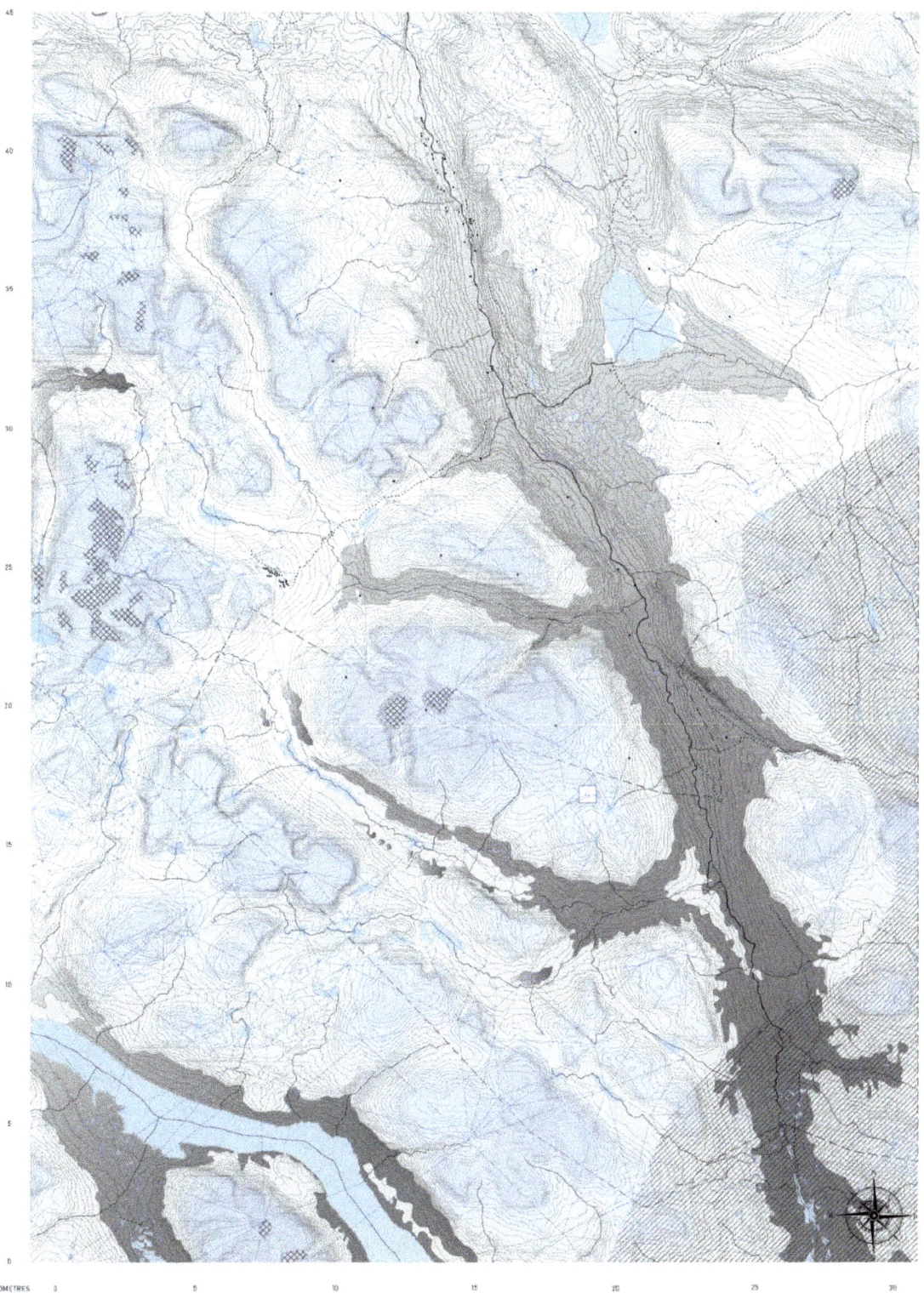

The Seeping City - Site location. Permafrost and thermokarst landscapes cartographies.

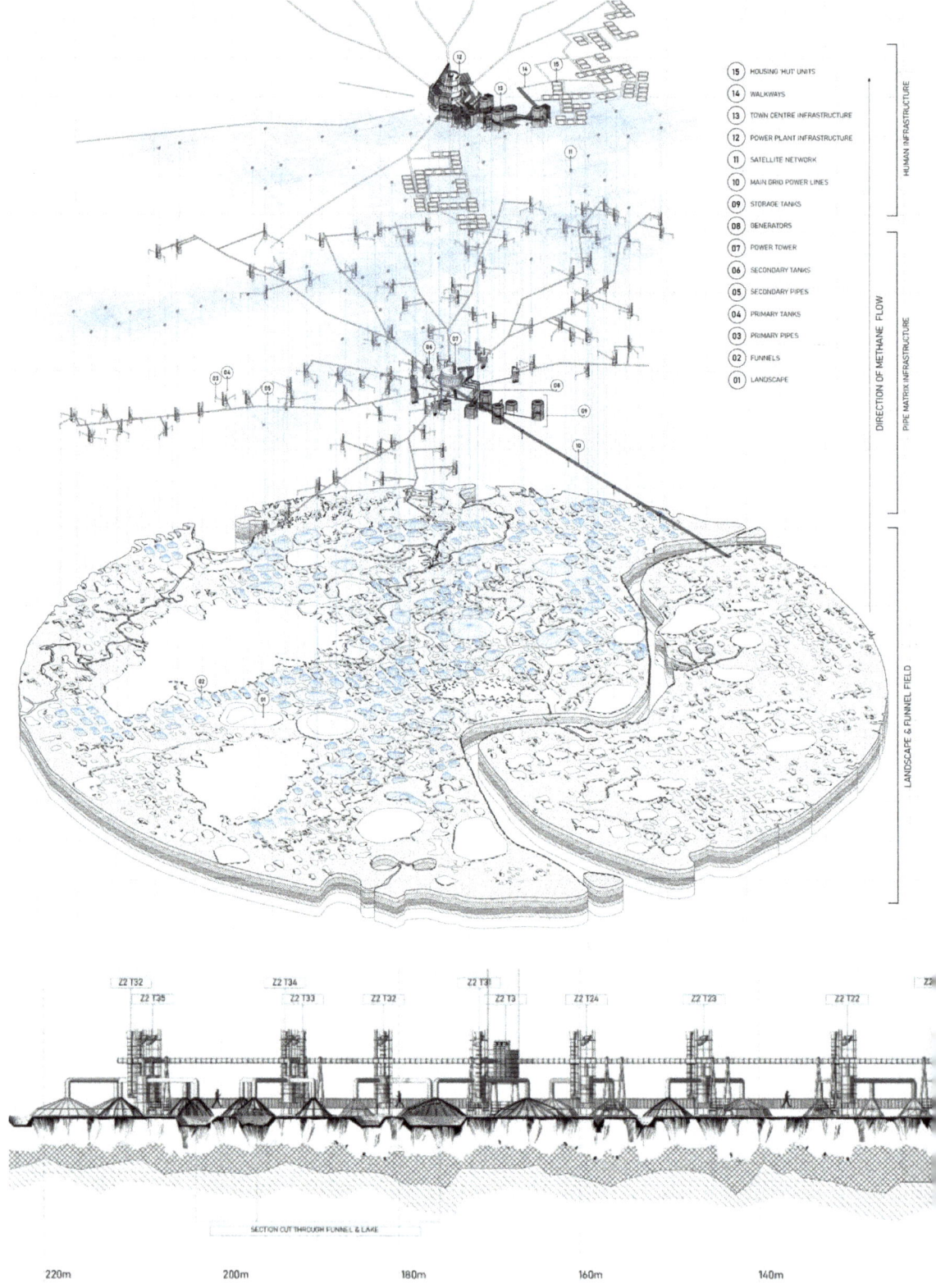

(top left) Exploded axonometric of the city and flow of methane. (top right) Site-wide masterplan. (bottom) Pipeline infrastructure across landscape.

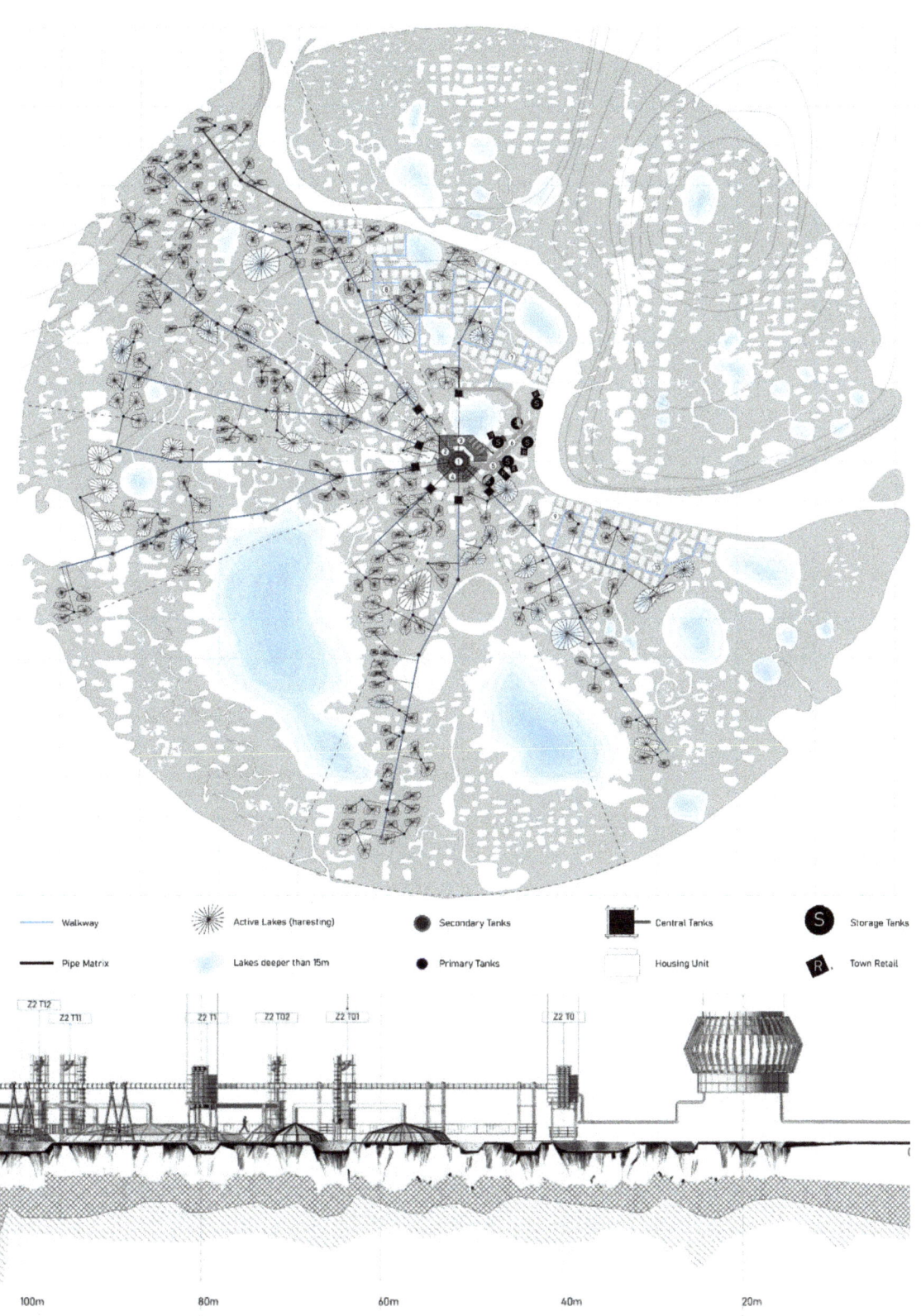

Carbon dioxide tanks perspective view.

(left) Power Tower. (right) Central pipe infrastructure funnel and pipe.

CLOUD FACTORY

DARIA - SUZANNE DONOVETSKY

Cloud climatology plays a critical role in addressing climate change, but accurately modelling clouds is challenging due to their dynamic nature, varying compositions, and altitudes. Their impact on climate fluctuates depending on time of day, geographic location, and whether they occur over land or water. High-altitude clouds like cirrus regulate heat transfer by reflecting and trapping radiation. These clouds form and dissipate rapidly under natural conditions, but human activities, particularly air traffic, disrupt this cycle. Aircraft emissions, especially particulate matter (PM 2.5) from burning kerosene, serve as nuclei for ice formation, leading to long-lasting contrail cirrus clouds. These human-made clouds persist longer, trapping more heat and exacerbating global warming.

Small particulate matter (SPM) extends cloud lifetimes, increases albedo, and leads to warming. In contrast, natural particles like salt and dust are larger, heavier, and less likely to form high-altitude clouds. They are more prone to precipitation, so they have more localised and transient effects, whereas SPM has a more widespread and sustained impact on the climate.

This research proposal aims to enhance the understanding of cloud feedback mechanisms and reduce uncertainties around climate sensitivity through advanced simulations and controlled cloud dynamics testing. It focuses on how natural and anthropogenic clouds, particularly those from aviation exhaust, interact.

Swansea, Wales, is an ideal location for atmospheric experiments due to its consistent wind patterns, air traffic corridors, annual temperatures, proximity to the sea, and polluted highways. These factors provide a mix of natural and artificial particles and favourable conditions for studying cloud dynamics using facilities like The Wet Chamber (cold, humid), The Condensers (hot, humid), and The Air Catchers (purified dry air).

The Cloud Factory is a proposed research facility and public space dedicated to cloud geoengineering and atmospheric modelling. It serves as both a scientific hub and a public engagement platform for exploring the contentious geoengineering technologies such as cloud seeding and cloud brightening. The facility integrates atmospheric modelling with public interaction, featuring an open-air amphitheatre and walkways where visitors can observe atmospheric conditions and air quality. Two towers will spray aerosols—one for controlled experiments and another for open-air experiments. Open-air experiments only proceed after closed-air tests confirm that the engineered particles are safe to release into the atmosphere, minimising their environmental impact.

The facility consists of seven buildings powered by renewable energy sources such as hydraulic systems and wind turbines. It captures aerosols up to 1,000 meters in the atmosphere, allowing researchers to analyse their impact on cloud formation and particulate matter's role in atmospheric systems.

The Cloud Factory aims to advance cloud climatology, improve climate modelling, and educate around the effects of geoengineering practices. Its ultimate goal is to create adaptive architecture that harmonises with the surrounding landscape while contributing to a deeper understanding of cloud dynamics and their impact on global warming.

(right) The Cloud Factory - Geoengineering Facility and Cloud Proving Ground.

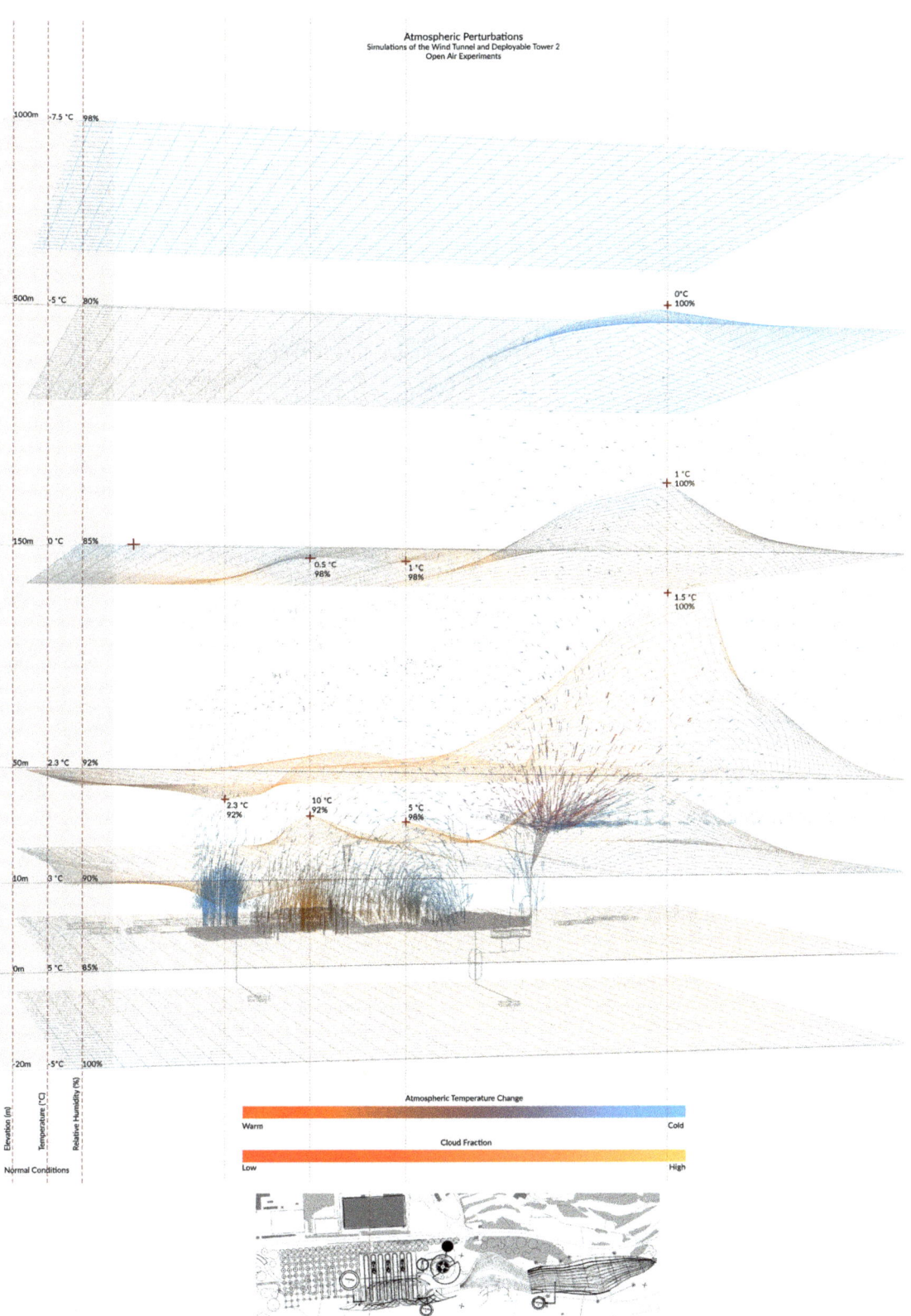

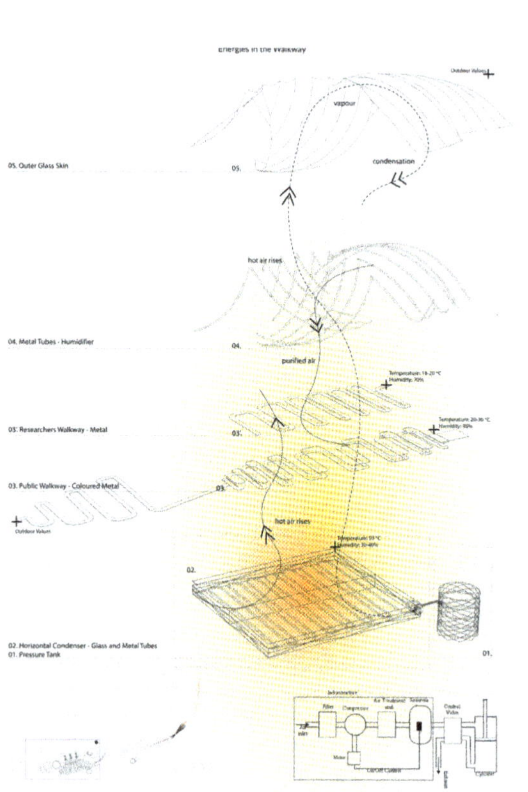

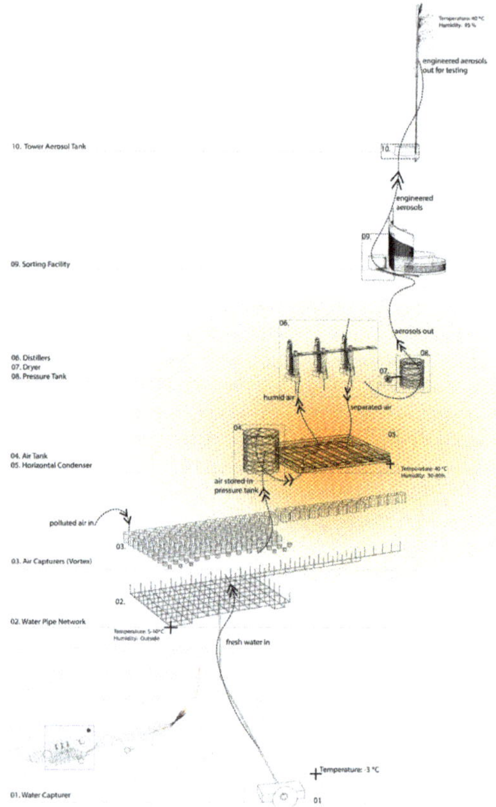

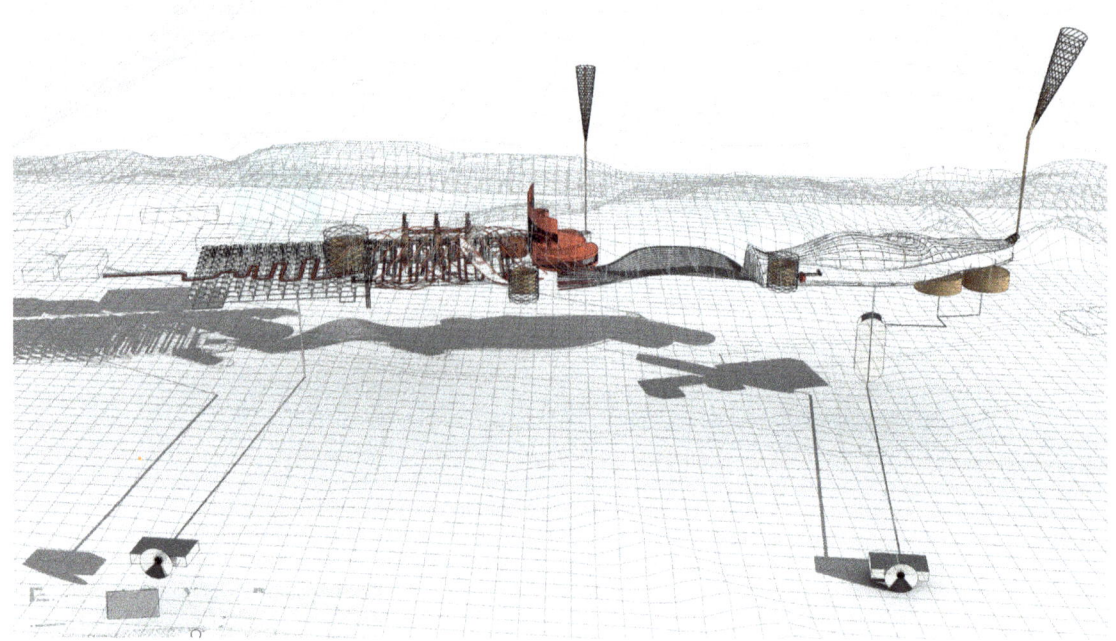

(top left) Energies in the Walkways (horizontal condenser and metal conduit) and (top right) Energies in the Condenser (air capturing and distillers).
(bottom) The Cloud Factory - Geoengineering Facility and Cloud Providing Ground.

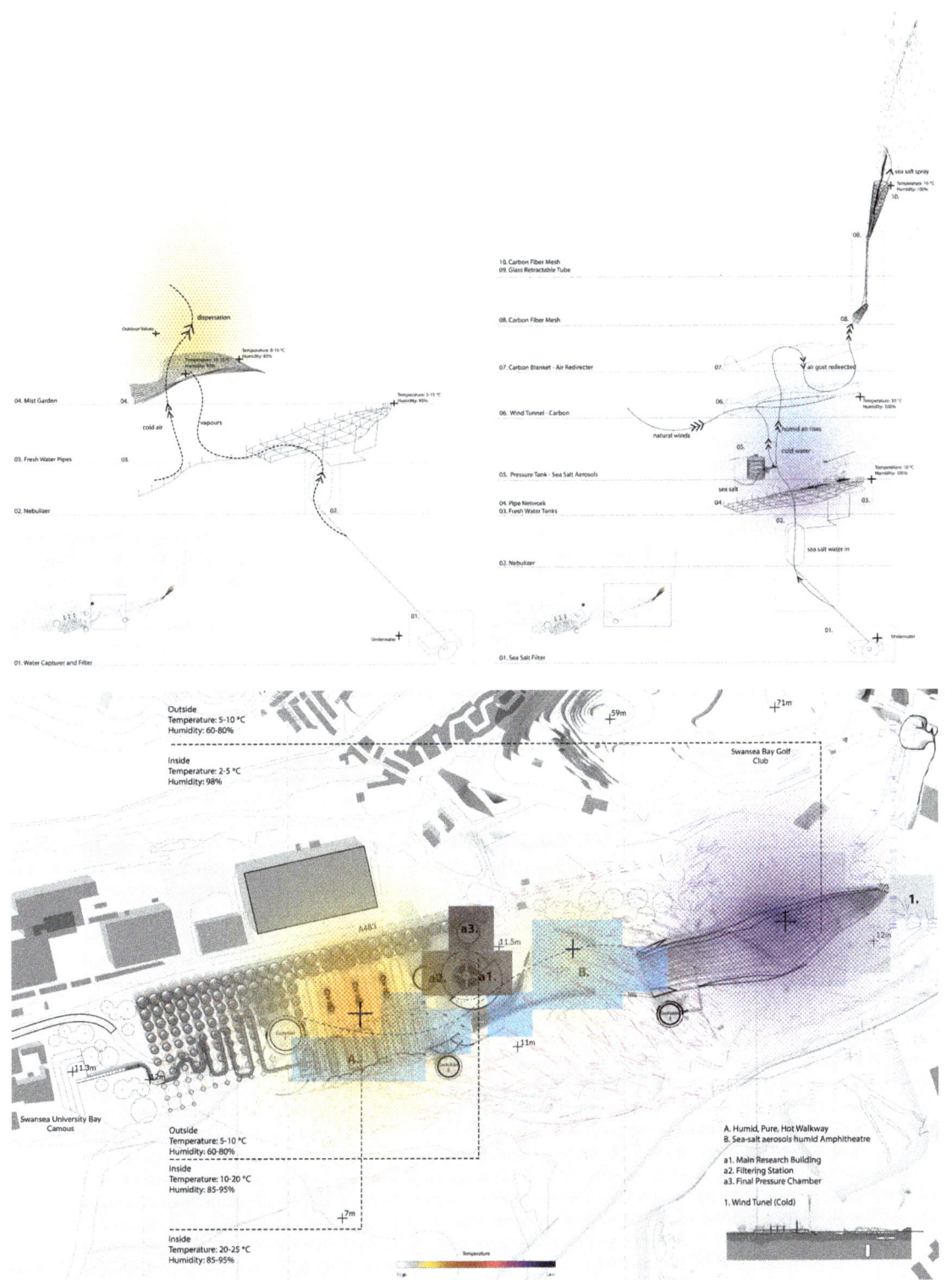

(top left) Energies in the Amphitheatre (the Mist Garden and Nabulizer pipes) and (top right) Energies in the Wind Tunnel (spraying mix for cloud formation).
(bottom) Vapour Floorplan - humid, hot and cold areas.

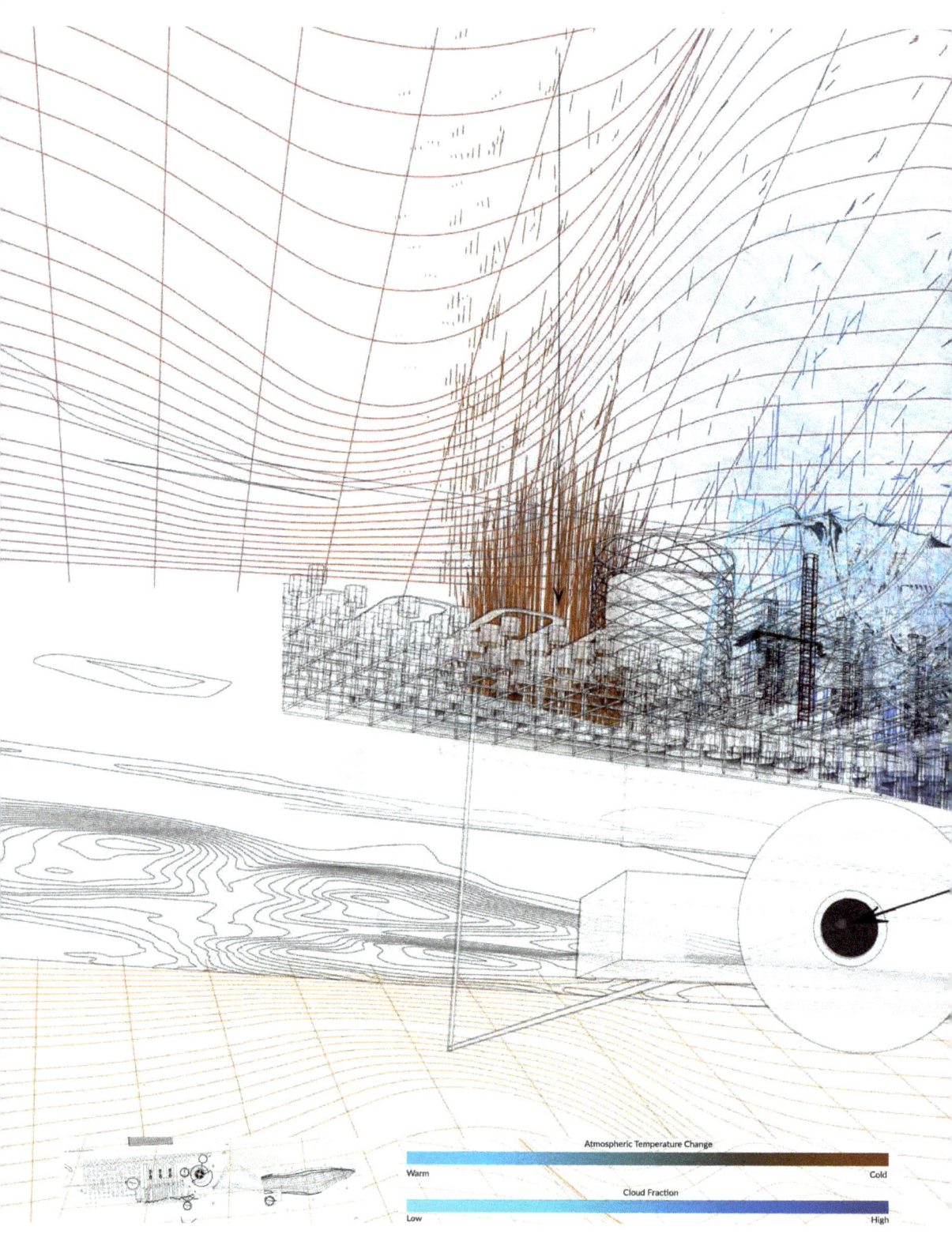

The Cloud Factory - Energy production, atmospheric temperature change and cloud fraction.

CARBON MONITORING STATION AND TERRITORIAL RE-WILDING

ELIZABETH TERRY

The Global North, and the richest 1% of the population, cause double the CO_2 emissions of the poorest countries in the Global South (Oxfam). Within this anthropogenic carbon system, the 'Carbon Credit' is a financial market tool, equating carbon emissions to an abstract value - giving those who can afford it, the right to emit. Offsetting schemes and trading provide a contradictory loop of potentially never ending emissions in the Global North; where there is an enormous local deficit of carbon. The UK government's agenda was to capture up to 10 million tonnes of carbon a year from 2023, only 2.7% of the total carbon emissions from 2018. Driven by this framing, the proposal aspires to generate a Carbon Re-wilding revolution; a decolonisation lead process of converting contentious territories owned by the Crown Estate (800,000 acres) and other privately owned land, into land for carbon capture and natural regeneration.

The Carbon Re-wiling Revolution strategy utilises the influence and popularity of the British Crown, and aims to create an exemplar model of their largest estate, Balmoral (situated in Scotland) by creating a typology that can be replicated across other sites and influential landowners. The proposal campaigns against current land fashioning techniques at Balmoral, such as deer stalking/hunting and heath burning, both influential in disrupting the climate. The Carbon Re-wilding Revolution provokes decolonisation and creates a new, naturally regenerated, climate conscious landscape through planting of high carbon absorbing, native tree species. Tree species were assessed based on their average size/weight and lifespan. Carbon represents approximately half of a tree's dry weight, this metric was used to calculate and compare the average carbon consumption of different tree species found in the UK, such as the native Scots Pine, Beech, English Elm etc. Following this method, a tree taxonomy was formed - species that had high carbon absorbing abilities as well as a longer life span were selected. The Re-wilding Revolution uses a digital cartographic tool that analyses existing land characteristics (such as proximity to infrastructure, soil contamination levels etc) to produce a gradient of re-wilding potential.

The Old Caledonian Memorial and Carbon Monitoring Station sits at the centre of the re-wilded landscape of Balmoral. The architecture promotes a symbolic gesture to the vulnerable, prehistoric 'Old Caledonian' forest of Scotland - the building itself echoes the structure and concept of the native Scots Pine tree. The architecture is made of 38 modules (representing the 38 remaining areas of Caledonian forest in Scotland) with three different module sizes - based on three growing stages of the Scots Pine tree. The module sizes mirror the tree during each phase, taking into consideration overall tree height, crown height, crown thickness and trunk thickness. The materiality of each module also reflects that of the tree, a primary branching glulam structure creates the skeleton of each module. Rammed earth walls infill the glulam to form a lower datum, mimicking the solidity of the tree trunks. Above this, a mixture of solid cork panels and glazing are used, creating a dappled effect of the forest.

The architecture and landscape work harmoniously together, the regenerated land provides the basis for the architecture, with facilities such as the wood lab, seed vaults and observatory, that record, monitor and preserve. The wood lab collects tree trunk boreholes from across the re-wielded landscape, measuring carbon absorption and creating key archival information. The seed preservation facilities collect and preserve each tree species and store these highly precious seeds in vaults beneath the ground, futureproofing the species and re-wilded landscape. The architecture cannot exist without the presence of the landscape; an inverted relationship of what is more commonly seen within contemporary architecture.

(right) The New Caledonian Carbon Forest, a re-wilded landscape of carbon absorption.

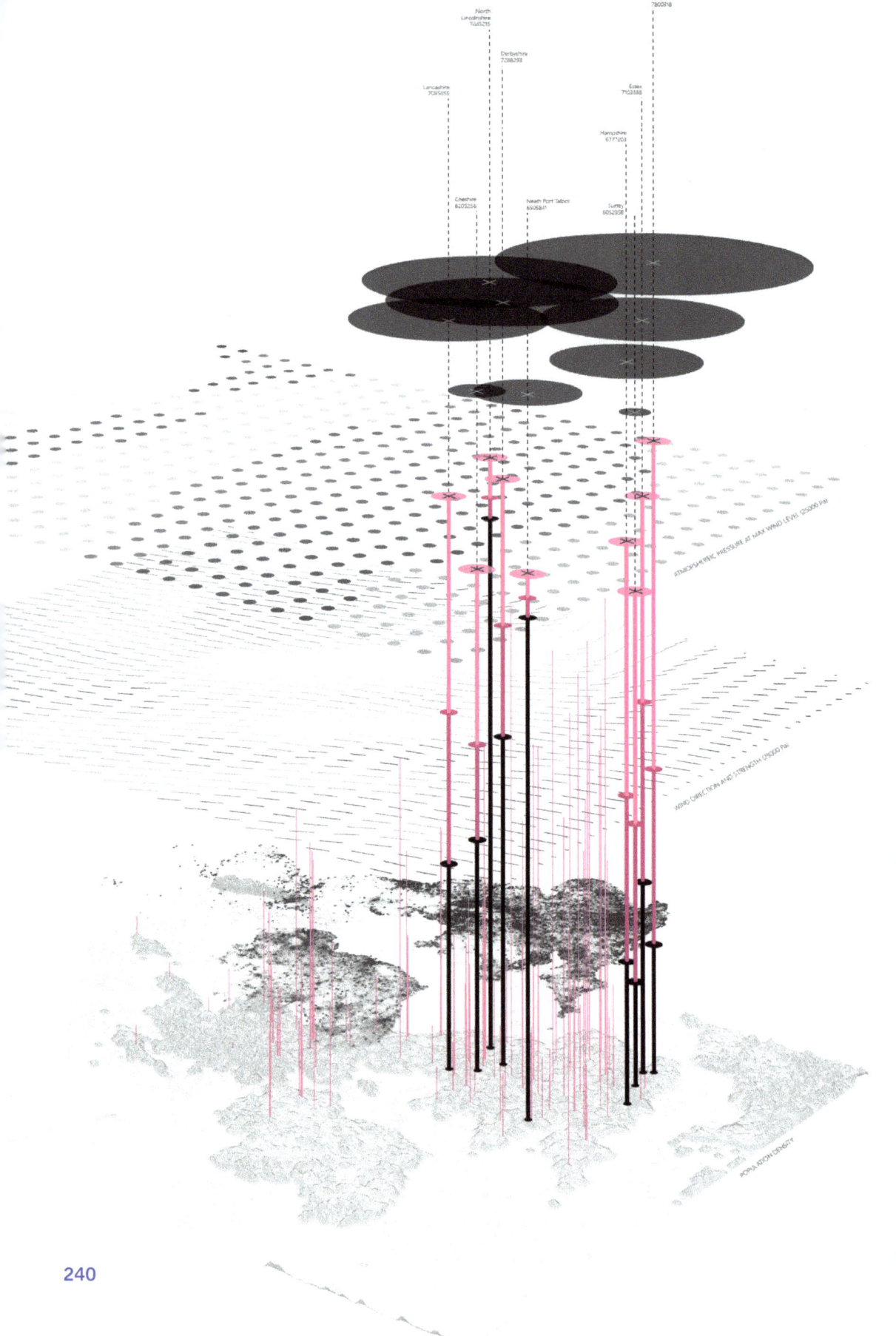

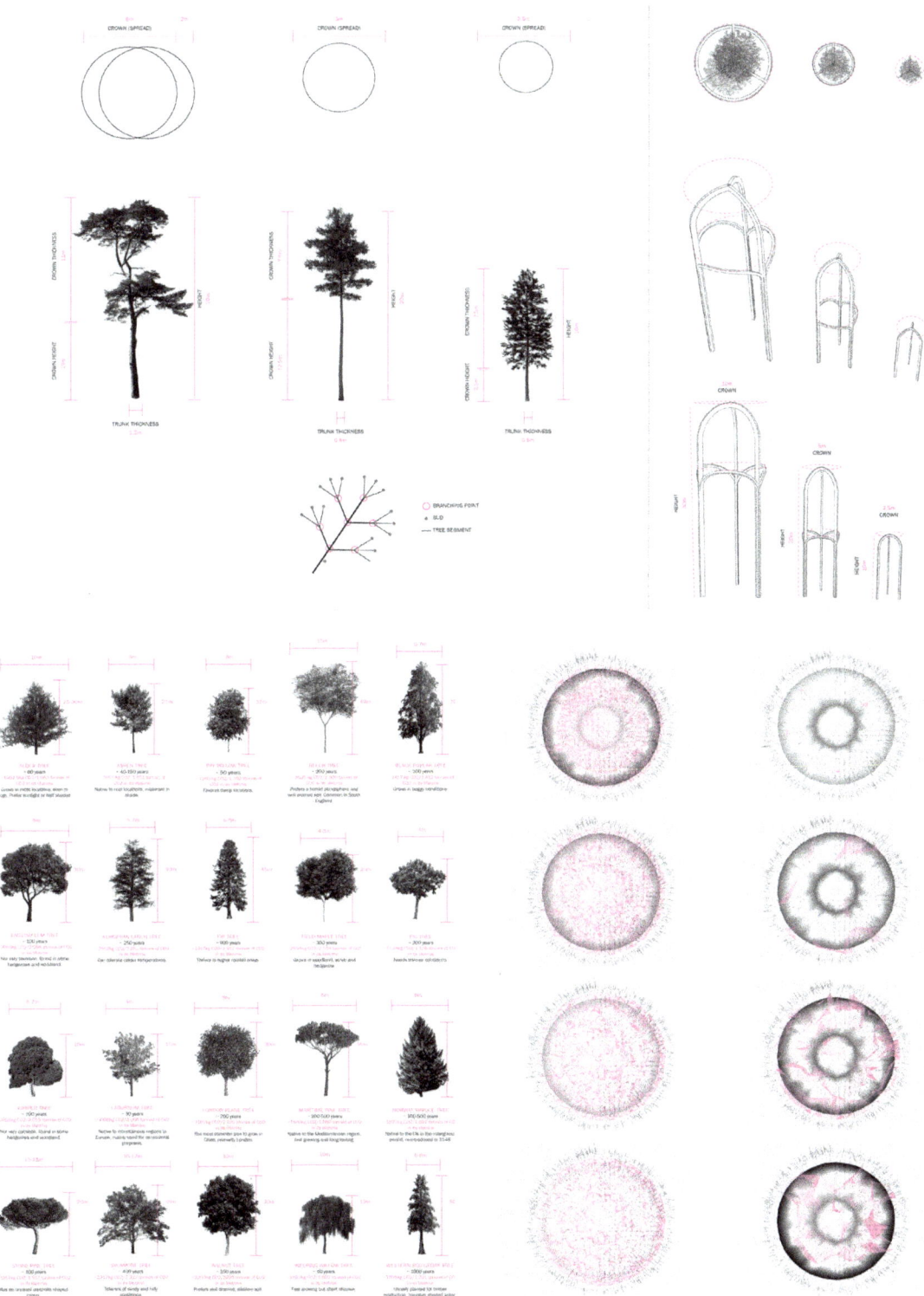

(left) Atmospheric conditions and CO_2 emissions in the UK.
(top) Measuring the Native Scottish Pine. (bottom left) Taxonomy of UK tree species and CO_2 class. (bottom right) Combustion and CO_2 simulation.

(top) Proposed floorplan. (bottom) The centre point of the Carbon Re-wilded Landscape - a view towards the Wood Lab.
(right) The Old Caledonian Memorial and Carbon Monitoring Station, overview.

FERREL PERIPHERY TRANSCRIBING THE JET STREAM

KIRSTEN DAVIS

Arctic amplification, linked to the weakening and fragmentation of the polar jet stream, has resulted in more frequent, stationary high-pressure weather systems associated with heatwaves, drought and frost. Their impact on UK infrastructure raises social and economic issues, thus the development of forecasting tools is critical, alongside strategies for adaptation to more turbulent weather patterns.

Situated at the most North-Westerly location in the UK, the remote islands of the Outer Hebrides are exposed to the harsh fronts of the polar jet stream, intensified ground level effects of these weather patterns and rising sea levels, and have historically experienced some of the most extreme of national pressure recordings. The lifestyle of local inhabitants is intricately linked to the weather, extending beyond physical experience to encompass local customs, mythology and a deep attachment to the place. Understanding the community's relationship with the weather has guided the development of an architecture that is both resilient and climate-responsive.

The proposal seeks to tangibly communicate both long-term patterns of climate, and the potential impact of global warming on the more localised, short-term weather systems. Through physical representation of data, and kinetic response to atmospheric pressure, the architecture engages with ground level aspects of weather and records patterns over time.

Paying homage to the Hebridean Neolithic stone circles, plinths of Lewisian gneiss are cut to size according to pressure recordings; using traditional skills serving as a community craft enterprise. Emerging from the rich geology of the South Uist hills, in full exposure to Westerly winds, sat just above the 1000mb pressure threshold, the building tunes into the elements to amplify the tangible experience of the jet stream.

At the periphery of the Ferrel Cell, at the intersection between world coordinate grid lines, the Jet Stream Archives will provide a facility for research, climate forecasting and political stratification; one that challenges the existing hierarchy associated with adaptation planning and rather seeks to respond to community initiatives.

(right) Hecla's Jet Stream Stone Archives; Of Stone, Earth and Wicker.

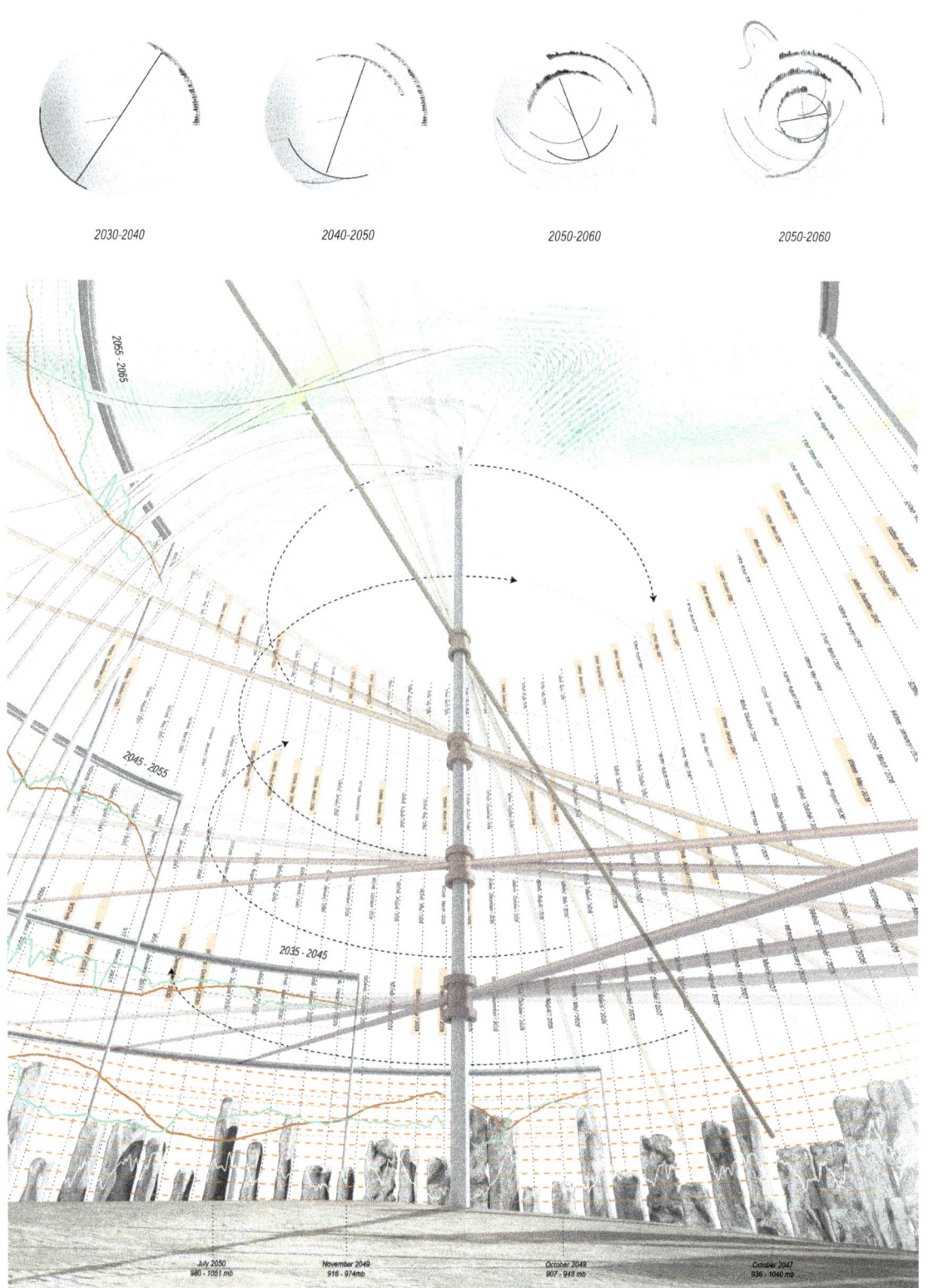

(top) Etching the weather variables into stone, diagrams. (bottom) Main climate conference room, the Register.

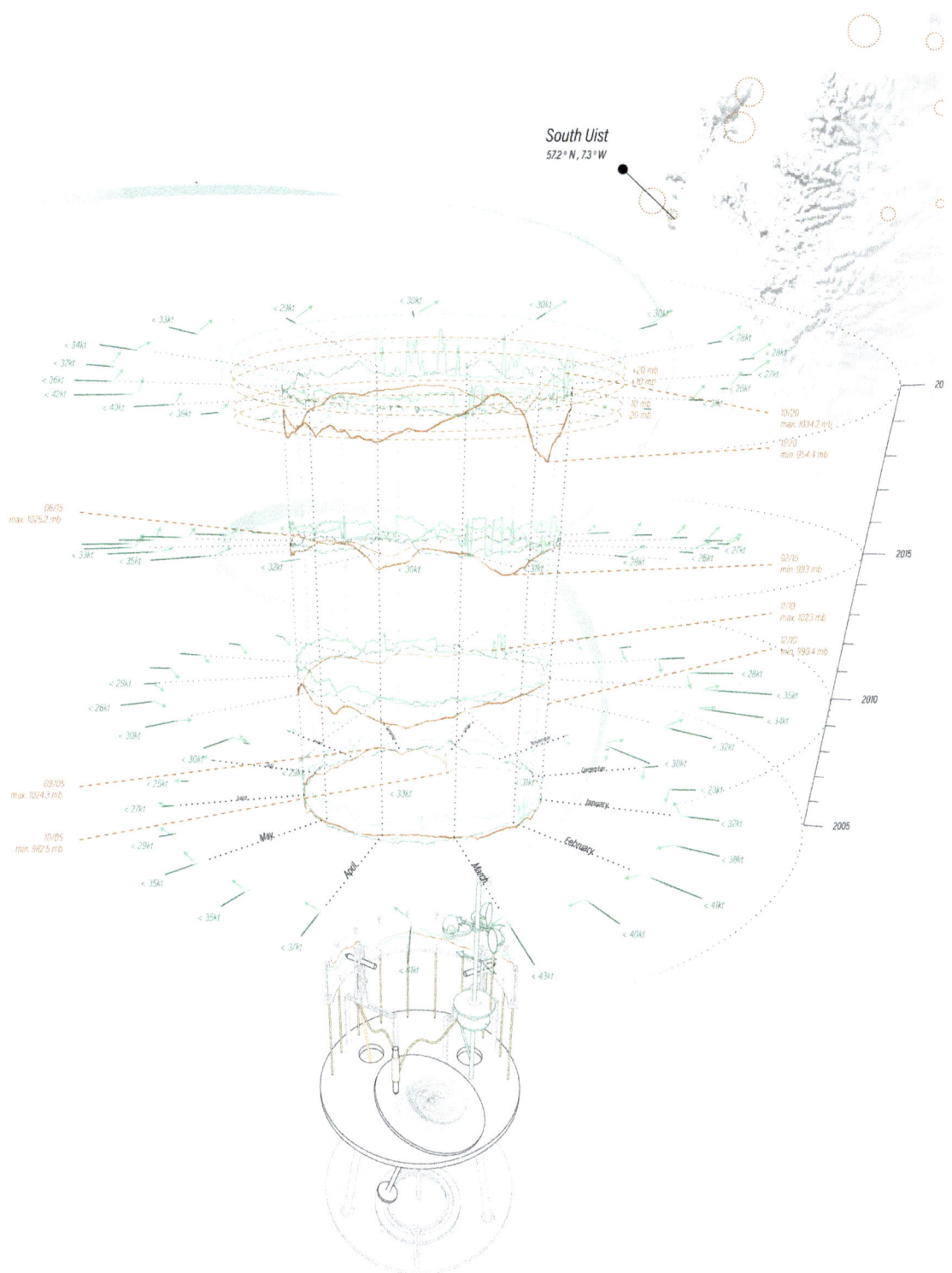

Variation and Unpredictability Archive.

(top) Aerial site section simulation. (middle) Archival site section. (bottom left) Hecla's Jet Stream Stone Archives, overview.

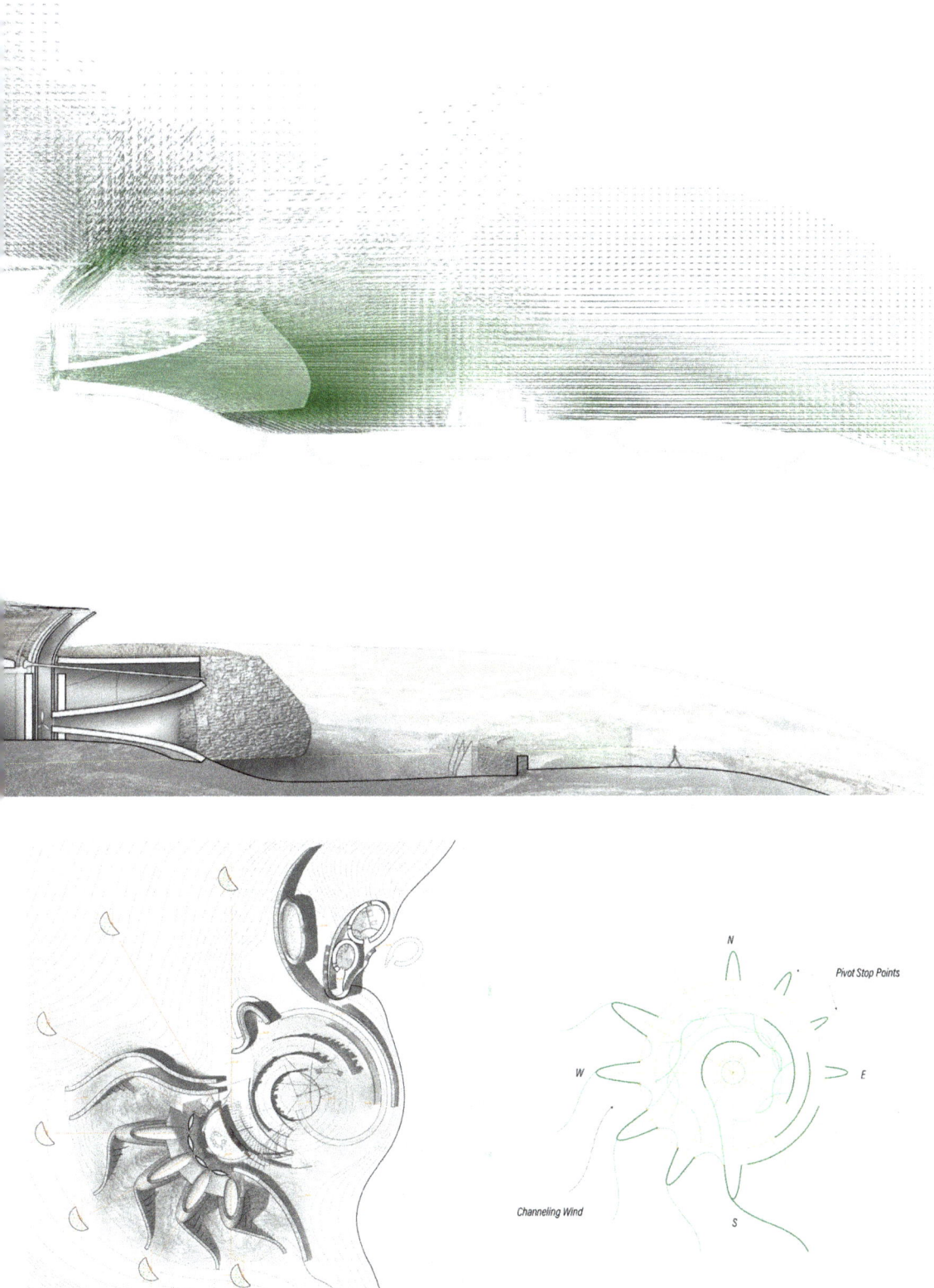

(bottom left) Proposed floorplan. (bottom right) Wind and pressure isocurve development.

SMOULDERING INTERFACE

CHADA ELALAMI

The Smouldering Interface project seeks to redefine life within a wildland-urban interface by embracing fire as an integral part of the environment—capable of both destruction and renewal.

Wildfires in the UK, though less frequent than in other parts of the world, are becoming increasingly severe and harder to control due to rising temperatures and changing human activity (such as land mismanagement and increased development near wildland areas). These factors contributed to the 2018 Saddleworth Moor fires in the Peak District, which burned for weeks, destroyed large areas of peatland, and required extensive firefighting efforts to contain. In response to the significant impact of this event, the project is located adjacent to a fire scar and aims to enhance fire resilience within the at-risk community. Departing from traditional approaches that simply reject fire, the proposal adopts a multifaceted perspective, embracing a paradigm of adaptation. It explores various fire interactions, including guidance, containment, rejection, protection, and educational utilisation, based on its specific position within a 'wildfire matrix'. This weighted probabilistic matrix, structured as a 50x50m grid, evaluates environmental and soil conditions such as vegetation density, wind speed, and terrain slope. It guides the placement of interventions by identifying areas categorised as high, medium, or low risk.

The project comprises of a series of interconnected interventions functioning as a holistic system, targeting three distinct phases across different scales: mitigating fire risk at the landscape level, responding to fires at the building scale, and supporting recovery through detailed building design and materiality. As a risk mitigation measure, sacrificial wooden interventions are strategically placed in the landscape to interact with climatic conditions and alleviate fire-prone conditions such as soil moisture and strong winds. These include 'guiding walls' scattered throughout the landscape, designed to direct the fire to strategic points where it is allowed to burn in a controlled manner to help contain it at sacrificial locations. Additionally, fire education and awareness serve as indispensable non-physical risk mitigation measures.

The architecture of the project is designed to tactically respond to fire, employing a range of fire-resistant properties. It utilises low fire resistance for wood elements and high fire resistance for the biopolymer material. The varying charring levels of the biopolymer orchestrate and choreograph fire dynamics intentionally. Moreover, the project introduces a new fire-resistant wood-based biopolymer as a material strategy for post-fire recovery. This biopolymer can be fabricated on-site by the community in designated workshop areas.

Overall, the Smouldering Interface project reimagines the relationship between communities and wildfire-prone landscapes, emphasising adaptation, resilience, and education. By incorporating locally produced materials, such as community-fabricated fire-resistant biopolymers, alongside holistic interventions at multiple scales, the project empowers at-risk communities to coexist with fire while reducing its impact. This approach, not only mitigates risk but also fosters a proactive and sustainable response to the challenges of living within a wildland-urban interface— therefore, rethinking how we design alternative spaces of thermal danger.

(right) The Smouldering Interface, overview.

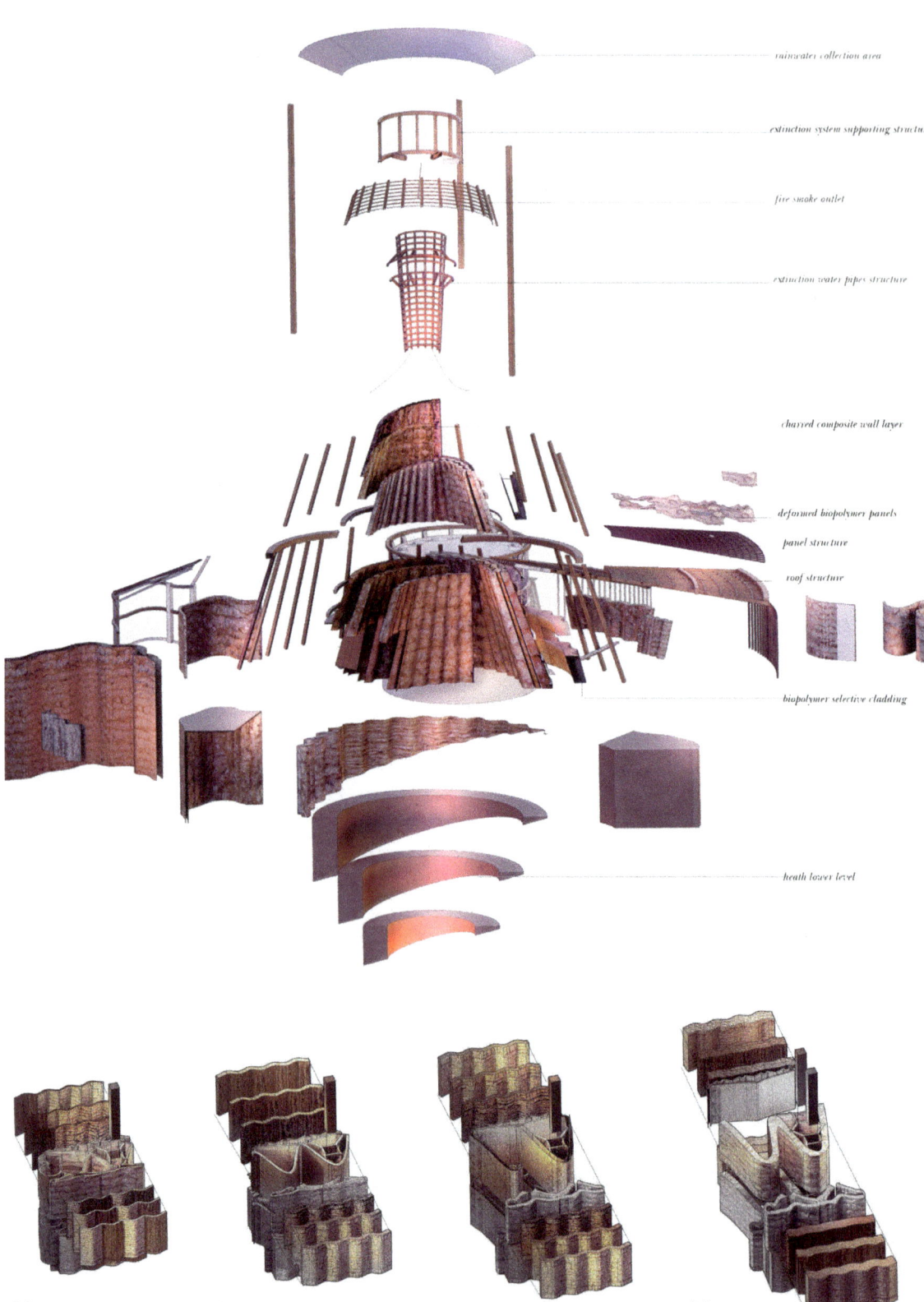

01 30 minute wall   *02* 1 hour wall   *03* 2 hours wall   *04* 3 hours wall

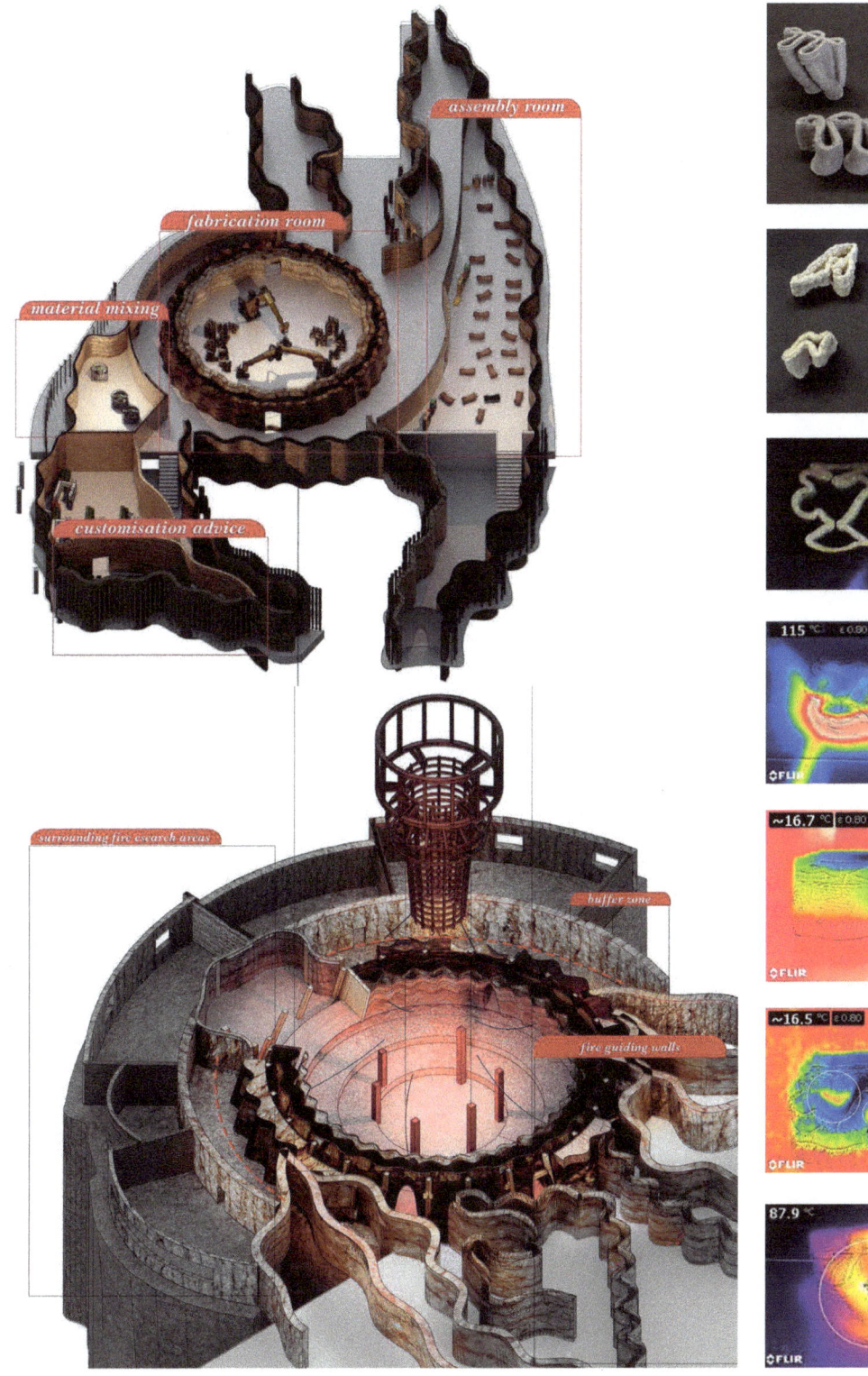

(top left) Dynamic and static fire layering strategy. (bottom left) Wall build-up overview.
(top) Proposed Material Workshop (bottom) Proposed Research Centre. (right) Thermal 3D printed samples for heat transfer.

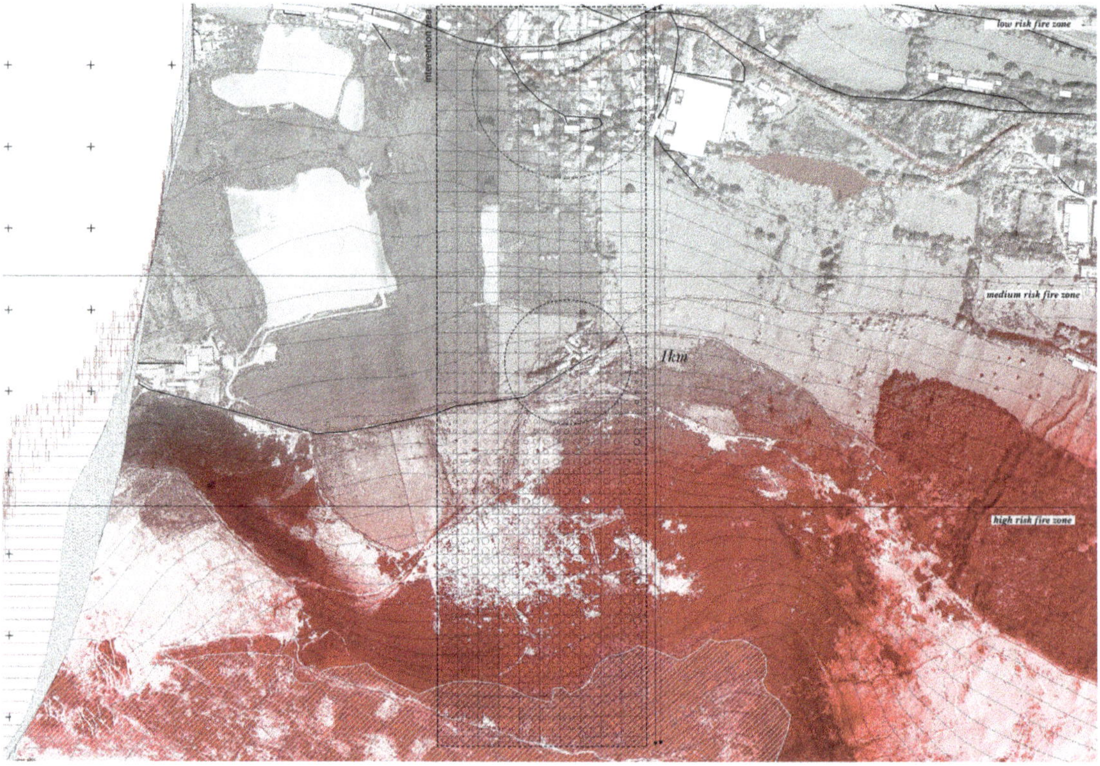

(top) Fire Probability Matrix - site, slope, wind analysis and fire propagation. (bottom) Wildfire mapping and risks.
(right) The Smoldering Interface, Landscape Prevention and Intervention.

ROMNEY MARSH THATCHERY

NICHOLAS TSANGARIS

The UK is suffering from widespread sewage pollution that is damaging our natural environment and everything in it. The ageing infrastructure, increased rainfall, lack of chemical access and profit driven companies, means that the issue is constantly getting worse. Taking into account for some of the Green New Deal objectives, Dungeness can become a test bed for a large-scale ecological sewage treatment plant.

The nature themed project will be based around the idea of an 100-year life span that will start with the re-forming of the landscape to facilitate reed beds and quickly shift standard sewage treatment towards them. The reforming will be achieved through the use of timber posts that will monitor, manage and access the reed beds as well as control waterflow and sedimentation. In turn, the thatch will be harvested, dried, processed and turned into a natural based typology for the site. This idea emphasizes the temporality of the scheme that may eventually wash away due to the low-lying land. The posts will eventually form the foundation for the structures on site which will facilitate the thatch processing, as well as space for training based around the contemporary and experimental use of thatch in buildings. The posts will also support new infrastructure for bird watching tourism generated from the large natural landscape.

The Romney Marsh Thatchery would employ workers from the decommissioned nuclear power station, workers from the old sewage plants and farmers from the land that is now used for the reed beds and allow them to retrain with professionals from the construction industry. These employment opportunities combined with an investment from a larger charity such as the RSPB for the visitor centre would help maintain the local community and boost their economy.

The core of the project is the central workshop space that will be used as a training facility for new thatching techniques which combines traditional and digital construction into a new thatching methodology. This in turn would be showcased through an ever-changing visitor centre and thatch processing facility that would reflect these updated uses of thatch and the natural weathering of the material.

(right) The Romney Marsh Thatchery overview.

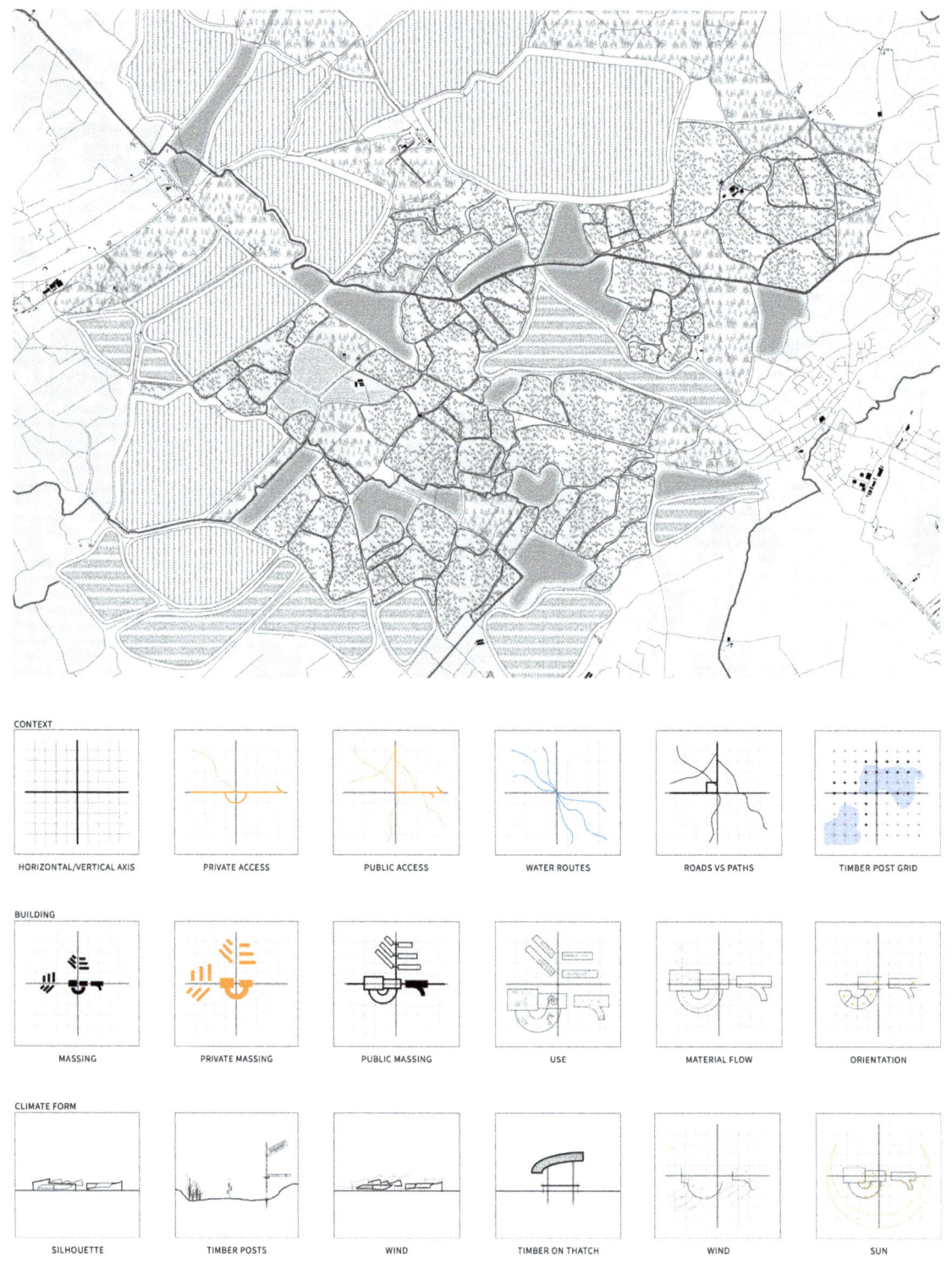

(top) The Romney Marsh Masterplan - consisting of constructed wetlands, forests, flower fields and water reservoirs.
(bottom) Key design decision matrix - split into context, building form and climate driven form.

(top) Seasonal changes in reed harvesting is reflected by the buildings canopies (before/after).

(bottom) Perspective view over the reed growing landscape of Dungeness.

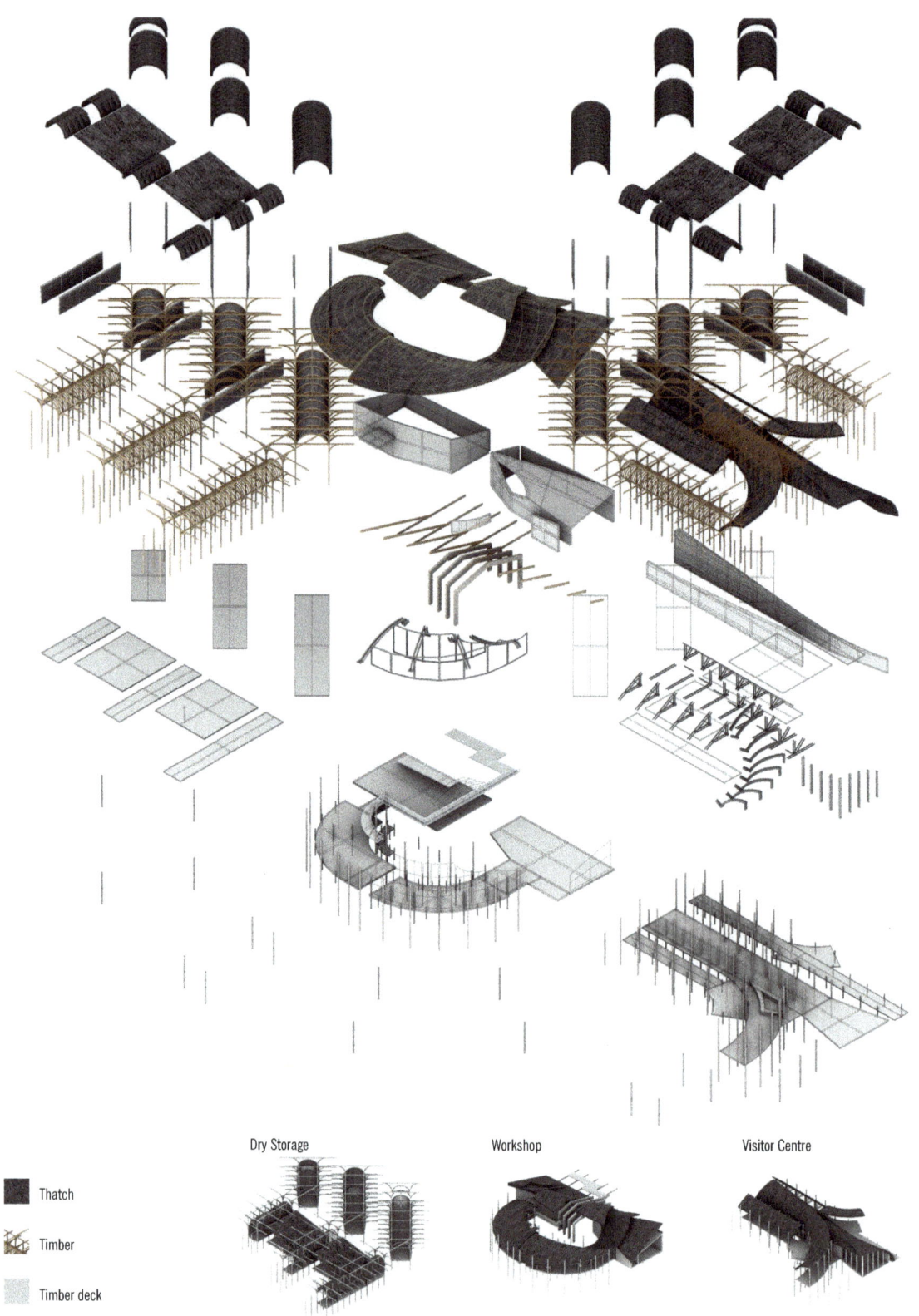

The Romney Marsh Thatchery exploded axonometric - The structure and modular roof system allow for the buildings to be adjusted and change depending on the users needs.

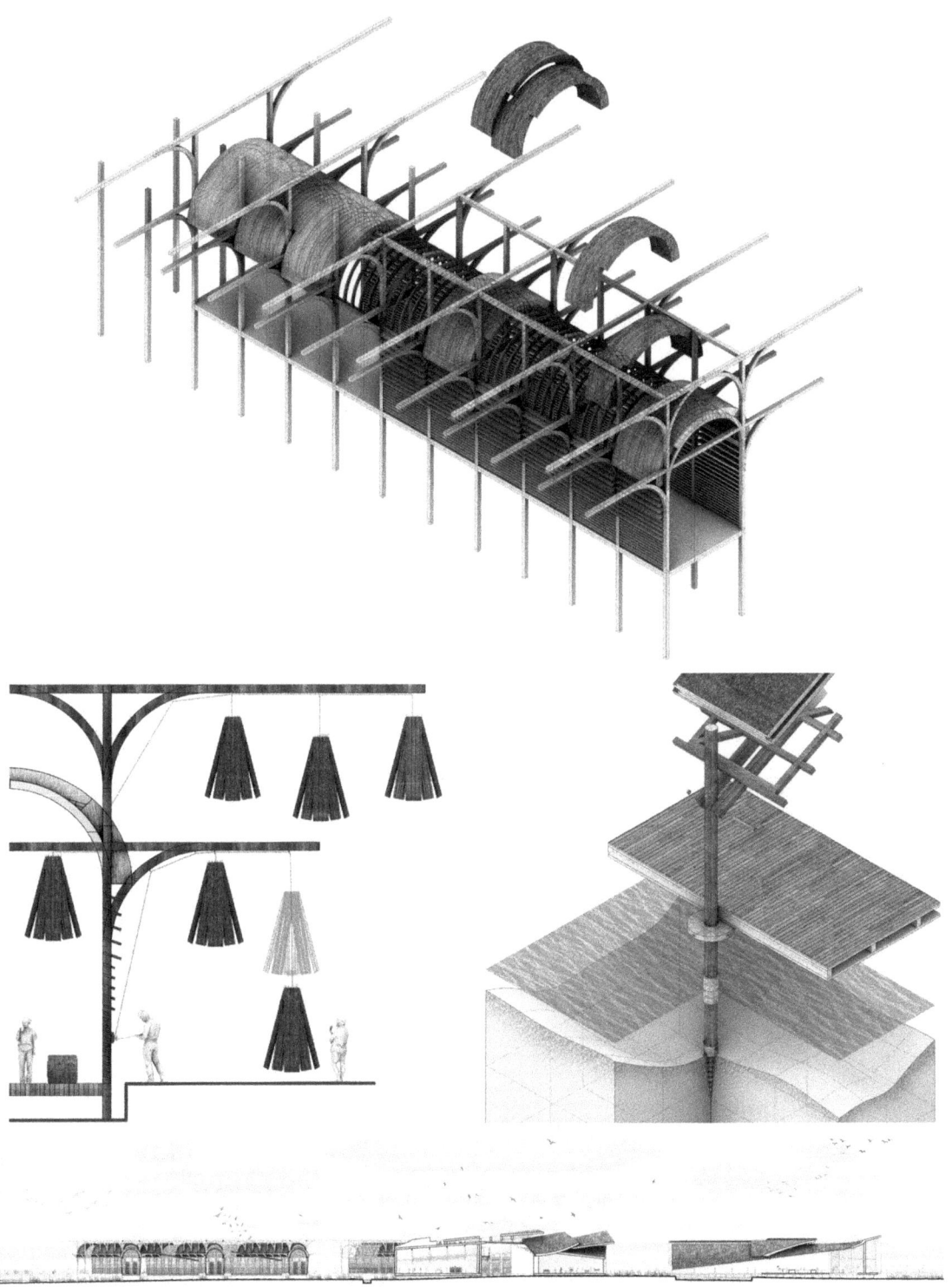

(top) Modular timber and thatch storage facilities that grow depending on storage needs. (middle left) The posts allow for easy adjustments to the buildings form, using a fully demountable structure. (middle right) Emphasis on low carbon and re-usable materials. (bottom) The journey of the thatch from the fields through the workshop and to the visitor centre.

LYCHEN INCUBATOR

JUSTYNA LESNY

Dungeness, a headland on the coast of Kent, in the UK, faces the growing threat of being submerged due to rising sea levels. While it presents an unforgiving landscape for many species, it is home to a surprising abundance of lichen. These cryptogams are both resilient and sensitive organisms, absorbing approximately 14 billion tons of carbon dioxide each year, playing a key role in mitigating the increasingly detrimental effects of human activity.

Lichens are incredibly adaptable organisms, capable of thriving in some of the harshest environments on Earth, from radiation-rich areas to regions with extreme variations in humidity, temperature, and light. This adaptability is not only a survival trait but also a key factor in their role as bioindicators of environmental health. With a diverse range of forms—ranging from crust-like patches to leafy or bushy structures—and vibrant colours, including bright greens, yellows, and deep reds, lichens are finely tuned to help them survive, reproduce, and thrive. Some species even possess the ability to glow in the dark, a phenomenon known as bioluminescence.

This project explores the impact of climate change, particularly how rising sea levels affect the biodiversity of Dungeness. It is informed by these resilient organisms, focusing on their carbon-capturing potential and their remarkable symbiotic relationship with fungi and algae—each taking exactly what it needs from the other to thrive.

Dungeness B, one of seven Advanced Gas-Cooled Reactors (AGRs) set to close by the end of this decade, has left behind a stagnant, available environment—especially its façade. This project leverages an in-depth understanding of lichen properties to retrofit Dungeness B, transforming it into a thriving habitat for a diverse range of lichen species. Through environmental analysis, and simulations of both air and daylight, a new façade system is developed to capture and cultivate airborne spores and cryptogams. The design integrates the growing logics of lichens into an architectural 'bioskin' tile that adapts in surface area, shading, material, and form depending on its placement on the Reactor's façade.

The Lichen Incubator is an intervention that seizes the opportunity to repurpose both the physical structures of these iconic buildings and the social and economic voids they leave behind. It indirectly challenges the future of nuclear architecture, questioning the legacy of such sites.

Within the walls of the Incubator, lichens' unique properties can be researched, harvested, and utilised to gradually remediate the environment. The empty reactor cores have been repurposed to house various microclimates. One such environment, the Incubator, is heated by the warm air from the dye extraction process in the dye house and perfumery below, creating ideal conditions for lichens that thrive in milder temperatures and higher moisture levels. Meanwhile, the other core holds the Spore Store and Growing Ceiling, where lichens native to the Dungeness area, such as those from the Cladonia genus, are observed, protected, and cultivated. It is not a profit-making enterprise, but a vessel to initiate lichen growth—some only used when required for research and extraction, while most will serve their primary purpose of capturing carbon and contributing to a more sustainable, balanced relationship with our natural assets.

(right) The Lichen Incubator. Retrofit concept diagram of AGR Power Station, Dungeness.

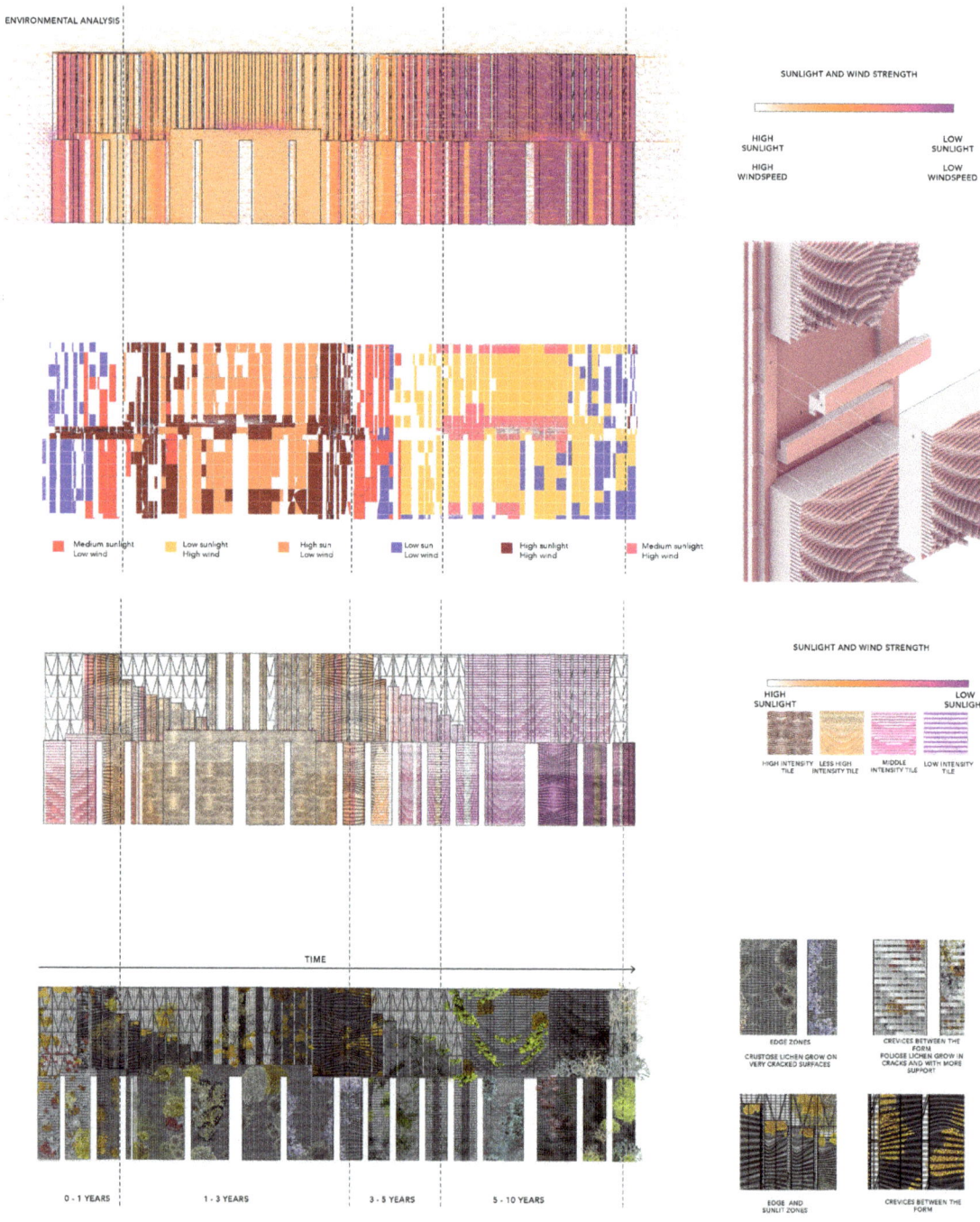

The Growing Facade. Unrolled logic elevations based on a combined analysis of the sunlight hours and wind velocity received by the existing facade on all sides.

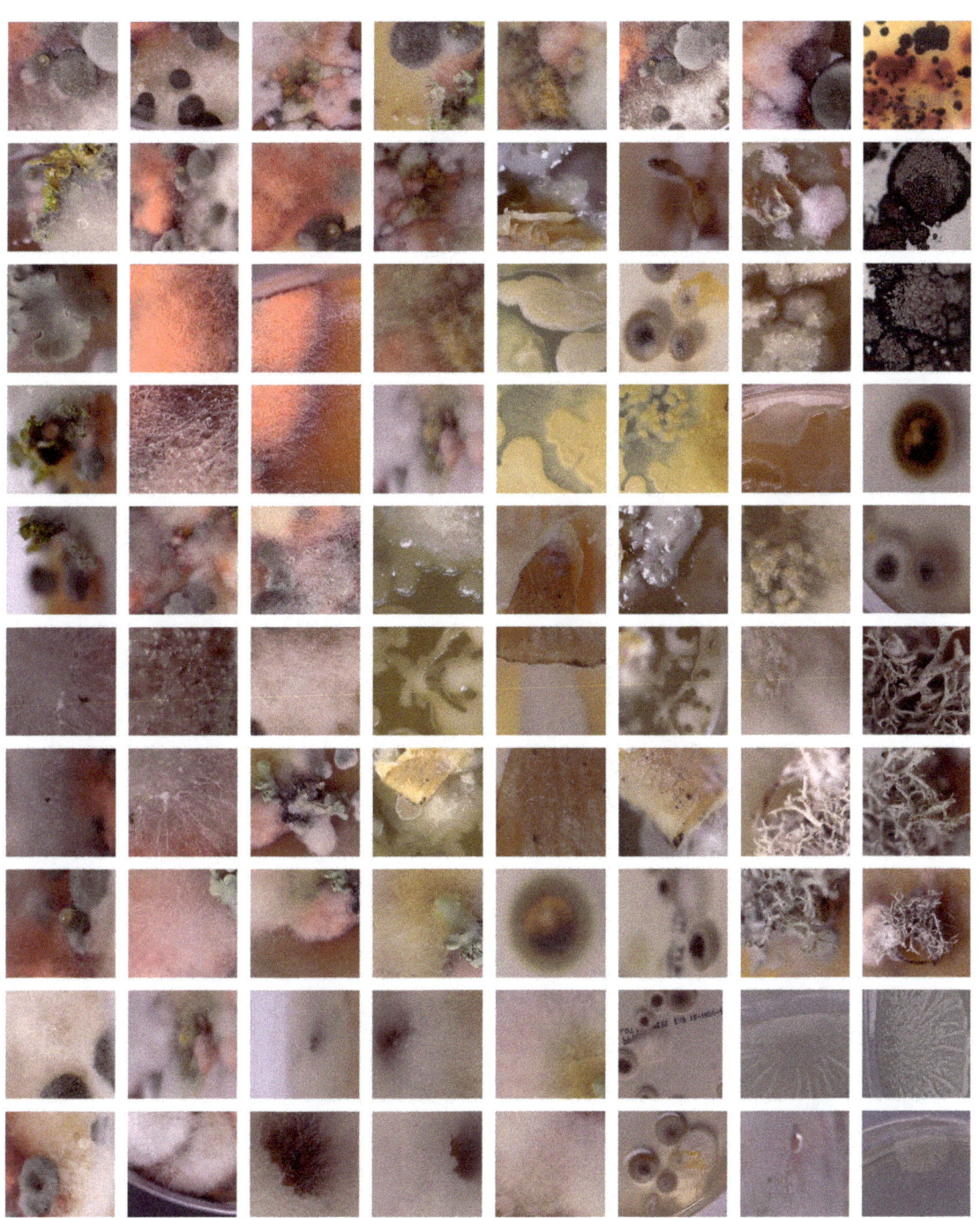

Micro-Growth Matrix. Mapping the textures of lichen and bacterial growth from 14 samples around Dungeness.

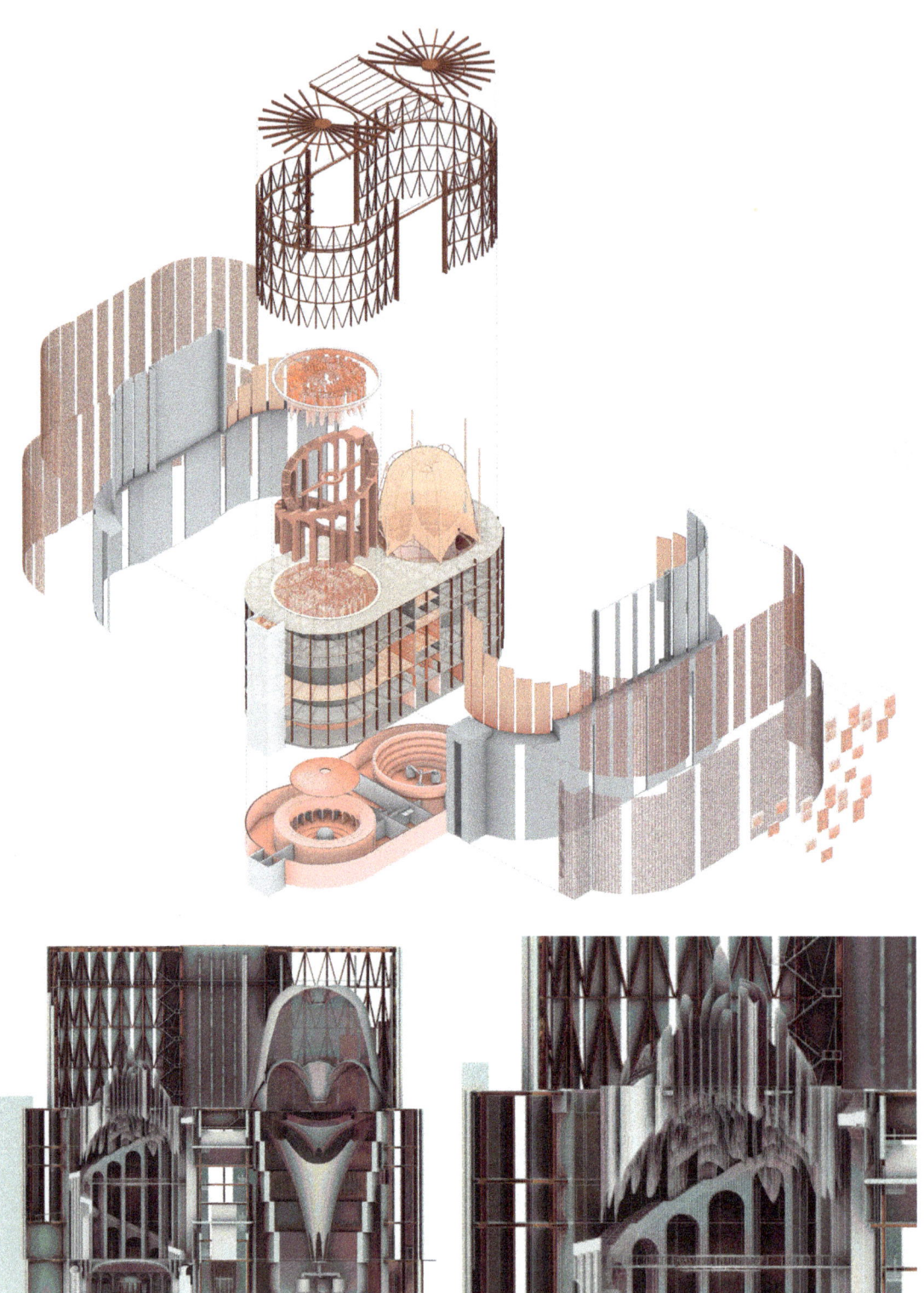

(top) Proposed retro-fit axonometric. (bottom) The reactor cores and façade have been re-imagined to house the bioskin tiles to increase facade surface area for spore collection. (right) The Growing Ceiling, internal view.

PEAT RECOVERY FACILITY
SENI AGUNPOPO

The project focuses on preserving and accelerating the restoration of damaged peatlands in Scotland, particularly in the Flow Country—home to one of the largest continuous peat bogs in Europe. Peatlands are among the world's most efficient carbon sinks, storing millions of tons of carbon dioxide. However, they are critically endangered by human activities such as agricultural farming, urbanisation, and even climate mitigation efforts like tree planting and wind farms when these are incorrectly sited on peatland. This project addresses the climatic and ecological challenges threatening peatlands and offers a comprehensive architectural response to facilitate their regeneration.

The concept explores a parametric masterplan integrating responsive systems that regenerate damaged peatlands by manipulating micro-environmental conditions. This includes modular interventions for monitoring and restoration, as well as adaptive blanket systems and probes designed to create conditions conducive to peat formation while safeguarding existing peat layers.

Peatlands play a critical role in global climate regulation, functioning as carbon sinks capable of storing more carbon than all the world's forests combined. However, rising temperatures, shifting rainfall patterns, and human activities are accelerating peat degradation. For example, the 2019 fire in Scotland's Flow Country burned over 5,300 hectares, releasing vast amounts of stored carbon into the atmosphere. Current legislative efforts to restore peatlands, such as banning commercial peat extraction, highlight the urgent need for innovative solutions to address these climatic and ecological crises effectively. Without intervention, the degradation of peatlands will not only reduce their capacity to sequester carbon but also release previously stored carbon, further exacerbating climate change.

This project proposes a multifaceted strategy to support peatland regeneration. A deployable modular research lab serves as the operational hub for scientists monitoring peat conditions and conducting restoration activities. These units are complemented by a responsive "blanket system" designed to retain soil moisture, stabilize temperatures, and enhance humidity in damaged areas, effectively mimicking a protective second skin for peatlands. Additionally, landscape probes are deployed to accelerate the conditions necessary for peat formation, such as regulating soil moisture and temperature to encourage the accumulation of organic matter.

The project not only aligns with Scotland's legislative priorities on landscape restoration but also serves as a scalable model for global peatland conservation. By combining architecture, environmental science, and responsive technologies, it demonstrates the critical role of interdisciplinary approaches in addressing climate challenges. This innovative intervention emphasises the importance of peatland regeneration as a key strategy in mitigating climate change and protecting one of Earth's most valuable carbon sinks.

(right) Deployment of the peat probes, landscape overview proposal.

(left) Exploded diagram of the blanket proposal, indicating moisture retention and quantifying absorption into peat. (top left) Technical close-up of the 'pippette' or probe.
(top bottom) CFD model of carbon in air transferred into ground.
Peat recovery facility - a landscape blanket proposal.

BEYOND STUDIO

ANTHROPOGENIC PEDAGOGIES AND EXPERIMENTAL MEDIA

LIDIA GASPERONI

We can conceptualise more than we can design, we can design more than we can imagine. But how can we imagine more than we can conceptualise and then think critically about what we imagine? In the contemporary era, the capacity to conceptualise has surpassed that of the capacity to design, and the latter has itself exceeded the former's limits of imagination, operating on the threshold between the visible and the invisible. A variety of disciplines and methodologies provide extensive conceptual frameworks that extend the field of signification, which can be generatively embedded into the design practice. Meanwhile, digital design tools operate at the level of semantics, overproducing images and representations. In particular, the use of digital technologies in design leads to the production of highly complex visualisations that appear to align with the imagination. However, human imagination is shaped by a hybrid use of media that co-design environments as a signifying dimension of intersectionality between diverse critical spaces and devices.

Architectural interventions operate on a complex scale of phenomena. They constitute a network of intersecting fields. These intersections provoke a continuous renegotiating of human positionality, thereby shifting local perspectives and global levels of impact that shape more-than-human life. In the Anthropocene, these entanglements – at once local and global – reach a level of technological complexity that seems to elude human perception. The pivotal question of the Anthropocene is whether the elusiveness that immerses humanity in the so-called technosphere should in fact entail a human (but not anthropocentric) project. If so, such a human project should include an attitude towards media practices across existing representations that helps elucidate the causes and consequences of human exploitation of environments and that opens up new approaches to more-than-human relationality and transscalarity. These approaches would be not just solutions, but novel attitudes of designing the environments that humans engage in. From this perspective, the (Post-)Anthropocene must be viewed as a critical and emancipatory project that does not neglect the role of human embodied cognition, which can be enabled by specific media practices. Understood as a medium, design needs to reposition human reflexivity and to rethink the institutional framework that humans developed in order to produce and transmit knowledge. This includes the possibility of transcending and hybridising spatial scales. The result is an operational field in which humans have a responsibility for action within the given institutional frameworks. One of such frameworks is academic education.

Architectural Pedagogy and the Question of Efficacy

In the field of architectural pedagogy, the urgency to experiment is connected to what Peggy Deamer in a recent essay on Ardeth defined as a problem of "efficacy", stating: "architectural academy is guilty of producing architects who might be competent, but are not effective in putting their training into socially relevant use." [01] Unlike mere competency and efficiency, the notion of efficacy questions the way in which design pedagogy is able to contribute to the transformation of the society in which architectural practice is situated, while also reflecting on the limits of its impact. These include the relationship between the training courses and the regulation of the professional figure of the architect – think of the different systems of qualification and accreditation of architects that differ from country to country. Another crucial issue is the role of the design studio as the core of the production of architectural knowledge and forms during training. For Deamer, there is a need to move beyond design that is focused on formal choices in order to include the complexity of real design: "A broader definition of design has the students consider what acts, if their hypothetical project were built, would be set in motion by their formal choices. This means, at the front end, imagining and designing the procurement process: who builds, with what materials, coming from what location, and by what means. It implies imagining the suppliers, fabricators, and labourers mobilised by the aesthetic choices being made." [02]

This means questioning the implicit dispositions underlying architectural pedagogy in the face of the urgent challenges of climate change and the need for a new pedagogy based on environmental and social justice. Effective architectural education in the state of climate emergency requires an experimental approach. It integrates the development of new technologies and materials, rethinking architectural practice as a process of synthesis capable of incorporating extra-disciplinary knowledge and facilitating real practice. In this perspective, architectural pedagogies engage with climate change in inventive and transformative ways, not in the form of a mere critique of the building practice but as a transformative "interferences" [03]. The latter prompts us not only to adapt architecture to construction methods and materials that are sustainable in time and space, but to turn the state of emergency into a field of transformative practices. There is thus a specific experimental need in the attempt to develop a new way of doing architecture by producing innovative technologies and materials and extending the efficacy of architecture as an environmental practice and model. [04]

Rethinking pedagogy on an experimental level means renegotiating a field of themes and practices to train architects capable of facing the challenges of the contemporary world and projecting those challenges into the future. This means to rediscover architectural pedagogies [05], question existing canons and implicit values [06], and expand the territorial borders of architectural pedagogies [07]. Issue 76 (2022) of the Journal of Architectural Education, dedicated to Pedagogies for a Broken World, declares the need to overcome pedagogical models based on supremacist and progressive visions. Instead, the editors propose an architectural pedagogy "centred around various forms of breakdown and related epistemologies" [08] that becomes a space of care and openness to the pluriverse of environmental actors and realities that it includes [09]. The introductory essay on Pedagogical Experiments in Architecture for a Changing Climate [10] emphasises the responsibility of pedagogy in architecture in re-establishing a critical relationship with the building sector and reconsidering its impact on the environment. In order to achieve this, "environmental architects" are able to engage in holistic and systematic imaginative abstraction. This capacity should be connected with the ability to simultaneously immerse oneself in and situate oneself within a given context. In order to facilitate this, it is necessary to reconsider the relationship between media practices and design processes, with a view to identifying alternative and transformative ways of making architecture. [11]

The Limits of Abstraction

A fundamental question arises with respect to the epistemic function of architecture, which is capable of generating knowledge without becoming a practice of mere abstraction – the reductionism of which is one of the main criticisms levelled at modernism. In the field of architectural pedagogy, Adrian Forty's essay on the notion of 'design' as a complex notion between drawing, design and form, highlights how a close link between the training of the architect – increasingly entrusted to university institutions – and the formal approach to design was at the basis of a profound caesura between design practice and material practice at the beginning of the 20th century. This separation between architecture as "mental product – which was taught" and architecture as "practice engaged with the material world" creates a progressive distance between education and practice: "In short," Forty states, "the category 'design' allowed architecture to be taught, rather than learned by experience." (12)

This caesura is also considered by Pier Vittorio Aureli with reference to abstraction as one of the cornerstones of capitalist society. According to Aureli, it is based on the division between manual and intellectual labour, which in architecture is manifested in the central role of form as the privileged method of abstraction. In this regard, Aureli, taking up the Vitruvian distinction between fabrica and ratiocinatio, critically investigates the development of geometric representation as a scientific objectification of space. (13)

Considering Forty's and Aureli's positions as two theoretical provocations, the question arises as to whether the architectural project can constitute a space of non-reductionist abstraction, i.e. whether it is able to incorporate extra-disciplinary, situated and specific knowledge, and at the same time become an epistemic artefact. (14) This issue is particularly pertinent when considering the utilisation and synthesis of complex data through the application of computational technologies and artificial intelligence. These facilitate a dynamic interface between empirical data and semantic criteria, thereby introducing a tension between real and fictional data that propose transformative visions of reality itself. What is the degree and legitimacy of abstraction inherent in this process?

Design Experimentation in Architectural Education and Design Studio 18

Design, as an institutionalized practice of teaching architecture, includes experimentation, which enables educators and students to develop specific modes of expression, media practices and methods of architectural materialisation. In this perspective, it is crucial to rethink the relationship between canonical and experimental practices to grasp the transformative potential of the architectural practice.

An 'experimental practice' is on the one hand a specific media practice as an intersection between sensory modalities and technological devices. (15) On the other hand it is a practice of expanding signification, rethinking the attitudes and implicit assumptions in the way we teach architectural design. The experimental value of a practice lies in its capacity to transform architecture, extending its sphere of signification through a specific expressive modality. Experimentation involves both the incorporation of extra-disciplinary knowledge and the transformative shift of established representational attitudes. The pivotal issue at hand is to comprehend how such media practices transcend the confines of an internal, protected and controlled domain within academic institutions. Instead, they can serve the function of exposure to the outside world, becoming a porous practice between the inside and the outside. To achieve this, it is essential to adopt a conception of experimental media practices that is neither instrumentalist nor technicist, but rather open to transformation and inclusivity. Questioning the representation(s) of more than human environments, overcoming a reductionist view of territorial and cartographic abstraction, is one of the prominent areas. As a transformative modality architectural design achieves the status of an environmental model that is both effective and inventive.

In this way, an experimental approach does not lead merely to the development of new representation techniques but also to a critical reflection on the ways in which representation is generated and on the agency of media. An experimental approach of representation thus includes a performative attitude, capable of understanding the empirical conditions – social, political, cultural – that underlie representations. The concept of performativity can be understood as a sphere of shifts, corrections, and repairs to representation, generating a dynamic space of representation in which to incorporate spheres of signification previously excluded from architectural representation.

The role of design, in my opinion, can only be rethought in the pedagogical sphere through specific teaching practices that engage with specific sites, themes, design practices and purposes. In this framework, my task as philosopher and architectural theorist is to gather, facilitate and question practices that try to respond to these challenges, to foster their criticalities through collaborative dialogues and shared platforms. In 2020, I initiated the Anthropocene Pedagogies in Architecture project as part of the Berlin-based association Fieldstations (16) and in collaboration with the Department of Architecture Theory at the Technical University Berlin. The project is meant to connect experimental teaching practices that share a specific transformative value in architectural pedagogy intersecting crucial fields of architectural education such as theoretical, material, digital and activistic practices. These practices enable future architects to respond to contemporary challenges related to the design of environmentally and socially sustainable spaces. They also involve experimental methods of teaching that significantly extend the media that are already part of design by creating hybrid practices at the intersection between architecture and other disciplines.

Design Studio 18 was from the beginning part of this initiative contributing in various ways, presenting and reflecting on their practices. DS 18 is committed to promoting design experimentation with the aim of producing "future scenarios". They constitute an interface of data and information, creating a multiscalar and multi-layered space of semantic interpretation of phenomena situated on the edge between visibility and invisibility. In this context, design can be considered as a research field characterised by a particular approach to data processing and visualisation. This research engages with the interdisciplinary fields of architecture, urbanism and landscape, addressing social, economic and political issues. It considers the ownership of air and its role in transcending political boundaries, demonstrating the global impact of situated processes. This practice of intersectionality informs architectural knowledge production, rethinking situatedness and illustrating the non-linearity of geological processes.

DS18 is a practice that engages with the microscale analysis of natural phenomena and the role that artistic and architectural practices can play in representing them. Rather than merely replicating or re-presenting phenomena that are perceptible to humans, this practice involves the generation of new representations that are informed by data. Simulation plays a crucial role in this process, allowing for the reassembly of data and the embedding of alternative data sets, thereby informing architectural design. This methodology, as an inventive exercise, also leads us to reflect on the relationship between data and scientific knowledge. A dataset is the product of a specific selection and the use of specific technologies for sensing and analysing data. This selection constitutes a potential plan of evidence and formulates specific questions for the analysis of climate change and the role of human life on the planet. However, the production of data, which enter into the field of visibility, generates a narrative of cause and effect that requires continual rethinking at a critical level. In this perspective, design fosters the production of scenarios as tools for critique and recontextualization. What degree of evidence and media of communication are required for visualisations? At different scales, the efficacy of visualisations – as open media – can be counterbalanced and renegotiated within the specific contexts (those of scientific, artistic, political production), in which architects act as mediators of efficacy.

Notes

(01) P. Deamer, 'Beyond Competency. Disciplinary Efficacy', *Ardeth 10-11*, 2022, p. 49.
(02) Ibid., p. 52.
(03) L. Gasperoni, 'Architecture as productive interference', *Stoa*, 9, 2024, pp. 26-39.
(04) See J. Graham, *Climates: Architecture and the Planetary Imaginary*, Lars Müller Publishers 2016.
(05) See the book "*Radical Pedagogies*" dedicated to the experimental practices of the 1960s and 1970s (B. Colomina, I.G. Galán, E. Kotsioris, A. Meister, Radical Pedagogies, The MIT Press 2022).
(06) C. Garcia, N. Frankowski, *A Manual of Anti-Racist Architecture Education*, WAI Architecture Think Tank, 2020.
(07) H. Harriss, A.M. Salama, A.G. Lara, *The Routledge Companion to Architectural Pedagogies of the Global South*, Routledge 2022.
(08) J. Cephas, I. Marjanović, A. Miljački (ed.), 'Pedagogies for a Broken World', *Journal of Architectural Education*, 76:2, 2022, p. 2.
(09) This agenda is already visible in the debate on pedagogy in architecture (see https://urgentpedagogies.iaspis.se/) and in alternative pedagogy projects, such as the Anthropocene Architecture School and the Floating University Berlin.
(10) T. Atak, L. Callejas, J.A. Scelsa, J.J. Tangberg (ed.), *Pedagogical Experiments in Architecture for a Changing Climate*, Routledge 2024, pp. 1-12.
(11) See L. Gasperoni, 'The Environmental Architect. Reflections on Media Performativity', in: C. Barioglio, D. Campobenedetto, A. A. Dutto, V. Federighi, C. Quaglio, E. Todella (ed.), *Innovation in Practice in Theory: Positioning Architectural Design and its Agency*, Applied Research and Design Publishing 2022, pp. 200-210.
(12) A. Forty, *Worlds and Buildings: A Vocabulary of Modern Architecture*, Thames and Hudson, 2004, p. 138.
(13) P.V. Aureli, 'Intangible and Concrete: Notes on Architecture and Abstraction', *e-flux*, 64, 3, 2015, pp. 1-10.
(14) See L. Gasperoni and M. Ballestrem, *Epistemic Artefacts. A Dialogical Reflection on Design Research in Architecture*, AADR 2023.
(15) See L. Gasperoni, 'Media of Change. Design as Generative Inquire', in: H. Groninger, S. Hensel, C. Klug (ed.) *Hybrid Tools for Thought*, RWTH Aachen University 2023, pp.16-27.
(16) Fieldstations is a non-profit association whose main function is to promote transdisciplinary research between art, architecture, natural sciences and the humanities within the Anthropocene: www.fieldstations.net. The 'Educational Platform – Anthropocene Pedagogies in Architecture' is co-curated with Jennifer Raum (Department of Theory and History of Modern Architecture, Bauhaus University Weimar), Andrea Rossi (Department of Experimental and Digital Design and Construction, Uni Kassel) and Till Zihlmann (Institute for Building Climatology and Energy of Architecture, TU Braunschweig): http://www.anthropocenepedagogies.net/.

ALTERNATIVE MODES OF SPATIAL PRACTICE

TRACING PATHWAYS OUTSIDE DS18

This chapter explores the professional trajectories of past students of DS18, offering insights into their evolving roles within and beyond architectural practice. Through a series of reflective impact interviews, we sought to uncover how their experiences within the studio influenced their career choices, skillsets, and design philosophies.

The interviews began with foundational questions about current roles and professional environments and how these align with or diverge from conventional architectural practice. Participants shared their journeys, detailing key moments and skills developed in DS18. These ranged from mastering innovative methodologies and approaches to materiality to transformative field trips, collaborative engagements, and exposure to novel design concepts.

The reflections extended beyond career specifics, delving into broader themes such as sustainability, digital innovation, ethical practice, and design's evolving role as an agent of care. By reflecting on how DS18's ethos shaped their paths, the interviewees highlighted the importance of interdisciplinary skills, adaptability, and critical thinking in navigating contemporary challenges.

The aim is to inspire prospective and current students while also serving as a resource for understanding the diverse ways alumni contribute to the wider profession.

1) Describe your current job/role.
2) Would you consider this 'traditional' or' typical architectural practice'? If not, how does it differ?
3) Is this something you do all the time or on occasion? Did your role change over time?
4) What key points or moments helped you transition into this line of work?
5) If there were any, what were the experiences in DS18 that contributed to this direction?
6) Are you furthering these skills with further training or application? What is the value of this?

Bio Materal experiments at the Norman Foster Foundation Sustainability Workshop in Madrid 2022.
Image Credits: Georgios Malliaropoulos

Georgios Malliaropoulos
Part II Architectural Assistant, Populous, UK.
DS18: 2021–2023

GM: I am currently working on the North Stand Expansion of Manchester City's Etihad Stadium. My tasks involve construction development, Part L Compliance, and designing solutions that integrate natural and technological systems. While my role follows conventional design processes, I also explore research-driven, experimental approaches - particularly in early-stage projects and competitions focusing on sustainability.

GM: DS18 has profoundly influenced this direction. The studio's data-driven design methods and advanced computational tools (Grasshopper and Computational Fluid Dynamics) were essential for exploring and modelling thermal conditions, as well as visualising complex building systems. Through these, I gained a deeper understanding of sustainable design principles and the analytical tools necessary to apprise more technical elements of thermal design.

GM: During my DS18 studies, I was selected as a research scholar for the Norman Foster Foundation's 2022 Sustainability Workshop in Madrid. This interdisciplinary forum examined how merging ecological, human, and technological perspectives could reshape architecture. Working with digital simulations to design soil morphologies for agricultural improvement, I harnessed fluid dynamics to optimise water enrichment and integrate biological processes into architectural systems – building on initial skills I had developed in DS18. Presenting my work to Lord Norman Foster and receiving feedback from architects such as Moshe Safdie and Mohsen Mostafavi highlighted the importance of sustainability-driven innovation.

GM: These experiences inform my current professional perspective. As I complete my Part 3 professional qualifications, I believe the convergence of design, research, and technology should evolve into a specialised field bridging architecture, ecology, and urban planning. Architecture extends beyond mere construction, yet conventional practice often limits its scope, restricting the profession's ability to address climate change, resource management, and the integration of natural systems effectively.

Computational Landscape, experimental workflows and geospatial analysis using Grasshopper.
Image Credits: Jamie Williams

Jamie Williams
Architect, Foster + Partners, UK.
DS18: 2019 - 2021

JW: As an architect at Foster + Partners, I have primarily led design feasibility studies, competitions, and early RIBA work stages on various international projects. My work involves navigating complex briefs and envisioning innovative design solutions to typically unique client requirements. While it has traditional aspects in its operational structure, its scale and portfolio diversity often breaks from the conventional ideas of architectural practice, due to the multidisciplinary nature of the practice, they have specialised sub-studios within the business to further refine the design process.

JW: The transition into this field was shaped by key opportunities to work on competitions and early stages of projects, where I could explore conceptual design and problem-solving. Through my studio projects and the conceptual explorations, a university environment enabled, I was able to refine my skills in managing complexity and interpreting project briefs creatively and efficiently.

JW: The scale and complexity of ideas which DS18 consistently discussed during my MArch, and the attention to detail holds similarities in the attentiveness of thinking at work, this has helped me adapt to life at Foster + Partners quicker than I would have imaged and think about "bigger picture" design as opposed to a more traditional role in architectural design, which often only considers its immediate contexts when rationalising design ideas.

JW: The skills I gained in studio continually evolve as I apply them to professional practice. For instance, I am deepening my understanding of digital tools and sustainable design approaches to address emerging industry demands. This alignment between technical proficiency and sustainability goals is pivotal as projects become increasingly complex and the architecture industry becomes increasingly demanding in these areas. Such roles could benefit from recognition as specialised disciplines. They serve as critical intersections of design, research, and policy, enabling architects to contribute meaningfully to global challenges, such as the climate and ecological crises, alongside increasing urbanisation.

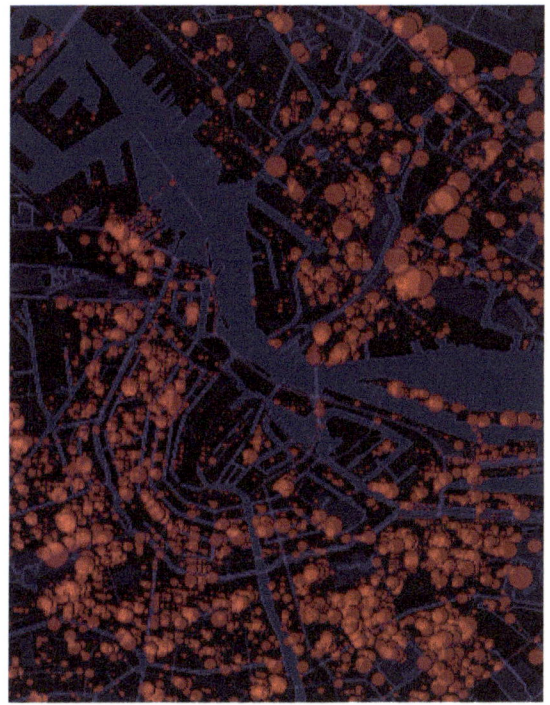 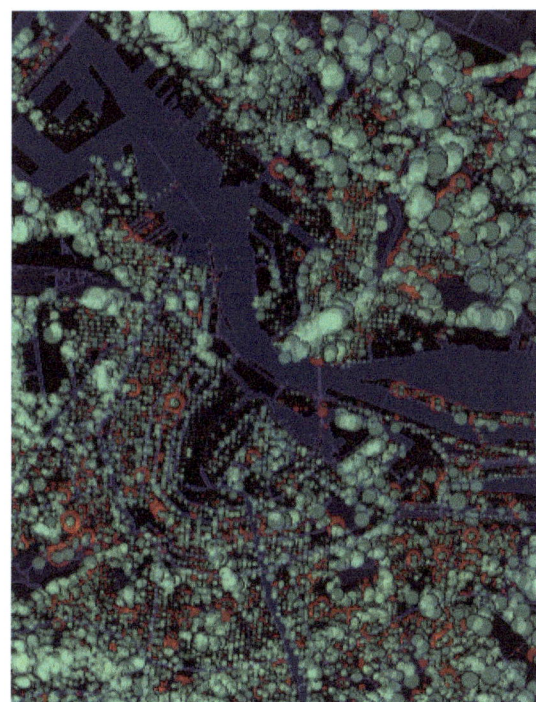

No "True" Greenery: Deciphering the bias of satellite and street view imagery in urban greenery measurement, Amsterdam
Image Credits: Senseable City Lab

Chada Elalami
Research Fellow at MIT Senseable City Lab, UAE.
DS18: 2022-2023

CA: I currently focus on various aspects of design at the research lab, including graphic design, physical product design, and other interdisciplinary forms. I also sometimes engage in research, mostly exploring how design can be informed by research findings and data to develop solutions that benefit urban life and infrastructure.

CA: I think that although my current role is not by any means 'architectural' per se, it definitely benefitted from an architectural background where I learnt a broad range of skills. Since the lab focuses on reimagining cities and urban life, I shifted my focus from a smaller scale - more of a building centric approach - to a wider urban-scale perspective.

CA: I don't know if I would've been able to contribute efficiently to this research lab had I not learnt the technical skills that I learned in DS18. In particular, we learned how to use geospatial tools and visualise data in an impactful and appealing way. This was also my first time interacting with data and I gained insights on how to find the value in it, how to find those useful 'nuggets of information' that need to be highlighted to tell a bigger story. And beyond that - the research mindset.

CA: For example, I entered my second year with the thought of ravaging wildfires fresh in my mind, as it came right after the 'fire season'. Every summer, news of destructive fires makes the headline - and that seems to be the case all over the world, from Mediterranean countries (where it is more common) to the UK. However, this topic is incredibly broad, so my job in DS18 involved breaking it down into distinct events and analysing it as a phenomenon driven by interconnected flows of energy, materials, and human activity. Once I had something concrete to work with, I could start mapping high-risk areas in the UK, digging into a specific fire event, and looking at its aftermath as part of a web of interconnected flows and effects.

CA: Due to the more complex nature of the data I am working with now, I have had to further my skills as I spend more time processing the data rather than just visualising it.

Astana, Kazakhstan. A city masterplan to with a view to increasing urban desnisty and connectivity.
Image Credits: Space Syntax

Oscar McDonald
Associate Director / Head of Studio, Space Syntax, UK.
DS18: 2014-2016

OM: For the last few years I've been leading city-scale strategic projects and masterplans with a focus on creating positive long-term outcomes such as sustainability and liveability, using an evidence-based approach. Coupled with this is trying to promote the need for evidence-based planning and design – which still has a long way to go!

OM: Day-to-day there is a lot more analysis and policy compared to traditional architecture, but it still needs creativity/design to turn it into something tangible and useful. I think there is also something different in dealing with complex systems in a way that isn't always in the foreground at the scales of traditional architecture - you can attempt to hold all variables for a building in your head - for a city, it is impossible, so you need good models and frameworks to deal with that.

OM: The transition point from traditional architecture was a clear one, co-founding 4D Island after my master's degree and using it as a vehicle to initially explore data-driven sustainability and resilience planning in the Maldives. Secondary to that and coming from a more traditional and less computational architectural background, an obvious turning point was how the studio engaged with complexity and systems thinking and how I was able to explore and realise these ideas through my design research projects.

OM: I think, in general, these skills and ways of thinking need to be far more widespread, particularly in larger scales of design, but everywhere really. We need an evidence-based approach because we can't afford to keep making so many mistakes in design (making places less sustainable as well as less human). And we need to be humble in the face of complexity - making resilient and flexible things, not pretending we can predict and control everything.

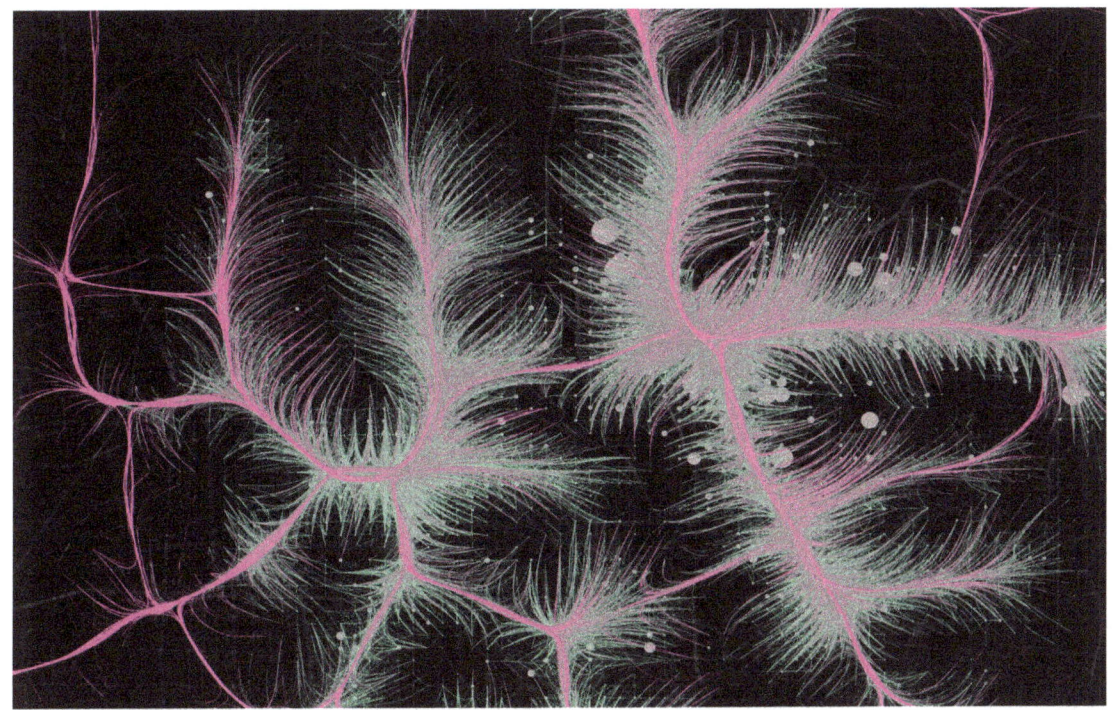

Potato Project: The study used mobile phone location data from 50 million individuals across 234 cities to understand commuting patterns (done while at MIT Senseable City Lab). Image Credits: Tom Benson.

Tom Benson
Lead of LabX at Dar, UK.
DS18: 2015-17

TB: I'm leading LabX at Dar, where we use advanced data analysis to generate actionable insights for the built environment. The aim is to rethink how cities are planned, focusing on sustainability and placemaking, not just efficiency. Alongside this, I'm building partnerships with organisations such as Siemens, MIT, and UCL to push the boundaries of what urban innovation can achieve.

TB: No, it's not traditional architectural practice, and honestly, that's what makes it exciting. Traditional practices often focus narrowly on designing buildings, whereas my work examines broader urban systems. It addresses questions that architecture alone can't solve, using data and interdisciplinary collaboration as the starting point.

TB: My career path has been far from traditional. At 16, I joined the British Army, driven in part by a lack of commitment to my studies at school during which I discovered a sense of purpose and a deep commitment to making a positive impact. It was here that I began to realise I had more to offer, and it shaped the values that continue to guide my work today. Following this and more academically, another defining moment came during my time in DS18. The studio's focus on combining innovative tools with climate challenges opened entirely new ways of thinking about architecture. It pushed me to look beyond the traditional boundaries of designing buildings and explore how data and technology could be applied to tackle systemic urban issues. This shift in perspective was transformative, setting me on the path I continue to follow in my career.

TB: This question highlights a broader issue: why hasn't architecture evolving to integrate roles like this into its core practice? Creating a separate discipline risk marginalising innovation rather than embedding it as a fundamental part of the design process. Data-driven approaches are essential for addressing today's complex challenges—pushing policy frameworks, tackling sustainability, or adopting a more holistic view of design. These roles shouldn't be siloed; teams would benefit from being omni-disciplinary, where different expertise comes together seamlessly to address problems comprehensively.

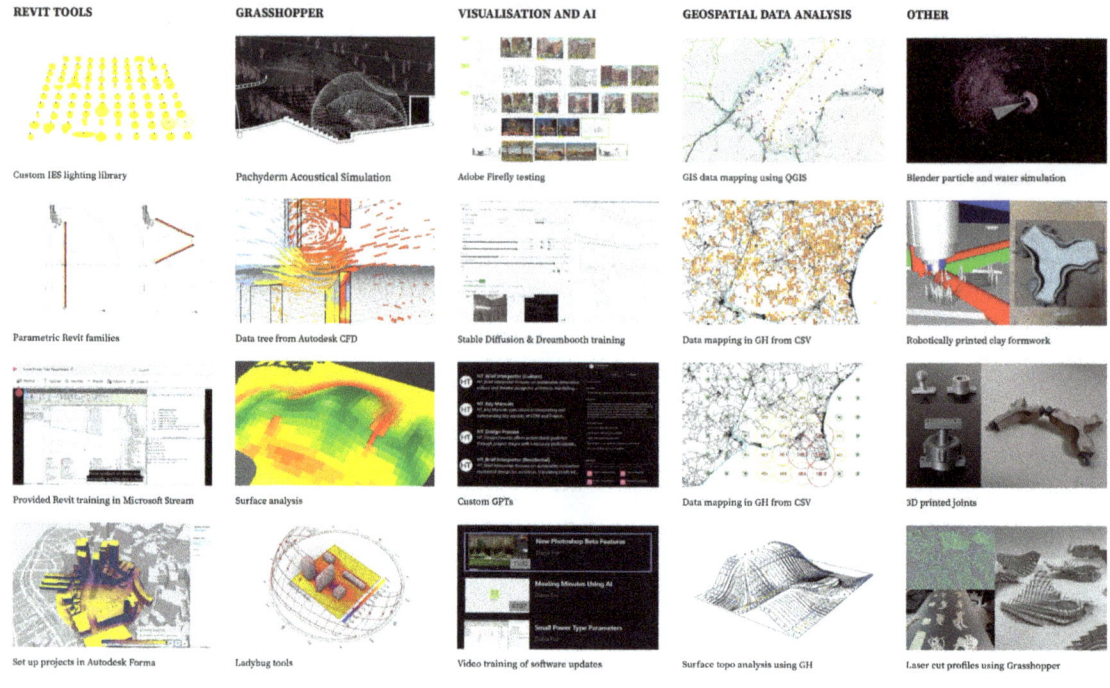

Computational design skills showcase
Image Credits: Diana Fox

Diana Fox
Computational Designer at Haworth Tompkins, UK.
DS18: 2023-24

DF: Computational Design is essentially a non-project-specific role where I utilise algorithms, simulations, and data analysis to assist architects in solving problems and developing designs across various projects and all RIBA stages. Additionally, I create and deliver specialised training content to colleagues, helping them learn and effectively use various software tools.

DF: In our practice, we never had a dedicated computational designer role, nor did we fully realise how beneficial it could be to have someone in this position. After working at HT for over four years, my role as an architectural assistant gradually became more software-focused and technical. This evolution led me to propose a formal shift in my role to become a computational designer, enabling me to contribute to multiple projects rather than being tied to a single one for an extended period.

DF: Throughout my architectural journey, I have always been more drawn to the software and tools themselves rather than traditional design approaches. I have always had a strong interest in learning new software and tools that enable designers to work more efficiently in developing their designs. With the constantly evolving software landscape, it is invaluable to have someone whose sole focus is on software - staying up to date with the latest updates, testing them, and implementing solutions on an office-wide scale.

DF: In other studios with a focus on traditional approaches to building design, DS18 placed greater emphasis on understanding the full range of tools available for creating adaptive, responsive, and parametric designs. I gained experience with various software, including QGIS, Autodesk CFD, Blender, and Grasshopper, which enabled me to develop several scripts that facilitated more sophisticated methods of design production. This process, along with the focus on these tools, has been a significant factor in my transition to the role I hold today.

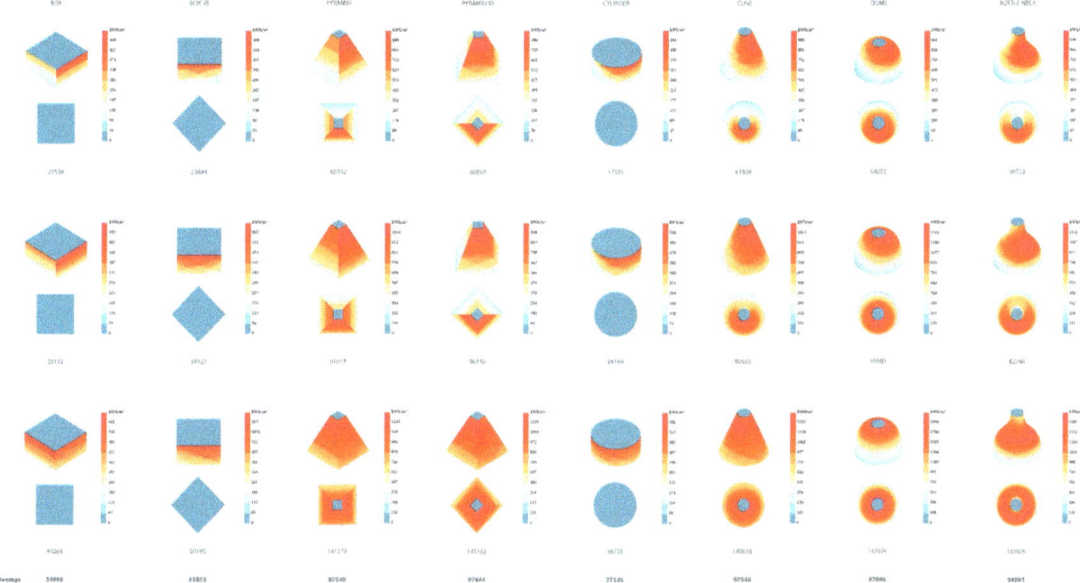

Evaluating the passive solar performance of project primitive forms.
Image Credits: Tom Wildbore

Tom Wildbore
Senior Architect & Sustainability Lead, Ayre Chamberlain Gaunt, UK.
DS18: 2015-2016

TW: A mix of traditional job running whilst leading on sustainability in the practice. This includes running project sustainability reviews, environmental analysis, practice carbon accounting and climate literacy.

TW: The 'Head of Sustainability' role has been formalised into a named role across more and more practices as the demand for leadership in this area across the industry has taken off. So, my role is not traditional but is fast becoming normal.

TW: I've always had a passion for sustainable design, but for the first few years of my career, I was engrossed in learning the core skills we need to be an architect. Things started to change very quickly about 6 or 7 years ago when the flaws in this approach (which are contributing to unsustainable buildings) became impossible to ignore. At the same time, some inspirational groups such as LETI, ACAN, and Architects Declare started to show how we needed to make changes in practice. Prior to this, DS18 encouraged us to explore how seemingly unconnected factors are related and to appreciate our complete interdependence with the natural world. This is crucial to properly understand how to design and build sustainable buildings and cities and live a sustainable lifestyle.
This analytical approach and also learning how to use Grasshopper for Rhino both for environmental analysis and wider conceptual design have been entirely fundamental to my career since graduation.

TW: Completing the Certified Passivhaus Designer qualification was a real eye-opener for me, and I would advise anyone who has the chance to, do it!

TW: The advancements we are seeing in sustainable building design are coming faster because of a greater awareness and improved skillset within architectural practice. For too long, data-driven environmental analysis has largely remained a compliance exercise to achieve undemanding Building Regulation standards, usually carried out by third-party consultants once major design decisions have already been made. We are now moving to a position where this analysis is recognised as a critical complementary early-stage activity to appraise design options.

4993 Feet Under, MIRO, CLAB (doom), (Tech Demo), (NewInc Performance).
Photo credit: clab.futurevisionlab

Calvin Sin
Project Designer, Morphosis Architects, Los Angeles, US.
DS18: 2015-2017

CS: I've been a Project Designer at Morphosis Architects for over three years, working on projects ranging from urban design for a new city to affordable housing for the homeless in Los Angeles. This covers competitions, as well as Stage 1-3 concept and schematic stages. I operate at the intersection of design and computational design, and I'm particularly interested in scalability and efficiency, as I believe these are critical to addressing the challenges we face in the AEC industry.

CS: The practice follows a traditional work culture, but the projects I've worked on often break away from conventional norms. This mix creates opportunities to explore new ideas and design approaches.

CS: My past experiences have significantly shaped how I approach concepts, particularly in developing skills and adopting tools like Grasshopper, which I use frequently in professional and personal work. These foundations have also made it easier for me to learn new software, such as Unreal Engine, and to find my own solutions to complex challenges.

CS: Being part of DS 18 influenced my perspective on the Anthropocene and our ecological connections, inspiring personal projects I wouldn't have considered otherwise. For example, 4993 Feet Under, a speculative research project with Ina Chen and Lu, explored oil's environmental and historical impact. While the final output was unique, the approach mirrored my academic methods, integrating science and history into design.

CS: These skills have been incredibly valuable in both architectural and non-architectural projects. My time in DS18 was a notable point in the journey as it exposed me to ways of thinking beyond traditional architecture design. It emphasized the importance of Creative Technologies and expanded my view of design in a broader context. This mindset has allowed me to collaborate with professionals across various fields and adapt to projects that go beyond the built environment. I've found that this approach has enabled me to engage with diverse teams, working on projects that span both architectural and non-architectural sectors.

Shaded 40°
Redesigning the external awning for the British context.

Aimée Daniel
Founder at Shaded, UK.
DS18: 2018-2020

AD: I recently founded my own company, Shaded, where I'm developing simple and cost-effective retrofit solutions for homes and buildings, with a focus on products to reduce overheating risks.

AD: Although I technically operate in the domain of the built environment, I consider my current role more aligned with entrepreneurship than architectural practice. There is design involved in developing and bringing a product to market, but my day to day now compared to when I was working in architectural practice is totally different! It's an interesting mix of learning how to run a business, being involved in discussions around climate change, public health, and policy, and designing something that feels, in my opinion, a lot less abstract than a building.

AD: It exceeded 40 degrees in London for the first time ever over summer 2022. As I roasted in my flat, I wondered why the UK hadn't embraced simple passive cooling solutions like shade and thought perhaps it was a design issue with currently available products. I put my idea to paper and won a UKRI-funded grant at the end of 2023 to pursue it. This was followed up by another grant funded by the LLDC in May 2024. This opportunity came at the right time for me, too. I finished my Part 3 in 2022 and was uncomfortable with how predictable a career in traditional architectural practice appears to be.

AD: The DS18 experience that had the strongest influence on my direction was probably just the ability to focus on climate themes more than architecture itself. When deciding what university to go to in the UK moving from the US, I specifically sought out climate-focused studios. I actually don't think an MArch needs to be about designing buildings, you can learn and do that in the workforce.

AD: Being an architect has given me a lot of credibility in the innovation space. Climate change and buildings are part of the same conversation. Based on personal experience, I worry that people might think they're 'in too deep' after doing three degrees and forget that they can and should bring their ideas and expertise to other lines of work!

APPENDICES

BIOGRAPHIES

LAURA NICA is a practicing architect, digital designer and researcher.

Laura is a doctoral scholar, recipient of the Techne Collaborative Doctoral Award (CDA) between the Zaha Hadid Foundation and the University of Westminster (UoW); investigating digital archives in architecture, by developing reverse-engineering techniques to describe alternative historiographies of Zaha Hadid's shift from analogue to digital. Previously she has taught *Material and Technical Studies* at UoW and the *Bio-Integrated Design* programme at UCL.

Her work has been published and awarded, including *Sir G. Iacobescu Award for Academic Excellence* (2025), *ACADIA conference* (2024), *Globally Engaged Research Scholarship* (2024), *Surface Design of the Year* (2024), Winner of the American Society of Maths Art Exhibition (2022), *Monsoon [+other] Waters* (2019), Detail Magazine Award (2016) and RIBA Bronze Medal Shortlist (2014).

Director of Laura Nica Studio, her architectural practice focuses on bespoke private residential projects, new buildings and small commercial developments across the UK and North America; ranging from conversions and extensions, to heritage restorations and creative installations. Laura has previously worked at Wilkinson Eyre (2014), Foster + Partners (2017), dRMM (2019), Giles Miller Studio (2020), and Fathom Architects (2021) on masterplans, large residential developments, bridge design, mixed-use buildings in the UK, China, Middle East, Thailand, USA and Mauritius.

Website: *www.lauranica.com and* Instagram: *@laura.nica.archi.*

JOHN COOK is an architect, researcher, and educator. His speciality lies in the visualisation and communication of environmental and climatic concerns across ranging scales and visual mediums, through the use of data, cartographic and computational means.

Having studied architecture at the University of Nottingham and Westminster, he went on to gain professional experience at Birds Portchmouth Russum Architects, contributing to a range of public competitions, master planning, and private residential projects. In 2018, John joined the multidisciplinary research team of the ERC-funded project *Monsoon Assemblages*, investigating the drivers and impacts of the changing South Asian Monsoon, as well as the human and non-human lives dependent upon it. Through field work, meteorological data, cartographic visualisations and multimedia installations, the project's outputs were published and exhibited internationally, notably at the Milan Triennale (2019), Venice Biennale (2021), and Lethaby Gallery in London (2022).

In 2022, supported by the UKRI and alongside Lindsay Bremner and Ben Pollock, he co-founded the non-profit design research studio *Climate Cartographics*. As Creative Director, John leads the development of innovative approaches to climate data aesthetics and visual communication strategies, delivering spatial decision making tools that make complex climate data accessible and actionable.

Website: *www.climatecartographics.*com and Monsoon Assemblages: *www.monass.org.*

BEN POLLOCK is an architect, researcher, and educator specialising in climate, ecology, data, and computational design. He has worked at Hopkins, Fletcher Priest, and Jestico + Whiles Architects, contributing to international and domestic educational and commercial projects. His experience includes large-scale commercial retrofits with a focus on sustainable and adaptive principles.

In 2020, he founded *4D Island* to address climate challenges in frontline communities in the Global South. The project gained recognition at COP26 for its innovative approach to adaptation, storytelling, and community engagement in the Maldives. Ben has contributed to education reform through ACAN, advocating for climate literacy and ecological priorities in architectural education.

Following a UKRI-supported Research Fellowship at the University of Westminster in 2023, he co-founded *Climate Cartographics*, a non-profit design research studio specialising in climate-focused data visualisation, mapping, and communications. As Strategy Director, he collaborates with local authorities and UK-based organisations to promote regenerative practices and leverage geospatial tools for better decision-making and public engagement. Fostering cross-disciplinary collaboration, bridging design, policy, and technology to amplify impact.

Website: *www.climatecartographics.com.*

ROBERTO BOTTAZZI is an architect, researcher, and educator based in London. He has studied in Italy and Canada before moving to London. He is Associate Professor and Director of the Master in Urban Design at The Bartlett, UCL. He previously taught Master studio at the University of Westminster and the Royal College of Art. He is the author of Digital Architecture beyond Computers: Fragments of a Cultural History of Computational Design (Bloomsbury, 2018) and co-editor of Walking Cities: London (Camberwell Press, 2017, Routledge, 2021).

LIDIA GASPERONI is Associate Professor, Co-Director of design and member of the Just Environments Cluster at the Bartlett School of Architecture (UCL). Between 2018 and 2024, she was a postdoctoral researcher and lecturer in the Department of Architectural Theory at TU Berlin. She is a philosopher and architectural theorist, specialising in architecture in the experimental relationship between theory and design practices with specific reference to the contemporary challenges of the Anthropocene.

OLIVIA EWING is a Senior Wind Engineer. Olivia is a Chartered Engineer with the Institute of Mechanical Engineers (IMechE) and a senior UK Wind Microclimate consultant. She specializes in external environment design and comfort modelling. Her work involves climate analysis as well as management and execution of wind engineering and environmental physics projects. Olivia is experienced in pedestrian wind comfort studies and wind climate analyses in the UK and internationally.

ANDREAS KÖRNER University College London and University of Innsbruck. Andreas' design research explores the relationship between the built and the natural environment through layering, materials, and ornament. Special interest is given to the impact of weather on surfaces and their textural articulations. The results are highly intricate interfaces that express invisible environmental parameters in the built environment. He holds a BSc in architecture from TU Vienna, an MArch pt2 from the Bartlett, and a PhD in architecture from the University of Innsbruck. Andreas is a lecturer at the Bio-integrated Design programme at the Bartlett and an assistant professor at the Department of Experimental Architecture in Innsbruck. Website: *www.krnr.at*.

SHAHID PADHANI is a Senior Engineer. Shahid is a fluid dynamics and building physics specialist. He has experience on building physics projects involving Computational Fluid Dynamic (CFD) modelling, Dynamic Thermal Modelling (DTM), and wind and microclimate projects. He has extensive experience in fluid dynamics obtained during the course of his PhD. His work regularly includes experimental design and technique, managing, processing, and analysing large data sets, and developing simple mathematical models.

DIMPLE RANA Associate. Dimple is an experienced engineer specialising in environmental and building physics. She provides consulting for both external and internal environments and the interaction between the two. She has worked on range of international commercial and technical projects and is experienced in using tools and techniques such as computational fluid dynamics, climate analysis, solar analysis, thermal analysis etc. She has a developing interest in microclimate work especially on a larger urban scale and in various different climate zones.

GUY SINCLAIR is a designer, lecturer and doctoral researcher in the School of Architecture + Cities at the University of Westminster. He has previously worked with Climate Cartographics as a research associate and as guest critic within the School of Architecture + Cities and the Architectural Association. His current research thesis focusses on the architectures of climate science and Catholic ecotheology, exploring how knowledge production of, with and through climate is spatialised.

URI WEGMAN is an architect and an educator. He taught at the Cooper Union, New York, EPFL, Lausanne and currently at the Faculty of architecture at Universite libre de Bruxelles where he is also conducting a doctoral research about the representation of air in architecture.

STUDENT LIST

2019 - 2020

Year 1
Denise Carcangiu
Elizabeth Terry
Gergana Georgieva
Hannah Pinsent
Helen Windsor
Jamie Williams
Nikhil Berwal
Rishi Mistry
Seni Agunpopo

Year 2
Aimée Daniels
Carolina Lopez
Charlotte Grasselli
Dagmara Dyner
Gabrielle Bucknall
Kate Hosking
Katherine Dechow
Sara Kosanovic
Tamanna Akhter
Una Osterhus Ledaal

2020 - 2021

Year 1
Chantal Barnes
Daria-Suzanne Donovetsky
Gary Chan
Justyna Lesny
Sulman Shaikh Muhammad
Muhtasim Mojnu

Year 2
Almudena Tesorero Garcia
Denise Carcangiu
Hannah Pinsent
Helen Windsor
Jamie Williams
Katarzyna Maskowicz
Elizabeth Terry
Nikhil Berwal
Seni Agunpopo
Seungmin Lee

2021 - 2022

Year 1
Kirsten Davis
Chada Elalami
Carl Fletcher
Georgios Malliaropoulos
Vilde Bakkeli Sand
Guy Sinclair
Yuechuan Xi

Year 2
Arvindaa Balamurugan
Gary Chan
Daria-Suzanne Donovetsky
Gary Chan
Justyna Lesny
Sulman Shaikh Muhammad
Muhtasim Mojnu
Nicholas Tsangaris

2022 - 2023

Year 1
Alice Own
Alistair Orchard-Mitchell
Farah Mussadiq
Naomi Punnett
Ollie Astley
Qingqing He
Ross Wilson
Vanessa Keung
Zixin (Tiffany) Yao

Year 2
Kirsten Davis
Chada Elalami
Carl Fletcher
Georgios Malliaropoulos
Guy Sinclair
Nat (Indy) Saligupta
Sian Sliwinska
Timea Iulia Kadar
Yuechuan Xi

AWARDS, TALKS AND PUBLICATIONS

2023
- Chada Elalami, *KooZA/Rch Portfolio: Rad(iation/ical) Atheneum and The Transient Estate*.
- Carl Fletcher, Scholar to the Norman Foster Foundation, *Energy Workshop*, Madrid.

2022
- Chada Elalami, Justyna Lesny and Kirsten Davis, *Radical Architecture Practice for Sustainability (RAPS)* Conference and Exhibition, Eindhoven (online).
- Kirsten Davis, Royal Academy Summer Show (Climate) - *Saline Experimentarium* model display.
- Georgios Malliaropoulos, Scholar to the Norman Foster Foundation, *Sustainability Workshop*, Madrid.
- Kirsten Davis, KooZA/Rch Portfolio: *Saline Landscapes*, Dungeness UK.
- Daria-Suzanne Donovetsky, KooZA/Rch Portfolio: *The Liquid Landscape*, Dungeness UK.
- Justyna Lesny, KooZA/Rch Portfolio: *The Lichen Incubator*, Dungeness UK.
- Jamie Williams, exhibited at *Imagine Glasgow 2021*, COP26 edition, New Glasgow Society.

2021
- Jamie Williams, MIT's Projection 16 – Visualising Cities Awards, 2021. Winner for Best Visualization Award: *The Atlas of the Carbon Economy*.
- Hannah Pinsent, Helen Windsor and Elizabeth Terry: *Radical Architecture Practice for Sustainability (RAPS)* Conference and Exhibition, Bristol.
- Daria-Suzanne Donovetsky, Hannah Pinsent, Jamie Williams, Elizabeth Terry, Nikhil Berwal, Muhtasim Mojnu, Seni Agunpopo: MIT Department of Urban Studies and Planning, Projections 16 | *Measuring the City: The Power of Urban Metrics*, Visualizing Cities.
- Katie Dechow, Hannah Pinsent, Jamie Williams, Elizabeth Terry, Helen Windsor, Nikhil Berwal, Kate Hosking, Gaby Bucknall, Seni Agunpopo: *A+CCxT Architecture + Cities Climate Action Taskforce Exhibition*, University of Westminster.
- Ben Pollock, Laura Nica, John Cook - Anthropocene Teaching Practices in Architecture. *Territorial Matters and Interfaces Workshop* (online), TU Berlin and Field Stations.
- Elizabeth Terry, KooZA/Rch Interview: *A Carbon Re-wilding: Decolonisation of Contentious Territories*.
- Seni Agunpopo, KooZA/Rch Interview: *Peat Observations*.
- Seni Agunpopo, Dezeen feature, University of Westminster.
- Helen Windsor, *Shoaib Rawat Award*, Third Place, UoW.
- Jamie Williams, KooZA/Rch Interview: *The Didactic Kingdom Of Nowhere in Particular*.
- Kate Hosking, KooZA/Rch Interview: *Black Ice Form*.

2020
- Ben Pollock, Laura Nica, Kate Hosking, Katie Dechow, Rachel Wakelin, Fiona Grieve, *100 Day Studio Talk*, Architecture Foundation, studio and student presentations; accessible at: *https://youtu.be/o7CixDJilFw?si=C1zo6hL2wwWIxWP4*.
- Katie Dechow, *Dezeen Virtual Design Festival*.
- Gaby Bucknall, *Architectural Journal - Student Prize for Sustainability*.

ACKNOWLEDGEMENTS

We would like to extend our thank you to our vast DS18 community - alumni, colleagues, practitioners, researchers, friends and mentors.

We never write a book alone, especially one that encapsulates the insights of a four-year-long project enriched by extended discussions and numerous guests. We extend our deepest gratitude to each other for the opportunity to work, think, compute, and discuss within our wider community.

We express our immense gratitude and heartfelt appreciation to Professor Dr. Lindsay Bremner and Dr. Roberto Bottazzi. Their unwavering trust in our capabilities and the transformative opportunity to continue Design Studio 18 have been invaluable. This book reflects the profound impact they have had on our academic and professional development, but also multiple generations of students, encapsulating the knowledge, themes, and innovative approaches they have generously shared with us.

We also extend our thanks to our talented past, present students, whose work represents the culmination of all of our collective efforts.

Laura Nica
John Cook
Ben Pollock

2019- 2020

Special Thanks:
Aurelien Thomas (Jestico + Whiles),
Kathryn Donnelly (FRAM),
Leonora Tarrason (Norwegian Institute for Air Research),
Namik Mackic (Oslo School of Architecture and Design),
Matthew Dalziel (Oslo Architecture Triennale, OAT)
Alex Gordon (Jestico +Whiles)
Alex Watts (Eric Parry Architects)
Ben Summers (RCKa)
Calvin Sin (SCI-Arc)
Carlos Bausa Martinez (Zaha Hadid Architects)
Charity Edwards (Monash University)
Cid Schuller (Undercover Architecture)
Constance Lau (UoW, DS03)
Corinna Dean (UoW, DS2.1)
Druv Gulabchande (HFM/ Narrative Practice)
Filip Visnjic (UoW, fvda /creativeapplications.net)
Fiona Grieve (Scott Brownrigg Architects)
Iulia Stefan (Ground Lab, AA Research Fellow)
James Mak (dRMM)
Jon Goodbun (UoW, Rheomode)
Jose Alfredo Ramirez (AA Ground Lab)
Katt Scott (dRMM)
Matthew Rosier (ACAN)
Mike O'Hanlon (DSDHA)
Oscar McDonald (Space Syntax)
Philip Hurrell (Millar+Howard Workshop)
Rachel Wakelin (Buckley Grey Yeoman)
Raymonde Bieler (White Arkitekter)
Richard Portchmouth (Birds Portchmouth Russum)
Roberto Botazzi (UCL, Bartlett B-Pro)

2020- 2021

Special Thanks: Ben Ashby and Shahid Padhani (ARUP)
Alice Thomson (MATA Architects)
Andreas Koerner (University of Innsbruck)
Andrei Jipa (ETH Zurich)
Andrew Madl (University of Tennessee)
Anthony Boulanger (UoW, DS16)
Ed Wall (University of Greenwich)
Calvin Sin (SCI-Arc)
Charity Edwards (Monash University)
Constance Lau (UoW, DS03)
Cristina Nan (Future//Fields, TU Eindhoven)
Dhruv Gulabchande (HFM / Narrative Practice)
Finbar Charleson (dRMM + AA Wood Lab)
Fiona Grieve (Scott Brownrigg)
Fraser Morrison (Future//Fields, Architecture 00)
Iulia Stefan (Ground Lab, AA Research Fellow)
James Mak (Of Architecture)
Joseph Musil (Foster + Partners)
Katie Dechow (Jo Cowen Architects)
Larisa Bulibasa (Project d'ARCHITECTURE)
Lindsay Bremner (UoW, Monsoon Assemblages)
Mitesh Dixit (DOMAIN Office & Columbia GSAPP)
Matt Rosier (Artist/ ACAN)
Michael O'Hanlon (DSDHA)
Oscar McDonald (Space Syntax)
Rachel Wakelin (Buckley Gray Yeoman)
Toby Burgess (UoW, DS10)
Tom Benson (Senseable City Lab, MIT)
Vlad Tenu (AHMM)

2021- 2022

Constantina Avraamides (CA Architecture)
Raul Bielsa (Prior+ Partners/ AAVS Transborder)
Roberto Bottazzi (UCL, Bartlett B-Pro)
Lindsay Bremner (UoW, Monsoon Assemblages)
Finbar Charleson (dRMM + AA Wood Lab)
Emma Colthurst (University of Greenwich)
Katie Dechow (Jo Cowen Architects)
Fraser Morrison (Future Fields/ Architecture 00)
Cristina Nan (Future//Fields, TU Eindhoven)
Justin Nicholls (Fathom Architects)
Iulia Stefan (AA Ground Lab)
Rachel Wakelin (Buckley Grey Yeoman)
Izabela Wieczorek (Atmospheric Architecture Agency/ Reading University)
Oscar Villareal (Lab 10 MX/ ecoLogicStudio/ UAL)
Francois Girardin (UoW, DS25)
William McLean (UOW, Technical Studies)

2022- 2023

Special Thanks: George Herrick (L&P Group)
Constantina Avraamides (CA Architecture),
Dhruv Gulabchande (Narrative Practice + HFM Architects)
Emma Colthurst (University of Greenwich)
Finbar Charleson (dRMM + AA Wood Lab)
Fiona Grieve (Scott Browning Architects)
Fraser Morrison (Future Fields)
Justin Nicholls (Fathom Architects)
Kate Hosking (Squires & Partners)
Lindsay Bremner (UoW, University of Westminster)
Omar Ibraz (Foster + Partners)
Oscar Villareal (Lab10 MX, UAL)
Rachel Wakelin (Buckley Grey Yeoman)
Raul Bielsa (Prior+Partners/ AAVS Transborder)
Roberto Bottazzi (UCL, Bartlett B-Pro)
Sho Ito (UoW, DS2.6)

OPEN EXHIBITION
2019 - 2020
Arctic Ecologies

Photo Credits: DS18 Students 2019-20.
Full Accessible website: designstudio18.com/Arctic-Ecologies-An-Atmospheric-Assemblage.

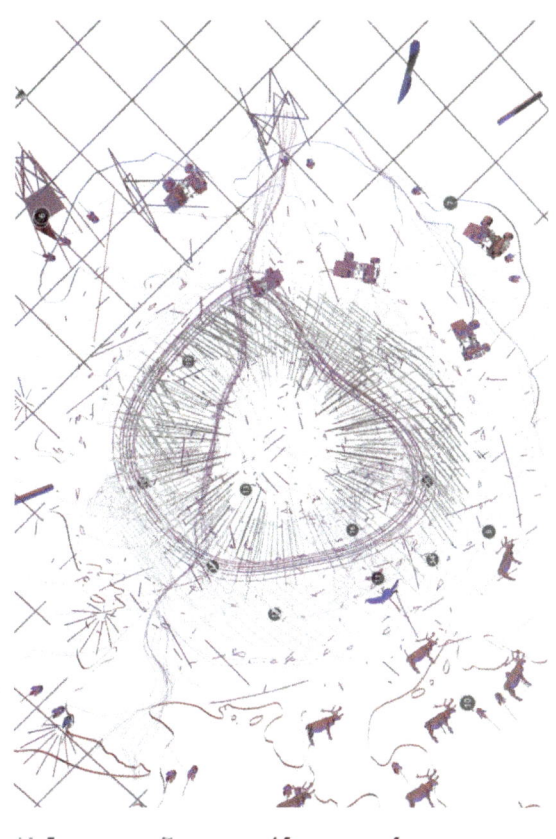
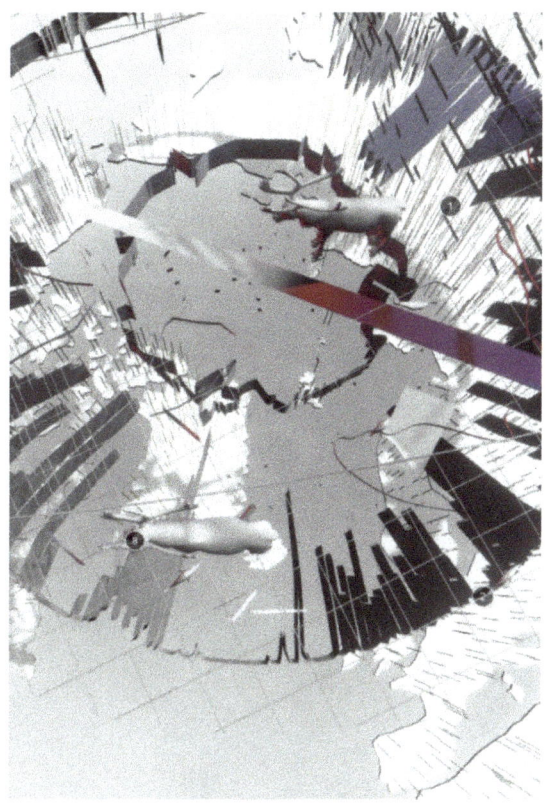
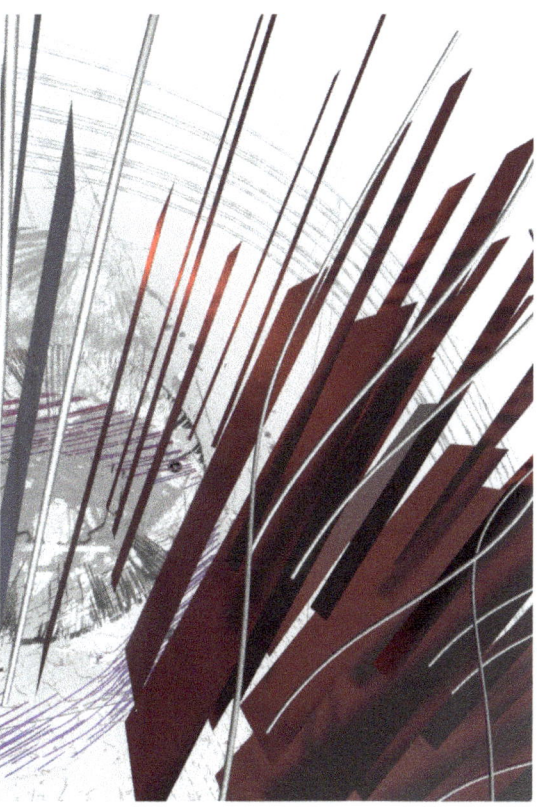

OPEN EXHIBITION
2020 - 2021
Carbon Transitions

Photo Credits: DS18 Students 2020-21.

Full Accessible website: OPEN '21 Studio website, accessible at: *www.openwestminster.london/open21-studio/?studio=DS%2018&v=one*.

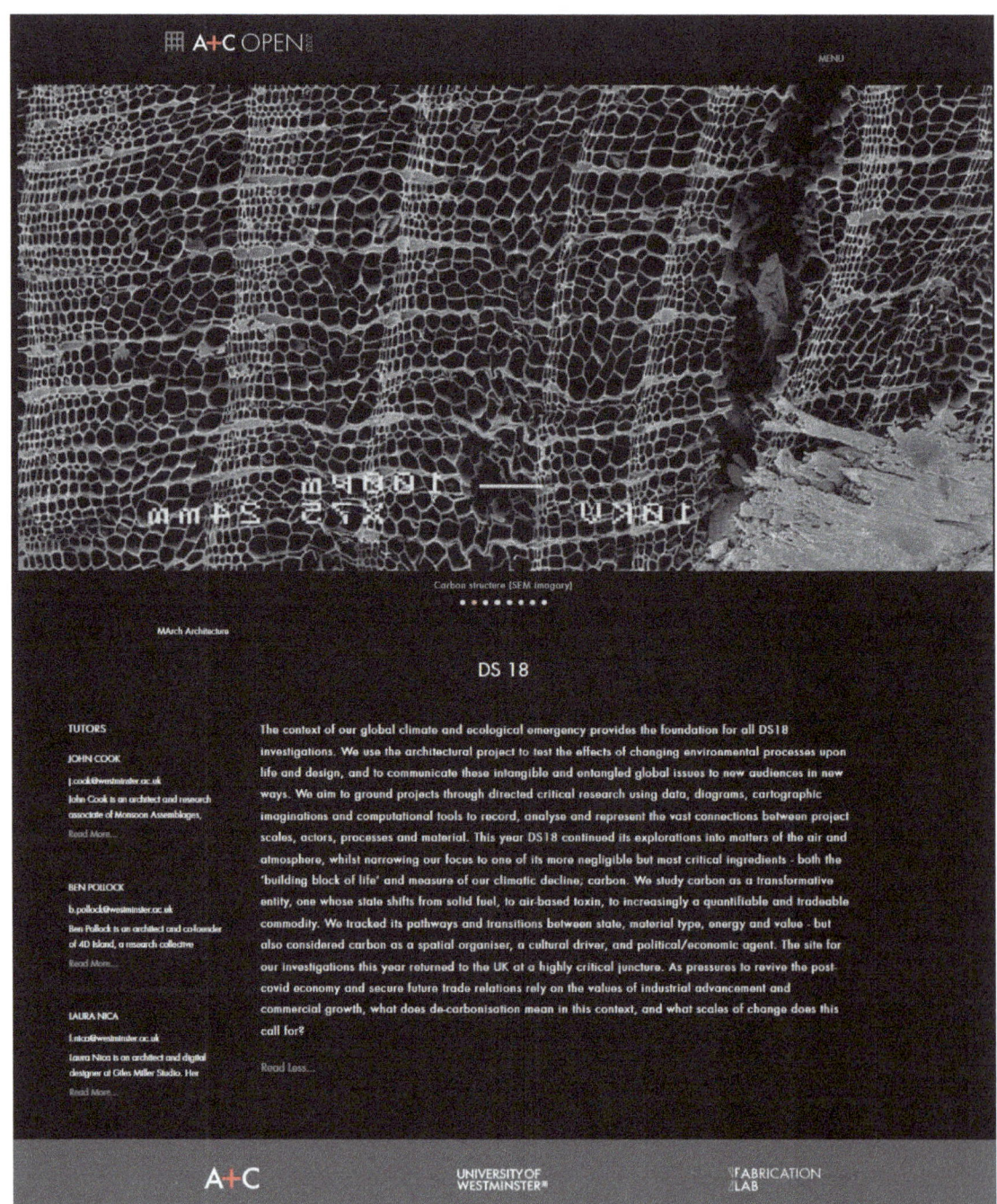

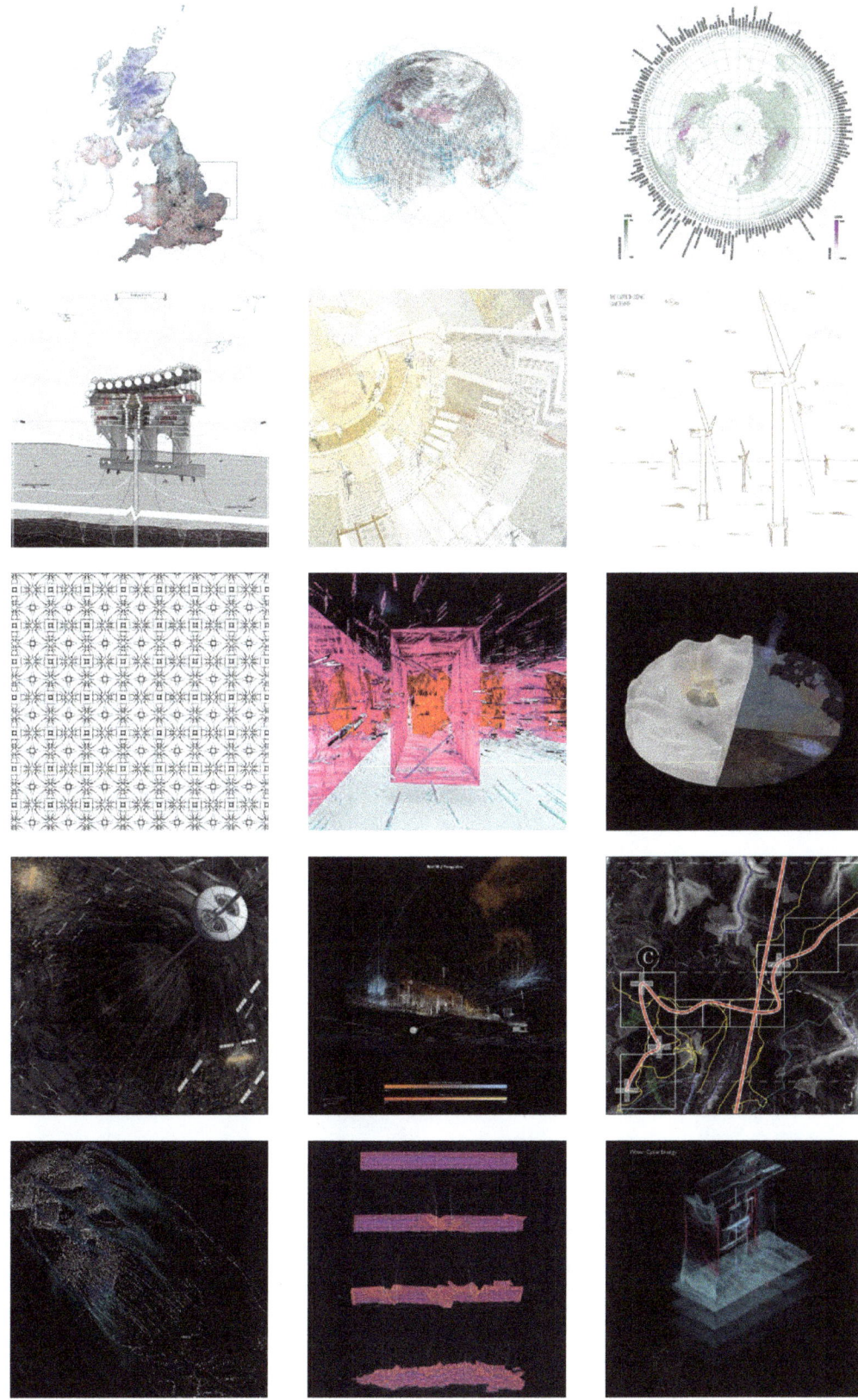

OPEN EXHIBITION
2021 - 2022
Climate Futures

Photo Credits: Laura Nica, Vilde Bakkeli Sand.

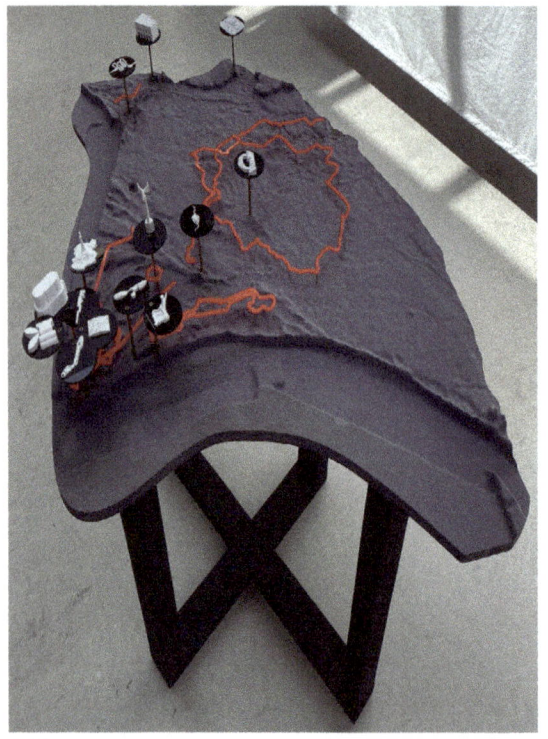

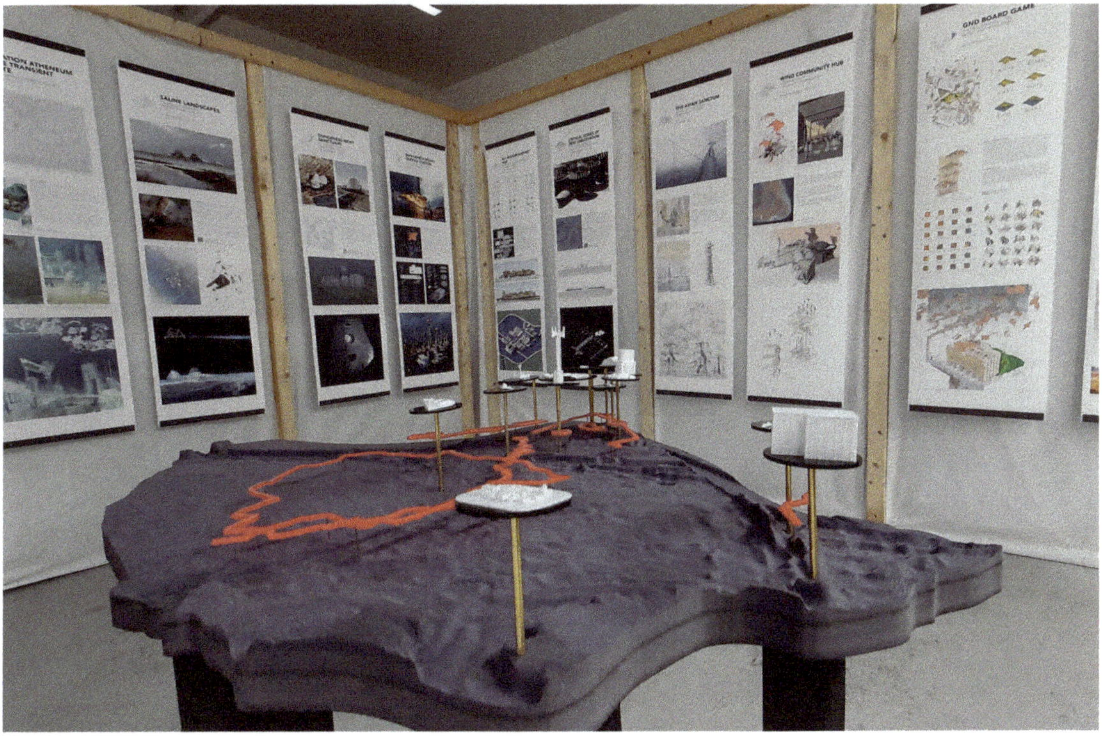

OPEN EXHIBITION
2022 - 2023
Thermal Domains

Photo Credits: Kevin Wong, Laura Nica.

AIR PHOTO ALBUM

Tromso, Norway - 69° 37' 44.3"; N 18° 55' 02.8"
November 2019

Photo Credits: Laura Nica, Aimee Daniels, Charlotte Grasselli, Denise Carcangiu, Jamie Williams, Katie Dechow, Sara Kosanovic.

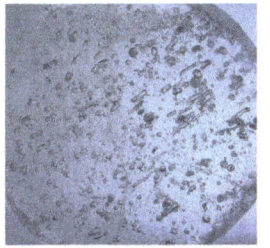
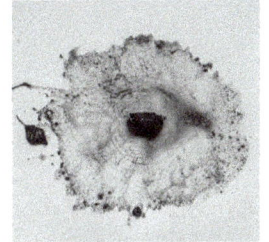

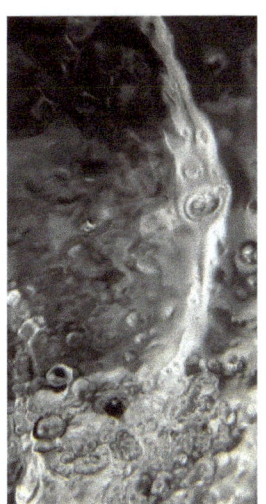
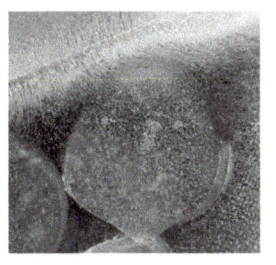

AIR PHOTO ALBUM

Dungeness, United Kingdom - 50.9193°
November 2021

Photo Credits: Laura Nica, Ben Pollock, Arvindaa Balamurugan, Guy Sinclair, Nicholas Tsangaris, Yuechuan Xi, Muhtasim Mojnu.

THEMATICS

The glossary of terms forms an evolving host of supplementary details, directions, and areas of interest that accompanied the explorations through these studio years. This list is intentionally broad, not comprehensive, to demonstrate the breadth of scale, sectors and processes that one could weave through and investigate.

Meteorological
Acid rains
Air Cells
Airspace classification
Albedo
Anti-cyclone
Astrology
Atmospheric 'river'
Chronobiology
Cloud Faction
Cloud seeding
Condensation
Electromagnetic radiation
Evaporation
Feedback Loops
Fog
Geofence-ing
Geological
Geomagnetic cusp
Grids
Heat bursts
Jet streams
Lightning Strikes
Lunar Cycles
Orographic Lift
Osmosis
Phonotelemetry
Precipitation
Pressure zones
Radiative Flux
Saharan Sands Deposition
Sky permeability
Solar cycles
Solar Radiation
Solar winds
Stratification
Sun glare
Temperature
Thermodynamics
Thunderstorms
UV systems
Vorticity
Weather Engineering

Chemical
Aerosols
Air based microplastics
Aircraft emissions
Batteries
'City Dust'
Corrosion
Fertilizers
Gases cycle (CO_2, NO_2, O_2)
Hydrogen
Light pollution
Methane
Nuclear Radiation
Pigments

Climate Processes
Acidification
Aerosol Cloud Interaction
Albedo
Cold/Heat trap
Crystallisation
Degradation & Decay
Dome Blockage
Effusivity
El Nino/ La Nina Oscillation
Evapotranspiration
Filtering
Hadley & Ferrel Cells
Heat flux
Heat Island
Heat Trapping Gases (HFA's)
Jet Stream anomalies
Katabatic/ Anabatic flow
Melting
Overheating
Polar Vortex
Radiant Heating
Solar radiation/ sun ray
Sun glare
Terrestrial Radiation
Thermal stress
UV system

Processes
Aerolipile
Atmospheric Ice Interaction
Burning
Compaction
Convection
Crystallisation
Diffussion
Deposition
Dust
Erosion
Evaporation
Filtering
Floods
Freezing
Frost/ Freezing
Heat Exchange
Incineration
Melting
Momentum exchange
Precipitation
Radiation/ Irradiation
Soil Acidification
Storms
Thermal effusivity
Vapour

Biological & Non-Human
Air-based bacteria
Breath
Coniferous Trees
Chronobiology
Disease
Eutrophication
Humpback Whales
Lichen spores
Metabolism
Microbial photosynthesis
Noonsphere
Pollen
Protozoan cysts
Spores
Tardigrades
Viruses

Territorial
Agriculture/ Aquaculture
Augmented landscapes
Bio-corridors
Climate Zones
Coal
Critical zones
Ecosystems
Forestry
Geo-engineering
Glaciers
Industrial landscapes
Landmass
Manufactured Landscapes
Permafrost
Ripparian buffers
'Sacrificial zones'
Seed Vaults
Shale gas fracking
The Tree Line
Transect
Watersheds

Ethnographical
Cloud Appreciation Society
Geo-glyphs
Indigenous People
Myths + Folklore
Population density
Religion
Settlements
Third Natures
'Umwelt'

Climate Politics
ACAN
Adaptation
Biotechnologies policies
COP 26
De-Carbonisation
De-Growth
EcoDesign Directives
Emergency Bill
Environmentalism

308

'Greenwashing'
Green New Deal
Greta Thunberg
'Insulate Britain!'
IPPC Report
LETI
Re-generation
Re-wilding
The Paris Agreement 2016

Carbon Planning & Regulation
Air Nuisance (odour, air toxicity etc.)
Biotechnologies policies
Carbon Benchmarking
Carbon Procurement
Eco-Regions
Free-marwket
Gardens Cities
Green Belts
'Green corridors'/ 'Sun corridors'
Low-Emission Zones
Part Z (building regulations)
Protected Lands
Retrofit framework

Digital
Air-balloons
Data Centres
EM Waves
Geo-tagging
Internet Connectivity
NOOA.com
Null Earth.com
Open-Weather
Radar
Radio waves
Satellite Relay Stations
Sensors
Weather Stations

Climate Renewal
Adaptation
Bioenergy
Carbon Capture + Storage
Carbon Capture and Storage
Carbon Negativity
Carbon Offsetting
Carbon Removal
Carbon Sequestration
Carbon Sinks
Enhanced weathering
Filtering
Negative Emissions Infrastructures
Ocean Fertilisation
Reuse/Recycling
Restoration
Resilience
Rewilding
Self-Sufficiency
Slow-building initiative
Sustainability Principles (Regenerate, Loop, Exchange, Recycle, Offset)
Waste Reduction & Recycling

Infrastructures
Airscapes
Airports
CERN Accelerator
HVAC system
Jet Propulsion Lab
Lake-loop cooling
'Space trash'
Steam Engine

Climate Economy
Carbon Credits
Carbon Offset Fund
Carbon Spike/ Carbon Debt
Carbon Tax
Circular Economy
Green Growth

Climate Measure
Anemometer
Argo Floats
Barometer
Carbon credits
Carbon footprint
Carbon sampling
DEFRA approved
Embodied Carbon
Energy codes
EN15804
EU's TEEB study etc.
Feedback Loops
Forecasting
Guides (*BREEAM, LEED, WELL, LETI* etc.)
Hygrometer
Life-span
Low Carbon Economy
Modelling
Net-Zero Energy
Operational Carbon
Passivhaus
Pyrometer
Radiosondes
Thermometer

Climate Change
Defoliation
Disease & Allergens
Drought
Extreme Weather Events
Floods
Heat Waves
Invasive Species
Landslides
Nutrient loss
Ocean Acidification
Saline Intrusion
Sea Level Rise
Soil Acidification
Super Bloom
Thermal Stress
Weathering

Art & Architecture
Amid.Cero9
Amy Balkin
Andres Jaque
Dark Matter Lab
David Gissen
Design Earth
Ecologic Studio
Geoff Manaugh
Hans Haacke
James Corner
James Lovelock
James Turrell
J.M.W. Turner
Julian Peschel
Mathur / Da Cunha
Monsoon Assemblages
Nerea Calvino
Olafur Eliasson
Philip Beesley
Philippe Rahm
Planet Labs
Rachael Armstrong
Sasha Engelmann
Sean Burhholden
Sean Lally
Smout Allen
Tega Brain
Terreform One
Territorial Agency
Thomas Ruff
Thomas Saraceno
Young & Ayata

Design Philosophy
Bruno Latour
Elise Iturbe
Eva Horn
Holly Jean Buck
Kate Raworth
Kiel Moe
Michael Pawlyn
Tim Ingold
Timothy Morton

Air, Architecture + Other Climates

DS18, 2019-2023
Edited by Laura Nica, John Cook and Ben Pollock

A University of Westminster,
School of Architecture + Cities Publication

Designed by Mark Boyce

All texts ©2025 Roberto Bottazzi, John Cook, Guy Sinclair,
Ben Pollock, Uri Wegman, Andreas Koerner, Laura Nica,
and Lidia Gasperoni.

This work is licensed under a CC BY-NC 4.0 license

ISBN 978-1-7385696-0-1

Books in the Studio as Book series are available to
purchase via OpenStudioWestminster here:
http://www.openstudiowestminster.org/studio-as-book/ or
from online book stores.

The editors have attempted to acknowledge all sources of
images used and apologise for any errors or omissions.

School of Architecture + Cities
University of Westminster
35 Marylebone Road
London
NW1 5LS